Rescue and Resistance:
Portraits of the Holocaust

MACMILLAN
PROFILES

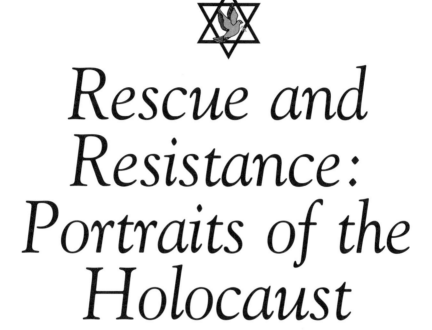

Rescue and Resistance: Portraits of the Holocaust

MACMILLAN LIBRARY REFERENCE USA
New York

Macmillan Library Reference USA
1633 Broadway
New York, New York 10019

Manufactured in the United States of America

Printing number
1 2 3 4 5 6 7 8 9 10

Cover design by Berrian Design

Library of Congress Cataloging-in-Publication Data

Rescue and resistance: portraits of the Holocaust.
      p.   cm. — (Macmillan profiles)
   Includes bibliographical references and index.
   ISBN 0-02-865362-9 (hc. : alk. paper)
   1. Holocaust, Jewish (1939–1945)—Biography.   2. Jews—Biography.
3. World War, 1939–1945—Jewish resistance.   4. Holocaust survivors—
Biography.   5. World War, 1939–1945—Jews—Rescue.   6. Righteous
Gentiles in the Holocaust—Biography.   I. Series.
D804.195L59   1999
940.53′18′0922—dc21   98-56458
[B]   CIP

Ref ✓

Front cover clockwise from top: Oskar Schindler (©UPI / Corbis-Bettmann); Anne Frank (©UPI / Corbis-Bettmann); Raoul Wallenberg (©Corbis-Bettmann); Elie Wiesel (©David Rubinger / Corbis)

This paper meets the requirements of ANSI/NISO A39.48-1992 (Permanence of Paper)

Contents

Macmillan Profiles: *Rescue and Resistance: Portraits of the Holocaust* is a unique reference featuring 167 profiles of men and women from all walks of life who fought against Germany's Third Reich and struggled to survive during the Holocaust. Macmillan Library Reference recognizes the need for reliable, accurate, and accessible biographies of notable figures in history. The Macmillan Profile series can help meet that need by providing new collections of biographies that were carefully selected from distinguished Macmillan sources. Macmillan Library Reference has published a wide array of award-winning reference materials for libraries across the world. It is likely that several of the encyclopedias on the shelves in this library were published by Macmillan Reference or Charles Scribner's Sons. All biographies in Macmillan Profiles have been tailored for a younger audience by a team of experienced writers and editors. In some cases, new biographies were commissioned to supplement entries from original sources.

Rescue and Resistance features moving profiles of important civic and military leaders who risked their lives to save Jews and fight the Nazis, artists, and writers who lived during the Holocaust and strove to record it, and the countless ordinary people who rose to heroic stature as they struggled to save their own lives and the lives of their families, friends, and communties. The article list was based on the following criteria: relevance to the curriculum, importance to history, and representation of as broad a cultural range as possible. The article list was refined and expanded in response to advice from a lively and generous team of librarians from high schools and public schools across the United States. The result is a balanced, curriculum-related work that brings these historical figures to life.

FEATURES

Rescue and Resistance: Portraits of the Holocaust is part of Macmillan's **Profiles Series.** To add visual appeal and enhance the usefulness of the volume, the page format was designed to include the following helpful features:

- ◼ Time Lines: Found throughout the text in the margins, time lines provide a quick reference source for dates and important events in the life and times of these important men and women.

- ◼ Notable Quotations: Found throughout the text in the margins, these thought-provoking quotations are drawn from interviews, speeches, and writings of the person covered in the article. Such quotations give readers a special insight into the distinctive personalities of these great men and women.

- ■ Definitions and Glossary: Brief definitions of important terms in the main text can be found in the margins. A glossary at the end of the book provides students with an even broader list of definitions.

- ■ Sidebars: Appearing in shaded boxes throughout the volume, these provocative asides relate to and amplify topics.

- ■ Pull Quotes: Found throughout the text in the margin, pull quotes highlight essential facts.

- ■ Suggested Reading: An extensive list of books and articles about the men and women covered in the volume will help students who want to do further research.

- ■ Index: A thorough index provides thousands of additional points of entry into the work.

ACKNOWLEDGMENTS

We thank our colleagues who publish the Merriam Webster's Collegiate Dictionary. Definitions used in the margins and many of the glossary terms come from the distinguished Webster's Collegiate Dictionary, Tenth Edition, 1996.

We are also grateful for the contributions of the following inimitable team of librarians who helped compile the article list. Their knowledge of school curriculum and reader interest were invaluable in shaping a volume of optimum usefulness to middle and high school students.

Rosalie Daniels, Mann Magnet Junior High, Little Rock, Arkansas
Dennis Donnelly, Hoover High School, San Diego, California
Kathy Labertew, Clairemont High School, San Diego, California
Dottie Renfro, Madison Middle School Library, Richmond, Kentucky
Merrill Stegal, Whitney Young High School, Chicago, Illinois
Civia Tuteur, retired librarian, Chicago, Illinois

The biographies herein were written by leading authorities at work in the field of history. *Rescue and Resistance* contains 72 photographs. Acknowledgments of sources for the illustrations can be found on page 361.

This work would not have been possible without the hard work and creativity of our staff. We offer our sincere thanks to all who helped create this marvelous work.

Macmillan Library Reference

Abegg, Elisabeth

1882–D. AFTER 1957

German Quaker who saved Jews in Berlin during World War II. Raised in Strasbourg (Alsace) when it was part of Imperial Germany, Abegg became involved in activities for the Quakers when she moved to Berlin. A history teacher at the Luisen girls' school, she was dismissed in 1933 by the Nazi school director for her pronounced anti-Nazi views.

In 1942, at the age of sixty and while looking after her bedridden mother and sick elder sister, Abegg began using her home in the Tempelhof district as a temporary shelter and assembly point for many Jews. She created a rescue network made up of friends from the Quaker movement, pastors, and former students, and over a period of almost three years helped dozens of Jews escape deprivation and deportation. Her activities included sheltering Jews either in her own home (in a building that also housed several Nazi party members) or in temporarily empty adjoining apartments in her care. Abegg found safe and permanent refuges both in Berlin and in

more distant locations such as Alsace and East Prussia; she sent provisions to enable those who escaped to survive and provided them with false identities. She helped others to escape across the Swiss border, selling her jewelry and other valuables in order to finance this work. She also tutored Jewish children at her home to compensate for their not being able to attend school. Bringing false identification papers, money, and provisions, she visited her charges in various locations.

In a booklet dedicated to her on her seventy-fifth birthday in 1957 entitled "And a Light Shone in the Darkness," her former charges offered profuse praise of Elisabeth Abegg's dedication, care, and humanity. ◆

Abugov, Aleksandr

1913–

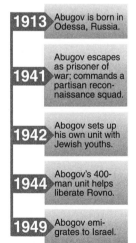

Russian Jewish partisan commander. A native of Odessa, Abugov grew up in Kirovograd and became a locksmith. After his army service he studied at the Kharkov sports academy and worked as a fencing instructor.

When the Germans invaded the Soviet Union on June 22, 1941, Abugov was called up and posted to the Ukrainian front, where he served as a second lieutenant in an armored-train unit. The unit was besieged and Abugov was taken prisoner of war. Seeing that the Germans were murdering the Jews among the prisoners, Abugov posed as an ethnic Russian. He passed through several prisoner-of-war camps—Uman, Vinnitsa, Shepetovka, Brest-Litovsk, and Kobrin—and finally reached the camp in Kovel, from which he made his escape. He joined a partisan unit in the village of Dolsk, in Polesye. By September 1942, the group had grown in size and Abugov commanded its reconnaissance squad.

At the end of 1942 the unit moved east, where Abugov encountered Jews fleeing from the Serniki and Dubrovitsa ghettos. He was deeply moved by the difficult situation of the Jews and decided, with several friends, to leave his unit and together with Jewish youths to set up his own partisan unit. At the request of General Vasily Begma, commanding officer of the two Rovno divisions, Abugov joined the Rovno division and was appointed commander of the reconnaissance battalion, a

400-man cavalry unit, with which he took part in the liberation of Rovno in February 1944. On his discharge he became the district sports officer. He married one of the young women who had served with him and, together with other members of his family, moved to Poland. In 1949 he emigrated to Israel. ◆

Adamowicz, Irena

1910–1963

Polish liaison officer among various ghetto underground movements. Born in Warsaw, Adamowicz was a pious Catholic and a member of the leadership of the Polish scout movement. She graduated with a degree in social work at Warsaw University. In the 1930s she was greatly attracted by the Ha-Shomer ha-Tsa'ir movement and even participated in its social and educational work. In the summer of 1942, Adamowicz carried out many dangerous missions for the Jewish underground organizations in the ghettos of Warsaw, Białystok, Vilna, Kovno, and Šiauliai. In addition to the important information she conveyed, her visits to the isolated ghettos brought moral encouragement to those imprisoned there. With her help, contact was established between the Jewish underground organizations and the members of the Armia Krajowa (Home Army).

After the war, Adamowicz maintained close relations with the survivors of the pioneer Zionist movements in Poland and with her friends from those movements in Israel. For her unique activity in the war years she was awarded the "Righteous among the Nations" medal by Yad Vashem in Jerusalem. ◆

1910 Adamowicz is born in Warsaw, Poland.

1942 Adamowicz carries out many dangerous missions for the Jewish underground.

1942 Adamowicz helps the Jewish underground contact the Home Army.

1963 Adamowicz dies.

André, Joseph

1908–1973

Belgian abbot who helped to rescue hundreds of Jewish children. In liaison with the Comité de Défense des Juifs, an underground Jewish organization searching for

1908 André is born in Belgium.

1944 Andre is liberated in Namur by the U.S. army.

1968 André is awarded Yad Vashem's "Righteous among the Nations" medal.

1973 André dies.

secure hiding places for Jews in distress, Abbé André coordinated his rescue activities out of his parish office, which was located next to the German military headquarters in Namur.

Abbé André found hiding places for many Jews. He kept an eye on all Jews whom he had directed to secure shelters. If convinced that a certain place had become unsuitable or that the treatment given was inadequate, he immediately took steps to have the Jew transferred to a new location. His role was especially significant in the rescue of children.

Traveling from place to place, he implored at monasteries, convents, and private homes that they take Jewish children under their protective wings. It did not take long for the Gestapo to realize that Abbé André was frustrating its designs for the deportation of all Belgian Jews, and they trailed his movements. He eventually became a marked man and had to go into hiding until the liberation of Namur by the United States Army in September 1944.

He then undertook the arduous task of gathering the children and returning them to their parents or to Jewish organizations. André never thought of trying to convert the children. On the contrary, he always emphasized the duty of maintaining every person's own faith, to the extent that many children under his care knew the "Hatikvah" (the Jewish national anthem).

Abbé Joseph André (front row, fourth from right) at Yad Vashem in 1968 with people he saved during the Holocaust.

Abbé Joseph André was recognized as one of the "Righteous among the Nations" by Yad Vashem in 1968. ◆

Anielewicz, Mordecai

1919 OR 1920–1943

Commander of the Warsaw ghetto uprising. Anielewicz was born into a poor family living in a Warsaw slum quarter; he graduated from the Laor Jewish secondary school and joined the Zionist Ha-Shomer ha-Tsa'ir movement, where he distinguished himself as an organizer and a youth leader.

On September 7, 1939, a week after the outbreak of the war, Anielewicz fled from Warsaw and, together with the senior members of his movement, made his way to eastern Poland, assuming that the Polish forces would establish their defense line there. On September 17, however, eastern Poland was occupied by the Soviet army. Aniel-ewicz reached the southern part of the Soviet-occupied area and tried to cross into Romania and establish a route for Jewish youth trying to get to Palestine. He was caught by the Soviets and put in jail; when he was released, he decided to return to Warsaw—by then under German occupation—and on the way he stopped at many towns and cities, visiting the Jewish communities. He stayed in Warsaw for a short while only and left for Vilna, which by then had been incorporated into Lithuania. It contained a large con-centration of refugees from Warsaw, among them members of the youth movements and political parties. Anielewicz called on his fellow Ha-Shomer ha-Tsa'ir members to send a team of instructors back to German-

occupied Poland, where they would resume the movement's educational and political activities in the underground. He and his friend Mira Fuchrer set an example by being the first to volunteer for this assignment.

By January 1940 Anielewicz had become a full-time underground activist. As the leader of the Ha-Shomer ha-Tsa'ir underground movement, he set up cells and youth groups, organized their activities, helped publish an underground newspaper, arranged meetings and seminars, and made frequent illegal trips outside Warsaw, visiting communities and his movement's chapters in the provincial ghettos. He also found time to study for himself, especially Hebrew, and read much history, sociology, and economics. It was in this period that, in his attempts to comprehend the situation, he crystallized his views, giving them expression in lectures and in articles that he published in the underground press.

Under the impact of the first reports of the mass murder of Jews in the east, following the German invasion of the Soviet Union in June 1941, Anielewicz revised his policy and concen-

Ghetto

The word "ghetto" referred to a city quarter or street in which only Jews lived, confined and separated from the other parts of the city. The term had its origin in Venice, where in 1516 the Jews were forced into a closed quarter called the Geto Novo (New Foundry). Other Italian cities also segregated their Jewish population into ghettos, and the practice was adopted by cities in France, Poland, Germany, and some other countries. The purpose of ghettoizing the Jews was to restrict contact between them and Christians and to confine the Jews to certain economic activities. Inside the ghettos, the Jews lived their lives in accordance with their traditional customs. From the end of the eighteenth century, the forcible restriction of Jews to ghettos was gradually abandoned. However, in many cities Jews continued of their own free will to live in separate quarters. In more recent times the term "ghetto" came to be applied to urban areas inhabited by blacks in the United States and South Africa and to quarters inhabited by any minority that was oppressed and living in slum conditions. None of these forms of ghettos can be compared to the ghettos established by the Germans in the countries they occupied in World War II. These were not designed to serve as a separate area for Jewish habitations; they were merely a transitional phase in a process that was to lead to the "Final Solution" of the Jewish question. The Nazi-instituted ghettos were, in fact, camps where the Jews were held under duress, with their internal life and organization imposed on them and enforced, through violent means, from the outside, by the Nazi regime.

trated on the creation of a self-defense organization in the ghetto. His first efforts to establish contacts with the Polish underground forces who were loyal to the Polish government-in-exile in London were unsuccessful. In March and April 1942 he joined others in the formation of the Antifascist Bloc; the bloc, however, did not fulfill the expectations of its Zionist components, and after a wave of arrests, including those of Communist activists in the bloc, it ceased to exist.

At the time of the mass deportation from Warsaw in the summer of 1942, Anielewicz was staying in Zagłębie (the south-western part of Poland, which had been incorporated into Germany). There he worked at transforming the underground youth movements into an armed resistance movement. On his return to Warsaw after the mass deportation, he found that only 60,000 of Warsaw's 350,000 Jews were left in the ghetto, and that the small Żydowska Organizacja Bojowa (Jewish Fighting Organization; ŻOB) in the ghetto lacked arms and was in a dire situation, having suffered failures and lost members. Anielewicz embarked upon a determined drive to reorganize and reinvigorate the ŻOB and achieved rapid results; following the mass deportation, there was far more support in the ghetto than previously for the idea of armed resistance and its practical organization. Most of the existing Jewish underground groups now joined the ŻOB, and a public council, consisting of authorized representatives, was established in support of the ŻOB (the Żydowski Komitet Narodowy, or Jewish National Committee, and the Coordinating Committee, the latter also including the Bund). In November 1942 Anielewicz was appointed commander of the ŻOB. By January 1943 several groups of fighters, consisting of members of the pioneering Zionist youth movements, had been consolidated, contact had been established with the Armia Krajowa (Home Army) command, and a small quantity of arms had been obtained from the Polish side of the city.

On January 18, 1943, the Germans launched the second mass deportation from the Warsaw ghetto. Caught unawares, the ŻOB staff was unable to meet in order to decide on what action to take in response, but in one part of the ghetto the armed groups of ŻOB fighters decided to act on their own. There were two foci of ŻOB resistance, with Anielewicz commanding the major street battle. The fighters deliberately joined the columns of deportees and, at an agreed signal, attacked the German escorts at the corner of Zamenhofa and

> *"My life's dream has come true; I have lived to see Jewish resistance in the ghetto in all its greatness and glory."*
>
> Mordecai Anielewicz, in a letter, 1943

Niska streets, while the rest of the Jews fled from the scene. Most of the fighters belonging to the Ha-Shomer ha-Tsa'ir group fell in that battle. Anielewicz was saved by his men, who came to his aid in the close-quarters fighting. The resistance action taken on January 18 was of great importance, because four days later the Germans halted the deportation, a step that the ghetto population interpreted as meaning that the Germans were drawing back in the face of armed resistance by the Jews. The following three months, from January to April 1943, were used by the ŻOB for intensive preparations for the decisive test ahead, under the supervision of the organization's headquarters, led by Anielewicz.

On April 19, the eve of Passover, the final deportation of Warsaw Jews was launched, an event that served as the signal for the Warsaw ghetto uprising. In the first few clashes, the Jewish resistance fighters held the upper hand and the Germans suffered losses. The clashes and street fighting in the ghetto lasted for three days. The Germans introduced a large military force, against which the few hundred Jewish fighters, armed only with pistols, had no chance whatsoever; but the fighters did not surrender. Neither, for the most part, did the Jews who were in the bunkers; the appeals and promises they heard from the Germans did not lure them out of their hiding places, and the Germans had to burn down the ghetto, house by house, in order to destroy the bunkers. The fighting in the ghetto went on for four weeks, in the course of which the Germans and their helpers suffered constant losses. It was only on May 16 that SS-Brigadeführer Jürgen Stroop, the commander of the German force, was able to report that the *Grossaktion* ("major operation") had been concluded and the ghetto conquered.

In the first days of the fighting, Anielewicz was in command, in the midst of the main fighting forces of the ghetto. When the street fighting was over, Anielewicz, together with his staff and a large force of fighters, retreated into the bunker at 18 Mila Street. This bunker fell on May 8, and the main body of the ŻOB, including Anielewicz, was killed. In his last letter, of April 23, 1943, to Yitzhak Zuckerman (a member of the ŻOB staff who was then on assignment on the Polish side), Anielewicz wrote:

> What has happened is beyond our wildest dreams. Twice the Germans fled from the ghetto. One of our companies held out for forty minutes and the other, for over six hours. . . . I have no

words to describe to you the conditions in which the Jews are living. Only a few chosen ones will hold out; all the rest will perish sooner or later. The die is cast. In the bunkers in which our comrades are hiding, no candle can be lit, for lack of air. . . . The main thing is: My life's dream has come true; I have lived to see Jewish resistance in the ghetto in all its greatness and glory.

Kibbutz Yad Mordecai in Israel has been named after Mordecai Anielewicz, and is the site of a memorial in his honor. ◆

Atlas, Yeheskel

1913–1942

Physician and partisan commander. Born in Rawa Mazowiecka, in the Warsaw district, Atlas studied medicine in France and Italy. The outbreak of war in 1939 found him in Kozlovshchina, near Slonim, in the area occupied by the Soviet army. His parents and sister died in the ghetto there on November 24, 1941, five months after the Germans had conquered the area. Atlas stayed on, serving the farmers of the neighborhood as a physician and giving medical assistance to Soviet troops who had survived in the forest. When the Derechin ghetto was liquidated, on July 24, 1942, Atlas organized those who escaped into a Jewish partisan company under his command. Numbering 120, the company was subordinated to a Soviet partisan leader named Bulat, who headed a battalion that fought in the Lipiczany Forest.

On August 10 Atlas initiated an attack on Derechin in which forty-four German policemen were captured and executed. Though the Soviet authorities wanted the "fight-

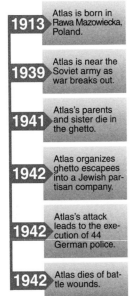

1913 Atlas is born in Rawa Mazowiecka, Poland.

1939 Atlas is near the Soviet army as war breaks out.

1941 Atlas's parents and sister die in the ghetto.

1942 Atlas organizes ghetto escapees into a Jewish partisan company.

1942 Atlas's attack leads to the execution of 44 German police.

1942 Atlas dies of battle wounds.

ing doctor" to practice medicine for the partisans, after the Derechin attack the partisan leadership, recognizing his gifts as a tactician, did not want to lose him as a combat commander. Atlas and his men blew up a train on the Lida-Grodno line, burned down a bridge on the Neman River, and, on September 5, launched an attack on Kozlovshchina in which over thirty Germans were killed.

The company gained fame throughout the region for its daring exploits and was mentioned in dispatches for its role in the Ruda-Jaworska battle of October 10, during which 127 Germans were killed, 75 captured, and a considerable amount of much-needed war material seized. Atlas also assisted the family camp attached to his company that housed escapees from nearby ghettos. Following the second *Aktion* that took place at Diatlovo, on August 6, its refugees too were helped by Atlas. His personality, military exploits, and acts of revenge made a profound impression on both the Jewish and non-Jewish partisans in the region.

On December 5, 1942, Atlas was wounded in a battle at Wielka Wola; after handing the command over to Eliyahu Lipshowitz, he died from his wounds. ◆

Barth, Karl

1886–1968

Swiss Protestant theologian. Barth was the most prominent theologian in the Reformed (Calvinist) tradition in the first half of the twentieth century. He was educated in Germany, but in 1914 turned against his theological mentors because of their uncritical support of German nationalism and war aims. His commentary on the Epistle to the Romans (1919) was an outright attack on the "cultural Protestantism" of the nineteenth century and denied the identification of the Kingdom of God with human or national progress. Theology, for Barth, consisted not in man's attempt to find God, but solely in describing God's justification of man through faith. From 1921 to 1935, Barth was a professor of theology in Göttingen, Münster, and Bonn, establishing his school of "dialectical" theology, which looked to biblical revelation as the sole source of authority in the church and rejected any accommodation with nationalist or racial ideologies. From 1933 on, Barth was the theological leader of the German Confessing Church (Bekennende Kirche), in opposition to the pro-Nazi "German Christians"; he was the principal author of the 1934 Barmen Declaration, in which the supporters of the Confessing Church joined to defend their position against the totalitarian demands of the state. In 1935 he was expelled from Germany and returned to his native Basel, where he continued working on his unfinished major work *Church Dogmatics* (13 vols.).

Barth's hostility to Nazi anti-Semitism was based on his biblical theology, though he did not at first recognize the need to

1914 Barth rejects his mentors who support German nationalism.

1919 Barth attacks "cultural Protestantism."

1921 Barth becomes a theology professor; rejects racial ideologies.

1933 Barth becomes leader of the German Confessing Church.

1934 Barth is principal author of the Barmen Declaration.

1935 Barth is expelled from Germany and returns to Basel.

1938 Barth's theology begins to affirm Christian-Jewish solidarity.

1942 Barth's second volume of *Church Dogmatics* supports connection with Israel.

solidarity: unity based on common interests.

dogmatics: a system of established principles and beliefs.

triumphalist: believing that one's religious creed is superior to all others.

exclusivist: tending to exclude others; believing that salvation is found only through faith in Jesus.

make the "Jewish question" the central point of church resistance. Following his expulsion from Germany, he became more outspoken on behalf of the Jews, and from 1938 on his theology clearly affirmed the **solidarity** of Christians and Jews as the common heirs of biblical revelation. The second volume of *Church **Dogmatics*** (1942) contained a pointed chapter on the church's indissoluble dependence on and foundation in Israel. In later volumes of this work, he strongly criticized traditional Christian **triumphalist** attitudes, regarded Christian missionary activity to the Jewish people as theologically inadmissible, and repudiated the view that the Christian church had displaced Judaism as the sole channel of salvation. Despite his dogmatic views on modern Judaism and his **exclusivist** Christology, Barth's influence in the postwar period was significant, particularly in such bodies as the World Council of Churches, in rethinking the theological relationship between Christianity and Judaism.

Barth's writings that bear on such matters include *Church Dogmatics* (London, 1936–69), *Der Römerbrief* (Oxford, 1933), and "The Jewish Problem and the Christian Answer," in *Against the Stream: Shorter Post-War Writings, 1946–1952* (London, 1954). ◆

Bartoszewski, Władysław

1922–

> "In the camp, where I saw and experienced the deepest human misery, I developed the conviction that helping the victims of Nazi terror was of the utmost important."
> Wladyslaw Bartoszewski, *The Warsaw Ghetto: A Christian's Testimony,* 1987

Polish anti-Nazi who aided Jews during the Holocaust. Bartoszewski was imprisoned in Auschwitz from September 1940 to April 1941, and from 1942 to 1945 he was a member of the Armia Krajowa (the Polish Home Army). He also belonged to the underground organization of young Catholics, the Front Odrodzenia Polski (Front for the Rebirth of Poland), and in September 1942 helped to set up a provisional committee that later became the Zegota welfare organization. When the latter's permanent council was set up, on December 4, 1942, Bartoszewski became one of the two Delegatura representatives who regularly attended Zegota's board meetings. He was active in the underground and helped transmit to the Polish government-in-exile reports on the Nazi terror against the Poles and on the situation of the Jews. In 1963 Yad Vashem designated him a "Righteous among the Nations."

A prolific writer and historian, Bartoszewski has published a number of books, dealing mostly with the history of Warsaw during the war, the Polish Jews, and the rescue of Jews by Polish gentiles. They include *Warsaw Death Ring, 1939–1944* (1968) and *Righteous among Nations: How Poles Helped the Jews, 1939–1945* (1969). Bartoszewski is the president of the PEN Club in Poland, serves as a professor on the faculty of the Catholic University of Lublin, and frequently lectures in many countries. ◆

Baublys, Petras

D. 1974

Pediatrician and head of an orphanage in Kovno, Lithuania. Upon being contacted by an underground Jewish organization operating in the Kovno ghetto, Baublys agreed to use the orphanage facility (located in the Slobodka section of the city, where the ghetto was situated) as a temporary shelter and a **conduit** for transferring Jewish children to permanent, safe locations. Dozens of children and infants were accepted into the orphanage, some abandoned on the doorsteps by fleeing Jewish mothers. Children knowing a smattering of Lithuanian were kept within the orphanage compound for relatively longer periods; others, as well as children over the permissible age, were quickly spirited to hiding places with Lithuanian families, with Baublys providing free medical care for the sick children he visited. In order to minimize the danger

conduit: a channel through which something passes.

of betrayal to the authorities, only a select group of the orphanage staff knew of this undertaking.

Baublys, his brother Sergejus, and his sister-in-law Jadvyga (who hid a Jewish child in their home) were recognized by Yad Vashem as "Righteous among the Nations" in 1977. ◆

Bauminger, Heshek Zvi ("Bazyli")

1919–1943

One of the commanders of the Iskra (Spark) fighting organization in Kraków. Bauminger, who was born in Kraków, received a Zionist religious upbringing and attended the Hebrew high school in Kraków. At the age of sixteen he joined Ha-Shomer ha-Tsa'ir, and he eventually became the head of the movement's branch in Kraków.

When World War II broke out he was drafted into the Polish army, ending up in Lvov. After the Germans invaded the Soviet Union on June 22, 1941, Bauminger was drafted into the Red Army and fell into German captivity. He managed to escape and make his way to Lvov, where fellow Ha-Shomer ha-Tsa'ir members provided him with Aryan papers. He then made his way back to Kraków on foot, reaching the ghetto in early 1942. There he met with the surviving members of his movement and with leaders of Akiva, reporting to them on the horrendous mass murders that the Germans had perpetrated on the Jews of Eastern Galicia and the Ukraine, and advocating an armed struggle against the enemy.

In mid-1942 a unified Jewish command, the Żydowska Organizacja Bojowa (ŻOB), was established;

headed by Bauminger, it included members of Akiva, Dror, Iskra, and other organizations. Using hit-and-run tactics, each movement engaged in its own sporadic actions, but major operations were carried out jointly and directed by the unified command. The most important of these, conducted on December 22, 1942, was called the "Cyganeria Night" (Cyganeria being the name of the café that was the target). Nine German officers were killed in the attack and thirteen wounded; this was the first time that Kraków residents saw Germans killed and wounded. The escape plan was for the He-Haluts ha-Lohem fighters to make their way back to their headquarters at 24 Skavinska Street, while the Iskra fighters were to go to their headquarters in Czerwony Pradnik, a Polish workers' section of the city, several kilometers from the ghetto. The Germans, however, found out about the meeting at the He-Haluts ha-Lohem headquarters. They broke in, killing some of the members and capturing the rest.

Bauminger and his men continued fighting the Germans, carrying out acts of sabotage on German installations in and outside the ghetto. In March 1943 the Germans broke into the place where he lived. Bauminger fired at them, saving the last bullet to shoot himself in the temple. ◆

1919 Bauminger is born in Kraków, Poland.

1941 Bauminger, drafted into the Red Army, falls into German captivity.

1942 Bauminger reaches the Kraków ghetto after escaping the Germans.

1942 Bauminger heads a resistance unit.

1942 Bauminger's unit kills nine German officers.

1943 Bauminger kills himself when the Germans invade his home.

Baur, André

1904–1943

Jewish leader in Paris. Born in Paris, Baur was reared in a distinguished Jewish family of rabbis and community figures, and he himself became the president of the Paris Reform synagogue (on Rue Copernic) in the late 1930s. A well-to-do banker, Baur could easily have left Paris during the great exodus of Jews in 1940 but opted to remain and serve the community.

In March 1941 the Comité de Coordination, the recently established umbrella organization of Jewish welfare societies in Paris, was at a crossroads, and new responsible Jewish personalities were needed to invigorate it. Called upon by his uncle Julien Weill, who was the Chief Rabbi of Paris, Baur entered the Comité and tried to turn it in constructive directions and

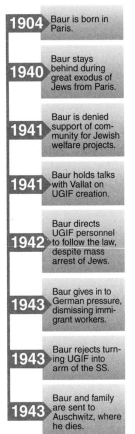

1904 Baur is born in Paris.

1940 Baur stays behind during great exodus of Jews from Paris.

1941 Baur is denied support of community for Jewish welfare projects.

1941 Baur holds talks with Vallat on UGIF creation.

1942 Baur directs UGIF personnel to follow the law, despite mass arrest of Jews.

1943 Baur gives in to German pressure, dismissing immigrant workers.

1943 Baur rejects turning UGIF into arm of the SS.

1943 Baur and family are sent to Auschwitz, where he dies.

increase relief to the Jews of the occupied zone. Although he succeeded in bringing together reputable individuals to head the Comité, he was unable to obtain the support of the community for his welfare schemes.

In the fall of 1941, Baur held talks with Xavier Vallat, head of the Commissariat Genéral aux Questions Juives (established by the Vichy government), on the creation of the Union Genérale des Israélites de France (UGIF), and he became its vice president. From the outset of the UGIF's existence, Baur directed it to abide by legal methods of operation, and even in moments of great crisis (such as the mass arrest of Jews in Paris in July 1942), he adhered strictly to this outlook, hoping thereby to alleviate the plight of the Jewish community. Constantly concerned with the needs of Jews, Baur went to great efforts to guarantee the UGIF's resources, even to the point of proposing a more "harmonized" and authoritarian organization that would have eliminated the autonomous existence of UGIF-South, the UGIF division in the unoccupied zone. Baur fought valiantly to save his immigrant employees from dismissal in early 1943, but gave in to the German pressure when it threatened the UGIF's continuation.

Baur was a man of principle, deeply devoted to succoring the needy. His policy came to an impasse in July 1943, when SS-Hauptsturm-führer Alois Brunner devised a scheme in which the UGIF would encourage relatives of interned Jews to unite voluntarily with their family members in Drancy. With the full support of his council, Baur rejected turning the UGIF into a police arm of the SS and sought the intervention of Prime Minister Pierre Laval. As a result of his objection to carrying out Brunner's plan, Baur, his wife, and their four children were arrested and sent to Drancy. From there they were deported in December 1943 to Auschwitz, where Baur perished. ◆

Beccari, Arrigo

P riest in Nonantola, near Bologna in northern Italy, who together with Giuseppe Moreali, a local physician, saved the lives of 120 Jews, mostly children. In July 1942 an initial group of fifty Jewish children arrived in Nonantola, after having resided for a while in the Italian zone of occupation in northern Yugoslavia. They had earlier been separated from their parents, whose whereabouts remained unknown. With the increase of partisan activity in the Italian zone, the friendly Italian authorities suggested to Josef Itai, the group leader, that he move his children to the safety of Italy proper (then at war on the side of Nazi Germany). With the aid of Delasem (Delegazione Assistenza Emigranti Ebrei), the Jewish welfare agency officially recognized by the Fascist government, the children were housed in Villa Emma, in the village of Nonantola. There they were joined by an additional fifty children, recent refugees from Nazi terror. When the Germans overran northern Italy on September 8, 1943, the children were no longer safe, and preventive measures had to be taken immediately to avoid their falling into German hands. Without seeking the approval of his superiors in Modena, Arrigo Beccari, an instructor in a nearby Catholic seminary whom Itai had earlier befriended, opened the seminary's doors to the children. Others were housed with surrounding villagers, while the food for all was prepared within the seminary walls. When the seminary rector first saw the children, who included girls, he crossed himself and exclaimed: "For a thousand years, a woman's foot has not trodden on these grounds, but let God's will be done."

With the Nazis intensifying their search for Jews in hiding, a plan was prepared to move the children and their adult caretakers, a total of 120 persons, out of the occupied zone. At first, the thought was to smuggle them across Allied lines south of Rome. But as this proved impractical, it was decided to transfer them to the Swiss border to the north. With the help of Giuseppe Moreali, the town doctor, false identities were provided and all 120 children and their caretakers were taken by train to the Swiss border, which they crossed on the eve of the Day of Atonement of 1943. The dangers attending the convoy of such a large group of children and their Italian guides on their trek to the Swiss border were great. The children, for instance, bore Italian names on their false credentials but were hardly proficient in that language.

The Gestapo, belatedly discovering the children's flight, seized Beccari and interrogated him to elicit the names of persons involved in the rescue operation and the location of other Jews in hiding. Beccari withstood the terrible ordeal of Nazi tor-

> When the seminary rector first saw the children, who included girls, he exclaimed: "For a thousand years, woman's foot has not trodden on these grounds, but let God's will be done."

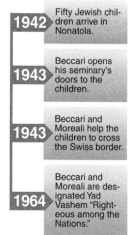

1942 Fifty Jewish children arrive in Nonatola.

1943 Beccari opens his seminary's doors to the children.

1943 Beccari and Moreali help the children to cross the Swiss border.

1964 Beccari and Moreali are designated Yad Vashem "Righteous among the Nations."

ture and was released after many months of incarceration in a notorious Bologna prison.

Arrigo Beccari and Giuseppe Moreali were recognized by Yad Vashem as "Righteous among the Nations" in 1964. ◆

Ben-Gurion, David

1886–1973

Prominent Zionist leader; first prime minister of Israel. Born in Płońsk, Poland, Ben-Gurion was a Zionist from his early youth and settled in Palestine in 1906. He was one of the founders of the socialist movement Po'alei Zion and subsequently of the Ahdut ha-Avoda and Mapai socialist political parties. In World War I he volunteered for the Jewish Legion, the volunteer formation in World War I that fought in the British army for the liberation of Palestine from Turkish rule. He was one of the founders of the Histadrut (the General Federation of Labor) and was its secretary-general from 1921 to 1935; in the latter year he became chairman of the Zionist Executive and of the Jewish Agency, holding both posts up to 1948. Ben-Gurion played a central role in the struggle for the establishment of a Jewish state, which he proclaimed on May 14, 1948. In the subsequent war he led both the political and the military struggles as prime minister and minister of defense, posts he retained until 1963.

Ben-Gurion's attitude toward European Jewry during the Holocaust period and the actions that he took for their rescue have been the subject of controversy. It has even been claimed that he consciously detached himself from the Holocaust events and concentrated on the building up of the Yishuv (the Jewish community in Palestine) and establishment of the state, almost to the exclusion of everything else. The views of scholars are divided: a minority holds that Ben-Gurion did in fact distance himself from the problem of European Jewry during the Holocaust; others maintain that from the early 1930s he was at all times pre-occupied with the current and potential threats facing Jewish existence in Europe. Most scholars dealing with the general history of the Yishuv tend to take a more balanced view, and reject a one-sided approach.

The situation was, in any case, extremely complex. On the one hand, the conditions facing the Jews of eastern and central Europe in the 1930s deteriorated rapidly; on the other, there was a crisis in the relations between the Zionist movement and the British government. It reached a climax in May 1939, when the White Paper—limiting future Jewish development, including immigration, in the country—was issued. The combination of circumstances caused Ben-Gurion to conclude that Zionism had to blaze a new political trail. He spent much of the first two years of the war in the United States, in order to mobilize American Jewry's support for a far-reaching new program. It was ratified by a special Zionist conference held in New York in May 1942 at the Biltmore Hotel, hence its name, the Biltmore Resolution.

The resolution called for Palestine to be opened for large-scale Jewish immigration and, after the war, to become a Jewish **commonwealth,** under Jewish authority. In this way, it would provide a solution to the problems of the Jews (even if it could not absorb them all), and the mass immigration would also be the basis for its political and economic status. The political solution would be the concern of the Zionist movement, while Jewish organizations in the free world—who had financial means and access to the centers of political power—would have the task of providing immediate aid to the Jews of Europe, and first and foremost to Polish Jewry.

In May 1942 reports of the mass murder of the Jews began to be published, and when in October of that year Ben-Gurion returned to Palestine, he was already in possession of information concerning a German master plan for the systematic annihilation of the Jews. Thus, the millions of Jews for whom the Biltmore program had been conceived were being killed. Ben-Gurion, however, clung to his program, believing that "disaster is the source of strength" that would spur the Jewish people and the Zionist movement to action.

"In Israel, in order to be a realist you must believe in miracles."

David Ben-Gurion, interview, 1956

commonwealth: a nation, state, or other political unit.

1886 Ben-Gurion is born in Plonsk, Poland.

1906 Ben-Gurion settles in Palestine.

1921 Ben-Gurion becomes secretary-general of Histadrut.

1935 Ben-Gurion becomes chairman of the Zionist Executive and the Jewish Agency.

1939 The White Paper is issued, limiting Jewish immigration to Palestine.

1942 Ben-Gurion's Biltmore Resolution is ratified.

1942 Reports of the mass murder of Jews begin to be published.

1942 Ben-Gurion helps to organize the Yishuv for rescue operations.

1943 Bermuda Conference reinforces Ben-Gurion's doubts about rescue efforts.

1948 Ben-Gurion proclaims the Jewish State of Israel.

1963 Ben-Gurion resigns as prime minister and minister of defense.

1973 Ben-Gurion is buried in Sde Boker.

From the end of 1942, Ben-Gurion took part in organizing the Yishuv for rescue operations. He did not permit the establishment of a broad rescue committee under Jewish Agency auspices, since he felt that the Yishuv should have its own official committee; but he did leave political action in the hands of Jewish Agency departments, under the direction and watchful eye of his confidants, among them Shaul Meirov (Avigur), Eliyahu Golomb, and Zvi Yehieli. Ben-Gurion consistently had reservations about mass demonstrations, which were intended to rouse public opinion in the free world and influence Allied governments to help in rescue efforts, because he did not expect them to be effective while the war was in progress. He was against using "national funds" for rescue operations, but was in favor of collecting money for that specific purpose, and himself took part in such fund-raising.

Ben-Gurion's attitude and actions appear to have been based on his conviction that even if the Yishuv were to use its best people and all the resources at its disposal, it would not be able to save many lives, both because of the relentless German annihilation machinery and because the Allied powers, especially Britain, managed to thwart one rescue plan after the other. These included proposals for exchange of Germans for Jews; provision of protective documents to Jews; emigration; cessation of the extermination process in exchange for financial remittances (the Europa Plan, for example); and the dispatch of parachutists from Palestine.

Ben-Gurion's doubts about the chances of success for rescue efforts were further reinforced by the Bermuda Conference of April 1943 and by various developments in 1944, such as the Allies' refusal to bomb Auschwitz; the failure of the arrangement concerning Hungarian Jewry, proposed by Adolf Eichmann and his aides, to exchange "blood for goods"; and, above all, Britain's attitude toward a plan on which Ben-Gurion had pinned great hopes—the rescue of thirty thousand Jewish children from German-occupied Europe. These disappointments led Ben-Gurion to concentrate on independent, smaller, and more realistic rescue programs.

This line of reasoning on Ben-Gurion's part and its practical consequences caused tension between him and a significant part of the Jewish population, and within the leadership itself. The approach was criticized not only by the opposition on the right but also by members of Mapai, Ben-Gurion's own party.

Moreover, Ben-Gurion did not publicly reveal his analysis of the situation, the intuition that he had, and the way in which he reached his conclusions. The impression created was that he lacked compassion for the suffering of European Jewry and that his course of action was not affected by the Holocaust. In fact, he was deeply moved by the enormity of the tragedy, and his policies were molded by his determination to alleviate the suffering and its root causes by finding long-term solutions. ◆

Benoît, Marie

1895–?

French Capuchin monk who rescued Jews during the Holocaust. In the summer of 1942, Benoît was a resident monk in the Capuchin monastery in Marseilles, France. Witnessing the spectacle of Vichy authorities rounding up thousands of non-French Jewish refugees and handing them over to the Germans for deportation, Benoît decided to devote himself to helping Jews escape from France to either Spain or Switzerland, both neutral countries. Under his guidance, the Capuchin monastery was transformed into a nerve center of a widespread rescue network, in collaboration with frontier smugglers (*passeurs*) and in coordination with various Christian and Jewish organizations. A printing machine in the monastery's basement turned out thousands of false baptismal certificates, which the fleeing Jews needed in order to procure other necessary documents.

With the occupation of Vichy France in November 1942, the escape routes to Switzerland and Spain became more difficult to negotiate. The nearby Italian zone of occupation now became the principal escape haven. Journeying to Nice, Benoît

1895 Benoît is born.

1942 Benoît transforms the Capuchin monastery into a widespread rescue network.

1942 Escape routes to Switzerland and Spain become tougher to negotiate.

1943 Benoît meets with the Pope to outline an escape plan.

1944 Benoît is hailed by the Jewish community after Rome's liberation.

1966 Benoît is given Yad Vashem's "Righteous among the Nations" title.

coordinated plans with local Jewish organizations. Accompanied by Angelo Donati, an influential local Jewish banker in Nice, he met with General Guido Lospinoso, the Italian commissioner of Jewish affairs (sent to Nice by Mussolini, under German pressure, for the express purpose of instituting anti-Jewish measures), and convinced him that the rescue of the thirty thousand Jews in Nice and its environs was the divine order of the day. Benoît was promised that the Italian occupation authorities would not interfere. Not satisfied with this commitment, and harboring presentiments as to the ultimate fate of the Jews in Nice, Benoît continued on to Rome, and in an audience with Pope Pius XII on July 16, 1943, he outlined a plan for transferring the majority of the thirty thousand Jews in the Nice region to northern Italy to prevent their falling into German hands. This plan was later expanded to provide for the Jews' transfer to former military camps in North Africa, now in Allied hands. The new Italian government of Marshal Pietro Badoglio (Mussolini had been deposed on July 25, 1943) was prepared to provide four ships for this giant undertaking, and ways were found to channel funds from Jewish organizations abroad. However, the premature publication of the Italian armistice on September 8 and the immediate German occupation of northern Italy and the Italian zone of occupation in France foiled this plan.

Benoît's activities now centered on helping Jews in Rome and its vicinity, with the Capuchin College inside the Vatican as his base of operations. To be able to deal effectively with the task of providing food, shelter, and new identities to thousands of Jewish refugees in Rome and elsewhere, he was elected a board member of Delasem (Delegazione Assistenza Emigranti Ebrei), the central Jewish welfare organization of Italy. When its Jewish president, Settimo Sorani, was arrested by the Germans, Benoît was nominated acting president; he chaired the organization's meetings, which were now held inside the Capuchin College. Benoît escaped several attempts by the Gestapo to arrest him, as his fame spread among Jews and non-Jews. He extracted letters of protection and other important documents from the Swiss, Romanian, Hungarian, and Spanish legations. These papers enabled thousands of Jews, under assumed names, to circulate freely in Rome. He also obtained a large batch of ration cards from the Rome police, ostensibly on behalf of non-Jewish homeless refugees stranded in the capital.

After Rome's liberation in June 1944, Benoît was hailed by the Jewish community at an official synagogue ceremony. With the war over and the Jews safe, he returned to his ecclesiastical duties. France awarded him various military decorations; Israel, through Yad Vashem, conferred on him the title of "Righteous among the Nations" in 1966. ◆

Berman, Adolf Abraham

1906–1978

Psychologist, Zionist activist in the Warsaw ghetto underground, and one of the leaders of Zegota (the Polish Council for Aid to Jews) in the Polish part of Warsaw. Berman obtained his Ph.D. degree at Warsaw University and was director of the Jewish center of psychological counseling clinics in Warsaw. He also taught in high schools and published articles dealing with social and educational psychology. From his early years, he was active in the Left Po'alei Zion. Under the German occupation, he was director of CENTOS (Federation of Associations for the Care of Orphans in Poland) in the Warsaw ghetto, a league affiliated with the Jewish self-help organization. Berman was active in the political underground and was one of the founders of the Antifascist Bloc, the precursor to the Żydowska Organizacja Bojowa (Jewish Fighting Organization; ŻOB) in the ghetto.

In September 1942 Berman moved to the "Aryan" side of Warsaw, together with his wife, Batya, who had been active in the ghetto underground as manager of a network of lending libraries. Posing as a Pole, Berman lived among the Poles up to the end of the war, making strenuous efforts to help the Jews, as representative of the Żydowski Komitet Narodowy (Jewish National Committee) and as secretary of Zegota. Owing to his connections and his non-Jewish appearance, he was able to move about freely and promote widespread efforts for the rescue of Jews surviving in Warsaw after the liquidation of the ghetto. He also helped to save the written records that had been hidden on the "Aryan" side, among them the last of the chronicles recorded by Emanuel Ringelblum. In January 1944 Berman fell

1906 Berman is born.

1942 Berman poses as a Pole to help the Jews.

1944 Berman is captured by Polish blackmailers, but escapes.

1950 Berman settles in Israel and is elected to the Knesset.

1971 Berman publishes *The Underground Period.*

1978 Berman publishes *In the Place Where Fate Brought Me: With the Jews of Warsaw.*

1978 Berman dies.

into the hands of Polish blackmailers, but was freed by the help of his Polish friends and the payment of ransom.

When Poland was liberated, Berman became the chairman of the Central Committee of the Jews of Poland and a member of the Polish parliament. In 1950 he settled in Israel, was active in the leftist political camp, was elected to the second Knesset (Israeli parliament), and was involved in the activities of survivors' organizations and former underground fighters living in Israel. His underground and public activities during the Holocaust period are described in his two books, *The Underground Period* (1971) and *In the Place Where Fate Brought Me: With the Jews of Warsaw, 1939–1942* (1978; both in Hebrew).

◆

Bernadotte, Folke

1895–1948

Swedish statesman; count of Wisborg and nephew of King Gustav V. During World War II Bernadotte represented the Swedish Red Cross in the exchange of prisoners between Germany and the Allies. In 1943 he became its vice president and in 1946 he was appointed its president. Bernadotte negotiated with Heinrich Himmler on behalf of the Swedish Red Cross, and in March and April of 1945 succeeded in persuading him to release more than seven thousand Scandinavian nationals who were being held in Nazi concentration camps; these included over four hundred Danish Jews imprisoned in Theresienstadt.

Following a meeting between Norbert Masur, the representative of the World Jewish Congress in Sweden, and Himmler, Bernadotte also succeeded in arranging for the release of ten thousand women from the

Ravensbrück concentration camp; two thousand of the women, who were nationals of various countries, were Jewish. Most of them were transferred to Sweden.

On May 20, 1948, the United Nations Security Council appointed Bernadotte as a mediator on its behalf between Israel and the invading Arab countries. He negotiated a four-week truce, beginning on June 11, 1948, but was unable to obtain from the Arab states an agreement for its extension. Bernadotte then worked out a plan for the settlement of the conflict based on Israeli concessions to the Arabs, but on September 17 of that year he was assassinated in Jerusalem by Hazit ha-Moledet (Fatherland Front), a group connected with the Loḥamei Ḥerut Israel organization.

The Jewish National Fund planted a forest in the hills of Jerusalem in honor of Folke Bernadotte. His book, *Instead of Arms*, was published in 1949. ◆

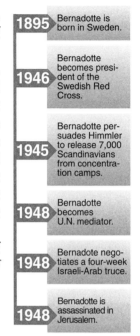

1895 Bernadotte is born in Sweden.

1946 Bernadotte becomes president of the Swedish Red Cross.

1945 Bernadotte persuades Himmler to release 7,000 Scandinavians from concentration camps.

1948 Bernadotte becomes U.N. mediator.

1948 Bernadote negotiates a four-week Israeli-Arab truce.

1948 Bernadotte is assassinated in Jerusalem.

Biberstein, Marek

D. 1944

Chairman of the Judenrat (Jewish Council) in Kraków. Before the war, Biberstein was a prominent figure in the life of the city's Jewish community. When Kraków was occupied by the Germans, he was appointed chairman of the provisional community administration, which before long became a Judenrat, with Biberstein remaining at its head. In this capacity, he did a great deal to alleviate the lot of the community by organizing aid to those in need and by frequently intervening for the release of Jews who for one reason or another had been seized by the Germans. In June 1941 Biberstein was arrested on the charge of having violated foreign-currency regulations, but the real reason seems to have been the Germans' dissatisfaction with his conduct and their desire to remove him from his post. He was kept in prison in Tarnów until the end of July 1942, when he returned to the Kraków ghetto, a sick and broken man. A few weeks later Biberstein and his family were taken to the Płaszów camp, where he perished on May 14, 1944. ◆

1941 Biberstein is arrested for allegedly violating foreign currency regulations.

1942 Biberstein returns to the Kraków ghetto from prison, a broken man.

1944 Biberstein dies at the Płaszów concentration camp.

Bielski, Tuvia

1906–1987

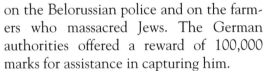

ewish partisan commander. Bielski's family were farmers in Stankiewicze, near Novogrudok. At the age of seventeen he joined the Zionist pioneering movement, and in 1928 he was mobilized into the Polish army, where he rose to the rank of corporal. He married in 1930 and settled in the village of Subotnik, where he opened a textile store. In September 1939 the area was annexed to the Soviet Union.

With the German invasion of the Soviet Union on June 22, 1941, Bielski was **mobilized.** When the Germans invaded the region he fled to the forest, and from there to his village of birth. After their parents and other members of their family were slaughtered in the Novogrudok ghetto, Bielski and his brothers, Zusya, Asael, and Aharon, escaped to the forests. Securing arms, they created a seventeen-member partisan core there, consisting mostly of members of Bielski's family. Elected as commander, Tuvia Bielski sent emissaries to the ghettos in the vicinity, inviting the inmates to join his group. Hundreds of the surviving Jews in the ghettos of the Novogrudok region—men, women, and children—streamed into Bielski's camp, and his partisan band grew daily.

Bielski learned to wage partisan combat, and he considered the saving of Jewish lives a supreme objective. His band inspired terror in the Novogrudok region as it took vengeance on the Belorussian police and on the farmers who massacred Jews. The German authorities offered a reward of 100,000 marks for assistance in capturing him.

With the creation of the band of Jewish partisans in the Naliboki Forest, Bielski won the trust of the Soviet partisan unit in the vicinity, and particularly of its commander, General Platon (Vasily Yehimovich Chernyshev). Bielski opposed the unit's intention of taking away his 150 fighters, leaving him with a civilian camp of refugees, and in order to frustrate this aim he made his camp a maintenance base for the Soviet fighters. His group was not a

mobilized: called into active military service.

partisan band in the regular sense but a Jewish community in the forest, with a synagogue, a law court, workshops, a school, and a dispensary.

In the summer of 1943, the Germans initiated a massive hunt through the Naliboki Forest in order to destroy the partisan forces, and in particular Bielski's band. The partisans retreated to the densest part of the forest, and the commander of Bielski's area ordered Bielski to pare down his unit to include only single people with arms; married men, women, and children were ordered to abandon the area where the unit had been staying and not follow the fighters to the center of the forest. Knowing that this instruction was a death sentence for the civilians in his group, Bielski disobeyed, retreating to the thickest part of the forest with his entire band. The fighters protected the civilians until they were able to emerge safely from the forest, evading the Germans who surrounded it. In the summer of 1944, with the liberation of the area, Bielski and his 1,230-strong partisan band, known as "Kalinin," marched into the town of Novogrudok. Asael Bielski was killed in battle as a soldier in the Soviet army at Königsberg in 1944.

After the war Bielski returned to Poland. That same year, in 1945, he immigrated to Palestine, and in 1954 he settled in the United States with his two surviving brothers. ◆

1928	Bielski is mobilized into the Polish Army.
1930	Bielski opens a textile store in Subotnik.
1939	Bielski's neighborhood is annexed to the Soviet Union.
1941	Bielski is mobilized with the German invasion of the Soviet Union.
1943	Bielski disobeys German orders and saves many lives.
1944	Bielski's brother Asael is killed in battle.
1945	Bielski immigrates to Palestine.
1954	Bielski settles in the United States with his surviving brothers.

Binkiene, Sofija

1902–1984

Rescuer of Jews in Kovno, Lithuania. The widow of a well-known Lithuanian author, Binkiene lived near the Kovno ghetto. Although she had had no previous contacts with Jewish circles and was tending a sick husband, she helped Jews by offering them temporary shelter in her home. Many Jews, fleeing from the Kovno ghetto, found initial refuge in her home. At times, especially during the final liquidation of the ghetto in 1944, Binkiene roved the streets near the ghetto in the hope of bringing straggling Jews into the safety of her home. Many scores of Jews were thus helped and saved.

In 1967 Sofija Binkiene edited a book on Lithuanians who rescued Jews, *Ir be ginklo kariai* (Vilna, 1962). She was awarded

1902 Binkiene is born.

1944 Binkiene saves many Jews in the Kovno ghetto.

1967 Binkiene edits a book on Lithuanians who rescued Jews.

1967 Binkiene is awarded Yad Vashem's title "Righteous among the Nations."

the title of "Righteous among the Nations" by Yad Vashem in 1967. ◆

Blum, Abraham "Abrasha"

1905–1943

Bund leader and member of the Żydowska Organizacja Bojowa (Jewish Fighting Organization; ŻOB) in Warsaw. Blum was born in Vilna into a middle-class family, attended a Yiddish secondary school, and graduated with a degree in construction engineering from a Belgian institute. As a young man he became active in the Bund's youth movement. In 1929 he moved to Warsaw and became a full-time party activist. In the 1930s he was a member of the national board of the Bund youth movement, Zukunft (Future), and was active in the Bund-sponsored school network.

In the early days of World War II, Blum was one of the few Bund leaders who did not leave Warsaw. He played a central role in the Bund's clandestine operations as soon as they were launched, and helped run the party's soup kitchens, underground press, welfare services, and political indoctrination efforts.

In the underground's debate concerning the formation of a united fighting organization, Blum, as of the spring of 1942, supported the stand that called for the Bund to join with the Zionist groups in such an organization. Marek Edelman, in the report on the Bund's underground operations, *Getto Walczy* (The Ghetto Fights), published in 1945, described Blum as "the spiritual father of our resistance . . . the only person [in the Bund] able to control the situation [during the mass deportation from Warsaw]," and stated: "We owe it to him that we survived that terrible period." In October 1942 the Bund joined the ŻOB, and Blum was appointed the party's representative on the coordinating committee of the Bund and the Jewish National Committee (Żydowski Komitet Narodowy), the two bodies that formed the political leadership of the ŻOB. He rejected an offer to cross over to the "Aryan" side, despite the fact that his wife and children had gone into hiding there.

During the Warsaw Ghetto Uprising in April 1943, Blum fought with a group of young people in the "Brushmakers" area. He was among the group that succeeded in escaping from the ghetto and reaching the Polish side by way of the city sewage system. For several days he was in hiding in the Kampinos Forest, and from there he returned to Warsaw. When his hiding place there was discovered, he tried to escape through a fourth-floor window by tying bed sheets together and climbing down, but the sheets tore; Blum fell and was injured. He was seized by the Germans and taken to the Gestapo, and all further trace of him was lost. ◆

1905 — Blum is born in Vilna into a middle-class family.

1929 — Blum moves to Warsaw and becomes a full-time activist.

1942 — Blum supports the Bund's joining with Zionist groups.

1942 — Blum rejects an offer to cross over to the "Aryan" side.

1943 — Blum escapes through the sewers and fights with young people.

1943 — Blum is never seen again after Germans seize him escaping.

1945 — Blum is described as "the spiritual father of our movement."

Bogaard, Johannes "Uncle Hannes"

1891–1974

Farmer in Nieuw Vennep (Haarlemmermeer), southwest of Amsterdam, who was responsible for the rescue of some three hundred Jews. Bogaard hid fugitive Jews on his farm, as well as on the farms of relatives and friendly neigh-

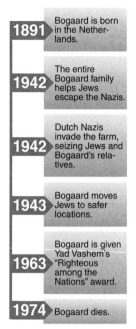

1891 Bogaard is born in the Nether-lands.

1942 The entire Bogaard family helps Jews escape the Nazis.

1942 Dutch Nazis invade the farm, seizing Jews and Bogaard's rela-tives.

1943 Bogaard moves Jews to safer locations.

1963 Bogaard is given Yad Vashem's "Righteous among the Nations" award.

1974 Bogaard dies.

bors, for long periods of time. Born into a strict Calvinist family of limited means, he was taught by his father to respect the Jews as the people of the Bible. After the deportation of Jews from the Netherlands began in July 1942, the entire Bogaard family of farmers devoted themselves to helping Jews escape the Nazi dragnet. When Jews were referred to Bogaard as being in need of help, Uncle Hannes ("Oom Hannes"), as he was affectionately known, traveled to Amsterdam once or twice a week to fetch the persons threatened with deportation and persuade them to follow him and place themselves under his care. Most were hidden in the vicinity of his farm, although at times there were up to one hundred Jews on his family's farm alone. He also collected money, ration cards, and identification papers from friends and acquaintances.

In November 1942 the Dutch Nazi police raided the Bogaard farm, capturing three Jews. Two more raids followed in the succeeding months, in which several dozen Jews were apprehended and a policeman was killed. Johannes's father, one of his brothers, and his own son Teunis were taken to a German concentration camp, where they perished.

By the end of 1943, Johannes Bogaard, until then operating largely on his own initiative, was able to link up with underground organizations, but most of his help still came from his own family. Alerted to the increased danger of detection by the authorities, most of the Jews in his charge were moved to other locations in the countryside for safe refuge. Bogaard probably saved more Jews, almost single-handedly, than any other person in the Netherlands. He was recognized by Yad Vashem as a "Righteous among the Nations" in 1963. ◆

Bonhoeffer, Dietrich

1906–1945

German Protestant theologian. Bonhoeffer's execution by the Nazis in the Flossenbürg concentration camp on April 9, 1945, in the closing stages of World War II, cut short his career as one of Germany's most significant twentieth-century theologians. After completing his studies at the University of Berlin (Ph.D., 1927) as a student of Adolf von Harnack, Germany's famous liberal theologian, Bonhoeffer became attracted to the more critical dialectical theology of Karl Barth.

Early in his career he realized the dangers of the extremism and racist bias of Nazi ideology, and in 1933 he became an outspoken opponent of the German Christian (Deutsche Christen) faction of the German Evangelical Church (Evangelische Kirche), which lauded Adolf Hitler and gave its support to the rise of the Nazi party. Because of this opposition, Bonhoeffer was sent to be chaplain of the German church in south London from 1933 to 1935, but he was later recalled to lead an illegal training institute for ordination candidates of the anti-Nazi Confessing Church (Bekennende Kirche), until it was suppressed by the Gestapo in 1938. During the war, he was recruited by Admiral Wilhelm Canaris, head of the Abwehr (the Wehrmacht intelligence service), for secret contacts with foreign churches, but was arrested in April 1943 and imprisoned in Berlin and Flossenbürg until his execution.

Bonhoeffer came from a Christian tradition that saw the Jews as accursed, as stated in his April 1933 essay "The Church and the Jewish Question." However, he was the first theologian to recognize the implications for Christian theology of the Nazi persecution of the Jews, and in 1933 he warned his fellow churchmen of the perversion of the Gospels that these racist attacks implied. He subsequently became involved in efforts to assist Jews to escape from Germany, including a successful scheme in 1942 to smuggle a party of fifteen Jews to Switzerland, which led to his arrest. Bonhoeffer's sense of moral outrage against the Nazi treatment of Jews was a major factor in his support of the German resistance movement, in which various members of his immediate family were involved and for which they were later executed.

In his theology, Bonhoeffer addressed the deeper causes of the alienation between Judaism and Christianity, showing that all attempts to curtail the theological significance of the Jewish heritage must be regarded as **heretical.** In his unfinished work *Ethics*, he began to define the basis for a new understanding of the theological solidarity between Christians and Jews, which went beyond sympathy based on humanitarian feelings. He was continually disappointed by the timidity of the Confessing Church in facing its obligations to the Jewish people. But his involvement in conspiratorial activities after 1939 prevented him from publishing any more outspoken attacks on the regime. There are, however, hints of new approaches in the series of his

"We have been silent witnesses of evil deeds: we have been drenched by many storms; we have learnt the arts of equivocation and pretence; experience has made us suspicious of others and kept us from being truthful and open; intolerable conflicts have worn us down and even made us cynical. Are we still of any use?"
Dietrich Bonhoeffer, "After Ten Years," *Letters and Papers from Prison*, 1942

heretical: opposed to the accepted beliefs of the church.

letters that were smuggled out of prison between 1943 and 1945. A collection of them was first published in 1951, under the title *Widerstand und Ergebung* (Resistance and Surrender). It appeared in English translation in 1953 as *Letters and Papers from Prison* and was published in many subsequent editions.

Bonhoeffer's courageous opposition to the Nazi regime and his subsequent murder greatly enhanced his reputation in the postwar period, and his theological influence has been significantly instrumental in the post-Holocaust rethinking of Christian relationships with the Jewish people. His other major works include *Nachfolge* (1937; published in English as *The Cost of Discipleship*, 1948) and *Sanctorium Communio* (1929; *The Community of Saints*, 1963). ◆

Bor-Komorowski, Tadeusz

1895–1966

Commander of the Armia Krajowa (Home Army) in Warsaw and of the Warsaw Polish uprising in 1944. Bor-Komorowski was born in Lvov. His actual name was Komorowski, "Bor" being his later code name in the underground. In World War I he was an officer in the Austro-Hungarian army, and after the war served as an officer in the Polish army, in which he became a colonel. In 1939 he took part in the battle against the German invaders.

At the beginning of the German occupation, Bor-Komorowski was one of the organizers of the Polish underground in the Kraków area. In July 1941 he became deputy commander of the Armia Krajowa and two years later was appointed its commander, the Polish government-in-exile promoting him to brigadier general. In his political views he was close to the National Democratic party (the

"Endeks"). It was he who gave the order for the Polish uprising in Warsaw, which he led from August to October 1944. When the rebellion was put down, Bor-Komorowski became a prisoner of war. He was liberated at the end of the war and spent the rest of his life in London, where he was active among Polish **emigrés.** He wrote the story of his experiences in *The Secret Army* (1951), in which he told about the aid offered and the actions taken by the Armia Krajowa in the face of mass deportations and the killing of the Jews. His contentions, however, have no basis in fact. ◆

emigré: a person forced to emigrate for political reasons.

Borkowska, Anna

D. 1988

Mother superior of a small cloister of Dominican sisters in Kolonia Wilenska, near Vilna, Lithuania. During the Ponary massacres of Jews in the summer months of 1941, Anna Borkowska agreed to conceal in her convent for brief periods seventeen members of Jewish Zionist pioneering groups, including Ha-Shomer ha-Tsa'ir. Later, she helped by smuggling weapons into the Vilna ghetto. Abraham Sutzkever, the Yiddish poet, related that the first four grenades received there were the gift of the mother superior, who instructed Abba Kovner in their proper use. She later supplied other weapons.

As Nazi suspicions of her mounted, the Germans had Anna Borkowska arrested in September 1943, the convent closed, and the sisters dispersed. One nun was dispatched to a labor camp. In 1984 Anna Borkowska was recognized by Yad Vashem as a "Righteous among the Nations." ◆

Brand, Joel

1907–1964

Member of the Relief and Rescue Committee of Budapest (known as the Va'ada) during World War II. Born in Năsăud, Transylvania, then under Hungarian

Jews could not remain in Hungary, for Eichmann had promised to make the country *judenrein* (cleansed of Jews).

rule, Brand embraced Zionism after a stint in the radical leftist movement in Weimar Germany. He returned to Transylvania after Hitler's seizure of power but eventually settled in Budapest, where together with his wife, Hansi Hartmann Brand, he operated a medium-sized glove-manufacturing plant. After the Anschluss and especially after the outbreak of World War II, the Brands became interested in refugee affairs, organizing a variety of rescue and relief activities.

When the Va'ada was established in January 1943 to aid refugees who had escaped from or were seeking to escape from Slovakia and Poland, Brand was chosen to head its Tiyyul (Trip) section, a border-crossing operation whose function was to smuggle Jews out of these countries.

After the German occupation of Hungary on March 19, 1944, the Va'ada's primary concern was the rescuing of Jews within Hungary. Brand was also engaged in the Re-Tiyyul (Return Trip) program, which enabled a number of Polish and Slovak refugees to return to Slovakia, where the situation of the remaining Jews was better, at least temporarily. While the first contact and rescue negotiations with the SS were established through Fülöp Freudiger, the Orthodox representative of the Jewish Council (Zsidó Tanács), and continued later by Rezső (Rudolf) Kasztner, it was Brand whom Adolf Eichmann summoned, on April 25, 1944, to offer his "Blood for Goods" arrangement. Under the arrangement, which was approved by the higher SS authorities, apparently including Heinrich Himmler, Eichmann expressed his readiness to exchange one million Jews for certain goods to be obtained from outside Hungary. These included 10,000 trucks that would be used for civilian purposes or only along the eastern front. Jews could not remain in Hungary, for he had promised to make the country *judenrein* ("cleansed of Jews"). But those covered by the bargain would be permitted to go into any Allied-controlled part of the world except Palestine, for the Nazis had promised the **mufti** of Jerusalem, Hajj Amin al-Husseini, not to permit this. To effectuate the deal, Eichmann was ready to allow Brand to go abroad to establish contact with the representatives of world Jewry and the western Allies.

mufti: a professional jurist who interprets Muslin law.

The true reason why Brand was chosen remains a mystery, but it appears that he had been recommended by Andor ("Bandi") Grosz, a doubtful character and minor intelligence agent who was in the service of anyone who paid him, including the Germans and the Va'ada. Grosz was reportedly employed by SS-Hauptsturmführer Otto Klages, the head of the SD (Sicherheitsdienst; Security Service) in Hungary; he was assigned to go together with Brand to establish contact with American and British intelligence officers in Istanbul and to discuss with them the possibility of a separate peace between Germany and the western Allies. Brand's mission, according to this scenario, was to camouflage Grosz's more important assignment.

Brand was informed about the completion of his travel arrangements on May 15, 1944, the day that mass deportations from Hungary began. Supplied with a German passport bearing the name Eugen Band, he left Budapest for Vienna in the company of Obersturmbannführer Hermann Krumey, a leading member of the Eichmann Sonderkommando, and Groz left two days later. On May 19 Brand and Grosz arrived in Istanbul, where they were met by local representatives of the Joint Rescue Committee of the Jewish Agency. Since Brand had no Turkish visa, the details of his mission were revealed to Laurence Steinhardt, the American ambassador in Ankara, and to the leaders of the Jewish Agency in Jerusalem by the Agency's representatives in Turkey.

By the end of the month, the leaders of the American and British governments were fully informed about Brand's mission. Grosz was arrested by the British on June 1, shortly after crossing the Syrian border. Thus, he was unable to meet with authorized Jewish and non-Jewish representatives and to complete his assignment. Equipped with a British visa, Brand left—ostensibly for Palestine—on June 5, but was arrested by the British at Aleppo two days later. On June 10 he was given an opportunity (while under arrest) to reveal the plight of Hungarian Jewry and the details of his mission to Moshe Shertok (Sharett), head of the Jewish Agency's Political Department. Shertok was very favorably impressed with Brand, as was Ira A. Hirschmann, the representative of the War Refugee Board, who interrogated him later in the month in Cairo. Before the month was over, Shertok and Hirschmnn revealed the details of their interrogations to the Yishuv leaders and to top figures of the American and British governments.

In spite of pleas by the Yishuv leaders, the British decided against having any dealings "with the Gestapo" and even permitting Brand's return to Hungary. Their decision was based on

1907 Brand is born in Nsud, Transylvania.

1943 Brand is chosen to help smuggle Jews over the border.

1944 Brand is arrested by the British after crossing the Syrian border.

1944 Brand reveals the details of his mission to Moshe Shertok.

1964 Brand regrets passing Eichmann's offer to the British.

1964 Brand dies.

many factors, among them the continuation of the "Final Solution" program in Hungary; the vehement opposition of the Soviets (who were officially informed about the offer in mid-June) to any discussion on this matter with the Germans; and the concern of the British over acquiring responsibility for one million Jews in case the Nazis kept their side of the bargain. The Americans were more flexible, advocating that the negotiations be continued in the hope of saving lives. Whatever hopes the Jewish leaders of the free world had for Brand's mission dissipated on July 19, when the BBC brought it to public attention. The following day, the British press emphasized that the "monstrous offer" of the Germans to barter Jews was a loathsome attempt to blackmail the Allies.

Immediately after his June 10 meeting with Shertok, Brand was taken to Cairo, where he was intensively debriefed and treated as a "privileged prisoner" until October, when he was allowed to go to Palestine. A frustrated and dejected man, Brand felt for a long time that because of the failure and shortcomings of the Jewish leaders and the passivity and insensitivity of the Allies, the chance to save a million Jews had been missed. However, shortly before his death in Tel Aviv in 1964, Brand came to believe that he had made a "terrible mistake" in passing to the British the Eichmann offer, and that Heinrich Himmler had merely sought to sow suspicion among the Allies as a preparation for his much-desired Nazi-Western coalition against Moscow. ◆

> Whatever hope the Jewish leaders of the free world had for Brand's mission dissipated on July 19, when the BBC brought it to public attention.

Choms, Władysława

1891–1966

Polish rescuer of Jews during the Holocaust. Choms headed the Lvov branch of Zegota (the Polish Council for Aid to Jews), a Polish underground organization based in Warsaw. Before the war, in Drogobych, Eastern Galicia, where she headed the municipal welfare department, and in Lvov, where she was active in combating anti-Semitism, she showed a particular concern for the welfare of the Jewish people. With the German occupation of Lvov in June 1941, she became wholeheartedly involved in charitable work on behalf of destitute Jews. Collecting jewelry and money from wealthy Jews, she created a fund for extending aid to Jews, and rallied around her a group of devoted persons.

Władysława Choms (front row, fourth from left) at Yad Vashem in 1963.

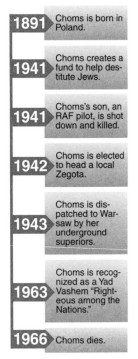

1891 Choms is born in Poland.

1941 Choms creates a fund to help destitute Jews.

1941 Choms's son, an RAF pilot, is shot down and killed.

1942 Choms is elected to head a local Zegota.

1943 Choms is dispatched to Warsaw by her underground superiors.

1963 Choms is recognized as a Yad Vashem "Righteous among the Nations."

1966 Choms dies.

Aid came in various forms: the forging of false documents for Jews living outside the restricted ghetto perimeter; provision of money, food, and medical care for Jews inside and outside the ghetto; and the removal of Jewish children and adults from the ghetto to secure shelters in convents and with private families. Some sixty Jewish children were under her personal supervision.

Sought by the Germans (her officer-husband and son had fled to England and were known to have enlisted in the struggle against Nazi Germany), Choms was constantly on the move, ever changing names and addresses. In November 1942, while supervising a well-established rescue network in Lvov, she was elected by the Warsaw-based Zegota to establish and head a local branch in Lvov. Nicknamed the "Angel of Lvov" by her Jewish beneficiaries, she continued her charitable activities until November 1943, when, with the increasing threat to her personal safety, she was dispatched to Warsaw by her underground superiors.

After the war, Choms learned that her son, a pilot in the Royal Air Force, had been shot down and killed in 1941. She was recognized as a "Righteous among the Nations," and planted a tree at Yad Vashem in Jerusalem in 1963. ◆

Cohn, Marianne

1924–1944

French Jewish underground activist. Born in Mannheim, Germany, Cohn was a member of the Eclaireurs Israélites de France (French Jewish Scouts) and in 1942 joined the Mouvement de la Jeunesse Sioniste (Zionist Youth Movement). She belonged to the underground sponsored by both organizations, which smuggled into Switzerland Jewish children whose parents had been expelled from France. On June 1, 1944, Cohn was seized by a German patrol, together with a group of twenty-eight children, and all were imprisoned in the town of Annemasse. The underground succeeded in establishing contact with Cohn and devised a plan to get her out of jail, but she was not prepared to escape, fearing that the

1924 Cohn is born in Mannheim, Germany.

1942 Cohn joins the Zionist Youth Movement.

1944 Cohn is seized by Germans and imprisoned in Annemasse.

1944 Cohn is killed by ax-wielding French militia.

children would suffer if she were to do so. On July 8, two members of the Nazi-sponsored French militia broke into the prison, took Cohn out, and killed her with an ax. The children were all saved. ◆

Deffaugt, Jean

Mayor of Annemasse, a French town on the Swiss border, where many clandestine escape routes for fleeing Jews converged. Deffaugt took it upon himself to visit Jews who were caught by the Germans while trying to cross the border and incarcerated in an annex of the Pax Hotel, where they had to withstand brutal interrogation of the Gestapo. He collected food, medicines, blankets, and other supplies, which he brought to the Gestapo prison to deliver to the inmates. Deffaugt pleaded with the Gestapo on behalf of the imprisoned Jews. As he later reminisced, "I was afraid, I admit. I never mounted the Gestapo stairways without making the sign of the

Jean Deffaugt and his wife.

41

> *"I was afraid, I admit. I never mounted the Gestapo stairways without making the sign of the cross, or murmuring a prayer."*
>
> Jean Deffaught

cross, or murmuring a prayer." On one occasion, the Gestapo agreed to release into Deffaugt's care a group of children under the age of eleven, arrested while on their way to the border, on the basis of the following statement: "I, Jean Deffaugt, mayor of Annemasse, acknowledge receiving from Inspector Mayer, chief of the Security Services, eleven children of Jewish faith, whom I pledge to return at the first order." Deffaugt soon placed them in the hands of a Father Duret, who hid them in Bonne-sur-Menoge until the Allied liberation in the following weeks.

With the liberation of Annemasse by the United States Army, all the children were reunited by Deffaugt and turned over to Jewish hands. Jean Deffaugt was recognized by Yad Vashem as a "Righteous among the Nations" in 1965. ◆

Douwes, Arnold

1906–

1906 Douwes is born in the Netherlands.

1945 Douwes is imprisoned in Assen, and awaits execution.

1956 Douwes moves to Israel.

1965 Douwes is recognized as a Yad Vashem "Righteous among the Nations."

Dutch rescuer of Jews during the Holocaust. The son of a pastor in the Dutch Reformed church, Douwes joined the Dutch underground and devoted himself to the rescue of Jewish adults and children. At first, he worked under the guidance of Johannes Post (an important underground figure who aided Jews), who was shot by the Germans. Douwes enlarged the scope of his mentor's rescue operations. Jewish families who had received notification to report for deportation to the Westerbork camp were referred to him by the Dutch underground. He concentrated his activities in the vicinity of the town of Nieuwlande, in the northeastern province of Drenthe. There, almost every household sheltered a Jewish person. Douwes looked after all the needs of these Jews, helping to supply them with food and other necessities, false identification papers, and financial support (through the underground). Together with Max Leons (nicknamed "Nico"), a Jew who posed as a Protestant colleague and friend of Douwes, he scoured the countryside and enlisted several hundred Dutch families in their mutual rescue activities.

Douwes personally met the children in Amsterdam, or at the train station upon their arrival in the Drenthe district. When the Germans staged raids in the vicinity, Douwes went for nocturnal rides on his bicycle, moving Jews—under the very noses of the Germans—to safer locations.

An operation of this magnitude could not go undetected for long, and Douwes was wanted by the authorities. To avoid arrest, he changed his appearance, growing a mustache and wearing a hat and eyeglasses. In spite of these precautions, he was apprehended in January 1945 and imprisoned in Assen, where he awaited his execution. The underground, however, succeeded in freeing him before that could take place. After the war, Douwes lived for a time in South Africa and then moved to Israel in 1956.

Arnold Douwes was responsible for saving the lives of hundreds of Jews, including some one hundred children. In 1965 he was recognized as a "Righteous among the Nations" by Yad Vashem. More than two hundred residents of the Nieuwlande area were later awarded the title as well. ◆

Draenger, Shimshon

1917–1943?

Underground leader. Draenger, who was known as Simek, was born in Kraków. At the age of thirteen he joined the Akiva Zionist youth movement, and later became one of its main leaders. Until the outbreak of World War II he edited the movement's journal, *Divrei Akiva*, and the weekly *Tse'irim*, a newspaper for young people. On September 22, 1939, a short time after the German occupation of Kraków, Draenger was arrested because of the articles of Irene Harand, an Austrian anti-Nazi, that he had published in *Divrei Akiva*. Together with his future wife, Gusta Dawidson, who was arrested at the same time, Draenger was held at the prison camp in Trop-

pau, Czechoslovakia. Following his release in December 1939, he reassembled his followers under the guise of educational activity, thereby reconstructing the Akiva cell in Warsaw. At the beginning of the war Draenger tried, unsuccessfully, to save the members of his movement by smuggling them into Slovakia. From December 1941 to August 1942 he managed a training farm at Kopaliny, which was a cover for Akiva and its underground activity.

Draenger was one of the youth movement activists who from the beginning of the war maintained that the Jews had no chance of survival under the Nazi occupation, and this approach dictated his radical position and methods of activity. In August 1942 he helped found He-Haluts ha-Lohem, a combat organization of Jewish pioneer youth, and was a member of its command. He set up the organization's Technical Office, which forged permits for the members giving entry to and exit from the ghetto, and sold these permits to finance arms purchases. He also edited the underground journal *He-Haluts ha-Lohem*.

In January 1943 Draenger was seized and was imprisoned in the Montelupich Prison, where he organized Bible and other study circles for his friends in jail. On April 29 of that year he escaped and was reunited with his wife, Gusta, who had also escaped from Montelupich. Both became partisans in the Wiśnicz Forest. There Draenger also resumed publication of *He-Haluts ha-Lohem*, exhorting the Jewish youth remaining in the forest to resist the Germans actively, urging the last residents of the ghetto to flee for their lives, and appealing to the Poles not to betray Jews to the authorities. His articles also sketched the history of the pioneer underground.

On November 8, 1943, Draenger was apprehended by the Germans and, presumably, was killed. ◆

"For an entire year, the ghetto's population had lived in constant dread of the night raids, when the police went from house to house, working from lists compiled with the aid of collaborators, picking up innocent people for slaughter."

Tova Draenger,
Justyna's Narrative,
1943

Draenger, Tova

1917–1943?

Underground member and chronicler. Draenger's maiden name was Gusta Dawidson. Born in Kraków, by 1938 she was one of the leaders of the Akiva movement there. Together with Shimshon Draenger (who became her husband early in 1940), she edited *Tse'irim*, a weekly for young people. During the Nazi occupation she was one of the founders of He-Haluts ha-Lohem, an underground combat movement in Kraków, and played an active role in its operations.

On September 22, 1939, she was arrested, together with Shimshon Draenger, and charged with belonging to the Austrian anti-Nazi Irene Harand group. In December 1939 they were released from the prison camp in Troppau, Czechoslovakia, where they had been interned. They resumed their activities in Kraków and Warsaw and, in 1940, reorganized Akiva in both cities.

In He-Haluts ha-Lohem, Draenger's main task was, with her husband, to produce forged documents for the organization's use. On January 18, 1943, having learned that her husband had been arrested, she surrendered to the Gestapo, as she and her husband had pledged to do if either was seized. She was put in the Montelupich Prison and, while there, until April 29 of that year, wrote her memoirs in the form of a diary, her purpose being to record the story of the final uprising in Kraków. Years later, these memoirs were published under the title *Justina's Diary*. She wrote on toilet paper, in several copies, helped by fellow members of the underground who shared the cell with her. The diary presents, in Draenger's own words, "the true story of the last and most daring revolt of the young fighters," and deals with the history of Akiva and He-Haluts ha-Lohem between April 1941 and March 1943. Miraculously, fifteen of the diary's twenty chapters were preserved, covering the period from August 23 to November 26, 1942.

Draenger escaped from prison on April 29, 1943, and, together with her husband, resumed underground activities, this time in the Wiśnicz Forest. The two also recommenced publication of *He-Haluts ha-Lohem,* the underground movement's journal.

On November 9 of that year, following her husband's arrest, Draenger again surrendered to the Nazis. Nothing is known of the subsequent fate of either, and it is assumed that they were both executed. ◆

Dubnow, Simon

1860–1941

Hasidism: concerning Hasidim, a mystical Jewish sect.

One of the great Jewish historians and thinkers of modern times and one of the founders of Autonomism, the movement that advocated Jewish national autonomy in the Diaspora. Dubnow was born in Mstislavl, Belorussia, received a traditional Jewish education, and acquired a broad general education on his own; he was close to the circle of the Jewish Enlightenment in Russia. Dubnow's first works on Jewish history were published in the 1880s. His greatest achievement was his pioneering approach to the study of the history of the Jews in eastern Europe and their spiritual and religious movements. In his research work, Dubnow stressed the periods of Jewish autonomy in Poland and Lithuania and the history of **Hasidism.** His major work was the ten-volume *Weltgeschichte des jüdischen Volkes* (World History of the Jewish People), which traced the history of the Jews from their beginnings to modern times; it was first published in its German translation between 1923 and 1929, and then in other languages, including the original Russian.

In his early work as a historian, Dubnow followed the trail of the nineteenth-century German Jewish historian Heinrich

Graetz, but he later discarded the view that saw the Jewish people as a unique phenomenon in history with its own spiritual and religious mission. He adopted instead a secular concept, which regarded the Jews as a national entity that, despite the passage of generations and the rise and fall of its "centers of hegemony," has preserved its autonomous spiritual framework. In Dubnow's view, it was the spiritual and cultural elements that represented the highest degree of a people's development. Since the Jews, thanks to their unique history, had retained their specific spiritual essence more than any other people, they were ripe to assume this highest level of a people in progressive human society.

This was the source of Dubnow's political philosophy, which regarded the Emancipation as a turning point in Jewish history and called for the granting of spiritual and cultural autonomy to the Jewish populations of Europe. Dubnow regarded such a grant of autonomy as providing the basis for national Jewish existence and for the realization of Jewish strivings, especially in the countries of eastern Europe. This political concept was the ideological base upon which Dubnow and his associates established the Jewish People's Party (Volkspartei) in 1906.

In 1922 Dubnow succeeded in leaving the Soviet Union and settled in Berlin. When Hitler came to power, Dubnow moved to Riga, the capital of Latvia, and continued his work. When Riga was occupied by the Germans in early July 1941, the eighty-one-year-old scholar was put in the city's ghetto, and his library was confiscated. In his final days he reportedly told the people he met, "Jews, make sure that everything is written down and recorded." According to one account, Dubnow was sick and feverish when he was shot to death while being taken out of the ghetto, in December 1941. ◆

1860	Dubnow is born in Mstislavl, Belorussia.
1906	Dubnow helps establish the Jewish People's Party.
1922	Dubnow settles in Berlin.
1923	Dubnow's 10-volume world history of the Jews is published.
1941	Dubnow is put in the Riga ghetto by Germans.
1941	Dubnow is shot to death by Nazis.

Duckwitz, Georg Ferdinand
1904–1973

German diplomat, one of the "Righteous among the Nations." Duckwitz was born in Bremen, the son of a prominent merchant family, and in the early 1930s was a businessman in Copenhagen. He joined the Nazi party in

1904 Duckwitz is born in Bremen, Germany.

1932 Duckwitz joins the Nazi party.

1933 Duckwitz begins serving in Alfred Rosenberg's office.

1943 Duckwitz foils German plans to deport Jews by warning Danish contacts.

1955 Duckwitz becomes German ambassador to Denmark.

1973 Duckwitz dies.

1932, and from 1933 to 1935 served in Alfred Rosenberg's foreign-policy office, but left that post of his own accord and took a civilian job in a shipping firm.

At the beginning of World War II, Duckwitz was posted to Denmark by the Abwehr, the German intelligence organization. When Denmark was occupied by the Germans, Duckwitz was appointed shipping attaché at the German mission in Copenhagen. He established ties with the leaders of the Danish Social Democrat party and gained their trust. When the Germans were about to deport the Jews of Denmark to Nazi camps in the east at the beginning of October 1943, Duckwitz informed his Danish contacts of the German plans. It was mainly this advance warning that enabled the Danes to organize the operation that saved the Jews by smuggling them out to Sweden. Duckwitz even went so far as to travel to Sweden, where he met with the prime minister, Per Albin Hansson, who promised that the Swedish government would help in the effort to rescue Denmark's Jews.

After the war, Duckwitz remained in the foreign service of the Federal Republic of Germany (West Germany), and from 1955 to 1958 he served as the German ambassador in Denmark. His last post was that of director-general of the Foreign Ministry. For Duckwitz's share in the rescue of the Jews of Denmark, Yad Vashem awarded him the title of "Righteous among the Nations." ◆

Dvoretski, Alter

1906–1942

Partisan commander. Dvoretski was born in Diatlovo (Zhetl), studied law at the University of Vilna, and was admitted to the bar in 1938. He was a member of Po'alei Zion, where his main interest was sports activities. Under the Soviet regime (1939–41) he practiced law in Novogrudok, in the Belorussian SSR.

At the beginning of the German occupation in 1941, Dvoretski settled in Diatlovo and was appointed chairman of its Judenrat (Jewish Council). Under the impact of the events he witnessed, he issued a call for rescue and revenge and organized an underground partisan group in the Diatlovo ghetto, with himself at the helm. He devised a plan to arm the Jewish youth in the surrounding towns and take them to the densely wooded Lipiczany Forest, in order to fight the Germans from there; this plan was also to be a means for saving Jews who were physically unfit for fighting.

Dvoretski met with the Germans from time to time, while organizing the acquisition of arms and smuggling them into the ghetto. At all times, he carried a loaded pistol so as to be prepared for any eventuality. He provided weapons to a group of Soviet prisoners of war who had escaped from the camps in which they had been held, and steered them to the Lipiczany Forest. Another group of Jewish youth—refugees with no local family ties or property—also made its way out of the ghetto with Dvoretski's support in the form of advice, arms, and clothing.

Dvoretski worked out a detailed plan for armed resistance in case the Germans tried to carry out a massacre in the ghetto, but the plan was foiled by an act of betrayal. When Dvoretski himself went to the forest, he tried to implement his daring plans of rescuing the Jews of Diatlovo and the neighboring ghettos, and he dreamed of forming Jewish partisan regiments. What he found in the forest, however, were small groups of Soviet partisans—former prisoners of war—who had few arms in their possession and were not prepared to take the initiative in genuine attacks on the Germans. They had no contact with Moscow, lacked a proper command, and were altogether undisciplined; many had anti-Semitic tendencies. Dvoretski pressured the commander of several partisan groups to agree to launch an attack on the Diatlovo garrison in order to liberate the Jewish youth who were confined in the ghetto.

On the night of April 29, 1942, the partisan group made its way to Diatlovo, coming to a halt at the Christian cemetery on the outskirts of the town. A local peasant was sent to reconnoiter, and he returned with a report that a strong German detachment had come to the town in order to massacre the Jews on the next day, April 30. The Soviet partisans were not ready to risk an attack, and made their way back to their refuge in the forest. The plan for saving the Jews of Diatlovo had been frustrated. The commanders of the various partisan groups treated Dvoretski's proposals with a mixture of fear and envy; in the end, the partisans set an ambush and murdered Dvoretski and one of his comrades.

1906 Dvoretski is born in Diatlovo.

1938 Dvoretski is admitted to the bar.

1939 Dvoretski begins to practice law in Novogrudok.

1941 Dvoretski settles in Diatlovo and becomes chairman of its Judenrat.

1942 Dvoretski is murdered in an ambush by Soviet partisans.

1942 More than 600 Jews can flee thanks to Dvoretski's activities.

1942 The Jews who survive the liquidation form a fighting battalion.

Dvoretski's activities in the ghetto enabled more than six hundred Jews from Diatlovo to flee during the liquidation of the ghetto on August 6, 1942, and to make their way to the Lipiczany Forest. There they formed a fighting battalion of partisans, commanded by Hirsch Kaplinski. This battalion eventually became a Jewish company (the third such) in the Soviet Orlianski-Borba battalion. ◆

Edelman, Marek

1921–

A commander of the Warsaw ghetto uprising. A native of Warsaw, Edelman was a member of Zukunft, the youth movement affiliated with the Jewish Socialist party, the Bund, and was one of its activists in the ghetto underground. When the relative standing of the young people in the underground gained in strength, Edelman became a member of the Bund's central institutions. In November 1942 he joined the Żydowska Organizacja Bojowa (Jewish Fighting Organization; ŻOB) and shortly afterward was appointed as his movement's representative in the organization's command.

In the Warsaw ghetto uprising of April 1943, Edelman was at first in charge of the "Brushmakers" area in the ghetto; following the withdrawal of the ŻOB forces, he and his men joined the group centered on 30 Franciszkanska Street. Edelman was among the last group of fighters to hold out in the ŻOB headquarters at 18 Mila Street, and he then crossed over to the "Aryan" side of Warsaw by way of the sewers, on May 10. In

August 1944 Edelman served in the ranks of the ŻOB company that took part in the Warsaw Polish uprising.

After the war, in 1945, Edelman published *The Bund's Role in the Defense of the Warsaw Ghetto*, in Polish and Yiddish. He also published *The Ghetto Fights* (1946), a short history of the uprising, in Polish, Yiddish, and English. He studied medicine and practiced it, remaining in Poland. From the early 1980s he was active in the **Solidarity** trade union movement. ◆

solidarity: unity based on common interests.

Edelstein, Jacob

1903–1944

Jacob Edelstein decided to do everything in his power to ensure that the Jews of Czechoslovakia would not be dispatched to Poland.

Chairman of the Judenrat (Jewish Council) in the Theresienstadt ghetto. Edelstein was born in Gorodenka, Galicia, and received a religious Zionist upbringing. During World War I his family moved to Brno (Ger., Brünn), the capital of Moravia, and from 1926 he was active in the Tekhelet-Lavan and He-Haluts Zionist youth movements. In 1929 he was elected Tekhelet-Lavan representative at the He-Haluts main office, and in 1933 he was appointed head of its Palestine Office in Prague. In the summer of 1937 Edelstein immigrated to Palestine and for three months worked there for Keren Hayesod (the Palestine Foundation Fund), but he was disappointed with that situation and decided to return to Prague, where he resumed his work as director of the Palestine Office.

On March 15, 1939, the day the Germans marched into Prague, the members of the Zionist leadership of Czechoslovakia held a meeting at which they decided that it was their duty to stay on and not abandon the Jewish population at a time of crisis. Edelsten became the leading personality in the Zionist leadership, was put in charge of emigration to Palestine, and before long became the official representative of the Jews in contacts with the Germans.

Until he was sent to Theresienstadt on December 4, 1941, Edelstein left the country for several trips abroad, with the Gestapo's permission, in order to look for ways and means to speed up the emigration of Jews. In May 1939 he visited Palestine, in November he was in Trieste, and at the end of that month he was in Vienna; in February 1940 he spent two days in Geneva and from there went to Berlin. He visited Bratislava in the fall of 1940, and in March 1941 he went to Amsterdam. In each of these placed Edelstein met with the Jewish community leaders and the Zionist leadership, shared his information with them, and warned them of possible future developments. He had several opportunities to stay abroad rather than return to Czechoslovakia, but he always went back to Prague.

On October 18, 1939, Edelstein, with a group of a thousand men from Moravská Ostrava, left for Nisko, on the San River, south of Lublin, in connection with a German plan for the "resettlement" of Jews in the Lublin district. This plan ended in failure, and some of the deportees were returned to their place of origin. Edelstein went back to Prague in November 1939. His Nisko experience gave him an idea of the conditions in the east and of what was happening there. He decided to do everything in his power to ensure that the Jews of Czechoslovakia would not be dispatched to Poland, since he doubted whether they could hold out in the harsh conditions prevailing in German-occupied Poland. It was now his major concern to persuade the Germans to let the Jews stay in the Protectorate of Bohemia and Moravia and to utilize them as manpower. Jewish labor as a means of saving Jewish lives became the core of Edelstein's policy, and this prompted him time and again to make proposals for the German exploitation of Jewish manpower.

In October 1941 the Germans decided on the establishment of the Theresienstadt ghetto as a temporary solution for the Jews of the Protectorate and a base for their future deportation to the east. The Jewish leadership, with Edelstein at its head, saw in the founding of Theresienstadt a personal achievement and the success of their efforts to gain permission for the Jews to stay in the Protectorate. They did not know that Theresienstadt was only a temporary arrangement. Edelstein arrived at Theresienstadt on December 4, 1941, and became the first chairman of its Judenrat. He was assisted by a deputy, Otto Zucker, and a council of twelve. The emphasis in the ghetto was on education of the young and on making the ghetto into a productive establishment. In January of 1943 Edelstein was dismissed from his post, on the charge that there was a discrepancy between the registered population of the Theresienstadt ghetto and the actual figure. On December 18, 1943, he was deported

1903 Edelstein is born in Gorodenka, Galicia.

1929 Edelstein is elected a representative in the youth movement office.

1933 Edelstein is appointed head of the youth movement's Palestine office in Prague.

1937 Edelstein immigrates to Palestine, but returns to Prague.

1939 Edelstein and 1,000 men leave for Nisko to resettle.

1939 Edelstein returns to Prague when the resettlement plan fails.

1940 Edelstein visits Geneva, Berlin, and Bratislava to speed Jewish emigration.

1941 Edelstein visits Amsterdam to warn Jewish leaders of possibilities.

1941 Edelstein is sent to the Theresienstadt ghetto and heads Judenrat.

1943 Edelstein is dismissed from his post.

1943 Edelstein is deported to Auschwitz.

1944 Edelstein and his family are shot to death at Auschwitz.

to Auschwitz, where he and his family were shot to death, on June 20, 1944.

Edelstein's activities in Theresienstadt have been the subject of dispute. Those who find fault with him charge him with cooperating with the Nazis and with misreading the fact of the situation; their criticism is directed at his policy, but no doubt has been cast on his personal honesty and integrity. Others regard Edelstein as a hero who sacrificed himself for the sake of his people. ◆

Ehrenburg, Ilya Grigoryevich

1891–1967

1891 Ehrenburg is born in Russia.

1940 Ehrenburg laments the Nazi persecution of the Jews in a poem.

1941 Ehrenburg denounces fascism and anti-Semitism in his book *Padenie Parizha*.

1944 Ehrenburg edits *Murders of Peoples*.

1945 Ehrenburg is officially criticized for his extreme anti-German stand.

1960 Six volumes of Ehrenburg's memoirs are serialized in a journal.

1967 Ehrenburg dies; bequeathes his entire archive to Yad Vashem.

1980 The complete version of *The Black Book of Soviet Jewry* is published.

Russian Jewish writer and journalist. Ehrenburg lived abroad for many years, mostly in Paris, and was a foreign correspondent for Soviet newspapers. After the German invasion of France in 1940, he returned to the Soviet Union. Although Ehrenburg was an assimilated Jew and was steeped in Russian culture, his writings often dealt with Jewish subjects. During World War II he became increasingly conscious of his Jewish identity and expressed these feelings in his publications. In *Padenie Parizha* (The Fall of Paris; 1941) he denounced fascism and anti-Semitism, and in a poem written in 1940 he lamented the Nazi persecution of the Jews. During the war years he was a correspondent for *Krasnaia Zvezda* (Red Star), the newspaper of the Red Army, and played a leading role in anti-Nazi propaganda in the Soviet Union and abroad.

Ehrenburg was one of the most prominent personalities to be appointed to the Jewish Antifascist Committee. In the committee's meetings and consultations he stressed the need to publicize the Jewish role in the war effort against the Nazis, and openly criticized manifestations of anti-Semitism among the Soviet population. He was one of the first in the Soviet Union to encourage the collection of documentary evidence on the murder of the Jews and on active Jewish resistance to the Nazis. Ehrenburg was the editor of *Merder fun Felker* (Murders of Peoples; 2 vols., 1944–45). Together with Vasily Grossman, he edited *Chernaya kniga* (The Black Book of Soviet Jewry), a collection of documents on the Holocaust in the Soviet Union.

He also co-sponsored *Krasnaya kniga* (The Red Book), which documented Jewish participation in the Red Army, the partisan movement, and the resistance to the Nazis in the ghettos. These books, however, were not released for publication, since it became Soviet policy to throw a veil over the Holocaust, a policy that became increasingly pronounced after the war. In the spring of 1945, official criticism was voiced against Ehrenburg's extreme anti-German stand.

The fate of the Jews during the war continued to preoccupy Ehrenburg in the postwar years. An abridged English translation of *Chernaya kniga* was published in New York in 1946, and the full version (which was smuggled out of the USSR) in 1980. Six volumes of his memoirs were serialized in the journal *Novyi Mir* between 1960 and 1965 under the title *Lyudi, gody, zhizn* (Men, Years, Life); at his death he was working on the concluding volumes. Ehrenburg bequeathed his entire archive to Yad Vashem, including a complete, uncensored edition of *Chernaya kniga* and many personal letters from survivors. ◆

> Ehrenburg's books were not released for publication when it became Soviet policy to throw a veil over the Holocaust.

Einstein, Albert

1879–1955

Physicist Einstein was born at Ulm, Germany, of an assimilated Jewish family. While working in a patent office in Bern, Switzerland, he published in 1905 three revolutionary papers; one of them, on his special theory of relativity, gained him international fame. He then taught physics at the universities of Bern, Zurich, and Prague. In 1914 Einstein was appointed professor of physics at the Berlin Academy of Science and the Kaiser Wilhelm Institute of Physics, where he published in 1916 an extended version of the theory of relativity. In 1921 he was awarded the Nobel prize in physics. When Hitler came to power in 1933, Einstein happened to be out of Germany; he never set foot in that country again. He resigned from the Prussian Academy of Science and eventually emigrated to the United States, where he worked at the Institute for Advanced Studies in Princeton, New Jersey, for the rest of his life.

> *"In a healthy nation there is a kind of dramatic balance between the will of the people and the government, which prevents its degeneration into tyranny."*
>
> Albert Einstein,
> *Out of My Later Years*, 1950

By his very nature Einstein was a fierce enemy of Nazism and all totalitarian regimes. Thus, in January 1933 he wrote: "My great fear is that this hate and power epidemic will spread throughout the world. It comes from below the surface like a flood, until the upper regions are isolated, terrified, and demoralized and then also submerged." The Nazis canceled his honorary citizenship (held from 1914, in addition to his Swiss citizenship), confiscated his property, and put a price of 50,000 reichsmarks on his head. In a statement to the Swiss press, he said: "As long as I have the choice, I shall live only in a land where political freedom, tolerance, and equality of all citizens reign."

In the United States, Einstein took part in Jewish rescue efforts, and in 1941 he tried in vain to influence President Franklin D. Roosevelt by writing to Eleanor Roosevelt, drawing her attention to the policy of the State Department, "which makes it all but impossible to give refuge in America to many worthy persons who are victims of the Fascist cruelty in Europe." Though Mrs. Roosevelt was ready to raise the issue with her husband, nothing came of it. After the war, Einstein also expressed criticism of Switzerland's policy toward refugees, stating that the country "behaved with unjust brutality . . . even towards those [refugees] whom it has allowed to enter its territory."

It was his hatred of Nazism that motivated Einstein, despite his pacifism, to warn Roosevelt, in August 1939, concerning the possibility that Germany might acquire sufficient quantities of uranium in the recently incorporated territory of Czechoslovakia to produce "extremely powerful bombs of a new type" that "might well destroy [a] whole port together with some surrounding territory." Einstein therefore recommended that the United States acquire uranium from the Belgian Congo. When the letter reached Roosevelt after the outbreak of the war, in

"If men as individuals surrender to the call of their elementary instincts, avoiding pain and seeking satisfaction only for their own selves, the result for them all taken together must be a state of insecurity, of fear, and of promiscuous misery."

Albert Einstein,
Out of My Later Years, 1950

October 1939, the National Research Defense Committee began to organize production of the atom bomb. In May 1946, after the war and the dropping of the first atom bombs, Einstein, presiding over the National Commission of Nuclear Scientists, declared: "The release of atom power has changed everything except our way of thinking, and thus we are being driven unarmed towards a catastrophe. . . . The solution of this problem lies in the heart of humankind." ◆

Elkes, Elchanan

1879–1944

Physician and chairman of the Ältestenrat (Council of Elders) in the Kovno ghetto in Lithuania. Elkes was born in the Lithuanian village of Kalvarija, close to the German border. He received a traditional Jewish and Hebrew education. While still a youngster, he was sent to Kovno to attend school. He completed his medical studies in Königsberg, Germany, and for seven years was village doctor in Berezino in Belorussia. During World War I, Elkes served as a medical officer in the Russian army, and he received numerous decorations. From the early 1920s, he headed the internal-medicine department in the Bikkur Holim Jewish hospital in Kovno. Reputed to be one of the best doctors in Lithuania, he numbered heads of state and diplomats among his patients.

Elkes was a Zionist, active on the Jewish cultural scene, and close to members of He-Haluts, the association of pioneering Zionist youth. During the period of Soviet rule (1940–41), he used his contacts as physician to Moscow's representative in Lithuania to help obtain exit permits for thousands of Polish Jewish refugees who were stranded in Lithuania.

On June 24, 1941, the Germans captured Kovno, and thousands of Jews were arrested and murdered by the invaders and their Lithuanian collaborators. The remaining thirty thousand Jews were ordered to move into a ghetto and to choose a head for the Ältestenrat. On August 4 an emergency meeting was called, and was attended by twenty-eight leading personalities from all walks of Jewish life in the city. At this meeting, the last of its kind in the Kovno Jewish community, Elkes was nomi-

> *"With my own ears I have heard the awful symphony of weeping, wailing, and screaming from tens of thousands of men, women, and children, which have rent the heavens. No one throughout the ages has heard such a sound."*
>
> Elchanan Elkes

Elchanan Elkes (left) in the Kovno ghetto with Dr. Moshe Berman, head of the ghetto hospital.

1879 Elkes is born in Kalvarija, a Lithuanian village near Germany.

1940 Elkes helps obtain exit permits for stranded Jewish refugees.

1941 The Germans capture Kovno.

1941 Thousands of Jews are arrested or murdered at Kovno.

1941 Elkes is chosen to head new ghetto.

1944 The Nazis liquidate the ghetto and transfer occupants to Germany.

1944 Elkes fails to convince commandant not to transfer occupants.

1944 Elkes dies of an illness after being transferred to Germany.

nated unanimously for the position and, with a heavy heart, he accepted the nomination. He was sixty-two years old and in failing health.

Elkes headed the Ältestenrat from its establishment until it was disbanded. All who came into contact with him attested to his impressive moral stature and devotion to the Jewish cause, his courage and dignity in his dealings with Nazi officials, his simplicity of manner with his fellow Jews, and his modest way of life. This was in sharp contrast to the corruption and haughtiness manifested by some of the Ältestenrat personnel. For these qualities Elkes was held in high regard by the Jewish ghetto population. He looked favorably on the anti-Nazi underground activity in the Kovno ghetto. Despite the danger involved, he was asked to organize supplies for the members of the General Jewish Fighting Organization (Yidishe Algemeyne Kamfs Organizatsye; JFO) who left the ghetto to fight as partisans in the forests. He declared: "Every opportunity for resistance should be exploited, especially in matters of honor." Elkes's stand influenced other members of the Ältestenrat to support the JFO.

At the beginning of July 1944, with the Red Army not far from Kovno, the Nazis proceeded to liquidate the ghetto and transfer its inhabitants to Germany. Elkes, at the risk of his life, appeared before the ghetto commandant, Obersturmbannführer Wilhelm Göcke, and suggested that Göcke drop the transfer plan, saying that this act would be held to his credit. Göcke refused bluntly, but allowed Elkes to leave unharmed. A few days later the ghetto was evacuated, and Elkes was transferred, with many of the surviving Jews, to the Landsberg concentration camp in Germany, where he was put in charge of the hospital hut. Soon afterward he fell ill, and died on October 17, 1944.

On October 19, 1943, while still in the ghetto, Elkes sent his children in England a final testament in Hebrew. He wrote: "With my own ears I have heard the awful symphony of weeping, wailing, and screaming from tens of thousands of men, women, and children, which have rent the heavens. No one throughout the ages has heard such a sound. Along with many of these martyrs I have quarreled with my Creator, and with them I cried out from a broken heart, 'Who is as silent as you, O Lord'" (a bitter allusion to a well-known prayer, "Who can compare to you, O Lord"). ◆

> *"There is a desert inside me. My soul is scorched. I am naked and empty. There are no words in my mouth."*
> Elchanan Elkes, 1943

Eppstein, Paul

1901–1944

A leader of German Jewry under the Third Reich. Eppstein was born in Ludwigshafen, and he majored in sociology at Mannheim University, where his teachers were Max Weber, Karl Jaspers, and Karl Mannheim.

At the age of twenty-six he became a lecturer in sociology at the business college in Mannheim. In 1929 he was appointed principal of the city's adult education college (*Volkshochschule*), which in less than four years developed into one of the most important institutions of its kind in Germany. When Hitler came to power in 1933, the college was closed down. Eppstein was asked to come to Berlin to participate in community activities on behalf of German Jewry, activities that under the new circumstances were in need of expansion and reorganization. His first appointment was with the Zentralausschuss der Deutschen Juden für Hilfe und Aufbau (Central Committee of German Jews for Relief and Reconstruction) and the Union of Jewish Communities of Prussia.

That same year, Eppstein was invited to join the board of the Reichsvertretung der Deutschen Juden (Reich Representation of German Jews), in which he was primarily occupied with administration and social activities. Following the *Kristallnacht*

> In 1938 Eppstein was invited to England to lecture in sociology, but he refused to leave Germany so long as the remaining Jews were in need of his services.

1901 Eppstein is born in Ludwigshafen.

1929 Eppstein is appointed principal of Mannheim's adult education college.

1933 The college is closed when Hitler comes to power.

1933 Eppstein moves to Berlin to serve Jewish organizations.

1938 Eppstein turns down job in England after *Kristallnacht*.

1940 Eppstein is arrested by the Gestapo.

1943 Eppstein is expelled to the Theresienstadt camp, where he is appointed head of Jewish elders council.

1944 Eppstein is executed the day after the Day of Atonement.

pogrom in 1938, Eppstein was invited to England to lecture in sociology, but he refused to leave Germany so long as the remaining Jews were in need of his services. He kept up his work in the new Reichsvereinigung der Juden in Deutschland (Reich Association of Jews in Germany; 1939–43); indeed, the scope of his responsibilities was enlarged, especially as regarded day-to-day contact with the authorities and his work in connection with emigration. As of the end of 1940, following the arrest of Otto Hirsch, Eppstein was the organization's sole executive director, under its presiding officer, Rabbi Leo Baeck.

In the years that he worked for the Reichsvereinigung, Eppstein was arrested several times by the Gestapo. One such arrest took place in the summer of 1940. When he was released, in October of that year, the Reichssicherheitshauptamt (Reich Security Main Office; RSHA) ordered him to desist from any further activity related to emigration, and henceforth he concentrated on administrative affairs. Late in January 1943, about six months before the abolishment of the Reichsvereinigung, Eppstein was expelled to the Theresienstadt camp, together with Leo Baeck. On his arrival, he was appointed chairman of the Ältestenrat der Juden (Council of Jewish Elders), together with Jacob Edelstein but in fact replacing him. Opinions vary on the way Eppstein carried out his task in Theresienstadt. In some quarters he has been criticized for not standing up to the German ghetto administration and for willingly submitting to its demands, as well as for alienating his fellow prisoners and standing aloof from them; others believe that he was a staunch spokesman for the Jews, both in Germany and in Theresienstadt. Eppstein was imprisoned in the summer of 1944, because (according to one version) the Germans found fault with a speech he had made before the ghetto prisoners. The day after the Day of Atonement, 1944, Eppstein was executed. ◆

Evert, Anghelos

1894–1970

Head of the Athens police during 1943. Inspired by Metropolitan Damaskinos's public denunciation of the persecution of Jews, Evert ordered that new and false credentials be issued by the police to all Jews requesting them. Hundreds of such credentials were thus made available to needy Jews, some of them personally issued by Evert (such as those of Haim Efraim Cohen, an attorney, to whom Evert personally handed a new identity card with the name Pavlos Georgiou Panopoulos). Thanks to this courageous decision by Evert (which, owing to his personal involvement, placed him in jeopardy of arrest and severe punishment by the Germans, in the event of disclosure), countless Jews were able to ride out the German occupation undetected, under new identities. For this deed, Anghelos Evert was recognized by Yad Vashem as a "Righteous among the Nations" in 1969. ◆

1894 Evert is born.

1943 Evert heads police force in Athens, Greece.

1943 Evert orders that fake credentials be given to all Jews.

1969 Evert is recognized as a Yad Vashem "Righteous among the Nations."

1970 Evert dies.

Feiner, Leon

1888–1945

Bund activist and member of the Jewish underground in Poland. Feiner was born in Kraków and studied law at the Jagiellonian University there. As a longtime member of socialist movements and a Bund activist in independent Poland, he frequently defended leftist political activists in court. Feiner came from an assimilated background and was well versed in Polish culture, but his loyalty to the Bund, as well as the increasingly anti-Jewish policy that Poland was pursuing, brought him closer to the Jewish masses and made him want to share their fate. In the second half of the 1930s he was imprisoned in Bereza-Kartuska, a Polish concentration camp in which a large number of opposition figures, of various shades of political opinion, were held.

When the war broke out, Feiner fled to the Soviet-occupied part of Poland, only to be put in prison. Following the German conquest of the area in 1941, he escaped and made his way back to Warsaw, where he lived under an assumed identity on the Polish ("Aryan") side of the city

and was an underground representative of the Bund and of the Jews in the ghetto. When the Bund joined the Żydowska Organizacja Bojowa (Jewish Fighting Organization; ŻOB), Feiner was appointed Bund representative on the "Aryan" side, and together with Abraham Berman (who represented the Żydowski Komitet Narodowy, or the Jewish National Committee), formed the coordinating committee for contacts with the Polish underground. In the fall of 1942 Jan Karski, a member of the Polish underground who was sent to London in its behalf, took a message from Feiner addressed to Samuel Zygelbojm, for transmission to all the Jews in the free world. Feiner asked Zygelbojm to tell the Jews "to lay siege to all important offices and agencies of the British and the Americans, and not to move from there until these Allied powers give guarantees that they will embark upon the rescue of the Jews. They [the demonstrators] should abstain from food and water, waste away before the eyes of the apathetic world, and starve to death. By doing so they may perhaps shock the conscience of the world." It was Feiner who drafted and forwarded to their destinations most of the Bund's reports and messages to London and the United States.

> *"They should abstain from food and water, waste away before the eyes of the apathetic world, and starve to death. By doing so they may perhaps shock the conscience of the world."*
>
> Leon Feiner

In the last few months of 1942, Feiner helped establish a Polish organization for giving aid to Jews and trying to rescue them, a project that had been initiated by various Polish circles— Catholics, liberal intellectuals, and representatives of political parties (mostly of the Center and the Left). From January 1943 to July 1944 Feiner was deputy chairman of Zegota, the Polish Council for Aid to Jews, and was its chairman from November to December 1944, until the liberation of Warsaw in January 1945.

After the liberation, Feiner, who was suffering from a malignant disease, was transferred to Lublin, the temporary seat of Poland's new regime. A month later he died. ◆

Filderman, Wilhelm

1882–1963

Romanian Jewish leader. Filderman was born in Bucharest. He studied law in Paris, earning a doctorate. In 1912 he was one of the few Jews granted Romanian nationality; this enabled him to earn his livelihood by practicing law. In the interwar period Filderman was a member of the Romanian parliament, and he served as chairman of most of the important Jewish organizations in the country, among them the Federatia Uniunilor de Comunitati Evreesti (Federation of Jewish Communities), the Uniunea Comunitatilor Evreesti din Regat (Union of Jewish Communities in the Regat [the Old Kingdom; Romania in its pre–World War I borders]), the Uniunea Evreilor Români (Union of Romanian Jews), the Joint Distribution Committee's office in Romania, and the Consiliul Evreesc (Jewish Council).

In the years following World War I, Filderman was active on behalf of the granting of Romanian nationality to the Jews of the Regat and in assisting the Jewish refugees from the Ukraine. He also aided in the preservation of Jewish rights in the face of the prevailing anti-Semitism in Romanian political and economic life, which also had its effect on Jewish religious life and education. Filderman persisted in this struggle even during the Iron Guard's regime of terror (September 6, 1940, to January 24, 1941) and during Ion Antonescu's dictatorship, notwithstanding the fact that Antonescu dissolved the existing Jewish organizations and in their place set up the Centrala Evreilor (Jewish Center). These activities finally led to Filderman's expulsion to Transnistria in May 1943; the immediate cause was his opposition to the collective ransom of 4 billion lei (about $40 million) that Antonescu imposed on Romanian Jewry. Even in Transnistria, however, Filderman maintained his activities, and in August of that year he was permitted to return from exile.

Throughout the war years Filderman maintained contact with senior officials, cabinet ministers, and Premier Ion Antonescu and his close associate Mihai Antonescu (who also held senior cabinet posts). The Romanian leaders were forced to accept Filderman as the authentic representative of the Jews (most of the leaders of the Jewish Center were Jewish converts to Christianity or collaborators who did not represent the Jews and had been appointed to their posts on the recommendation of the German legation). Filderman also earned the respect of Romanian opposition leaders, who cooperated with him; they included such renowned figures as Iuliu Maniu, head of the Peasants' Party (Partidul National Taranesc), and Dinu Bratianu, head of the National-Liberal Party (Partidul National-Liberal). During the spring and sum-

1882 Filderman is born in Bucharest, Romania.

1912 Filderman is one of few Jews granted Romanian nationality.

1940 Filderman persists in Jewish struggle during Reign of Terror.

1941 Filderman fails to prevent the deportation of Jews to Transnistria.

1942 Filderman forms a clandestine Jewish leadership; helps foil plans to send Romanian Jews to extermination camps.

1943 Filderman is exiled to Transnistria, but allowed to return.

1944 Filderman fights for the restoration of Jewish rights and property.

1948 Filderman flees to France.

1963 Filderman dies.

mer of 1942 Filderman formed a clandestine Jewish leadership, the Jewish Council, composed of representatives of the Zionist Organization and other Jewish bodies. The Jewish Council sought to save the Jews of Romania from deportation to Poland and to alleviate the daily life of the Jewish population, then suffering from the effects of countless anti-Semitic laws and regulations.

In the fall of 1941, when he was still chairman of the Federation of Jewish Communities, Filderman failed in his efforts to prevent the deportation to Transnistria of the Jews of Bessarabia and Bukovina. He played a decisive role, however, in foiling the plans to deport the entire Jewish population of Romania to the extermination camps in Poland in the fall of 1942, and in preventing the expulsion of Jews from neighboring countries who had taken refuge in Romania. In August and September of 1941, as a result of Filderman's intercession with Ion Antonescu, the decree on wearing the yellow badge was abolished in the Regat. For two years, from the end of 1941 to the end of 1943, Filderman persisted in a struggle for the right to send aid to the Jews who had been deported to Transnistria, and he followed up by campaigning for their repatriation to Romania, meeting with partial success.

After the fall of the dictatorial regime in August 1944, Filderman continued his public activities. In the following three years, from 1944 to 1947, he fought for the restoration of Jewish rights and Jewish property, and against the drafting of Jews into the ranks of the anti-Semitic Romanian army. In pursuing his aims, Filderman exploited every available legal loophole, and **echelon:** a level of authority. he also lobbied in the senior **echelons** of the regime. He saved the Romanian Jews from deportation to the extermination camps by making this a national Romanian issue and by persuading the leaders of the regime that compliance with the German demand for deportation would be a violation of Romanian **sovereignty:** freedom from outside control. **sovereignty.**

After the war, the Jewish Communists campaigned against Filderman, as part of their efforts to gain control of the Jewish organizations in Romania. Filderman was forced to resign from all his positions of leadership, and in early 1948 he fled to France, where he remained for the rest of his life. ◆

Fleischmann, Gisi

1897–1944

Zionist activist in Slovakia; leader of the Women's International Zionist Organization and of the Pracovná Skupina (Working Group).

When the Ústredňa Židov (Jewish Center) was established in Slovakia in 1940 on order of the authorities, Fleischmann was appointed head of its Aliya (immigration to Palestine) section. This section became the cover for the continuation of Zionist activities among the youth and of the *hakhshara* (agricultural training) network; it also provided vocational training.

Among Gisi Fleischmann's early achievements was the aid she helped organize for 326 Jews from Prague. These men had been interned in a camp in Sosnowiec, Poland, and had made their way to Slovakia early in 1940. Fleischmann managed to convince the Slovak government to allow the men to remain in Slovakia temporarily while she searched for a more permanent haven for them. They were housed in a camp at Vyhne. With the help of Richard Lichtheim (the Jewish Agency representative in Geneva) and Henry Montor (of the United Palestine Appeal in New York), she found safer places for them. Eventually, almost all of the men reached Palestine or other free countries before the deportations from Slovakia began in the spring of 1942.

Early that spring, a group of Slovak Jewish leaders had come to the conclusion that in order to help rescue

1897 Fleischmann is born.

1940 Fleischmann becomes head of Jewish Center's Palestinian immigration section.

1940 Fleischmann convinces Slovak government to give temporary haven to Jews.

1942 Slovakia starts deporting Jews.

1942 Fleischmann's group tries to stop deportation by bribing Eichmann's representative.

1944 Fleischmann declines an offer to be hidden from the Germans.

1944 Fleischmann is arrested, but allowed to stay in Bratislava.

1944 Fleischmann is deported to Auschwitz and gassed on arrival.

the Jewish population in Slovakia and other occupied countries, underground methods would have to be employed. Fleischmann was one of the early founders of this "Working Group," as it came to be called. After the deportation of Slovakia's Jews began, in March 1942, the Working Group tried to stop it by bribing Adolf Eichmann's representative in Slovakia, Dieter Wisliceny. In order to raise the required funds, the group entered into an exchange of letters with Nathan Schwalb of the American Jewish Joint Distribution Committee's office in Geneva. When the first wave of deportations ceased (there were to be none from October 1942 to the fall of 1944), the Working Group was greatly encouraged and came up with an even bolder proposal, the Europa Plan. This called for the cessation of deportations from all parts of German-occupied Europe in exchange for foreign currency or goods that would be transmitted to the Germans by Jews in free countries. The proposal was submitted to Wisliceny. Fleischmann played a major role in formulating the plan, in bringing it to fruition, and in establishing contacts for this purpose with individuals and organizations abroad. Not taking the proper precautions, she was arrested by the Gestapo and held in prison for four months, rejecting all efforts made in this period to enable her to leave Slovakia. On her release she resumed her previous work.

After the SS entry in force into Slovakia in the summer of 1944 and the suppression of the Slovak National Uprising in October of that year, Fleischmann sought to obtain an appointment with Alois Brunner, another representative of Eichmann. She also tried to persuade Kurt Becher to discontinue the deportations; both these efforts were unsuccessful. Fleischmann turned down an offer to be hidden from the Germans in a Bratislava bunker.

On September 28 of that year, most members of the Working Group, including Fleischmann, were arrested during an SS raid. They were all taken to the Sered labor camp except for Fleischmann and one other member of the group, who were permitted to stay behind in Bratislava to take care of the needs of the detainees and to close down the Jewish Center's affairs.

At the beginning of October 1944, Fleischmann was deported to Auschwitz in one of the last transports of the war, with a special instruction to the Auschwitz authorities labeling her as "RU" (*Rückkehr unerwünscht*, "return undesirable"). She was gassed on arrival in the camp. ◆

Fomenko, Witold

1905–1961

A "Righteous among the Nations." Born in Warsaw into a Ukrainian family, Fomenko was still a child when he moved with his family to Chełm, where he grew up in a Jewish neighborhood, learning to speak and write Yiddish. In 1924 the family moved to Lutsk, where Fomenko played in a military band and gave music lessons. Many of his students were Jewish, and through them he came to know the Stoliner Rebbe, Rabbi Yohanan Perlov, and composed tunes for Perlov's Hasidic songs. In the mid-1930s Fomenko had to give up his musical activities on doctors' orders, and with the help of Jewish friends he learned to be a barber.

In 1941, following the occupation of Lutsk and the establishment of a ghetto in the city, Fomenko began providing help to the Jews, bringing into the ghetto food, medicines, firewood, and other supplies, mainly for the soup kitchen where the needy received their meals. Fomenko paid for these purchases with his own income from the large barbershop he had opened, which had Jews among its employees. Whenever he visited the ghetto he tried to raise the morale of the Jews by telling them jokes and good news, and by singing anti-Nazi songs he had composed.

On the eve of the liquidation of the Lutsk ghetto, Fomenko began helping Jews to leave the ghetto and providing them with false "Aryan" documents that he had acquired or had had his Christian friends prepare for him. Following the arrest of a Jewish woman who had one of these documents in her possession and was tortured by her captors, Fomenko and his father were arrested, but the military commander of the city, who was a customer of Fomenko's, intervened on their behalf and they were released. Fomenko kept up his aid and rescue efforts even after the ghetto's liquidation, for those Jews who were being held in a labor camp in the city. When that camp was also liquidated, in December 1942, Fomenko concentrated on finding hiding places for Jews with Christian families in Lutsk, in most cases paying the families for their trouble. He also provided refuge for many Jews in his own house and among the members of his family in the city. Not all the Jews whom Fomenko helped survived

1905 Fomenko is born in Warsaw into a Ukrainian family.

1924 Fomenko moves to Lutz and plays in a military band.

1941 Fomenko begins providing help to Jews following Lutz's occupation.

1942 Fomenko finds hiding places for Jews after the ghetto's liquidation.

1961 Fomenko dies in Israel, where he received Yad Vashem's award.

the war—only thirty-six of them were still alive on the day the city was liberated.

After the war, Fomenko married one of the Jewish women he had saved, and with her made his home in Israel. He was awarded the "Righteous among the Nations" medal of Yad Vashem, and planted a tree on Righteous among the Nations Avenue on Remembrance Hill in Jerusalem. ◆

Frank, Anne

1929–1945

This entry is divided into three parts. The first tells about Anne Frank's family and recounts the story of her life; the second describes her diary. The third part is about the Anne Frank House in Amsterdam.

Family

Otto Heinrich Frank (1889–1980) was born in Frankfurt, Germany. He grew up in an assimilated, liberal Jewish environment, attended high school, and trained for a while at Macy's department store in New York. During World War I he was a reserve officer in the German army. After the war Frank started his own business, with mixed success. In 1925 he married Edith Holländer, the daughter of factory owners in Aachen. The couple had two daughters, Margot Betti (born February 16, 1926) and Annelies Marie (born June 12, 1929), called Anne.

Soon after the Nazis came to power in January 1933 and the first anti-Jewish measures were announced, the Frank family decided to leave Germany. Otto Frank went to Amsterdam. He knew the city well from frequent visits and had several good friends there. After finding an apartment he brought over the rest of his family. He set up a company, Opekta, that made and distributed pectin for use in homemade jams and jellies. In 1938, together with Hermann van Pels, Frank started a second company, Pectacon, which specialized in the preparation of spices for sausage making. Van Pels, his wife, Auguste, and their son, Peter, had recently fled to Amsterdam from Osnabrück in Germany.

> *"Dear Kitty, I've only got dismal and depressing news for you today. Our many Jewish friends are being taken away by the dozen."*
>
> Anne Frank, diary

Dit is een foto, zoals
ik me zou wensen,
altijd zo te zijn.
Dan had ik nog wel
een kans om naar
Holywood te komen.
Anne Frank.
10 Oct. 1942

(translation)
"This is a photo as I would wish
myself to look all the time. Then
I would maybe have a chance to
come to Hollywood."
Anne Frank, 10 Oct. 1942

Anne and Margot quickly adapted themselves to their new life. They learned Dutch and attended the local Montessori school. The Franks joined the liberal Jewish congregation of Amsterdam.

This relatively carefree existence came to an end on May 10, 1940, when the Germans invaded and occupied the Netherlands. The invasion was soon followed by anti-Jewish measures. That October a law was passed requiring all Jewish-owned businesses to be registered. With the help of non-Jewish friends and colleagues both Opekta and Pectacon were "Aryanized" on paper, and the businesses continued. Another law stipulated that Jewish children could attend only Jewish schools, and Anne and Margot switched to the Jewish **lyceum.**

lyceum: a secondary school.

Meanwhile, Otto Frank, who had no illusions about the Nazis, had begun preparations to go into hiding, if this proved necessary. Little by little, the family's possessions were brought to the vacant annex to Frank's office at Prinsengracht 263. Four employees were informed of his plans and agreed to help: Victor Kugler, Johannes Kleiman, Elli Voskuijl, and Miep Gies (born Hermine Santrouschitz). Miep had worked with Otto Frank for years and had become his right hand. Born in Vienna, she had been one of the many thousands of Austrian children who after World War I were taken into Dutch foster homes to improve

---

Anne Frank Dramatized

On October 5, 1955, *The Diary of Anne Frank* opened on Broadway. The play, written by Hollywood screenwriters Frances Goodrich and Albert Hackett, was based on the edited version of Anne Frank's diary that was released in the United States in 1952. Actress Susan Strasberg played the role of Anne. *The Diary of Anne Frank* was a great critical success, running for 717 performances and winning the Pulitzer Prize, the Tony Award, and the New York Critics' Circle Award for best play of the year. A film version of the play, starring Millie Perkins as Anne and Shelley Winters as Mrs. Van Daan, opened in 1959 and was subsequently nominated for eight Academy Awards. Although both the play and the film were commercial successes, many have criticized their creators for sentimentalizing the story and downplaying the darkness and fear inherent in Anne Frank's diary. In 1997 playwright Wendy Kesselman revised Goodrich and Hackett's original script to reflect more honestly and accurately Anne Frank's writings as published in the 1989 *Critical Edition* and the 1995 *Definitive Edition* of the diary. The new *Diary of Anne Frank* opened at New York's Music Box Theater in December 1997 and ran for seven months. Israeli-born film actress Natalie Portman starred as Anne.

---

annex: a wing or room added to an existing building.

their health. Miep had stayed on, and in 1941 she married Jan Gies.

The Franks' hiding plans went into high gear on July 5, 1942, when Margot received a registered letter from the Zentralstelle für Jüdische Auswanderung (Central Office for Jewish Emigration), a Nazi bureau. Margot, then sixteen years old, was ordered to register for what the letter called "labor expansion measures." After consultation with the van Pels family, the Franks decided to go into hiding immediately. The next day they moved into the **annex,** followed a week later by the van Pels family and their fifteen-year-old son, Peter. On November 16, 1942, they were joined by an eighth *onderduiker* (lit., "one who dives under"), the dentist Fritz Pfeffer, who had fled from Berlin in 1938. These eight people were to spend two years living in a few cramped rooms made in an attic. As food and clothing became scarce and could be bought only with coupons, which Jews in hiding could not obtain, the four helpers in the office managed somehow to buy enough supplies to feed and clothe eight additional people, often at great risk to their own lives.

On August 4, 1944, the SD (Sicherheitsdienst; Security Service) in Amsterdam received an anonymous phone call—it has never been established from whom—with information about Jews in hiding at Prinsengracht 263. A police van imme-

diately drove to the Prinsengracht, and the eight Jews were
found and arrested. A policeman named Silberbauer demanded
money and jewelry; to hide these he emptied an attaché case
full of papers, which he threw on the floor. Among the papers
was Anne Frank's diary. Also arrested were Kleiman and Kugler,
two of the employees who had assisted the families. After the
police left, Miep Gies and Elli Voskuijl went back to the annex
to pick up many personal items, such as photographs, books,
and other papers. A few days later all the furniture and clothing
were hauled away from the annex, a customary procedure after
an arrest. During the arrests Miep Gies had realized that Silberbauer, like her, came from Vienna. This may have been why he
did not arrest her, although he made it clear that he suspected
her as well of having helped the Jews. The next day Miep sought
him out to see if there was a way the prisoners could be set free,
but Silberbauer indicated there was nothing he could do. Kugler
and Kleiman were taken to the concentration camp in Amers-
foort, in the Netherlands. Kleiman suffered a hemorrhage of the
stomach, and through the intervention of the Red Cross was
sent home in September 1944. Kugler was able to escape during
a transport in March 1945 and remained in hiding until the liberation of the Netherlands in May.

The Jewish prisoners arrived at the Westerbork transit camp
on August 8, 1944. From there a full trainload of prisoners left for
the extermination camps every week. On September 3 the last
transport to leave Westerbork for Auschwitz departed. According
to the meticulously kept transport lists, there were 1,011 people
on board, among them the Franks, the van Pels family, and Pfeffer. On arrival at Auschwitz-Birkenau, 549 of them were immediately gassed. Hermann van Pels was one of these. Edith Frank,
her daughters, Margot and Anne, and Auguste van Pels were
interned in the Frauenblock. Pfeffer was the next to die. He is
listed in the death book of the Neuengamme camp on December
20, 1944. Edith Frank perished at Auschwitz-Birkenau on January 6, 1945. It has not been established where and when Auguste
van Pels died, but it is assumed that it was at the end of March or
early April, somewhere in Germany or Czechoslovakia. Peter van
Pels was one of the many thousands of prisoners who, because of
the advancing Russian army, were put on death marches. He died
shortly before the liberation in May 1945 in the Mauthausen
camp in Austria.

Anne and Margot were sent to Bergen-Belsen at the end of
October 1944. This camp filled up with thousands of prisoners

> *"I wander from one room to another, downstairs and up again, feeling like a song-bird whose wings have been brutally clipped and who is beating itself in utter darkness against the bars of its cage."*
>
> Anne Frank, diary

from other camps that were being vacated as the Russians advanced. Housing, food, and medicine became totally inadequate, and many prisoners weakened from hunger and the cold. A typhus epidemic took many victims. Margot died of typhus around the beginning of March; Anne, who believed that both her parents had perished, died a few days later. Two sisters from Amsterdam who had been with the Frank sisters in both Westerbork and Auschwitz later stated that they had carried Anne's body from the sick barrack. She was buried in one of the mass graves at Bergen-Belsen. Otto Frank was the only survivor of the eight in hiding. The Soviet army liberated Auschwitz on January 27, 1945, and Frank returned to Amsterdam the following June. After Anne's death had been confirmed, Miep Gies returned to him the papers she had kept.

Diary

On June 12, 1942, her thirteenth birthday, Anne received from her father a red-checked diary. That same day, Anne wrote on the first page:

> I hope I shall be able to confide in you completely, as I have never been able to do in anyone before, and I hope that you will be a great support and comfort to me.

In letters to her imaginary friend, Anne painted a picture of herself and of her personal development in the context of the problems and fears of eight Jews trying to hide from deportation. The frightening news about the developments on the outside reached those in hiding through the radio and through their helpers. On October 9, 1943, Anne wrote:

> Dear Kitty, I've only got dismal and depressing news for you today. Our many Jewish friends are being taken away by the dozen. These people are treated by the Gestapo without a shred of decency, being loaded into cattle trucks and sent to Westerbork, the big Jewish camp in Drente. Westerbork sounds terrible: only one washing cubicle for a hundred people and not nearly enough lavatories. . . . It is impossible to escape; most of the people in the camp are branded as inmates by their shaven heads and many also by their Jewish appearance.
>
> If it is as bad as this in Holland whatever will it be like in the distant and barbarous regions they are sent to? We assume

that most of them are murdered. The British radio speaks of their being gassed.

Perhaps this is the quickest way to die. I feel terribly upset.

When Pfeffer arrived at the annex, Anne noted:

> Pfeffer has told us a lot about the outside world, which we have missed for so long now. He had very sad news. Countless friends and acquaintances have gone to a terrible fate. Evening after evening the green and gray army lorries trundle past. The Germans ring at every front door to inquire if there are any Jews living in the house. If there are, then the whole family has to go at once. If they don't find any, they go on to the next house. No one has a chance of evading them unless one goes into hiding. Often they go around with lists, and only ring when they know they can get a good haul. Sometimes they let them off for cash— so much per head. It seems like the slave hunts of old times. But it's certainly no joke; it's much too tragic for that. In the evenings when it's dark, I often see rows of good, innocent people accompanied by crying children, walking on and on, in the charge of a couple of these chaps, bullied and knocked about until they almost drop. No one is spared—old people, babies, expectant mothers, the sick—each and all join in the march to death.

"The Germans ring at every front door to inquire if there are any Jews living in the house. If there are, then the whole family has to go at once. If they don't find any, they go on to the next house. No one has a chance of evading them unless one goes into hiding."
Anne Frank, diary

Still, the *onderduikers* tried to lead a normal life. For Anne as well as Margot and Peter, this meant doing homework with the help of their old schoolbooks and new books borrowed from the library by Miep and Elli.

Fear of discovery created enormous pressure on those in hiding. During the day they could not move around or use the bathroom because not everyone in the office below was aware of their presence. The close quarters and constant tensions were often too much for Anne. On October 29, 1943, she wrote:

> I wander from one room to another, downstairs and up again, feeling like a song-bird whose wings have been brutally clipped and who is beating itself in utter darkness against the bars of its cage. "Go outside, laugh, and take a breath of fresh air," a voice cries within me, but I don't even feel a response any more; I go and lie on the divan and sleep, to make the time move quickly, and the stillness and the terrible fear, because there is no way of killing them.

Anne described the difficulties with her mother, her special relationship with her father, her sexual development, and her efforts to improve her character. She fell in love with Peter but later wrote about her disappointment in him.

Anne's diary is also a monument to the helpers who for two years struggled to obtain food and clothing and provided spiritual support:

> Our helpers are a very good example. They have pulled us through up till now and we hope they will bring us safely to dry land. Otherwise, they will have to share the same fate as the many others who are being searched for. Never have we heard one word of the burden which we certainly must be to them, never has one of them complained of all the trouble we give. They all come upstairs every day, talk to the men about business and politics, to the women about food and wartime difficulties, and about newspapers and books with the children. They put on the brightest possible faces, bring flowers and presents for birthdays and bank holidays, are always ready to help and do all they can. That is something we must never forget; although others may show heroism in the war or against the Germans, our helpers display heroism in their cheerfulness and affection.

On March 28, 1944, Anne heard over the British radio about a plan to gather diaries and letters about the war. "Of course, they all made a rush at my diary immediately," she wrote the following day. "Just imagine how interesting it would be if I were to publish a romance of the 'Secret Annex.' The title alone would be enough to make people think it was a detective story." On May 11 she wrote:

> Now, about something else: you've known for a long time that my greatest wish is to become a journalist some day and later a famous writer. Whether these leanings towards greatness (of insanity?) will ever materialize remains to be seen, but I certainly have the subjects in my mind. In any case, I want to publish a book entitled *Het Achterhuis* [The Annex] after the war. Whether I shall succeed or not, I cannot say, but my diary will be a great help.

Anne prepared a list of pseudonyms for possible publication: Van Pels became Van Daan, Pfeffer became Dussel, and so on.

Anne observed herself and her environment, made plans for the future, commented and criticized, and did not spare herself in that regard. In the high-pressure situation of the annex, she changed from a shy young girl to a young woman. Superfi-

> *"No one is spared—old people, babies, expectant mothers, the sick—each and all join in the march to death."*
>
> Anne Frank, diary

cial comments about girlfriends and admirers made place for philosophical statements about herself and the world around her. One of the last entries in the diary is from July 15, 1944:

> That's the difficulty in these times: ideals, dreams, and cherished hopes rise within us, only to meet the horrible truth and be shattered. It's really a wonder that I haven't dropped all my ideals because they seem so absurd and impossible to carry out. Yet, I keep them, because in spite of everything I still believe that people are really good at heart. I simply can't build up my hopes on a foundation consisting of confusion, misery, and death. I see the world gradually being turned into a wilderness, I hear the ever-approaching thunder, which will destroy us too, I can feel the sufferings of millions, and yet, if I look up into the heavens, I think that it will all come right, that this cruelty too will end, and that peace and tranquillity will return again. In the meantime, I must uphold my ideals, for perhaps the time will come when I shall be able to carry them out. Yours, Anne.

Apart from the diary, Miep had also saved a book of stories ("Stories and Adventures from the Annex") and the "Book of Beautiful Phrases." In this Anne had copied quotations that had pleased her.

Friends of Otto Frank's to whom he had shown some of the passages from Anne's diary persuaded him to find a publisher. After the historian Jan Romein published an article in which he related his emotions on reading parts of the diary, the publisher Contact approached Otto Frank, and *The Annex* appeared in June 1947 as edited by Frank, who had deleted several passages that he deemed either offensive or too personal. Several pieces from the "Story Book" were added to the diary.

The book went through many reprints. In 1950 it appeared in Germany and France, and in 1952 in England and the United States. For the American edition, Eleanor Roosevelt wrote in the preface: "This is a remarkable book. Written by a young girl—and the young are not afraid of telling the truth—it is one of the wisest and most moving commentaries on war and its impact on human beings that I have ever read."

The diary has been published in more than fifty editions; the total number of copies printed amounts to almost twenty million. Dramatic presentations have also reached a large public. The stage version by Albert Hackett and Frances Goodrich premiered on Broadway on October 5, 1955, and received the

> *"I am not a hero. I stand at the end of the long, long line of good Dutch people who did what I did or more—much more—during those dark and terrible times years ago, but always like yesterday in the hearts of those who bear witness."*
> Miep Gies, *Anne Frank Remembered,* 1987

Throughout the world, Anne Frank has become a symbol of the millions of victims of the Holocaust. For many people, Anne's diary is the first confrontation with the Nazi persecution of the Jews.

Pulitzer prize for the best play of the year. The film version followed in 1959.

Numerous other artists, including sculptors, painters, composers, and choreographers, have been inspired by Anne Frank. Many schools have been named after her. Anne's wish—"I want to live on, even after my death"—has become a reality. Throughout the world she has become a symbol of the millions of victims of the Holocaust. For many people, Anne's diary is the first confrontation with the Nazi persecution of the Jews. The influence of the diary is such that those who try to deny the Nazis' crimes also denounce the diary as a fraud. To counter such efforts, the Rijksinstituut for Oorlogsdocumentatie (Netherlands State Institute for War Documentation) in Amsterdam published in 1986 an annotated edition of both versions of Anne's diary, the earlier edition with passages deleted, and the later complete version. The English translation appeared in 1989.

After Otto Frank's death in 1980, Anne's papers went to the Rijksinstituut. The diary is on loan to the Anne Frank House, and is on display there. The copyright is owned by the independent Anne Frank Foundation in Basel.

The Anne Frank House

After the publication of *The Annex* many visitors found their way to the house at Prinsengracht 263, which was still being used as an office. In 1957 there were plans to raze the house to make room for a new building, but the public outcry prevented this action. The owner of the building then donated the house to the newly established Anne Frank Foundation on condition that the building be open to visitors.

The museum opened its doors in 1960. Besides the maintenance of the Annex, it has as its second goal the struggle against anti-Semitism and racism. It was Otto Frank's wish that the museum not become a memorial to Anne but instead contribute to an understanding of prejudice and discrimination. The Anne Frank Foundation maintains a documentation center on anti-Semitism and racist groups in Western Europe and the United States. It produces teaching aids and organizes traveling exhibits in various languages. The foundation has an office in New York City.

The number of visitors to the Anne Frank House continues to increase each year. In 1988 there were a total of 550,000 from around the world. The impact of Anne's diary has not diminished and continues to confront readers with the cruel truth: "Six million Jews were not murdered. One Jew was murdered, six million times over" (Abel Herzberg, survivor of Bergen-Belsen). ◆

Frankfurter, David

1909–1982

1909 Frankfurter is born in Daruvar, Croatia.

1929 Frankfurter begins to study medicine.

1934 Frankfurter moves to Switzerland.

1935 The Nuremberg Laws are enacted.

1936 Frankfurter shoots and kills Wilhelm Gustloff.

1945 Frankfurter is pardoned, but expelled from Switzerland.

1969 Frankfurter is allowed to return to Switzerland.

1982 Frankfurter dies.

Medical student. Born in Daruvar, Croatia, Frankfurter was the son of the local rabbi, Dr. Moshe Frankfurter. In 1929 David Frankfurter began to study medicine, first at Leipzig and later at Frankfurt; he witnessed the Nazi rise to power and their persecution of the Jews in the first years of their rule. In 1934 he moved to Bern, Switzerland, to continue his studies, while maintaining his interest in the events taking place in Nazi Germany. The Nuremberg Laws, enacted in September 1935, strengthened his conviction that he had to make a move against the Nazis that would arouse the world's attention. In November of that year he began to follow the activities of Wilhelm Gustloff, the National Socialist leader of Switzerland; on the evening of February 4, 1936, he shot and killed Gustloff at Davos, the famous resort town, and then surrendered to the police.

Frankfurter's trial before a court at Chur, in the Graubünden canton, began on December 9, 1936. His action was received with great admiration by wide circles of the Swiss population, but Switzerland, apprehensive about its Nazi neighbor, did all it could to restrict the trial to its criminal aspect. The prosecution and the court both rejected the modest effort made by the defense to raise the issue of a young Jew's reaction to the Nazis and their anti-Semitic policy. Frankfurter was convicted and sentenced to eighteen years in prison.

On February 27, 1945, as Germany was on the verge of collapse in the war, Frankfurter applied for a pardon, which was granted on June 1. He was released, but was expelled from Switzerland and went to Palestine, where he settled in Tel Aviv.

It was only September 1969 that Switzerland rescinded Frankfurter's banishment from the country, after friends had interceded on his behalf. His memoir of the events appeared in English (published in *Commentary*) in February 1950 and in Hebrew (*First of the Nazi Fighters*) in 1984. ◆

Freudiger, Fülöp

1900–1976

1900 Freudiger is born in Budapest, Hungary.

1939 Freudiger becomes head of the Orthodox Jewish community.

1943 Freudiger founds committee to help illegal Jewish refugees.

1944 Freudiger is appointed to the Judenrat.

1944 Freudiger rescues 80 prominent Orthodox Jews by bribing an official.

1944 Freudiger and family escape to Romania.

1961 Freudiger serves as prosecution witness in the Eichmann trial.

1976 Freudiger dies.

Hungarian Jewish leader. Born in Budapest to a well-to-do family ennobled by Emperor Franz Josef, Freudiger succeeded his father, Abraham, as the head of the Orthodox Jewish community of Budapest in 1939. As a founder and leading figure of the Orthodox Relief and Rescue Committee of Budapest in 1943 and 1944, he helped many of the illegal foreign Jewish refugees in Hungary. After the German occupation of the country on March 19, 1944, he was appointed to the Central Jewish Council (Központi Zsidó Tanács), the Judenrat of Budapest—a position he retained after the council's reorganization on April 22.

Through the intermediacy of Rabbi Michael Dov Weissmandel of Bratislava, Freudiger established close contact with Dieter Wisliceny of the Eichmann Sonderkommando almost immediately after the occupation. He also received from Weissmandel a copy of the Auschwitz Protocols (a report by two Auschwitz escapees), and disseminated information about the mass killings taking place at Auschwitz to Jewish and non-Jewish leaders in Hungary. By bribing Wisliceny, Freudiger succeeded in rescuing eighty prominent Orthodox Jews from various ghettos in Hungary. Partly with Wisliceny's aid, he and his family escaped to Romania, on August 9, 1944. Freudiger eventually settled in Israel, where his role in the Central Jewish Council and his escape were subjects of controversy. He served as a prosecution witness in the Eichmann trial in 1961. ◆

Galen, Clemens August Graf von

1878–1946

Catholic bishop in Münster; one of the most prominent Catholic opponents of Adolf Hitler. In 1933 Galen became an archbishop, and at the end of World War II he was raised to the rank of cardinal.

When the Nazis came to power, Galen pledged his loyalty to the new regime, hoping that the Nazis would retrieve for Germany the honor lost in its World War I defeat. Before long, however, his support of the Nazis turned to opposition, on account of the anti-Catholic propaganda that they were conducting and the pagan concepts that he discovered in Alfred Rosenberg's book *Der Mythus des 20. Jahrhunderts* (The Myth of the Twentieth Century; 1930). Galen launched a sharp attack against that book by the Nazi party's chief ideologue because of its racist views.

The single most significant act in the record of Galen's campaign against Nazism was his courageous denunciation of the Euthanasia Program; in a sermon he gave on August 3, 1941, he declared that euthanasia was simply murder. There is a widely held belief that Galen's public statements on the subject caused Hitler to put an end to the project (although the killing of the chronically ill was not completely abandoned). Some scholars believe that public opinion in Germany, at a time when the Third Reich's military success was at its height, had an effect on Hitler's decisions. The fact is, however, that no such public protest was made, by the churches or by any other

> *"Woe to mankind, woe to our German nation if God's Holy Commandment 'Thou shalt not kill,' which God proclaimed on Mount Sinai amidst thunder and lightning, which God our Creator inscribed in the conscience of mankind from the very beginning, is not only broken, but if this transgression is actually tolerated and permitted to go unpunished."*
>
> Clemens von Galen, August 3, 1941

German institutions, against Nazi policy on the Jews and the "Final Solution." In the eyes of the Nazi leadership the archbishop's statements on euthanasia were tantamount to an act of treason; his life was saved only because Hitler did not want to clash openly with the Catholic church. Following the July 20, 1944, attempt on Hitler's life, Galen was imprisoned in the Sachsenhausen camp. He was held there until the war came to an end. ◆

Gamzon, Robert

1905–1961

French partisan commander. Gamzon, who was born in Paris, founded the Jewish scout movement in France (Eclaireurs Israélites de France), guiding it to become a pluralist organization attracting young Jews from different countries and backgrounds and with various shades of political opinion. In 1939 and 1940 Gamzon, who was an electronic-sound engineer, served as communications officer in the French Fourth Army headquarters. Following the French surrender in June 1940, Gamzon reestablished the Jewish scout movement's institutions in the cities of unoccupied France into which Jewish refugees were pouring, as well as in Algeria. He took the initiative in establishing children's homes, welfare centers, workshops, and agricultural training farms in the villages (the last so as to provide an educational network for the Jewish youth). He also arranged courses in Jewish culture and tradition for youth instructors. In January 1942 Gamzon was appointed to the executive board of the Union Genérale des Israélites de France (UGIF) in southern France and was active in the organization up to the end of 1943. In order to help Jews escape the Gestapo manhunts, Gamzon formed a clandestine rescue network in the summer of 1942 code-named "The Sixth" (La Sixième), which produced forged identity papers, found asylum for children and teenagers in non-Jewish private homes and institutions, and smuggled Jews of all ages across the borders into Spain and Switzerland. In May 1943 Gamzon, in his capacity as a member of the UGIF board, went to Paris, where he helped coordinate clandestine operations.

In December 1943 Gamzon (who by now had the code name "Lieutenant Lagnès") formed a Jewish partisan unit in the Tarn district of southwest France, which graduates of the village workshops and the Jewish scout movement came to join. By entering the command of the Armée Juive, Gamzon helped unify all the Jewish armed organizations in France; he then took over command of the partisan unit he had set up in Tarn. This became, by June 1944, a trained and disciplined military unit of 120 men, affiliated with the Forces Françaises de l'Intérieur; the unit bore the name of Marc Haguenau, who had been the leader of "The Sixth" and had committed suicide when he fell into Gestapo hands. Following the orders of the underground district military commander, Gamzon received the parachute drops for Allied saboteurs and large quantities of light and medium arms for use in ambushing German patrols. On August 19, 1944, the Jewish scout unit seized a powerful German armored train, and on August 21 it liberated two cities, Castres and Mazamet.

In 1949 Gamzon settled in Israel together with a group of fifty graduates of the Jewish scout movement in France, who followed his lead. ◆

1905 Gamzon is born in Paris, France.

1939 Gamzon becomes a communications officer in French army.

1940 Gamzon helps establish centers for Jewish refugees.

1942 Gamzon joins executive board of UGIF; forms a clandestine rescue network, "The Sixth."

1943 Gamzon forms a Jewish partisan unit in the Tarn district.

1944 Gamzon's Jewish scout unit liberates cities and seizes armored train.

1949 Gamzon settles in Israel.

1961 Gamzon dies.

Gebirtig, Mordecai (Mordecai Bertig)

1877–1942

Yiddish folk poet. Born in Kraków to a poor family, Gebirtig attended a Jewish school only up to the age of ten. He became a carpenter and plied this trade for the rest of his life, even when he had gained great fame. At an early age

1877 Gebertig is born in Kraków, Poland, to a poor family.

1938 Gebertig writes a poem that becomes popular with ghetto youth.

1939 Gebertig spends his time in occupied Kraków.

1940 Gebertig flees from Kraków and takes refuge in Lagiewniki.

1942 Gebertig, in the Kraków ghetto, writes somber, fearful songs.

1942 Gebertig is killed.

1943 Gusta Dawidson Granger translates "S'Brent" into Polish.

1946 Gebertig's poems are published in S'Brent.

1967 Ha-Ayara Bo'eret is published in Israel.

he took an interest in theater, poetry, literature, and music, becoming acquainted with Yiddish literature as an amateur actor and through the Jewish workers' movement. In World War I Gebirtig worked as a medical orderly in a Kraków military hospital, where he heard the songs of the many peoples of the Habsburg Empire serving in its army—Czechs, Hungarians, Romanians, Ukrainians, Serbs, and Croatians. Gebirtig could not read music, and the tunes for his poems were composed by others; he wrote the lyrics after first learning the tune.

Gebirtig wrote of the simple Jewish folk, and his talent lay in his ability to give expression to the sentiments felt by the Jewish masses of eastern Europe. His poems, set to music, were performed in theaters, concert halls, and on the radio, and were sung at public meetings, by street singers, and by ordinary Jews. During World War II they were sung in the Kraków and other ghettos and in the concentration camps. In his lifetime Gebirtig wrote about one hundred poems.

Of the poems he wrote during the Holocaust period, fifteen to twenty are known; most of them were published in Kraków in 1946 in a special volume, *S'Brent (1939–1942)*, with a foreword by Joseph Wolf. Wolf, who was a member of the Kraków ghetto underground from 1941 to 1943 and was close to Gebirtig, relates that Gebirtig was very pleased to hear from him that "S'Brent" (a poem Gebirtig had written in 1938, under the impact of the pogrom that took place that year in Przytyk) was highly popular with the young people in the ghetto, inspiring them to take up arms against the Nazis and serving as a slogan for their appeals to the Jewish population at large. Other settings for his poems were sung in the Kraków ghetto and also in the Warsaw ghetto theater, as revealed by an exchange of letters between Gebirtig and Diana Blumenfeld, an actress in the Warsaw ghetto. Just as his poems before 1939 had reflected the life of his people, those he wrote during the Nazi regime are a direct expression of pain, despair, hope, anger, and the desire for revenge.

Gebirtig's writings during the war cover three different periods, corresponding to his fate and that of the Jews of Kraków. First was the period from September 5, 1939, to October 24, 1940, which he spent in occupied Kraków. An outstanding example from this period is "S'Tut Vey," a song of rage and anger, in which he indicts the Poles who, despite the bitter fate they shared with the Jews at the hands of the joint Nazi enemy, could not help gloating over the sufferings of the Jews. Other poems from that period express both pain and hope. In the second period, from October 24, 1940 (when he had to flee from Kraków and took refuge in Lagiewniki, a nearby village), until the spring of 1942, Gebirtig wrote poems of revenge, such as "A Tog fun Nekome" (A Day of Revenge), as well as poems of hope and yearning. The third period covers the time Gebirtig spent in the Kraków ghetto, from April 1942 to June 4, 1942, the day he was killed. In that period his songs became somber, dominated by gloom and fear. He was then sixty-five years old, and in these last months of his life his spirits were raised by a report that the fighters of the underground had made "S'Brent" their anthem. In January 1943 or later, after Gebirtig's death, Gusta Dawidson Draenger, then in the Montelupich Prison, translated "S'Brent" into Polish. It became a folk ballad, sung in the ghettos and forests of occupied Poland and, after the war, by Holocaust survivors.

The 1946 Kraków edition of Gebirtig's writings, which contains nearly all his known work from the Holocaust period, cannot be regarded as definitive. The poem "Minuten fun Yiush" (Moments of Despair), which Gebirtig wrote a year after the war had started, was excluded, probably because it expressed the poet's momentary weakening of faith and his heretical thoughts about God.

In 1967, *Ha-Ayara Bo'eret* (The Town Is Burning) was published in Israel, containing a selection of Gebirtig's poems in Yiddish together with Hebrew translations. The book also contains photocopies of Gebirtig's manuscripts of poems from the Holocaust period, as well as an account of the manuscripts' history and how they were saved. ◆

> In the last months of his life, Gebirtig's spirits were raised by a report that the fighters of the underground had made one of his poems their anthem.

Gens, Jacob

1905–1943

Head of the Judenrat (Jewish Council) in the Vilna ghetto. Gens was born in Illovieciai, a village in the Šiauliai district of Lithuania. In 1919, when Lithuania was fighting for its independence, he volunteered for the Lithuanian army. Sent to an officers' training course, he gradu-

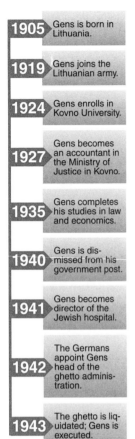

ated as a second lieutenant, and was sent to the front to join the fight against Poles. He served in the army until 1924. (In the late 1930s, as an officer in the reserves, he was sent to a staff officers' course and promoted to captain.) In 1924 Gens enrolled in Kovno University, earning his living as a teacher of Lithuanian and of physical education in the Jewish schools of Ukmerge and Jurbarkas. Three years later, he became an accountant in the Ministry of Justice in Kovno. He completed his university studies in law and economics in 1935.

In July 1940 when Lithuania became a Soviet republic, Gens was dismissed from his post. A Zionist who was close to the Revisionists, Gens feared that he was in danger of being arrested in a campaign that was being waged against anti-Soviet elements, and he moved to Vilna, where he was not known. A Lithuanian friend who headed the municipal health department there helped him obtain work as an accountant in the department.

When the Germans occupied Vilna in late June 1941, his Lithuanian friend appointed Gens director of the Jewish hospital. At the beginning of September, when a ghetto was set up in Vilna, Anatol Fried, chairman of the Judenrat, who had become acquainted with Gens as a patient in the Jewish hospital, appointed Gens commander of the ghetto police. Gens set up the police force, organized it, and made it into an orderly and disciplined body. The Jewish police were assigned a role in the *Aktionen* that were conducted in the ghetto from September to December 1941, in which tens of thousands of Jews were killed. According to most of the evidence available, Gens, within the framework of his job, did his best to help the Jews. He became the predominant personality in the ghetto and its de facto governor. His direct contact with the German authorities, bypassing the Judenrat, added to his prestige among the Jews in the ghetto. Gens involved himself in affairs that had nothing to do with the police: employment, cultural activities, and other aspects of ghetto life.

In July 1942 the Germans dismissed the Judenrat and appointed Gens head of the ghetto administration and sole representative of the ghetto (*Ghettovorsteher*), thereby making official his de facto position. Gens promoted the idea of "work for life," meaning that the survival of the ghetto Jews depended on their work and productivity. He believed that efforts had to be made to gain time and keep the ghetto in existence until Germany was defeated in the war, and that this could be achieved by working for the Germans. He constantly sought to increase the number of Jews in such positions. In the last few months of the ghetto's existence, 14,000 out of the total ghetto population of 20,000 were employed inside or outside the ghetto. On one occasion, Gens was ordered by the Germans to send the Vilna ghetto police to the Oshmiany ghetto, to carry out a *Selektion* there and to hand over 1,500 children and women who were not employed. Instead, Gens delivered to the Germans 406 persons who were chronically ill or old. He justified this action to the Jews by claiming that if the Germans and the Lithuanians had done the selecting, they would have taken the children and the women, whom he wanted to keep alive for the sake of the future of the Jewish people.

Gens's attitude toward the ghetto underground was ambivalent. On the one hand, he maintained contact with the underground leaders and declared that when the day of the ghetto's liquidation arrived, he would join them in an uprising; but on the other hand, when the underground's activities endangered the continued existence of the ghetto, he opposed it, and he complied with a German demand to hand over to them the underground commander, Yitzhak Wittenberg.

Once the process of liquidating the ghetto had been set in motion, in August and September 1943, Gens knew that his life was in danger. His Lithuanian wife and his daughter were both in Vilna, where they lived outside the ghetto. He had several offers from his Lithuanian relatives and friends to leave the ghetto and take refuge with them, but he refused, believing that in his role he was engaged in a mission on behalf of the Jewish people. On September 14, 1943, nine days before the final liquidation of the ghetto, Gens was summoned to the Gestapo. The previous day, he had been warned that the Germans were planning to kill him, and had been urged to flee. He replied that his escape would mean disaster for the Jews who remained in the ghetto.

Gens reported to the Gestapo on September 14, and at 6:00 P.M. he was shot to death in the Gestapo courtyard. News of his death reached the ghetto at once, and the Jews who were still alive mourned his passing. Gens's belief that if the ghetto were productive its Jews would be saved proved baseless; but under the terrible conditions prevailing at the time, he did his best, as he understood it, to save as many as possible. ◆

Gens promoted the idea of "work for life," meaning that the survival of the ghetto Jews depended on their work and productivity.

Gepner, Abraham

1872–1943

Businessman and public figure; member of the Warsaw ghetto Judenrat (Jewish Council). Gepner was born in Warsaw, into a poor family; his father died when Abraham was still a boy, and his studies had to be cut short. Owing to his drive and diligence, he rose from errand boy to become the owner of a trading firm and a number of factories in the metals industry in Poland, with far-flung international ties.

Gepner was a fervent Polish patriot and in his youth was inclined to join the **assimilationists.** In 1912, when the Polish nationalists declared an economic boycott of the Jews, Gepner abandoned assimilation and became active in the Jewish community. For many years he played a leading role in the Association of Jewish Businessmen in Poland, serving as its chairman from 1935 to 1939. He was a member of the Warsaw city council, and became known for his generous support of orphanages and vocational training institutions and for his efforts to raise productivity. Gepner was known for his austere private life; he set himself the rule of tithing, contributing a tenth of all his income to charity and welfare.

When World War II broke out, Gepner was sixty-seven years old. He and Samuel Zygelbojm were the two Jews among the twelve hostages whom the Germans seized in Warsaw when they captured the city in October 1939. Gepner was a member of the Judenrat from its inception and was close to Adam Czerniaków, the Judenrat chairman. From the beginning, Gepner assisted in organizing Jewish self-help, and when the ghetto was set up in November 1940, he was appointed head of the supply department (Zakład Zaopatrywania). This department had the task of supplying food and other essential items to the ghetto—under the prevailing conditions, a most delicate and responsible task. Gepner was not able to prevent hunger and mass deaths from starvation, but he had the ghetto population's confidence, and his organization was efficient (in relative terms); as a result, the supply organization was the target of far less criticism than the other Judenrat departments.

In the ghetto, too, Gepner was involved in aid and welfare; his main concern was children, and especially orphans. Early in

assimilationist: one who supports the gradual absorption of the Jewish community into the larger, more dominant culture.

"If I have succeeded in drying a single tear—that is my reward. I have a daughter living in the United States. Tell her that I served my people faithfully."

Abraham Gepner, 1943

Judenrat

The name Judenrat (plural: Judenrate) refers to the Jewish councils established on German orders in the Jewish communities of occupied Europe. Judenrate were first instituted in occupied Poland in 1939, and subsequently in other countries conquered by Germany. The Judenrate did not have a uniform structure; some of them held authority in one location only, while others administered Jewish communities throughout a district or even an entire country. The Judenrate were responsible for the implementation of German policy regarding the Jews and were made up of influential people and rabbis. In this way, the Jewish communities had forced upon them a body whose function was to receive German orders and decrees and be responsible for carrying them out. The inclusion of prominent Jewish people in the Judenrate had a dual purpose: to ensure that German orders were implemented to the fullest possible extent, and to discredit Jewish leadership in the eyes of the Jewish population. The role played by the Judenrate in Jewish public life during the Holocaust is one of the most controversial issues relating to the period; some historians believe that the institution of the Judenrate had a debilitating effect on the inner strength of the Jewish communities, whereas others maintain that the Judenrate reinforced the Jews' power of endurance in their struggle for survival.

the ghetto's existence, Gepner established contact with the Jewish political underground, lent support to the clandestine pioneer movements, and kept track of the latter's activities. He was in favor of youth movements and aided them even after the Żydowska Organizacja Bojowa (Jewish Fighting Organization; ŻOB) was established and preparations were under way for the ghetto uprising.

When the revolt broke out, on April 19, 1943, Gepner at first refused to take refuge in a bunker, but he gave in to his friends' appeals and together with his family went into the bunker of 30 Franciszkanska Street, where the staff of the supply department had gathered in the last days of the ghetto's life. On May 3 the Germans dragged Gepner, together with many others, out of the bunker and killed him. A letter he wrote on January 1, 1943, contains the following passage: "I have no regrets about staying in the ghetto, nor about any of the decisions that I made. Recently I reached the age of seventy, and remaining in the ghetto, together with my brothers and sisters, I regard as the most important step I took in my life. If I have succeeded in drying a single tear—that is my reward. I have a daughter living in the United States. Tell her that I served my people faithfully." ◆

"I have no regrets about staying in the ghetto, nor about any of the decisions that I made."
Abraham Gepner, 1943

Getter, Matylda

D. 1968

Mother superior of the Warsaw branch of the Order of the Franciscan Sisters of the Family of Mary, a Polish religious order that carried on educational work, mainly among orphans, and cared for the sick in hospitals. In 1942 Sister Matylda decided to accept all the Jewish children fleeing from the Warsaw ghetto who were brought to her and to shelter them in the order's many locations, but especially in its branch at Pludy, some 7.5 miles (12 km) outside Warsaw, on the right bank of the Vistula River.

> It is estimated that Sister Matylda was instrumental in rescuing several hundred Jewish children from certain death.

It is estimated that Sister Matylda was instrumental in rescuing several hundred Jewish children from certain death. Her principal aim was not to gain new souls for the church, but to rescue human lives. She was accused by some of unnecessarily endangering the lives of the many non-Jewish orphans in the order's homes by harboring Jewish children in their midst. Her reply was that by virtue of the Jewish children's presence, God would not allow any harm to befall the other children. Special precautions were taken to remove the too obviously Jewish-looking children for temporary shelter elsewhere when Sister Matylda was alerted to possible Gestapo raids on the orphanages. When time proved too short for this, children with a more Jewish appearance would have their heads or faces partially bandaged, to look as though they had been injured. Sister Matylda was at the time an elderly person and ill with cancer. After the war, the children were released to their parents or relatives.

Sister Matylda Getter was posthumously recognized by Yad Vashem as a "Righteous among the Nations." ◆

Gildenman, Moshe "Uncle Misha"

D. 1958

Partisan commander. A resident of the town of Korets in eastern Volhynia, Gildenman was an engineer by profession. After the Nazis' first *Aktion* in Korets on May 21,

1942, in which his wife and daughter died, Gildenman, together with his son, Simha, organized a rebel unit. On September 23 of that year, on the eve of the final liquidation of the Jews of Korets, Gildenman, Simha, and ten young men left for the forests, armed with two revolvers and a butcher knife. After wandering northward for about two weeks, they took in the survivors of an armed group of Jews in the Klesov area, together with whom they made their base in the wooded and swampy terrain north of the Sarny-Rokitno railway track. All of the unit members armed themselves with weapons taken in battles, attacked German farms and Ukrainian police centers, and took revenge on collaborators.

In late January 1943, the unit joined General Aleksandr Saburov's partisan group. The resulting company that Gildenman formed was initially entirely Jewish, but as it grew the Jews became a minority. The company operated independently in the northern area of the Zhitomir district until its liberation in October 1943. Early that month, Gildenman rescued beleaguered units of the Thirteenth Soviet Army; he went on to volunteer for the Soviet army and served as a captain in the engineer corps until the end of the war. He subsequently described the exploits of his unit in articles and in books (*On the Road to Victory: Types of Jewish Partisans*, 1946; and *The Destruction of Korets*, 1949; both in Yiddish). In the early 1950s Gildenman emigrated to Israel; he died in Rehovot. ◆

Gitterman, Yitzhak

1889–1943

Director of the American Jewish Joint Distribution Committee (the Joint) in Poland, an organizer of Jewish welfare in occupied Poland, and an active member

1889 Gitterman is born in Horonstopol, a town in Ukraine.

1921 Gitterman is appointed head of the Joint in Warsaw.

1926 Gitterman works in relief for Jews during dire economic crisis.

1940 Gitterman returns to Warsaw from prison-of-war camp.

1942 Gitterman joins ZOB financial subcommittee.

1943 Gitterman is killed during the second *Aktion* in the ghetto.

pauperization: process of becoming very poor.

vocational: relating to a trade or occupation.

of the underground and the Żydowska Organizacja Bojowa (Jewish Fighting Organization; ŻOB). Born in Horonstopol, a town in the Ukraine, Gitterman at an early age aided in organizing support to refugees and victims of persecution. In World War I war refugees from towns in Galicia and Lithuania benefited from his assistance, which also included facilitating their emigration from war-torn Europe. In 1921 he was appointed head of the Joint in Warsaw and took part in the postwar rehabilitation of the Jewish population and the establishment of welfare institutions. He was deeply involved in the relief efforts designed to alleviate the grave problems caused by the economic crisis of 1926 and its disastrous effect on the position of the Jews. Gitterman created a network of institutions that provided interest-free loans, the Centralna Kasa Bezprocentowa covering every city and town in Poland. This became an important instrument in Polish Jewry's defense against economic discrimination and boycott. There were places where no organized Jewish community existed, but the loan institution was there, representing every public institution whose services were required by a Jewish community. In the 1930s Gitterman was able to slow down somewhat the rapid **pauperization** process of Polish Jewry through **vocational** retraining and the introduction of new occupations.

When World War II broke out, Gitterman made his way to Vilna, which had a large concentration of refugees, and set up aid operations. He was on his way to Sweden to appeal for help when the boat on which he was sailing was seized by the Germans on the high seas. Gitterman was interned in a prisoner-of-war camp and returned to Warsaw in April 1940. He lost no time in taking over responsibility for the major functions of the Jewish Self-Help Society (Żydowska Samopomoc Społeczna) and the Jewish Mutual Aid Society (Żydowskie Towarzystwo Opieki Społecznej). When the Joint's financial resources were exhausted, Gitterman and his associates in the Joint leadership turned to the Jews of Poland themselves with an appeal for financial contributions.

As soon as the Jewish underground was set up, it benefited from Gitterman's support. The Self-Help Society, in which Gitterman played a prominent role, also had an underground council, made up of the leaders of the political underground in the Warsaw ghetto. Gitterman took a direct part in underground activities, together with Emanuel Ringelblum (a close friend), in the clandestine cultural programs and in social work for the underground organizations and youth movements. He was a member of the Oneg Shabbat and Idische Kultur Organizacje (Yiddish Culture Organization) executive boards.

When the first reports came in of the mass murder of Jews in eastern Europe, Gitterman lent his support to the emerging ŻOB, and provided funds to the Białystok ghetto fighters for the acquisition of arms. When the ŻOB was established in Warsaw in October 1942, Gitterman joined its coordinating committee's financial subcommittee, whose main task was to obtain funds for the purchase of arms.

Gitterman was killed on January 18, 1943, the first day of the second *Aktion* in the Warsaw ghetto. ◆

Glasberg, Alexandre

1902–1981

French priest, born a Jew in Zhitomir, in the Ukraine. Glasberg wandered about central Europe, converted, and became a priest in France. In 1940, after the German conquest of France, he established a charitable organization, Amitié Chrétienne (Christian Friendship), to help the victims of the anti-Jewish measures. Under the patronage of Cardinal Pierre-Marie Gerlier, the head of the Catholic church in France, Glasberg's organization set up shelter institutions that took in hundreds of Jewish prisoners who had been released from internment camps run by the French authorities.

When the mass arrests and deportations of Jews began in the summer of 1942, Glasberg turned his rescue efforts into clandestine operations. He cooperated closely with the Jewish rescue organizations, taking special care to ensure that no attempt was made to influence the religious convictions of the persons who were in the care of his institutions. In December 1942, when the Gestapo discovered his activities, Glasberg joined the French partisans, under an assumed name. After the war he played an important role in the operations of the Mosad Aliya (the organization that dealt with the "illegal" immigration of Jews into Palestine) in France and Iran. ◆

1902 Glasberg is born in Zitomir, Ukraine.

1940 Glasberg, now a priest, establishes a Jewish aid charity.

1942 Glasberg turns his rescue efforts into clandestine operations.

1942 Glasberg joins the French partisans under an assumed name.

1981 Glasberg dies.

Glazer, Gesja

D. 1944

Underground fighter in Lithuania. Before World War II Glazer was a member of the Communist party in Kovno, and she spent years in jail and concentration camps on account of her party activities. When the Germans invaded the Soviet Union on June 22, 1941, Glazer fled to the Soviet interior. From Moscow she was dispatched to Lithuania (dropped by parachute), where she became active in setting up an underground and partisan movement to fight the German invaders. On one occasion she entered the Kovno ghetto and, in the name of the Communist party, handed a pistol to the committee of the Antifascist Organization, in appreciation of its operations; she suggested that she would be prepared to lead fighting units of the Jewish underground into the Augustów forest and establish partisan bases there. According to her plan, the bases were to take in the entire membership of the ghetto underground.

After a week Glazer departed for the forest, remaining in touch with the ghetto underground until February 1944. She then left to take part in the Vilna underground operations. When she saw the German police closing in on her, Gesja Glazer committed suicide. ◆

Glazman, Josef

1913–1943

Jewish underground and partisan leader. Born in the town of Alytus, in southern Lithuania, Glazman was given a nationalist and traditional upbringing and was active in the Betar Zionist youth movement. In 1937 he was appointed Betar leader for Lithuania, retaining the post until July 1940, when the Soviets dissolved all Jewish political movements in the country. In the first phase of Soviet rule in Lithuania, from July 1940 to the end of June 1941, Glazman was one of the underground leaders of the Revisionist party. When the Germans occupied Lithuania, Glazman was in Vilna, where he was apprehended and sent on forced labor in nearby Reise. In early November of 1941 Glazman returned to the Vilna ghetto, where he organized an underground group made up of Betar members. In order to aid his underground activities he joined the Jewish ghetto police, and at the end of November 1941 he was appointed its deputy chief.

Glazman was one of the founders of the Fareynegte Partizaner Organizatsye (United Partisan Organization; FPO) of the Vilna ghetto and participated in its founding meeting on January 21, 1942. He became the FPO's deputy commander and was also in charge of its intelligence section and commander of one of its two battalions. His official post as deputy chief of the ghetto police was of great help to the underground's operations. Glazman also took an active part in the ghetto's educational and cultural activities. In June 1942, when the ghetto administration was reorganized, Glazman left the police and was appointed head of the ghetto housing department within the Judenrat (Jewish Council).

1913 Glazman is born in Alytus, Lithuania.

1937 Glazman is appointed Betar leader for Lithuania.

1940 Glazman becomes an underground leader of the Revisionist Party.

1941 Glazman is appointed deputy chief of the Jewish ghetto police.

1942 Glazman helps found the FPO and becomes its deputy commander.

1942 Glazman leaves police force to head Judenrat ghetto housing.

1942 Glazman is arrested and dismissed from his post.

1942 Glazman is released from jail.

1943 Glazman leaves the ghetto to form a partisan group.

1943 Glazman and comrades are killed by Germans.

Glazman's relations with Jacob Gens (chief of the ghetto police and, as of July 1942, ghetto head) were strained because of Glazman's underground activities and their differences over policy. At the end of October 1942, Glazman was arrested on Gens's orders and dismissed from his post. He was released in mid-December 1942 after spending several weeks in jail; at the end of June 1943 he was again arrested and sent to the Reise labor camp, on Gens's orders. His arrest was accompanied by a clash between FPO members and the ghetto police.

A few weeks later, Glazman was returned to the ghetto. In the wake of the Wittenberg affair (July 15, 1943), Glazman left the ghetto, leading the first group of FPO members into the forest in order to establish a partisan base there. On the way they fell into a German ambush and in the ensuing fight the group lost a third of its men. At the end of July, Glazman and his men reached the Naroch Forest, where he formed the Nekama (Revenge) Jewish partisan unit of the partisan brigade commanded by Fyodor Markov. At the end of September the Soviet command decided to dissolve the Jewish unit. As a result of this decision the unit also lost most of its arms. Glazman and a group of his comrades went over to the Lithuanian partisan command.

At this time the Germans launched a determined drive against the partisans in the Naroch and Kozhany forests. Glazman and a group of thirty-five Jewish partisans tried to break through to the Rudninkai Forest in the south in order to join up with FPO members who had gone there from the Vilna ghetto. On October 7, 1943, Glazman and his men were encircled by a superior German force. In the fierce struggle that followed he and his comrades were killed; only one member of the group, a young girl, was saved. ◆

Glik, Hirsh (Hirshke)

1922–1944

Poet and partisan in Lithuania. Born in Vilna, Glik began working at the age of fifteen. He joined the Ha-Shomer ha-Tsa'ir Zionist youth movement, and in 1935, when he was only thirteen, he began to write Hebrew poems. Later he wrote mostly in Yiddish; in the period preceding the war he was the most outstanding member of the Yungwald (Young People) group of young writers (named after the literary journal of that name). In 1940 he published poems in *Vilner Emes* (Vilna Truth) and in the Kovno *Naye Bleter* (New Bulletin).

When Vilna was occupied by the Germans at the end of June 1941, Glik and his father were among the Jews who were seized at random and taken to labor camps, to work in the peat deposits at Biała-Waka and Rzesza. Even there Glik continued to write prodigiously, and the Vilna Writers' and Artists' Association awarded him a prize for a play he wrote that dealt with the life of the Jews working in the **peat bogs.**

In early 1943, when the Biała-Waka camp was liquidated, Glik was moved to the Vilna ghetto. He joined the Fareynegte Partizaner Organizatsye (United Partisan Organization; FPO), and continued his writing. At this time he wrote *Di Balada fun Broynem Teater* (The Ballad of the Brown Theater), a macabre work that describes the terrible suffering of the Jews in the Lukishko prison before they were sent to their death at Ponary. On September 1, 1943, the FPO unit to which he belonged was captured and Glik was deported to Estonia, where he was imprisoned first in the Narva camp and then in the Goldfilz camp. In the summer of 1944 Glik broke out from the camp together with eight other FPO men, but all were killed by the Germans while trying to make their escape.

Even in the camps Glik did not cease writing, and he recited his poems to his comrades. Among the poems he wrote there were "In Gehenem bay Leningrad" (In Hell near Leningrad) and "Der Fay fun Mototsikl," (The Five from Mototsikl), a sarcastic verse composition about the Narva camp commandant, as well as poems about Vilna and hiding places in the ghetto. None of these works survived.

Glik's poems are very musical, and during the Holocaust years he composed poems that were to be sung. Most of these were designed to raise morale among the Jews, to glorify the deeds of the partisans, and to strengthen the Jews' faith and hope in the future. He gained fame with his "Song of the Partisans," which began: "Zog nisht keynmol az du geyst dem letztn Veg" (Never say that you are on your last journey). Glik based the song on a tune by two Soviet Jewish composers, the brothers Dimitri and Daniel Pokras. It became the partisan anthem as soon as it was written, and was sung in many places under Nazi

peat bog: a marsh area containing partly rotted plants that are used for fertilizer and fuel.

1922 Glik is born in Vilna.

1935 Glik begins to write Hebrew poems.

1940 Glik publishes poems in two periodicals.

1941 Glik is forced to work in peat bogs.

1943 Glik is moved to the Vilna ghetto; is deported to Estonia and imprisoned.

1944 Glik is killed while escaping from camp.

rule. After the war it was translated into numerous languages and became popular among Jews all over the world. ◆

Goldmann, Nahum

1895–1982

<blockquote>
"Although I was always conscious of the power discrepancy, I cannot remember any encounter, whether with Mussolini or Prince Regent Paul, with General Gamelin, the French Chief of Staff, or with American presidents or British foreign ministers, when I had the least feeling of inferiority. I recognized that they were different, and in most cases more powerful, but never that they were superior."

Nahum Goldmann, *Autobiography*, 1969
</blockquote>

Jewish and Zionist leader. Goldmann was born in Lithuania and taken to Germany when he was five years old. He studied at German universities, obtaining doctorates in humanities and law. At the outbreak of World War I, he joined the staff of the German Foreign Ministry's Jewish section. With his friend, the philosopher Jacob Klatzkin, Goldmann formed Eshkol Publishing House for the publication of the *Encyclopaedia Judaica*. The encyclopedia's completion was prevented by Hitler's rise to power, and only ten volumes in German and two in Hebrew were issued. In the 1960s Goldmann initiated the publication of the English-language *Encyclopaedia Judaica*, which appeared in 1971.

Forced to leave Germany when Hitler came to power in 1933, Goldmann settled in Switzerland and, at the end of that year, was elected chairman of the Committee of Jewish Delegations, which had come into existence after World War I to present the Jewish case at the Paris Peace Conference. In the summer of 1932 the leaders of the Committee of Jewish Delegations and of the American Jewish Congress, aware of the significance of the Nazi menace, had called the first preparatory conference for the World Jewish Congress (WJC). At that conference, warnings concerning the Nazi danger had been voiced by the WJC's future leaders Stephen S. Wise and Nahum Goldmann. The new organization, founded after several more preparatory conferences, in August 1936 called for the mobilization of the Jewish people and of democratic forces against the Nazi onslaught; the struggle for equal political and economic rights everywhere, particularly for the Jewish minorities in central and eastern Europe; and support for the Jewish national home in Palestine. The WJC was established as a worldwide Jewish representative body, democratically organized and based on the concept of the unity of the Jewish people.

The United States Holocaust Memorial Museum

The United States Holocaust Memorial Museum, located 400 yards from the Washington Monument in Washington, D.C., is America's only national institution for the documentation, study, and interpretation of Holocaust history. Chartered by an act of congress in 1980, the Holocaust Museum opened its doors to the public in April 1993. Architect James I. Freed, himself a child refugee from Nazi Germany, designed the museum building to resonate with abstract symbolic references to the Holocaust. A deep crack that runs down one side of the main hall symbolizes the rupture of civilization that occurred during the Holocaust. The six-sided shape of the museum's Hall of Remembrance represents the six million Jews murdered in the Holocaust. The museum's permanent collection of Holocaust-related artifacts, oral histories, documentary film, and photographs focuses on the tragic story of the Jews who died, but also describes the experiences of Gypsies, Poles, Soviet prisoners of war, homosexuals, Jehovah's Witnesses, and other victims of Nazi persecution. In addition, the exhibition depicts the rise of Nazi terror, the failure of the free world to stop it, and the inspiring story of resistance and rescue. The Holocaust Museum includes an interactive Learning Center that allows museum visitors to access maps, texts, videotapes, and music associated with the Holocaust. Students and scholars can visit the museum's Holocaust Research Institute, a comprehensive library and archive dedicated to the history of the Holocaust.

Goldmann was elected chairman of the WJC's Administrative Committee and until 1939 was its representative at the League of Nations; from 1934, he also represented the Jewish Agency for Palestine at the league. In this capacity he led the WJC's efforts with governments and the League of Nations to obtain prolongation of the Minority Rights Agreement covering Upper Silesia and thereby prevent the application of Nazi discriminatory measures in that region. When the government of Octavian Goga introduced anti-Jewish measures in Romania in 1937, the WJC petitioned the League of Nations, whose condemnation of Romania led to Goga's resignation early in 1938. Before and after the Anschluss, the WJC repeatedly appealed to the League of Nations for protection of the Jews of Austria.

Goldmann represented both the WJC and the Jewish Agency at the ill-fated Evian Conference, held in 1938, of which he later wrote: "The Evian Conference is an irrefutable indictment of the civilized world in its attitude to the Nazi persecution of the Jews." To facilitate the immigration to Palestine of Jews from Nazi Germany, Goldmann, who proclaimed a Jewish anti-Nazi boycott, was instrumental in concluding the

> *"The Evian Conference is an irrefutable indictment of the civilized world in its attitude to the Nazi persecution of the Jews."*
> Nahum Goldmann

Haavara Agreement between the Jewish Agency and Nazi Germany.

Goldmann moved to the United States in June 1940, and throughout the war worked for both the WJC and the Jewish Agency. With Stephen S. Wise, he tried to mobilize American Jewry and public opinion to help the Jews in Nazi-occupied Europe, keeping in close contact with WJC offices in Geneva and London, and through these offices monitoring the havoc wrought by the Nazis. When in August 1942 Dr. Gerhart Riegner, the WJC representative in Geneva, cabled news of the "Final Solution," Goldmann and Wise broke the media silence on the mass annihilation of Jews and bombarded President Franklin D. Roosevelt and the administration with pleas for help. This activity led to a December 1942 collective Allied condemnation of the Nazi extermination policy toward Jews and a stern warning of retribution.

An Advisory Council on European Jewish Affairs, under Goldmann's chairmanship, was set up in New York with representative committees from eighteen European countries. Tens of thousands of individual parcels were sent to concentration camps, and tons of food and medicines to Jewish communities in occupied Europe. A far-reaching rescue program was submitted to the 1943 refugee conference in Bermuda; a memorandum on Jewish aspects of relief and rehabilitation was submitted to the first session of the United Nations Relief and Rehabilitation Administration (UNRRA) in 1943; and in December 1943 a license was obtained from the United States Treasury to transmit funds to Europe for the rescue and assistance of persecuted Jews, a step leading to the eventual establishment of the War Refugee Board.

At the 1944 WJC War Emergency Conference in Atlantic City, Goldmann presented the first comprehensive program for the postwar rehabilitation of the Jewish people, including calls for Reparations and Restitution from Germany to Jews, use of heirless Jewish property for Jewish rehabilitation, and punishment of Nazi persecutors of Jews. With the end of war in Europe, Goldmann was in the forefront of the struggle for the admittance into Palestine of the survivors, and for the reconstruction of destroyed Jewish communities. As chairman of the Conference on Jewish Material Claims against Germany, which he created, he led the negotiations for restitution and indemnification to Israel and to individual victims of Nazi persecution.

Looking back on the years of the Holocaust, Goldmann said that the greatest tragedy of all was that both the Jews and the democratic world failed to realize the magnitude and the depth of evil that Nazism embodied. He acknowledged the failure of his generation to stand up to the challenge.

After the war, Goldmann was co-chairman of the executive of the World Zionist Organization (1948–56), its president (1956–68), and president of the WJC (1953–77). He published his recollections in *The Autobiography of Nahum Goldmann: Sixty Years of Jewish Life* (New York, 1969), *Mein Leben als deutscher Jude* (My Life as a German Jew; Munich, 1980), and *Mein Leben: U.S.A.—Europa—Israel* (Munich, 1981). ◆

Gräbe, Hermann Friedrich

1900–1986

A "Righteous among the Nations." Born in Solingen, Germany, Gräbe was a member of the Nazi party for a few months, but he later spoke out against the Nazi regime and served a short prison term. A construction worker, he was employed as a foreman at the Jung Company in Solingen. In October 1941 he was entrusted with setting up a branch of Jung in Zdolbunov, Volhynia, for the construction and repair of buildings used by the railway directorate in the Reichskommissariat Ukraine. Thousands of Jews were employed by Gräbe, and he insisted that his subordinates treat the workers properly. An intervention on his part with the Zdolbunov district commissar resulted in the cancellation of fines that had been imposed on the Jews; he also saved his Jewish employees from the *Aktionen* in Rovno in November 1941 and July 1942, not hesitating to intervene with the SD (Sicherheitsdienst; Security Service) commander in Rovno for this purpose.

Several dozen Jewish men and women were employed by Gräbe in the company's head office. In the summer of 1942, when they were seen to be in danger, they were given "Aryan" papers and sent to Poltava to work in what was purported to be a company branch; in actuality, it had been established by Gräbe without the authorization or knowledge of his employers, and it was maintained out of his own funds.

1900 Gräbe is born in Solingen, Germany.

1941 Gräbe employs thousands of Jews and saves them from the *Aktionen* in Rovno.

1942 Gräbe arranges for Jewish employees to have "Aryan" papers.

1942 Gräbe witnesses the murder of Dubno's Jews.

1966 Gräbe is designated a Yad Vashem "Righteous among the Nations."

1986 Gräbe dies.

In October of that year, alerted by his Jewish secretary, Gräbe went to Dubno, where he witnessed the murder of the city's Jews.

Gräbe saved the lives of dozens of Jews. At the Nuremberg Trial, where he gave evidence on the crimes committed by the Nazis in Volhynia, his description of the slaughter of the Dubno Jews made a deep impression. This created widespread animosity against him in Germany, and with the help of Jewish organizations he emigrated with his family to the United States, settling in California. In 1966 Gräbe was invited to Israel to be presented with the "Righteous among the Nations" award. There he planted a tree on the Avenue of the Righteous at Yad Vashem in Jerusalem. ◆

Grobelny, Julian

1893–1944

Polska Partia Socjalistyczna (Polish Socialist Party) activist. From 1919 to 1921 Grobelny strove for the annexation of Silesia to Poland. Subsequently employed in Łódź, he was active in the organization of social assistance. In 1940 he joined Wolność, Równość, Niepodległość (Freedom, Equality, Independence), the right-wing faction of the Polish Socialist party, and was a member of the party's regional labor committee in the Warsaw suburbs (he was known by the code name "Trojan").

Under Grobelny's chairmanship, from January 1943, Zegota, the Polish Council for Aid to Jews, greatly expanded its activity and increased its budget. Grobelny was of great assistance to the large group of people in the organization's care, and he was particularly sensitive to the distress of the children.

Arrested in March 1944 and imprisoned, Grobelny developed tuberculosis and was admitted to the prison hospital. After about a month he was smuggled out by the Polish underground and went into hiding in Mińsk Mazowiecki. After the liberation he became mayor of that town. ◆

Grosman, Haika

1919–

Underground activist and partisan. Born in Białystok, Grosman became a member of the Zionist youth movement Ha-Shomer ha-Tsa'ir at an early age. At the outbreak of World War II she moved to Vilna and helped to concentrate members of the pioneering Zionist youth movements in that city. Following the German invasion of the Soviet Union (June 22, 1941), Grosman returned to Białystok, where she became one of the organizers of the underground there. Posing as a Polish woman, she went on many underground missions to various cities and ghettos, including the Warsaw ghetto. She belonged to the "Antifascist Białystok" cell and, together with five other young women who posed as Poles—Marila Ruziecka, Liza Czapnik, Hasya Belicka (Borenstein), Ana Rud, and Bronka Winicki (Klibanski)—gave assistance to the Jewish underground and to the partisans who were then organizing themselves in the forests around Białystok. She participated in the Białystok ghetto revolt in August 1943 and was a member of a Jewish partisan unit that operated in the area.

> "My mind became absolutely alert. I must not give in. The movement needed me, our ranks were growing thinner. I did not want to die."
> Haika Grosman,
> *The Underground Army*

After liberation, Grosman served as the Ha-Shomer ha-Tsa'ir representative in the institutions set up by the remnants of the Jewish population in Poland. She settled in Israel in 1948, joining Kibbutz Evron in western Galilee. Grosman became politically active in Israel and was a member of the Knesset (the Israeli parliament) from 1969 to 1981, and again from 1984. She is the author of *People of the Underground* (published in English as *The Underground Army*, 1988), which contains memoirs and chapters on the struggle of the Białystok Jews. ◆

Grossman, Mendel

1917–1945

Photographer in the Łódź ghetto. Grossman commemorated the horrors of the Łódź ghetto in more than ten thousand pictures taken throughout the ghetto's existence. Since Jews were forbidden to photograph in the ghetto, he risked his life carrying out the task. He used his position in the ghetto's statistics department, where he received photographic materials and was permitted to keep a camera. Upon the liquidation of the ghetto he was sent to the Königs Wusterhausen labor camp, where he secretly continued photographing, but not developing and printing. When the war front advanced and came closer, and the prisoners of the camp were taken out on the liquidation march, Grossman collapsed and died with his camera on him. The negatives of his photographs, hidden by him in the ghetto, were found and sent to Israel, but most of them were lost during the War of Independence. Those photographs that were saved were used in the book *With a Camera in the Ghetto* (New York, 1977). ◆

Grüninger, Paul

1891–1972

Local police commandant of the Saint Gall canton in Switzerland, on the Austrian frontier, who was responsible for assisting thousands of Jewish refugees.

After Austria's annexation by Germany in March 1938, the stream of Jewish refugees seeking to leave the Reich increased, and many sought to gain access to Switzerland. But at this crit-

Paul Grüninger (left) in police uniform in 1934.

ical juncture, the Swiss government closed its borders to Jewish refugees. Grüninger was instructed on August 18, 1938, to refuse entry to refugees fleeing Germany for racial reasons. Confronted by an unending wave of Jewish refugees at his border post, he defied his government's instructions and allowed all the Jews crossing the border at his checkpoint entry into the country. As a coverup, he predated official seals in the refugees' passports to indicate that their holders had entered the country prior to the August 1938 government ruling. Thus, from August through December 1938, when he was summarily suspended, Grüninger allowed some thirty-six hundred persons (according to the state prosecutor) illegal entry into Switzerland.

Alerted by the German legation in Bern, the Swiss government in January 1939 opened an inquiry into Grüninger's activities, and charges were filed against him. Found guilty of insubordination, he was sentenced in 1941 to a stiff fine and the forfeiture of all retirement and severance payments. Grüninger was later denied access to other suitable positions in the government and the private sector, and he was never fully rehabilitated by the Swiss government. In 1971 he received recognition from Yad Vashem as a "Righteous among the Nations." ◆

1891 Grüninger is born in Switzerland.

1938 Switzerland closes its border to Jewish refuges.

1938 Grüninger defies orders and allows all Jews into Switzerland.

1938 Grüninger is suspended from his post.

1939 The Swiss government files charges against Grüninger.

1941 Grüninger is convicted of insubordination and fined.

1971 Grüninger is designated a Yad Vashem "Righteous among the Nations."

1972 Grüninger dies.

Hautval, Adelaide

1906–

1906 ▸ Hautval is born into a Protestant family in France.

1942 ▸ Hautval is arrested trying to cross to the unoccupied zone.

1942 ▸ Hautval protests the Gestapo's harsh treatment of Jewish prisoners.

1943 ▸ Hautval is sent as a doctor to Auschwitz.

1944 ▸ Hautval is transferred to Ravensbrück.

1945 ▸ Hautval is liberated.

1964 ▸ Hautval testifies that it is possible to bypass SS commands.

1965 ▸ Hautval is designated a Yad Vashem "Righteous among the Nations."

French physician. Born into a Protestant family, Hautval studied medicine in Strasbourg and later worked in several psychiatric clinics in Strasbourg and Switzerland.

In April 1942 Hautval was arrested trying to cross without a permit from the occupied to the unoccupied zone in France in order to attend her mother's funeral. Awaiting trial in the Bourges prison, she vehemently protested to the Gestapo against the harsh treatment of Jewish prisoners incarcerated with her. In reprisal, she was transferred to the Romainville prison with other political detainees, and eventually sent as a doctor to Auschwitz with a convoy of Jewish women, arriving there in January 1943. She reportedly bore a yellow badge attached to her overcoat, with the inscription "A friend of the Jews."

At Auschwitz, she helped hide a group of women afflicted with typhus on the top floor of her block and treated them as well as conditions allowed. She was later approached by SS-Hauptsturmführer Dr. Eduard Wirths, the garrison doctor (*Standortarzt*), and asked to practice gynecology. Aware of the sterilization experiments practiced in Block 10, Hautval accepted in order to gain a firsthand view of the Nazi procedure. She soon discovered that in this block Wirths was in charge of a team of doctors (Horst Schumann, Carl Clauberg, and Władysław Dering) who used women as guinea pigs, sterilizing them by means of X rays and ovariectomy (surgical removal of ovaries). These experiments were part of a large-scale plan: sterilization was intended to be applied (worldwide) to all half and

quarter Jews who were left alive after the Nazi victory. Hautval expressed her complete opposition and refused to participate in these experiments (in which Dr. Josef Mengele was also involved). She feared retribution, but was not punished.

After her confrontation with Wirths, Hautval continued practicing medicine in the nearby Birkenau camp (Auschwitz II) as best she could until August 1944, when she was transferred to the women's camp at Ravensbrück. She survived and was liberated in April 1945.

libel: a false or damaging statement about a person.

A **libel** trial (*Dering* v. *Uris*) was held in London in 1964, at which Dering claimed that the author Leon Uris had slandered him in his book *QB VII*. At the trial, Hautval refuted Dering's claim that it was futile to refuse to obey orders in Auschwitz, maintaining that one could bypass SS commands to remove women's ovaries and still manage to avoid punishment. The presiding judge, Justice Frederick Horace Lawton, in his summation to the jury called Hautval "perhaps one of the most impressive and courageous women who have ever given evidence in the courts of this country."

Hautval received recognition by Yad Vashem as a "Righteous among the Nations" in 1965. ◆

Helbronner, Jacques

1873–1943

Jewish leader in Vichy France. The son of a distinguished lawyer, Helbronner was born in Paris. In 1927 he was appointed to the Conseil d'Etat (Council of State), in which he too became a noted lawyer. During the 1930s, Helbronner was an active member of the Consistoire Central des Israélites de France (Central Consistory of French Jews), becoming its vice president. Deeply rooted in French society and culture, Helbronner was well qualified to represent the native French Jews, who maintained close contacts and associations with the French bureaucracy.

With the fall of Paris in June 1940, the Consistory joined other major Jewish organizations in the mass exodus to the unoccupied southern zone. Since the president of the **Consistory** had succeeded in leaving France, Helbronner quickly emerged as his successor, a choice no doubt reinforced by his close personal relations with the French chief of state, Marshal Philippe Pétain. There is evidence that during the first year and a half of the occupation, Helbronner met privately with Pétain twenty-seven times and continued his adoration of the World War I hero, after whom he had named his own son. A sense of trust in the French leader and his principles helped shape the direction in which Helbronner guided the Consistory in the face of Vichy's anti-Jewish laws. Reasoned but impassioned pleas that invoked the spirit of the glorious French traditions and were directed to the "father of the homeland" (*père de la patrie*) characterized Helbronner's approach as president from the first official meeting of the Consistory after the armistice, in March 1941. In this same vein, Helbronner, who was seemingly the first Jewish leader in the south to learn of the intention to establish a compulsory Jewish organization (later to be called the Union Générale des Israélites de France, or UGIF), stood on principle and legal precedents and succeeded in negotiating a special status for the Consistory that kept it independent of the UGIF throughout the war. Simultaneously, he counseled Jewish leaders to refrain from joining the UGIF and pursued an active campaign against its supporters. Defying the racial and national definition of Jews propounded by Vichy, Helbronner continued to adhere to the Consistory's historical definition of Judaism as a religion alone.

Helbronner's leadership of the Consistory came under strong criticism from various sectors of the Jewish community in the wake of the mass deportations of Jews from the south of France in August 1942. Attacked for timidity and for disregarding the plight of foreign-born Jews in France, Helbonner persisted in upholding his elitist and legalistic orientation and remained at his post. Signs of a changing perspective appeared only after the German occupation of most of southern France in November 1942. Helbronner advanced the negotiations that had been taking place between members of the Consistory and the UGIF, and looked for ways to widen the scope of aid to the

consistory: a group of counselors.

1873	Helbronner is born in Paris.
1927	Helbronner is appointed to the Council of State.
1940	Paris falls to the Germans.
1942	Large groups of Jews are deported from the south of France.
1942	Helbronner reconciles with the UGIF; is sent to Auschwitz.
1943	Helbronner dies at Auschwitz.

Encumbered by his trust and confidence in France and its head of state, Helbronner directed the Consistory on the path of least resistance.

needy community. A telling blow, the roundup of native and foreign Jews in Marseilles in January 1943, impelled Helbronner to a clear act of reconciliation with the leaders of the UGIF and to cooperation with them. Throughout this trying period, Helbronner protested sharply to the French authorities against the deterioration of Jewish life in France and raised his voice against the arrests of the UGIF leaders in the summer of 1943. These protests seem to have contributed to his eventual arrest on October 19 of that year and to his deportation a month later, together with his wife, to Auschwitz, where they were killed.

A man of sixty-eight when he assumed the presidency of the Consistory, Helbronner regarded himself as the spokesman of the Jews "of old vintage" (*de vieille souche*) and throughout the difficult years in Lyons he remained anchored in legalistic diplomacy. Encumbered by his trust and confidence in France and its head of state, Helbronner directed the Consistory on the path of least resistance, which began to change course with his deportation. ◆

Helmrich, Eberhard

"*We figured that after we had saved two people, we'd be even with Hitler if we were caught, and with every person saved beyond that, we were ahead.*"
Eberhard and Donata Helmrich

German who rescued Jews in Poland during the war. Helmrich had the rank of major. As head of a farm at the Hyrawka labor camp in Drogobych (Pol., Drohobycz), Eastern Galicia, he had the task of supplying German army units with foodstuffs. Helmrich used this opportunity to employ Jewish men and women from the Drogobych ghetto, who constituted over half of the nearly three hundred workers on his farm—most with no previous farming experience. He protected them from deportation roundups, hiding some in his home and helping to release others already arrested, with the excuse that they were needed for the proper functioning of the farm.

Realizing that the Germans were planning the liquidation of all the Jews in his region, Helmrich devised a plan—together with his wife, Donata—by means of which he succeeded in spiriting about twelve Jewish girls out of Poland. Provided with false credentials that he himself helped manufacture, the girls were sent to Germany as Ukrainian and Polish housemaids with German families. Helmrich coordinated this underground operation with his wife over vast distances—between Drogobych and Berlin. Donata Helmrich looked after her charges, making sure that they were not placed as domestics near Ukrainian and Polish women, so that there would be no suspicion as to their origins.

When asked about their motivation, after the war, the Helmrichs answered: "We were fully aware of the risks and the clash of responsibilities, but we decided that it would be better for our children to have dead parents than cowards as parents. After that decision, it was comparatively easy. We figured that after we had saved two people, we'd be even with Hitler if we were caught, and with every person saved beyond that, we were ahead."

Eberhard and Donata Helmrich were recognized by Yad Vashem as "Righteous among the Nations." ◆

> *"We were fully aware of the risks and the clash of responsibilities, but we decided that it would be better for our children to have dead parents than cowards as parents."*
>
> Eberhard and Donata Helmrich

Hirsch, Otto

1885–1941

Chairman of the Reichsvertretung der Deutschen Juden (Reich Representation of German Jews). Hirsch was born in Stuttgart, the capital of Württemberg, and studied law. He joined the civil service, first on the municipal and later on the provincial level.

In 1919 Hirsch represented Württemberg at the Weimar National Assembly and the Paris Peace Conference. Active in Jewish affairs, he became one of the leaders of the Centralverein Deutscher Staatsburger Jüdischen Glaubens (Central Union of German Citizens of Jewish Faith), and was among those of its members advocating that the Centralverein promote Jewish settlement in Palestine. Hirsch was on the committee that prepared for the establishment of the Jewish Agency, a Zionist organization; he also belonged to the Committee of Friends of the Hebrew University and the Provincial Council of Württemberg Jews, whose chairman he became in 1930. A meeting with Martin Buber aroused his interest in adult education, and on Hirsch's initiative a Lehrhaus (Bet-Midrash, or Jewish house

1885 Hirsch is born in Stuttgart, the capital of Württemberg.

1919 Hirsch represents Württemberg at the Weimar National Assembly.

1930 Hirsch becomes chairman of the Provincial Council of Württemberg Jews.

1933 Hirsch helps to found the Reichsvertretung and becomes chairman.

1935 Hirsch is arrested in connection with a sermon.

1938 Hirsch is arrested at the time of *Kristallnacht.*

1938 Hirsch holds meetings with representatives of aid organizations.

1941 Hirsch is arrested and taken to Mauthausen concentration camp, where he is tortured to death.

of study) was established in Stuttgart, with Buber as one of its lecturers. Hirsch headed the Lehrhaus board together with Jews of various shades of opinion.

In 1933 Hirsch was among the founders of the Reichsvertretung (as of 1939 the Reichsvereinigung der Juden in Deutschland) and became its chairman. He played a major role in the Reichsvertretung's activities: economic aid to Jews, vocational training and retraining, expansion of the Jewish network of schools, and Jewish emigration. He also had a part in the establishment and operation of the Center for Jewish Adult Education, headed by Buber. Hirsch was a courageous representative of the Reichsvertretung vis-à-vis the German authorities. He guided the organization through its internal problems, successfully mediating between opposing views and conflicting demands. An authority on organization and budgeting, he was the liaison between the Reichsvertretung and Jewish aid organizations abroad, especially the British Council for German Jewry and the American Joint Distribution Committee, gaining their full confidence as a representative of German Jewry.

In the summer of 1935 Hirsch was arrested for the first time, in connection with a sermon that the Reichsvertretung had prepared to be read out in all the synagogues of Germany on the Day of Atonement. Refusing to go into hiding at the time of the *Kristallnacht* pogroms in November 1938, Hirsch was arrested for a second time and held for two weeks in the Sachsenhausen concentration camp. On resuming his post, he focused most of his efforts on emigration and rescue. His plan was to establish transit camps for refugees in Britain and other countries; he hoped that this would facilitate and speed up the release of the many thousands of Jews who had been arrested in Germany and that it would bolster the rescue efforts. He held numerous meetings in Britain and the United States in 1938 and 1939 with representatives of aid organizations and government officials, and was the Reichsvertretung delegate to the Evian Conference.

On February 16, 1941, Hirsch was again arrested, and a few months later was taken to the Mauthausen concentration camp, despite the fact that his wife had obtained an entry visa for him to the United States. He was tortured to death in the camp, and his family was later informed by the camp administration that he had died on June 19, 1941. After the war, a memorial to Otto Hirsch was erected in his native city of

Stuttgart and in Shavei Zion, a settlement in northern Israel founded by Jews from Württemberg. ◆

Hirschler, René

1905–1944

Chief Rabbi of Strasbourg on the eve of World War II, prominent in welfare activity in Vichy France. Born in Marseilles, Hirschler became an important figure for Jewish youth in Alsace in the 1930s as the editor of *Kadimah,* a French-language periodical that both supported Zionism and advocated increased Jewish involvement in community affairs. Hirschler was instrumental in organizing the welfare structure for the thousands of Jews from Alsace-Lorraine who fled to the south of France with the outbreak of war in September 1939 or were evacuated to that region in the summer of 1940. Acutely aware of the needs of the Jewish refugees in the south, he also encouraged Isaïe Schwartz, the Chief Rabbi of France, to unite the various Jewish welfare societies in an umbrella organization. Herschler emerged as the chief figure in the Commission Centrale des Organisations Juives d'Assistance (CCOJA), established on October 30–31, 1940, in Marseilles. He called upon the community leaders and their constituents to build a strong and effective organization in anticipation of the dire days ahead, but his call fell on deaf ears, and notwithstanding his efforts, the CCOJA remained an insignificant body.

In early 1942, Hirschler turned his energies to establishing the Aumônerie Générale Israélite (Jewish Chaplaincy), which diligently served the Jews in French internment camps in the south of France. He developed a wide network of rabbis and laymen who traveled throughout the camps, assigned residences, hospitals, and so on, and offered both religious support and general relief. Although often at odds with the Consistoire Centrale des Israélites de France, his supporting agency, Hirschler was undaunted in pursuing his relief goals, even to the point of overriding the chief rabbi's directives. His wide-ranging activity and forceful interventions with the authorities eventually led to his arrest, on December 22, 1943. Together with his wife and

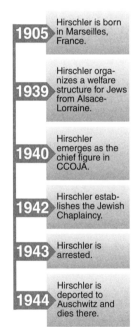

1905 Hirschler is born in Marseilles, France.

1939 Hirschler organizes a welfare structure for Jews from Alsace-Lorraine.

1940 Hirschler emerges as the chief figure in CCOJA.

1942 Hirschler establishes the Jewish Chaplaincy.

1943 Hirschler is arrested.

1944 Hirschler is deported to Auschwitz and dies there.

close collaborator Simone Hirschler, he was deported to Auschwitz on February 3, 1944, and perished there. ◆

Hirschmann, Ira A.

1901–1989

American business executive; vice president of Bloomingdale's department store in New York City from 1936 to 1946. In 1935 Hirschmann served as board chairman of the University in Exile (of the New School for Social Research), which offered positions to exiled German scholars.

In the summer of 1943, Hirschmann was asked by the Emergency Committee to Save the Jewish People in Europe of the Bergson Group to investigate rescue possibilities in Turkey. After delays, he reached Ankara in February 1944 as the special attaché of the War Refugee Board (WRB) to the United States embassy. Hirschmann and Ambassador Laurence Steinhardt exploited Balkan fears of postwar Allied retribution to obtain rescue of or improved conditions for thousands of Jews in Romania, Bulgaria, and Hungary. Hirschmann also helped

The Museum of Jewish Heritage—a Living Memorial to the Holocaust

The Museum of Jewish Heritage—a Living Memorial to the Holocaust opened to the public in New York City on September 15, 1997. The museum is located on the southwestern tip of Manhattan, on the shoreline directly opposite the Statue of Liberty and Ellis Island. The Museum of Jewish Heritage includes a memorial room, galleries for permanent and temporary exhibitions, a learning center, an auditorium, classrooms, archives, and a reference library. The name "Living Memorial" expresses two distinctive features of this institution. First, its primary purpose is to provide public education, rather than to be a major repository or research center. Second, the museum focuses on the nature and significance of modern Jewish civilization, and its continuity throughout the world, despite the devastation of the Holocaust. Thus, the four main themes of the museum's exhibitions and educational programs are The World Before (European and North African Jewish life in the late nineteenth and early twentieth centuries); The Holocaust; The Aftermath (depicting the efforts by Holocaust survivors and others to rebuild Jewish life and communities around the world); and Renewal in America (which traces Jewish immigration to and settlement in the United States from 1654 to the present).

Steinhardt overcome Turkish reluctance to allow refugees to land in Turkey. Nearly seven thousand Jews reached Turkey and Palestine under the WRB's aegis during the tenures of Hirschmann and his successor, Herbert Katzki.

Hirschmann contributed to a spectacular success in March 1944 when he helped persuade the Romanian ambassador to Turkey, Alexander Cretzianu, to prevail upon the Romanian government to transfer the remaining forty-eight thousand Jews in Transnistria to the Romanian interior. In June, Hirschmann interviewed Joel Brand in Cairo and recommended that the Allies continue negotiations in order to win time for the Hungarian Jews. Hirschmann contributed to additional successes that summer, including the provision of baptismal certificates by apostolic delegate Monsignor Angelo Roncalli (later Pope John XXIII) for Hungarian Jews in hiding, the Romanian government's agreement to allow Hungarian Jews to escape secretly to Romania and continue to Turkey, and the Bulgarian government's August 31 decision to abrogate its anti-Jewish laws.

In May 1946 Hirschmann was appointed special inspector general for the United Nations Relief and Rehabilitation Administration (UNRRA) to examine the conditions of Jewish Displaced Persons in Germany. He described his experiences in *Lifeline to a Promised Land* (1946) and *Caution to the Winds* (1962). ◆

"Hearing Adolf Hitler personally pronouncing the death sentence he was preparing for the Jewish people propelled me into an active concern for their welfare which continues to this very day."
Ira Hirschmann, *Obligato*, published posthumously in 1994

Jarblum, Marc

1887–1972

Jewish leader in Vichy France. Born in Warsaw, Jarblum came to Paris at the age of twenty and soon became a central figure in Po'alei Zion, a Socialist Zionist movement. In the interwar period he was also active in various immigrant organizations, while maintaining close ties with the French Socialist movement. After the fall of France, Jarblum attempted to coordinate welfare activity in the occupied zone and supported the creation of the Commission Centrale des Organisations Juives d'Assistance, attempting unsuccessfully to make it the political representative of the Jewish community in France. Jarblum found himself at odds with the French-born Jewish leaders and often condemned their lack of concern for the immigrant Jews in France. When the Union Générale des Israelites de France (UGIF) was proposed, he immediately opposed it, led the campaign against its creation, and refused to be nominated to its council.

Following the deportations from France in the summer of 1942, Jarblum channeled the activities of the Fédération des Sociétés Juives de France into "illegal" welfare work, though the federation continued to maintain an official position within the UGIF. He also encouraged Jews to flee to the Italian zone after November of that year, when the south of France was conquered by Germany and Italy; he himself was pursued by the Nazi-sponsored French militia and the SS for his anti-Vichy activity and escaped to Switzerland in spring 1943. While in Switzerland, Jarblum collected funds for Jewish organizations in southern France to enable them to extend their illegal work and

1887	Jarblum is born in Warsaw.
1942	Jarblum channels UGIF's activities into "illegal" welfare work.
1943	Jarblum escapes to Switzerland.
1945	Jarblum publishes *La lutte des Juifs contre les Nazis*.
1955	Jarblum emigrates to Israel.
1972	Jarblum dies.

free themselves from the UGIF's guardianship. Various projects to save Jewish children, either by hiding them in France or by helping them escape to Spain, were high on the list of his priorities. Jarblum survived the war and continued his Zionist activity in France before immigrating to Israel in 1955. His writings include *La lutte des Juifs contre les Nazis* (1945). ◆

Jefroykin, Jules "Dika"

1911–1987

Jewish resistance leader in Vichy France. The son of Israel Jefroykin, a prominent figure in the eastern European Jewish community in interwar France, Jules Jefroykin, together with Simon Levitte, was instrumental in organizing the Mouvement de la Jeunesse Sioniste (Zionist Youth Movement; MJS) in the winter of 1941–42. Open to Jewish youth of every persuasion, the MJS spearheaded cultural and social work in southern France, both officially and clandestinely. Jefroykin later became the Joint Distribution Committee's representative in southern France and was, with Maurice Brener, responsible for diverting the Joint's funds to "illegal" work. Jefroykin also participated in the underground operations of the Organisation Juive de Combat, most daringly in efforts to smuggle Jewish children and youth across the Pyrenees into Spain. ◆

Kaczerginski, Shmaryahu (Shmerke)

1908–1954

Jewish writer, poet, and partisan. Kaczerginski attended the Talmud Torah (religious school) in Vilna and then received vocational training, becoming a **lithographer.** While still at school he wrote poems and stories, and in the late 1920s was one of the founding members of Yung-Vilne (Young Vilna), a group of modernist Yiddish writers. He was arrested a number of times for his activities among the underground Communist youth. His revolutionary poems became popular folk songs in Poland, and prior to World War II he published poems, stories, a novel (*Yugnt on Freyd* [Youth without Joy]), and articles. He was also a correspondent of *Morgn Frayhayt,* the New York Yiddish daily.

After the German invasion of the Soviet Union in June 1941, Kaczerginski tried unsuccessfully to escape to the Soviet interior, and for a year he roamed about Vilna, posing as a deaf-mute. In the spring of 1942 he entered the Vilna ghetto and took an active part in its cultural life and the education of the youth. He directed the programs of the Yugnt Klub, a club for youth of school age. He also joined in the preparations for the formation of the Fareynegte Partizaner Organizatsye (United Partisan Organization; FPO), the ghetto's movement for armed resistance to the Nazis. The poems that Kaczerginski composed at the time relate to these activities. Some of them became popular in the ghetto and have survived, such as the lullaby "Shtiler, shtiler" (Softly, Softly) and "Yugnt-Himen" (Youth

lithographer: someone who makes prints from flat metal or stone plates that have been covered with ink.

Anthem). In addition to poems, Kaczerginski wrote articles and lectured extensively to ghetto audiences. His writings include an essay on the poet Abraham Sutzkever and a 300-page monograph on Chaim Grade, the Yiddish poet and novelist.

The Germans made use of Kaczerginski in sorting out valuable books in the library of Vilna's Yivo Institute for Jewish Research (YIVO) for confiscation by them. The library was situated outside the ghetto; this enabled Kaczerginski to establish contacts for obtaining arms and smuggling them into the ghetto, and also to save books and manuscripts from the Germans. Together with Sutzkever and others, Kaczerginski saved some eight thousand items in the Vilna ghetto archives, among them the diary of Herman Kruk. This collection is now in the possession of YIVO in New York.

On September 12, 1943, Kaczerginski, together with a group of FPO members, succeeded in leaving the ghetto clandestinely. For ten months, until the liberation of Vilna (July 13, 1944), he served with the partisans of the Voroshilov Brigade in the Naroch Forest. The brigade commander appointed Kaczerginski and Sutzkever official historians of the partisan movement in the region; their task included interviewing partisans and recording their statements on the partisan operations. Among those they interviewed were Jews who had taken refuge in the forest or were serving in the brigade. The impression made by these encounters is reflected in poems and stories about partisans that Kaczerginski wrote, especially in 1943. He also made translations from Russian into Yiddish.

In 1948 Kaczerginski published a collection of 250 Yiddish poems that had been composed in the ghettos and the camps, including notes on the fate of the authors, music to about 100 songs, and his own introduction. This is still the largest and most important collection of its kind. In 1950 Kaczerginski emigrated to Argentina, where he lost his life in an airplane accident. ◆

Kahn, Franz

1896–1944

Czechoslovak Zionist leader, born in Plzeň (Pilsen), in Bohemia. In 1916, while serving as a captain in the Austro-Hungarian army on the Russian front, Kahn was wounded and lost his left arm. After World War I he became active in the Zionist Tekhelet-Lavan (Blue-White) movement, and completed his law studies. In 1921, when the Zionist Organization of Czechoslovakia moved its headquarters to Moravská Ostrava, Kahn also moved to that city as the organization's secretary, and later became one of the leaders of Zionism in the country. At the end of 1938, following the Munich Conference and the truncation of Czechoslovakia, Kahn returned to Prague and was coopted to the Zionist Action Committee.

When Bohemia and Moravia were occupied by the Germans in March 1939, Kahn, unlike other members of the Zionist leadership, refused to abandon Protectorate Jewry and save himself by leaving the country; nor did he seek to exploit his privileged status as a disabled war veteran. He did arrange for his son and daughter to immigrate to Palestine. As the son of an American citizen, Kahn could have applied for repatriation to the United States, but he refused to affix his signature to such a request. He believed that this step might bar him from representing the Jews vis-à-vis the Germans, which he felt to be his duty, despite the loathing he felt whenever he had to meet with Germans.

In January 1943, Kahn and his wife were moved to the Theresienstadt camp. He did not join the camp's Ältestenrat (Council of Elders), but accepted the post of director of the cultural section and devoted himself to work among the youth in the camp. The many efforts made to rescue Kahn, by Nahum Goldmann and Stephen S. Wise in the United States, and by Chaim Weizmann and Moshe Shertok (Sharett) in London and Jerusalem, were of no avail. In October 1944 he was deported to Auschwitz, as were most of the other Jewish leaders in Theresienstadt and their families, although as a rule, disabled war veterans in Theresienstadt were not subject to further deportation. That same month he was killed in Birkenau. ◆

Kalmanowitz, Abraham

1891–1964

rabbinical: having to do with the Jewish clergy.

yeshiva: a Jewish school.

Rabbi of Tiktin, Poland. Kalmanowitz played a leading role in the rescue from Vilna to Shanghai of the Mir yeshiva (**rabbinical** academy) and in the activities of the Va'ad ha-Hatsala of the Orthodox rabbis in the United States. After the outbreak of World War II he escaped to Vilna, and from there he went to the United States in early 1940. Immediately upon his arrival in America, he assumed a leadership role in the Va'ad ha-Hatsala and traveled to numerous cities to raise funds for its work. After the United States entered World War II, he maintained contact with and sent relief to the hundreds of rabbis and **yeshiva** students stranded in Shanghai, by means of clearance arrangements via Uruguay and Argentina. Kalmanowitz was recognized for his expertise in influencing government officials and political leaders. He was also known for the fact that on several occasions he publicly rode vehicles on the Sabbath to stress the urgency of the predicament of European Jewry under Nazi rule. ◆

Kaplan, Chaim Aaron

1880–1942

Author of a Warsaw ghetto diary. Born in a village near Baranovichi, Belorussia, Kaplan became the principal of a Hebrew school in Warsaw. He kept a detailed personal diary (starting apparently in 1933) written in Hebrew, which is one of the rare original documents of its kind that has survived the Nazi era. It describes the decline of Jewish Warsaw and the Holocaust period in general. The diary, as Kaplan put it, became "my soul brother, my colleague and companion." Until the beginning of World War II it was a private personal account; but when the war broke out the diary changed its character, and in addition to his own experiences and troubles, Kaplan recorded the story of the Jews of Warsaw, his own speculations on future developments, the behavior and policies of the Germans as they unfolded before his eyes, and his opinions about the Poles.

Kaplan had a penetrating mind and a sharp eye, and his diary faithfully reflects the events of most of the ghetto's existence. The war diary begins on September 1, 1939, and ends on August 4, 1942, the day when the mass deportation was at its height. Kaplan evidently made his final entry a day or two before his own deportation to Treblinka. "When my end comes—what will happen to the diary?" reads the last sentence.

Kaplan's war diary was discovered almost intact after the war on a farm outside Warsaw, preserved in a kerosene can; the notebooks were legible and in good condition. The diary was published in Hebrew (*Megilat Yisurin, Yoman Geto Varsha— September 1, 1939–August 4, 1942*, with introduction and notes by A. I. Katsh and N. Blumental; Tel Aviv and Jerusalem, 1966) and in two English editions. The second contains all the pages of the diary that were recovered (*The Warsaw Diary of Chaim A. Kaplan*, translated and edited by A. I. Katsh; New York, 1965, 1973). ◆

> *"Never before was there a government so evil that it would forbid an entire population to pray. But never before in our history, drenched in tears and blood, did we have so cruel and barbaric an enemy."*
>
> Chaim Aaron Kaplan, diary 1940

Kaplan, Josef

1913–1942

> "He was an excellent organizer and an ideal underground operator, painstaking and resourceful in all humdrum day-to-day affairs, and with a clear and inspiring approach to matters of principle, of life and death."
>
> Irena Adamowicz, describing Josef Kaplan

A leader of the Warsaw Jewish underground and a founder of the Żydowska Organizacja Bojowa (Jewish Fighting Organization; ŻOB). Kaplan was born in Kalisz, in western Poland, into a poor family and a strict religious atmosphere. Early in his youth he was drawn to secular education and culture and joined the Ha-Shomer ha-Tsa'ir Zionist youth movement in the town. In the late 1930s he was one of the leaders of that movement in Poland. During the first few days of World War II, in September 1939, Kaplan joined the flood of refugees to the east, and took charge of the illegal border-crossing point at Lida on the Polish-Lithuanian border. At the beginning of 1940 he returned to Nazi-occupied Poland from Vilna (which in the meantime had been incorporated into Lithuania), in order to take charge of the underground Ha-Shomer ha-Tsa'ir movement. From that moment on, Kaplan devoted all his time to the underground. He consolidated the movement's structure in the various ghettos and ensured the continuation of agricultural training even on a clandestine basis; he published and distributed underground newspapers, and was his movement's representative in the overall Jewish underground organizations and institutions.

In the spring of 1942 Kaplan embarked upon the formation of a Jewish body that would fight against the Nazis. He took part in the activities of the Antifascist Bloc in Warsaw and, in July of that year, in establishing the ŻOB in Warsaw. On September 3, 1942, in the midst of the mass deportation of Jews from Warsaw, the Nazis caught Kaplan in the act of preparing forged documents for a group of fighters who were about to join the partisans, and he was killed.

Kaplan kept a diary, but it was not preserved. Irena Adamowicz, who knew him well, described him in the following terms: "The activist who had been likable but quite average turned into a great man, very strong . . . and very calm. He was an excellent organizer and an ideal underground operator, painstaking and resourceful in all humdrum day-to-day affairs, and with a clear and inspiring approach to matters of principle, of life and death." ◆

1913 Kaplan is born in Kalisz, Poland, into a poor family.

1939 Kaplan takes charge of an illegal border crossing point.

1942 Kaplan works to form a Jewish group to fight the Nazis.

1942 Kaplan is killed by the Nazis.

Kaplinski, Hirsch Zvi

1910–1942

Underground leader and partisan commander. Born in Diatlovo (Zhetl), in the Novogrudok district of Poland, Kaplinski was the secretary of the local Tarbut (Zionist-oriented) school and took an active part in Zionist and Jewish public life in the town. After World War II broke out, he served as a sergeant in the Polish army and then joined the underground in the Diatlovo ghetto. His parents, wife, and son were killed in the second *Aktion*, on August 5, 1942; together with comrades Kaplinski escaped from the ghetto to the Lipiczany Forest.

Kaplinski was a founder and commander of the Jewish partisan battalion known as the "Kaplinski Battalion." Consisting of 120 men, it was later incorporated in the Borba (Struggle) unit, as a company. The battalion took punitive action against peasants who had collaborated with the Nazis, fought the German militia in Mirovshchina, Zykovshchina, Nakryshki, and Mutsevichi, blew up bridges, and collected captured arms (in the Ruda-Jaworska battle).

During the German attack on the Lipiczany Forest, on December 10, 1942, Kaplinski was ambushed while on his way to division headquarters, and in the course of the fight was severely wounded. Apparently, the Russian partisans whom Kaplinski asked for help disarmed and killed him. ◆

1910	Kaplinski is born in Diatlovo.
1942	Kaplinski's family is killed in the *Aktion*.
1942	Kaplinski escapes from the ghetto to the forest.
1942	Kaplinski is ambushed and severely wounded.
1942	Kaplinski is killed by Russian partisans he asked for help.

Karski, Jan (real surname, Kozielewski)

1914–

Polish non-Jew who brought information on the Holocaust to the West. Born in Łódź, Karski completed his studies in demography at Lvov University in 1935 and worked in the Polish Foreign Office. After the occupation of

Poland in September 1939, he joined the Polish underground and was a courier for the Polish government-in-exile.

In 1942 Karski was sent on a mission to London, the head-quarters of the government-in-exile, to transmit a report on the situation in occupied Poland, and in particular on the situation of the Jewish population there. To be able to give authentic testimony, Karski twice visited the Warsaw ghetto, where he met with two Jewish leaders, Menahem Kirschenbaum of the General Zionists and Leon Feiner of the Bund. They asked him to inform world leaders of the desperate situation of Polish Jewry.

In November 1942 Karski arrived in London, transmitted the report to the Polish government, and met with Winston Churchill and other statesmen, journalists, and public figures. Basing itself on Karski's report, the Polish government-in-exile called on the Allied governments in December of that year to take steps that would compel Germany to halt the massacres of the Jews.

Following this mission, Karski left London for the United States. There he met with President Franklin D. Roosevelt and other statesmen, and tried to arouse public opinion against the massacres being carried out by the Germans. After the war, he remained in the United States.

Karski wrote a book about his experiences, *The Story of a Secret State* (1944). In 1982 he was awarded the title of "Righteous among the Nations" by Yad Vashem. ◆

1914 — Karski is born in Lodź.

1935 — Karski completes his studies at Lvov University.

1939 — Karski joins the Polish underground.

1942 — Karski is sent to London and America to report on the Polish situation.

1944 — Karski publishes *The Story of a Secret State*.

1982 — Karski is named "Righteous among the Nations."

Kasztner, Rezső (Rudolf or Israel)

1906–1957

Journalist, lawyer, and Zionist leader. Kasztner was a Labor Zionist activist, first in his hometown of Cluj and then, after the annexation of Transylvania by Hungary in 1940, in Budapest. In early 1943 he became the vice chairman, in fact the guiding spirit, of the Relief and Rescue Committee of Budapest of the Zionist movement, under Ottó Komoly. The committee maintained contact with the Slovak Pracovná Skupina (Working Group), which included Gisi Fleischmann and Rabbi Michael Dov Weissmandel; through it with Poland; and with a group of Palestinian emissaries in Istanbul, among whose founding members were Haim Barlas, Menachem Bader, and Venja Pomerantz.

The committee was well aware of the Holocaust in Poland and elsewhere, and tried to spread information about it, which was disbelieved in spite of the accounts of Polish Jewish refugees arriving in Hungary after 1942. In 1943 the committee was instrumental (through the work of Joel Brand) in smuggling refugees from Poland and Slovakia into Hungary. Despite internal **dissensions,** the committee tried to prepare for the eventuality of German occupation, even attempting to organize armed resistance. Such resistance, however, proved illusory in Hungary, owing to pervasive anti-Jewish hostility on the part of the population, the lack of any local anti-German resistance, and the fact that most young Jewish men were compelled to serve in the labor service system under Hungarian army control.

dissension: disagreement.

When the Germans occupied Hungary in March 1944, the committee made contact with the SS group in charge of the future extermination program under Adolf Eichmann. Similar contacts had led to ransom negotiations in Slovakia, where the Jewish negotiators believed they had resulted in the rescue of the remnant of Slovak Jewry and had led to the negotiations of the Europa Plan. Kasztner believed that in Hungary, the only avenue for rescue was negotiation with the Germans. Consequently, sums of money were paid to the SS, and Joel Brand was sent to Istanbul in May to negotiate the release of large numbers of Jews in return for trucks and other materials (the operation was called "Blood for Goods"). Brand was accompanied by Andor (Bandi) Grosz, a **quadruple** agent who served German, Hungarian, and other masters.

quadruple: serving four countries or groups.

Historians differ as to the seriousness of the proposal brought by Brand, but there is no doubt that it was originally formulated by Heinrich Himmler himself. When Brand was detained by the British and could not return as promised, his wife, Hansi, and Kasztner took over direct negotiations with Eichmann. At the end of June, a train with 1,684 Jews chosen by a committee headed by Komoly and Kasztner left Hungary, ostensibly for Spain or Switzerland; it was, however, directed to the Bergen-Belsen camp, where these Jews were intended. On the train were Kasztner's family and friends from Cluj, but in the main the group consisted of representatives from all political and religious factions, as well as wealthy people who had paid large sums subsidizing the others. Kasztner's idea was that this exodus would serve as a precedent for undoing the murder program, and that more trains would follow. However, none did.

In July an SS officer, Kurt Becher, received Himmler's permission to negotiate with Kasztner. As a result, Brand's negotiations were continued with the Joint Distribution Committee representative in Switzerland, Saly Mayer, on the Swiss border. The first meeting, on August 21, 1944, led to Himmler's order to refrain from deporting the Jews of Budapest, and 318 Jews in Bergen-Belsen from the "Kasztner train" were released to Switzerland. In December of that year the remainder of the Bergen-Belsen internees were also sent to safety, and Becher became obligated to the Jews by his contacts with Kasztner. At Kasztner's prodding, he intervened in favor of the Budapest Jews. Becher appeared to have acted from a variety of motives, but the outcome was an increase in Himmler's willingness to make some lifesaving gestures here and there, against the background of the approaching German defeat. The Jewish negotiators utilized the Germans' illusion that there might exist a possibility for negotiating with the West for a separate peace.

After the war, Kasztner was called to Nuremberg to help the investigators in their work with Nazi criminals. His written testimony in favor of Becher undoubtedly helped to save the latter from a closer investigation into less savory aspects of his wartime career. (Becher had served in some notorious SS units in the Russian campaign in 1941 and 1942. He had confiscated the Manfred Weiss industrial concern, resulting in a huge sum paid to the SS, in return for allowing some members of the Weiss-Chorin family to escape to Lisbon.) Kasztner also testified in favor of other Nazis, such as SS-Obergruppenführer Hans Jüttner, chief of the SS-Führungshauptamt (SS Operational Main Office), who had made the rather meaningless gesture of disapproving of the death march from Budapest in November 1944. Kasztner's line seems to have been one of *noblesse oblige:* once the war was over, any Nazi who had made a gesture or taken action in favor of Jews should be recognized for it.

In 1954 Kasztner brought a suit against one Malkiel Grünwald, who had accused him of being a traitor and causing the deaths of many Jews. The trial, in Israel, became instead a trial of Kasztner himself. Shmuel Tamir, Grünwald's attorney, steered the trial in the direction of an indictment of the Mapai Labor party, which had placed Kasztner on its list of candidates

1906 Kasztner is born in Transylvania.

1943 Kasztner becomes vice chairman of the Relief and Rescue Committee of Budapest.

1944 Kasztner begins negotiations with SS officer Kurt Becher.

1954 Kasztner brings a suit against accusations that he was a traitor.

1957 Kasztner is murdered in Israel by nationalist extremists.

noblesse oblige: the obligations imposed on an honorable person.

for the Knesset elections. The judge, Benjamin Halevi, accepted most of Tamir's arguments and summed up the court's opinion of Kasztner by accusing him of having "sold his soul to the devil." This referred both to the negotiations with the Nazis and to the train, which was seen as an avenue of rescue for Kasztner's relatives and friends and a German sop to Kasztner in return for his refraining from warning Hungarian Jewry of the impending disaster. The Israeli Supreme Court was debating Kasztner's appeal when he was murdered by nationalist extremists who took Halevi's words literally. In a final verdict, the court exonerated Kasztner from all accusations except the charge that he had helped Nazis to escape from justice.

Given the conditions in Hungary at the time, negotiations with the Nazis were in actuality the only way in which Jews might have been saved. The train could just as well have arrived in Auschwitz, and perhaps by putting his relatives on it, Kasztner persuaded many others to board it; in any case, he saw this as a breakthrough for future rescues. In the winter of 1944–45, when he was already safe in Switzerland, Kasztner voluntarily returned to Germany, and with Becher went to Berlin to try and save the Jewish remnants in the concentration camps. His intervention was possibly instrumental in securing the surrender of Bergen-Belsen to the British without the bloodbath that could have taken place there.

The most difficult problem is the charge that he did not warn Hungarian Jewry. Kasztner was totally unknown, was not in control of the Hungarian Jewish Council (Zsidó Tanács), and was in no position to warn anyone. In Cluj, where he was known, a rescue committee composed of important local citizens failed to convince all but a very few to escape for their lives to neighboring Romania, a mere ten miles away. Kasztner's tragic figure has been the subject of plays and stories, and continues to engender heated controversy. ◆

> The judge summed up the court's opinion of Kasztner by accusing him of having "sold his soul to the devil."

Katzenelson, Itzhak

1886–1944

Poet, playwright, and educator. Katzenelson was born in Korelichi, in the district of Minsk, Russia, where his father was a writer and teacher. In 1886 the family moved to Łódź. Katzenelson began writing poetry at an early age, and throughout his life he wrote in both Yiddish and Hebrew. His first book of Hebrew poems, *Dimdumim* (Twilight), appeared in 1910; earlier, in 1908, he had begun to write comedies in Yiddish, which he himself translated into Hebrew. Several of his Yiddish plays were performed in Łódź even before World War I. In 1912 he founded a theater, Ha-Bimah ha-Ivrit (The Hebrew Stage), in Łódź and took it on tours of cities in Poland and Lithuania. Before World War I Katzenelson undertook the creation of a network of Hebrew schools in Łódź, from kindergarten to high school, which functioned until 1939. He was the author of textbooks, biblical plays, and children's books. Beginning in 1930 he belonged to the Dror movement in Łódź and to the He-Haluts movement, the latter operating a training kibbutz (Kibbutz Hakhsharah) in Łódź.

Katzenelson's work in the interwar period was based on his sense that Jewish life in the Diaspora was incomplete; this belief also motivated his participation in cultural and other public affairs in those years. Such feelings appear in his works in the form of somber symbols of death, boredom, and silence. In his Yiddish play *Tarshish*, Katzenelson deals with the roots of anti-Semitism in Poland and with the utter hopelessness of Jewish life on Polish soil.

In late November 1939 Katzenelson fled from Łódź to Warsaw, where he lived and wrote (in Yiddish) until April 20, 1943, the day following the outbreak of the Warsaw ghetto uprising. Then, for several weeks, he was in hiding on the "Aryan" side of Warsaw. In May the Germans discovered his real identity, but since he held a Honduran passport he was sent to the Vittel camp in France, where he stayed for a year, keeping up his writing. In April 1944 he and his surviving son were deported to their death in Auschwitz.

Katzenelson's work clearly reflects the shifts in the situation of the Warsaw ghetto; indeed, his literary output of that period reflects the events that were taking place. From the very first day of his stay in the ghetto, he contributed to the underground press and participated in educational and cultural activities— teaching in the high school and in the underground seminars conducted by Dror, founding and directing a Yiddish dramatic troupe and a Hebrew theater circle, advising the elementary school teachers, involving himself in the cultural program of the orphanages, and so on. By public readings from his works,

1886 Katzenelson is born in Korelichi, Russia.

1886 Katzenelson's family moves to Łódz.

1908 Katzenelson begins to write comedies in Yiddish.

1910 Katzenelson's first book of Hebrew poems is published.

1912 Katzenelson founds a theater in Łódz.

1930 Katzenelson joins movements in Łódz.

1939 Katzenelson flees Łódz for Warsaw.

1942 Katzenelson's wife and two sons are deported to Treblinka.

1943 Katzenelson hides for several weeks on the "Aryan" side.

1944 Katzenelson is deported to his death in Auschwitz.

Auschwitz

Auschwitz was the largest and harshest of the Nazi concentration and forced-labor camps, and the largest camp at which Jews were exterminated by means of poison gas. Auschwitz was located near the town of Oswiecim in Poland. It consisted of three sections—Auschwitz I, built in 1940 under orders from Heinrich Himmler; Auschwitz II, called Birkenau, built in 1941; and Auschwitz III, called Monowitz, built in 1942. The gas chambers and the crematoria of the Auschwitz complex were located in Birkenau. Prisoners (mostly Jews, but also Gypsies, Soviet prisoners of war, and some political prisoners) were transported to Auschwitz via train. As trains stopped at the railway platform in Birkenau, the people inside were brutally forced to leave the cars and directed to form two lines, men and women separately. Nazi officials then conducted the *Selektion*, directing the people either to one side for the gas chambers, or to the other side for forced labor. Those who were sent to the gas chambers were killed that same day and their corpses were burned in the crematoria. Those not killed were sent to a part of the camp called the "quarantine," where their clothes and personal belongings were taken from them, their hair was shorn, and they were given striped prison garb. In the quarantine, a prisoner, if not soon transferred to forced labor, could survive only for a few weeks. In the labor camps the average life expectancy was extended to a few months. Prisoners who left quarantine for labor received numbers tattooed on their left arm. Auschwitz operated until Soviet soldiers liberated the camp in January 1945. The number of men, women, and children killed in the gas chambers of Birkenau or who died in Auschwitz from starvation, disease, or exhaustion has been estimated at one and a half million. Today, Auschwitz is a museum and memorial maintained by the Polish government.

through the Bible study groups that he organized, and with the help of his close ties with Dror, Katzenelson was able to convey to the public his thoughts and feelings, as expressed in his poetry, plays, essays, and lectures. In this way his literary creations came to have an impact on day-to-day life in the ghetto.

Katzenelson spent much of his time in translating sections from the biblical prophetic books into Yiddish for his reading public, and in writing plays for children or about children's life in the ghetto. In the first nineteen months of the Nazi occupation of Warsaw, Katzenelson sought to strengthen the ghetto population's resilience by interpreting contemporary reality in the light of the past history of the Jewish people—consoling them and offering the hope that "this too shall pass"—until the terrible truth dawned on him that the Nazis were aiming at the total destruction of the Jewish people.

In February and March of 1942, the mood of his writings became sharply more pessimistic, as reports came in of the mass

elegist: a writer of sad, mournful poems.

indictment: a formal accusation.

murder being committed in the Chełmno camp. After that, his writing addressed itself to the confrontation with death—the death, as he expected, of all the Jews of Poland. For the next two years, Katzenelson was the **elegist** of the Jewish people that was being driven to its death and also the prosecutor on its behalf, calling for the **indictment** of Western Christian civilization and for the punishment of the Germans, as a nation, for their crimes. Katzenelson's comprehensive reaction to the events finds its expression, above all, in the poem *Dos Lid funem Oysgehargetn Yidishn Folk* (The Song of the Murdered Jewish People; English ed., 1980), written in Vittel during the last year of his life. The poems that he composed in his last year in the Warsaw ghetto attempt to define and depict the essence of Jewish heroism (*Dos Lid vegn Shloyme Zhelichowski* [The Poem about Shlomo Zhelichowski] and *Dos Lid vegn Radziner* [The Poem about the Radzin Rebbe]). In that same year, he also elegized his wife and two of his sons, who had been deported to Treblinka in the mass deportation of the summer of 1942 from the Warsaw ghetto.

Two days before that deportation was begun, Mordechai Tenenbaum hid portions of Katzenelson's works, together with the Dror archive, in a subterranean hideout; of the works that he composed in the Vittel camp, the Holocaust researcher Miriam Nowitz was able to save a part. The Ghetto Fighters' Museum (Bet Loḥamei ha-getta'ot) at Kibbutz Loḥamei ha-Getta'ot in Israel is named after Itzhak Katzenelson. It has made extensive efforts to collect his manuscripts and to translate his works into English and other languages, and has published three editions of his last writings, consisting mostly of Hebrew translations of his Yiddish works and the Hebrew works that he wrote in the Holocaust period. Katzenelson's *Vittel Diary* was published in English (Tel Aviv, 1964). ◆

Kogon, Eugen

1903–1987

Journalist and political scientist; prisoner in the Buchenwald concentration camp. Kogon studied economics and sociology in his native Munich, as well as in Florence and

Vienna, and earned a doctor's degree in law and political science. A Catholic, he was critical of the church, a view reflected in the articles he published in various (mostly Catholic) Austrian magazines; he also acted as adviser to the Christian trade unions in Austria.

Kogon's anti-Nazi positions led to his arrest when the Nazis marched into Austria in 1938, and, in 1939, to his imprisonment in Buchenwald. For several years he was on hard labor of different types. In 1943 he became the medical clerk in the camp, remaining in that post until April 1945. From this vantage point Kogon was able to gain insight into the medical experiments being performed on the prisoners. Prompted by the humane instincts that he retained throughout the years of his imprisonment, Kogon tried to use his position to alleviate sanitary conditions in the camp and save the lives of individual prisoners. He cooperated with the underground in the camp (most of whose leaders were German Communists). Kogon was one of forty-six Buchenwald prisoners whom the Gestapo planned to kill on the eve of liberation, but he managed to be smuggled out of the camp in a locked container on April 12, 1945. Once outside, he put pressure on the camp commandant, by means of a fabricated threatening letter, to behave properly. He also persuaded American troops who were approaching the camp to liberate it without delay.

After the liberation, Kogon drew up a report on Buchenwald for the Psychological Welfare Branch at the Allied Forces Headquarters. He later elaborated his report into a book that became the first comprehensive description of the Nazi concentration camps, *Der SS-Staat: Das System der deutschen Konzentrationslager* (1946; published in English as *The Theory and Practice of Hell: The German Concentration Camps and the System behind Them*, 1950). Containing the first fundamental analysis of the concentration camps, the book has since gone through several editions and has been translated into many languages. Among other things, it analyzes from sociological and psychological perspectives the means used by the SS to divide the prisoners into various groups and thereby facilitate control over them.

In 1946 Kogon helped found the journal *Frankfurter Hefte*, and he remained one of its editors and contributors until his death. His articles dealt mostly with the nature of Nazism and the development of the Federal Republic of Germany. From 1951 until his retirement in 1968, Kogon was a professor of

"Thought and action securely anchored in humanity provide the only protection against the racist mania and all its consequences; humanity is also the source of the right normative perceptions on which all existential decisions should be based. This applies to the individual, to society, to the State."
Eugen Kogon,
1983

political science at the College of Engineering in Darmstadt. Politically, he was active on behalf of the European Movement, which advocated a united Western Europe, serving as chairman of the German European Union from 1949 to 1953. He was also chairman of the German Political Science Association.

Basing his efforts on his idealistic humanist convictions, Kogon continued to call for the complete investigation and publicizing of the nature and meaning of Nazism and its racist ideology. As he stated in *Nationalsozialistische Massentötung durch Giftgas* (Nazi Mass Murder by Poison Gas; 1983), which he coedited, "Thought and action securely anchored in humanity provide the only protection against the racist mania and all its consequences; humanity is also the source of the right normative perceptions on which all **existential** decisions should be based. This applies to the individual, to society, and to the State." ◆

existentialism: a 20th-century philosophical movement centering on analysis of individual existence in an unfathomable universe.

Kolbe, Maximilian

1894–1941

Polish monk, philosopher, priest, and Catholic saint. Kolbe was born in Zduńska Wola, in the Łódź district. His Christian name at birth was Raymond; at the age of seventeen he entered the Franciscan order and became Friar Maximilian. In 1912 he went to Rome to study theology and philosophy. He founded the Order of the Knights of the Immaculata in 1917, and was ordained a priest the following year; he returned home in 1919. In Poland, which by then had gained independence, Kolbe served as a priest; in 1927 he founded the City of the Immaculata (Pol., Niepokalanow), a center near Warsaw that was to disseminate the Catholic faith in the spirit of the Virgin Mary. By 1939 the number of the faithful at the center, followers of Kolbe, had grown to seven hundred. In 1930, in spite of being afflicted with tuberculosis, Kolbe went to the Far East, together with several assistants, to establish a Catholic mission. Located at Nagasaki, Japan, the mission was modeled on the Niepokalanow Center in Poland. Kolbe named it Mugenzai no Sono (Jpn.; Garden of the Immaculata). In 1936 Kolbe was summoned back to Poland, where he was

When the man cried out, "What will happen to my wife, to my children?" Kolbe stepped out of the line and declared that he wanted to take the man's place.

appointed head of the Niepokalanow Center and its operations. His special interest was the center's publications network, which included a monthly, a youth magazine, and a popular newspaper, *Mały Dziennik* (Small Daily). Kolbe was very active in disseminating his religious views and his social ideas in speech and writing, and he gained a reputation for his piety and devotion.

Early in the German occupation, Father Kolbe was arrested and removed from Niepokalanow, but by December 1939 he was allowed back to his "city," where he set up an institution for the care of refugees from Poznań and its environs and, it was reported, also extended help to Jewish refugees. In February 1941 Father Kolbe was again arrested, and put into the Pawiak prison. Three months later he was deported to the Auschwitz extermination camp. According to eyewitness accounts by other prisoners, Father Kolbe remained true to his faith and sought to bring comfort to many other victims. In July 1941 a prisoner from Kolbe's block succeeded in escaping from the camp, and as punishment the SS decided to execute every tenth prisoner in the block. Standing in line next to Kolbe was a Polish workingman by the name of Gajowniczek, to whose lot it fell to be one of the victims. When the man cried out, "What will happen to my wife, to my children?" Kolbe stepped out of the line and declared that he wanted to take Gajowniczek's place. The Germans agreed, and Kolbe was moved to a starvation cell, where he was later put to death with a phenol injection.

In 1971 the Vatican proclaimed the beatification of Father Kolbe (a step below sainthood), and in October 1982 he was canonized as a saint of the Catholic church. Since 1971, and with greater intensity after his canonization, a debate has raged in Poland, Austria, the United States, and Britain concerning Kolbe's personality and work. It was claimed that while Kolbe was to be admired for what he did in his life and for his act of self-sacrifice, he had also been contaminated with anti-Semitic views, and the newspapers that he published had an anti-Jewish slant.

The ensuing examination of these claims showed that the newspapers published under Kolbe's supervision, and especially the daily, which had had a wide circulation, did indeed have a strong anti-Semitic flavor. While Kolbe had tried to restrain the daily's extreme anti-Semitism, his own letters and writings had an anti-Semitic tone, and he had justified the exclusion of the

1894 Kolbe is born in Zdunska Wola.

1912 Kolbe goes to Rome to study theology and philosophy.

1917 Kolbe founds the Order of the Knights of the Immaculata.

1918 Kolbe is ordained a priest.

1927 Kolbe founds the City of the Immaculata.

1930 Kolbe establishes a Catholic mission in the Far East.

1936 Kolbe becomes head of the Niepokalanow Center in Poland.

1939 Kolbe is allowed back to his "city" after being arrested.

1939 Kolbe extends help to Jewish refugees.

1941 Kolbe is arrested and put into Pawiak prison.

1941 Kolbe is deported to Auschwitz, where he volunteers to be killed in place of a family man.

1971 Kolbe is beatified by the Catholic church.

Jews from the Polish economy. Kolbe's brand of anti-Semitism was not racist, and he preached that the Jews should convert; some of his expressions against Jews and Freemasons, however, were quite extreme, and his writings contain references to the Protocols of the Elders of Zion. ◆

Komoly, Ottó (also Nathan Kahn)

1892–1945

Hungarian Jewish leader. Komoly was born in Budapest and studied engineering. During World War I, he became a highly decorated officer. An active Zionist, he was elected deputy chairman of the Hungarian Zionist Federation late in 1940. Toward the end of 1941, he was drawn to the activities of Rezső (Rudolf) Kasztner, who was trying to form a committee around Social Democrats and Liberal Jews to help Jewish refugees arriving in Hungary. Although the committee did not really coalesce, Komoly, Kasztner, Samuel Springmann, Joel Brand, and several other Zionists continued to proffer aid to the refugees.

Following a suggestion by the YISHUV's recently organized rescue committee under Itzhak Gruenbaum, the Relief and Rescue Committee of Budapest was formally established, with Komoly and Kasztner at its head, early in 1943. In his capacity as a leader of the committee, Komoly took part in relief work and in attempts to smuggle Jewish refugees into Hungary. In the committee's major achievement, about eleven hundred Polish Jews were brought to Hungary through the Tiyyul ("Excursion": the code name for the operation of smuggling Polish Jews into Hungary) from Poland. With the help of Orthodox Jewish elements, Zionist youth movement members, and the Pracovná Skupina (Working Group), the Relief and Rescue Committee began to send messengers to Poland in the spring of 1943 to locate surviving Jews. Once found, they were smuggled to safety in Hungary, usually by way of Slovakia. This rescue work gained momentum in the autumn of 1943 and continued until the German occupation of Hungary in March 1944.

After the Germans entered Hungary, Komoly focused on efforts to convince the more moderate elements of the Hungar-

1892 Komoly is born in Budapest.

1940 Komoly is elected deputy chairman of the Hungarian Zionist Federation.

1941 Komoly is drawn to Jewish refugee aid activities.

1943 Komoly co-heads a new relief and rescue committee.

1944 The rescue work ends when the Germans occupied Hungary.

1944 Komoly strives to help Jews through his diplomatic contacts.

1944 Komoly sets up houses for Jewish refugee children.

1945 Komoly is executed by the Arrow Cross.

ian leadership to protect the Hungarian Jews. As a head of the Relief and Rescue Committee, he also played a role in the Brand mission, the "Kasztner train," and other negotiation attempts between Hungarian Jews and the Nazis.

From the summer of 1944 until his death in January 1945, Komoly strove to help Jews through his contacts with neutral diplomats in Budapest. In September of that year, Friedrich Born, the representative of the International Red Cross in Hungary, appointed Komoly head of Section A, the Red Cross department established to help Jewish children. Together with Born and members of the Zionist youth movement, Komoly set up children's houses under international protection, beginning in the summer of 1944 and continuing more intensively after the Arrow Cross Party coup of October 15, 1944. After that month, Section A expanded its activities to include provision of food and other supplies for the Jews of Budapest. As head of the Relief and Rescue Committee and Section A, and because of his contacts, Komoly emerged as a central figure in the rescue activities in Budapest during the Arrow Cross reign of terror.

Apparently because of his rescue activities, the Arrow Cross executed Komoly, shortly before the conquest of Budapest by the Red Army. He was posthumously awarded the Hungarian Order of Freedom. In Israel, Moshav (cooperative settlement) Yad Natan was named after Komoly. ◆

Korczak, Janusz (Henryk Goldszmit)

1878 OR 1879–1942

Physician, writer, and educator. Korczak was born in Warsaw, the son of an assimilated Jewish family. His father was a successful attorney who became mentally ill when Korczak was eleven; this was a heavy blow to the family's financial situation, and a trauma that cast its shadow over Korczak throughout his life.

Even while still a student of medicine at Warsaw University, Korczak was drawn to circles of liberal educators and writers in

Janusz Korczak and
some of his young wards.

1878 Korczak is born in Warsaw.

1901 Korczak publishes *Children of the Streets.*

1904 Korczak is drafted into the Russian Army.

1906 Korczak publishes *A Child of the Salon.*

1908 Korczak begins to work with orphans.

1912 Korczak is appointed director of a new Jewish orphanage.

1914 Korczak is called into military service.

1923 Korczak publishes *King Matthew the First.*

1925 Korczak publishes *When I am Small Again.*

1929 Korczek publishes *The Child's Right to Respect.*

1934 Korczek visits Palestine.

1942 Korczek turns down an offer of asylum.

1942 Korczek is deported to Treblinka, where he is killed.

Poland. When he entered medical practice, he did his best to help the poor and those who suffered the most; at the same time he began to write. His first books, *Children of the Streets* (1901) and *A Child of the Salon* (1906), aroused great interest. In 1904 he was drafted into the Russian army as a doctor, and was posted to East Asia.

Both as doctor and as writer, Korczak was drawn to the world of the child. He worked in a Jewish children's hospital and took groups of children to summer camps, and in 1908 he began to work with orphans. In 1912 he was appointed director of a new and spacious Jewish orphanage in Warsaw, on Krochmalna Street. Throughout his life, his partner in his work was Stefania Wilczyńska, a superb educator, the daughter of a wealthy Jewish family who dedicated her life to the care of orphans and greatly influenced Korczak and his career as an educator. In the orphanage, Korczak studied the secret depths of the child's soul, and it was in the orphanage that he made practical application of his educational ideas.

The Words "Holocaust" and "Shoah"

The word "holocaust" is derived from the Greek word *holokauston*, which originally meant a sacrifice totally burned by fire. The word was used in the translation of 1 Samuel 7:9 for "a burnt offering to God." In the course of time "holocaust" came to be used to describe slaughter on a general or large scale, and, especially, destruction of masses of human beings. In the 1950s the term came to be applied primarily to the attempt by the Nazi German state to destroy European Jewry during World War II. The use of the Hebrew word "*shoah*" to denote the destruction of Jews in Europe during the war appeared for the first time in the booklet *Sho'at Yehudei Polin* (The Holocaust of the Jews of Poland), published in Jerusalem by the United Aid Committee for the Jews of Poland in 1940. The booklet contains reports and articles on the persecution of Jews in eastern Europe from the beginning of the war. Up to the spring of 1942, however, the term was rarely used. The Hebrew term that was first used was *hurban*, which means "destruction" or "catastrophe," with it's historical Jewish meaning deriving from the destruction of the Temple. It was only when leaders of the Zionist movement and writers in Palestine began to express themselves on the destruction of European Jewry that the Hebrew term "*shoah*" became widely used. One of the first to use the term in the historical perspective was the Jerusalem historian Ben-Zion Dinur (Dinaburg), who, in the spring of 1942, stated that the Holocaust was a "catastrophe" that symbolized the unique situation of the Jewish people among the nations of the world.

Korczak called for an understanding of the emotional life of children and urged that children be respected. A child was not to be regarded as something to be shaped and trained to suit adults, but rather as someone whose soul was rich in perceptions and ideas, who should be observed and listened to within his or her own autonomous sphere. Every child, he maintained, has to be dealt with as an individual whose inclinations and ambitions, and the conditions under which he or she is growing up, require understanding. In several of his books—such as *King Matthew the First* (1923), *When I Am Small Again* (1925), and the short theoretical work *The Child's Right to Respect* (1929)—Korczak stressed the social conflict between child and adult in a situation when power and control are in the hands of the adult, even when the adult does not understand or refuses to understand the child's world, has no respect for the child, and deliberately deprives the child of his or her due. In Korczak's view, "to reform the world" meant "to reform the educational system."

In 1914 Korczak was again called up for military service in the Russian army, and it was in military hospitals and bases

"It is now the year 1942. The month of May. The month of May is cold this year. And tonight is the quietest of all nights. It is five in the morning. The little ones are asleep."

Janusz Korczak, diary

that he wrote his important work *How to Love Children*. After the war he returned to Poland—now independent—and to his work in the Jewish orphanage, but he was also asked to take charge of an orphanage for Polish children and to apply there the methods he had introduced in the establishment on Krochmalna Street. The 1920s were a period of intensive and fruitful work in Korczak's life. He was in charge of two orphanages (where he also lived), served as an instructor at boarding schools and summer camps and as a lecturer at universities and seminaries, and wrote a great deal. In the late 1920s he was able to put into effect his longtime plan to establish a newspaper for children as a weekly added to the Jewish daily in the Polish language, *Nasz Przegląd*; it was written by children, who related their experiences and their deepest thoughts.

> *"It's been a long time since I have blessed the world. I tried to tonight. It didn't work."*
> Janusz Korczak, diary, August 1, 1942

In the mid-1930s Korczak's public career underwent a change. Following the death of the Polish dictator Józef Piłsudski, political power in the country came into the hands of radical right-wing and openly anti-Semitic circles. Korczak was removed from many of the positions in which he had been active, and he suffered great disappointment. As a result, he took a growing interest in the Zionist effort and in the Jewish community in Palestine. He visited Palestine twice, in 1934 and 1936, showing particular interest in the state of education, especially the cooperative educational achievements of the kibbutz movement; but he was also deeply impressed by the changes he found in the Jews living there. On the eve of World War II, Korczak was considering moving to Palestine, but his idea failed to reach fruition.

From the very beginning of the war, Korczak took up activities among the Jews and Jewish children. At first he refused to acknowledge the German occupation and heed its rules; he refused to wear the yellow badge and as a consequence spent some time in jail. When, however, the economic situation took a sharp turn for the worse and the Jews of Warsaw were imprisoned in the ghetto, Korczak concentrated his efforts on the orphanage, seeking to provide the children there with food and the basic conditions of existence. He was now an elderly and tired man and could no longer keep track of the changes that were taking place in the world and in his immediate vicinity, and he shut himself in. The only thing that gave him the strength to carry on was the duty he felt to preserve and protect his orphanage, where old rules continued to apply: it was kept clean, the duty roster was observed, there were close relations between the staff and the children, an internal court of honor had jurisdiction over both children and teachers, every Sunday a general assembly was held, there were literary evenings, and the children gave performances. Polish friends of Korczak's reported that they went to see him in the ghetto and offered him asylum on the Polish side, but he refused, not prepared to save himself and abandon the children.

During the occupation and the period he spent in the ghetto, Korczak kept a diary. At the end of July 1942, when the deportations were at their height—about ten days before he, the orphans, and the staff of the orphanage were taken to the Umschlagplatz—Korczak wrote the following entry: "I feel so soft and warm in the bed—it will be hard for me to get up. . . . But today is Sabbath—the day on which I weigh the children, before they have their breakfast. This, I think, is the first time that I am not eager to know the figures for the past week. They ought to gain weight (I have no idea why they were given raw carrots for supper last night)."

On August 5 the Germans rounded up Korczak and his two hundred children. A witness to the orphans' three-mile march to the deportation train described the scene to the historian Emanuel Ringelblum as follows: "This was not a march to the railway cars, this was an organized, wordless protest against the murder! . . . The children marched in rows of four, with Korczak leading them, looking straight ahead, and holding a child's hand on each side. . . . A second column was led by Stefania Wilczyńska; the third by Broniatowska (her children bearing blue knapsacks on their backs), and the fourth by Sternfeld, from the boarding school on Twarda Street." Nothing is known of their last journey to Treblinka, where they were all put to death.

After the war, associations bearing Korczak's name were formed in Poland, Israel, Germany, and other countries, to keep his memory alive and to promote his message and his work. He became a legendary figure, and UNESCO named him "Man of the Year." Books and plays have been written about Korczak, and his own writings have been translated into many languages. ◆

"I should like to die consciously, in possession of my faculties. I don't know what I should say to the children by way of farewell. I should want to make clear to them only this—that the road is theirs to choose, freely."
Janusz Korczak, diary, July 21, 1942

Korczak-Marla, Rozka

1921–1988

Underground fighter and partisan. Korczak-Marla was born in Bielsko, Poland, and until the outbreak of World War II lived in Płock. At that time she went to Vilna, where she joined the leadership of the left-wing Zionist movement Ha-Shomer ha-Tsa'ir, with Abba Kovner and Vitka Kempner. When Vilna's Ghetto No. 1 was liquidated and forty thousand Vilna Jews were killed, Korczak-Marla agreed with Kovner that the surviving Jews should offer armed resistance in the ghetto. Kovner made this proposal at a meeting of the movement's activists that Korczak-Marla attended. His proposal was approved at the meeting, and was followed by a manifesto drafted by him and published on January 1, 1942.

Rozka Korczak (left) with Abba Kovner and Vitka Kempnet as partisans after the liberation of Vilna in 1944.

Korczak-Marla was active in the Fareynegte Partizaner Organizatsye (United Partisan Organization). After Yitzhak Wittenberg's self-surrender to the Germans, when a decision was made to leave the ghetto for the forests, Korczak-Marla was among those who went to the Rudninkai Forest. There, the creation of autonomous Jewish partisan units was initiated.

In July 1944 Korczak-Marla returned to Vilna, which by then had been liberated, and she immigrated to Palestine on December 12, 1944. She joined Kibbutz Eilon and reported to the Jewish leaders on the Jewish resistance movement and the atrocities committed during the war. Later, she moved to Kibbutz Ein ha-Horesh, together with a group of ex-partisans that also included Kovner and Kempner. Korczak-Marla took part in educational projects and in the work of Moreshet, the memorial museum named after Mordecai Anielewicz. She helped to establish the Holocaust studies centers at Givat Haviva and Yad Mordecai.

A book by Korczak-Marla, *Lehavot be-Efer* (Flames in the Ashes), was published in 1964. ◆

1921 Korczak-Marla is born in Bielsko, Poland.

1944 Korczak-Marla returns to liberate Vilna from the forest.

1944 Korczak-Marla immigrates to Palestine and joins a kibbutz.

1964 Korczak-Marla publishes *Flames in the Ashes*.

1988 Korczak-Marla dies.

Kossak-Szczucka, Zofia (maiden name, Szatkowska)

1890–1968

Polish Catholic writer. Kossak-Szczucka's novels were in the main historical, among them *Krzyżowy* (The Crusaders) and *Złota Wolność* (Golden Freedom). During the German occupation of Poland, she led the Catholic underground organization, Front Odrodzenia Polski (Polish Resistance Front), which conducted social and educational activities and, from 1942, assisted Jews. In September 1942 Kossak-Szczucka helped found the Tymczasowy Komitet Pomocy Żydom (Temporary Committee for Aid to Jews). That December the committee became the Rada Pomocy Żydom (Council for Aid to Jews), known as Zegota. Kossak-Szczucka then moved to the Społezna Organizacja Samoobrony (Civic Self-Defense Organization), where she continued to care for Jews in hiding. In September 1943 she was arrested under an assumed name, and the Germans did not identify her. She was interned

1942 Kossak-Szczucka leads the Polish Resistance Front.

1942 Kossak-Szczucka founds the Temporary Committee for Aid to Jews.

1943 Kossak-Szczucka is sent to Auschwitz.

1957 Kossak-Szczucka returns to Poland from Great Britain.

in Auschwitz until July 1944, and wrote a chronicle of this period, *Z otchłani* (From the Abyss). After the war she settled in Great Britain, returning to Poland in 1957. ◆

Kovner, Abba

1918–1988

> *"Let us not go like sheep to the slaughter. We may be weak and defenseless, but the only possible answer to the enemy is resistance!"*
>
> Abba Kovner

Underground leader and partisan commander, one of the architects of the Beriḥa, poet, and writer; influential figure in Israel's cultural and political life.

Kovner was born in Sevastopol, Russia, attended a Hebrew secondary school in Vilna, and studied plastic arts; from his youth he was a member of the Ha-Shomer ha-Tsa'ir Zionist youth movement. During the period when Vilna was the capital of the Lithuanian SSR (1940–41), he was active in the underground. When the city was captured by the Germans at the end of June 1941, Kovner, together with a group of his comrades, found temporary refuge in a Dominican convent on the outskirts of the city. On returning to the ghetto he learned of the massacres of the Jews, came to the realization that resistance was the only response, and decided to apply himself to the creation of a Jewish fighting force. At a meeting of the He-Haluts movement in Vilna, held on the night of December 31, 1941, a manifesto that Kovner had drawn up was read out. It stated (in part): "Hitler plans to kill all the Jews of Europe . . . the Jews of Lithuania are the first in line. *Let us not go like sheep to the slaughter.* We may be weak and defenseless, but the only possible answer to the enemy is resistance!" This was the first time that the mass killing of Jews by the Einsatzgruppen was analyzed as being part of a master plan for the destruction of European Jewry, and also the first time that Jews were urged to offer organized fighting resistance to the Nazis.

On January 21, 1942, a Jewish combat organization, the Fareynegte Partizaner Organizatsye (United Partisan Organization; FPO), was founded in Vilna, made up of youth movements and the various political parties. Kovner was a member of the FPO leadership, and in July 1943, when its first commander, Yitzhak Wittenberg, fell into the Nazis' hands, Kovner took his place (using the *nom de guerre* "Uri"). During the final deportation from Vilna in September 1943, he directed the FPO's operations and the escape of the ghetto fighters into the forests. In the Rudninkai Forest, Kovner commanded a Jewish unit made up of Vilna ghetto fighters, as well as the Jewish camp's "Revenge" battalion.

After liberation, Kovner became one of the architects of the Beriḥa escape movement and was the moving spirit in the Organization of Eastern European Survivors. This was a suprapartisan organization comprising various Zionist factions that called for the unity of all forces, a call based on "the lesson of the Holocaust" and the dangers still threatening the Jewish people. In July 1945 Kovner arrived at the Jewish Brigade Group base camp at Treviso, Italy, where he addressed an assembly of Jewish soldiers and, in moving and penetrating words, described the Holocaust and the Vilna uprising.

Kovner arrived in Palestine in the second half of 1945, on a short visit, in order to solicit support and resources for revenge operations in Europe against persons who had carried out murders or had been responsible for them. On his way back to Europe he was arrested by the British and returned to Palestine, where he spent some time in jail. After his release in 1946, Kovner joined Kibbutz Ein ha-Horesh, together with his wife, Vitka Kempner (who was also his partner in the underground and in the fighting), and a group of former partisans. During the Israeli War of Independence (1947–49), Kovner was the education officer of the Givati brigade and produced the brigade's publication, *Battle Page*.

When the War of Independence came to an end, Kovner went back to his kibbutz and devoted his time to writing. He published two volumes of prose writings in the Panim el Panim (Face-to-Face) series and issued collections of his many poems, among them the partisan poems *Ad Lo Or, Mi-Kol ha-Ahavot*, and *Ahoti ha-Ketanna*. In 1970 he was awarded the Israel Prize in Literature. Kovner was chairman of the Israel Hebrew Writers' Association and the founder of Moreshet (the institute for Holocaust research in Givat Haviva, Israel) and of the Mordecai Anielewicz Communities House. He shaped the character of the contents of Beth Hatefutsoth, the Nahum Goldmann Museum of the Jewish Diaspora, in Tel Aviv. A collection of his statements on current issues was published in the book *Al ha-Gesher ha-Zar* (1981). ◆

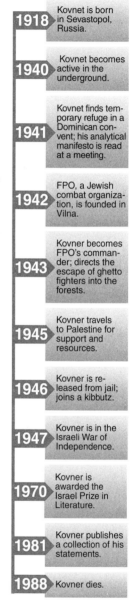

1918 Kovnet is born in Sevastopol, Russia.

1940 Kovnet becomes active in the underground.

1941 Kovnet finds temporary refuge in a Dominican convent; his analytical manifesto is read at a meeting.

1942 FPO, a Jewish combat organization, is founded in Vilna.

1943 Kovner becomes FPO's commander; directs the escape of ghetto fighters into the forests.

1945 Kovner travels to Palestine for support and resources.

1946 Kovner is released from jail; joins a kibbutz.

1947 Kovner is in the Israeli War of Independence.

1970 Kovner is awarded the Israel Prize in Literature.

1981 Kovner publishes a collection of his statements.

1988 Kovner dies.

Kovpak, Sidor Artemevich

1887–1967

1887 Kovpak is born in the village of Kotelva.

1940 Kovpak becomes the mayor of the Putivl municipality.

1941 Kovpak and Semyon Rudnev organize a partisan battalion.

1942 Kovpak sets off on a combat expedition.

1943 Kovpak reaches northern Volhynia.

1943 Kovpak goes to the Carpathian Mountains.

1944 Kovpak is wounded.

1947 Kovpak becomes deputy chairman of the Supreme Soviet of the Ukraine.

1965 Kovpak publishes *Our Partisan Course.*

1967 Kovpak dies.

Soviet partisan commander in World War II. Kovpak was born in the village of Kotelva, in the Poltava district. During the Civil War he was a partisan fighter for the Reds, and he subsequently fought under Vasily Chapayev in the Red Army. Between the two world wars, Kovpak was employed in party and administrative offices, and in 1940 he was the mayor of the Putivl municipality in Sumy Oblast (district).

As the Germans drew near to the Sumy district in late September of 1941, Kovpak and Semyon Rudnev organized a partisan battalion that developed into a division. On October 26, 1942, at the head of his fifteen hundred fighters, Kovpak set off on a combat expedition to the west, and in early 1943 he reached northern Volhynia; in the second half of that year he conducted combat expeditions through Volhynia and Polesye. On June 12, 1943, he went on an expedition to the Carpathian Mountains, with two objectives: to demonstrate a Soviet presence in Eastern Galicia, where the Ukrainska Povstanska Armyia (Ukrainian Insurgent Army) was in power, and to blow up oil installations in the Drogobych region. On his way, Kovpak liberated Jews from the Skalat labor camp, and a group of young people joined the division as a Jewish company under the command of veteran Jewish partisans. After bloody battles, the division was obliged on its way back to split into small groups. Many died during the retreat, and only part of the division reached the assembly point in north-eastern Volhynia.

In January 1944 Kovpak was wounded and flown to the hinterland. He was twice awarded the Soviet medal for heroism, and was promoted to the rank of major general. His division was named the "Kovpak First Ukrainian Partisan Division," and placed under the command of Lieutenant Colonel Petro Vershigora. On January 5, 1944, it began a campaign through Volhynia, Eastern Galicia, the Lublin district, Brest-Litovsk, and Pinsk. At the end of the campaign it was dismantled. In 1947 Kovpak was appointed deputy chairman of the Supreme Soviet of the Ukrainian SSR. His account of his partisan activities was published in *Our Partisan Course* (1965). ◆

Kowalski, Władysław

1895–1971

Pole who saved Jews during the Holocaust. A retired colonel in the Polish army at the time of the German occupation, Kowalski was the Warsaw representative of the Dutch-based Philips concern. Nazi Germany's interest in the Dutch-owned company facilitated the mobility of its foreign representatives, affording Kowalski freedom of circulation in all parts of Warsaw, including the closed-off Jewish ghetto. His first opportunity to help Jews took place outside the ghetto, on the "Aryan" side, when he encountered Bruno Borl, a ten-year-old boy wandering the streets of Warsaw in September 1940, seeking food and shelter. Taking the boy home, Kowalski fed him and provided him with a new identity and a home with friends.

This led to a series of bolder undertakings. Two brothers named Rubin, a lawyer and a dentist, were helped to find a new location after their hiding place was uncovered by an informer. Exploiting his freedom of movement, Kowalski smuggled seven Jews out of the Warsaw ghetto in February 1943 by bribing the Polish guards at the gates, and found safe havens for the Jews on the "Aryan" side. In November of that year he helped a family of four move from the Izbica area to a safer place with friends in Warsaw. He also offered refuge to twelve Jews in his Warsaw home. Roman Fisher, a construction worker whom Kowalski had rescued, built an underground shelter with material that Kowalski surreptitiously brought with him inside heavy suitcases. From late 1940 until August 1944, Kowalski paid for the upkeep of those of his charges for whom he had arranged hiding places. The group hiding in his home was kept busy manufacturing toys that Kowalski sold in the market, thus helping defray maintenance costs. After the suppression of the Warsaw Polish Uprising in October 1944, and the forcible evacuation of all the Warsaw residents by the Germans, Kowalski converted a basement in a ruined building into a bunker and hid there along with forty-nine Jews. Their daily ration consisted of three glasses of water, a modicum of sugar, and vitamin pills. They stayed hidden for 105 days; by the time they were liberated by the Russians in January 1945, they were reduced to eating fuel.

1895 Kowalski is born.

1943 Kowalski smuggles Jews out of the ghetto by bribing guards.

1944 Kowalski and 49 Jews hide in a basement bunker.

1945 Kowalski and Jews are liberated when resorting to fuel as food.

1947 Kowalski marries a Jewish woman he had rescued.

1957 Kowalski and his wife emigrate to Israel.

1963 Kowalski is designated a Yad Vashem "Righteous among the Nations."

1971 Kowalski dies.

More than fifty Jews benefited from Kowalski's help during the occupation period.

In 1947 Kowalski married one of the Jewish women he had rescued, and they emigrated to Israel in 1957. In 1963 he was recognized by Yad Vashem as a "Righteous among the Nations." ◆

Kruk, Herman

1897–1944

> "There is no doubt: Vilna will be occupied, the Germans will make it fascist, the Jews will be put into a ghetto, and I shall record all these events."
>
> Herman Kruk

Chronicler of the Vilna ghetto. Born in Płock, Poland, Kruk as a young man joined a Jewish socialist youth group that was close to the Bund. Under the influence of the Russian Revolution he joined the Polish Communist party, but was soon disillusioned by the party's stand on Jewish issues. In the 1920s, he found his way back to the Bund and was active in Tzukunft, the Bund's youth movement. Moving to Warsaw, he devoted himself primarily to educational and public activities, helped establish workers' libraries, contributed to *Volkstzeitung*, the Bund newspaper, and became one of the leaders of the movement in Poland.

In September 1939, when the Germans invaded Poland, Kruk fled from Warsaw and made his way to Vilna, which in October came under Lithuanian control. A large number of refugees from Poland had gathered there, and Kruk helped to organize their everyday life. Meanwhile, Lithuania was annexed by the USSR, in August 1940. With the help of the Bund, Kruk obtained a visa to the United States, but the Soviet authorities did not permit him to leave. In June of 1941, when the Soviet Union was invaded and German forces were approaching Vilna, Kruk decided to stay in the city under German rule and to record the events that were taking place. At the beginning of his diary, he wrote:

> I don't have the strength to become a wanderer once again. I am staying . . . and since I am staying and will be a victim of fascism, I will at least take up my pen and write the city's chronicle. There is no doubt: Vilna will be occupied, the German's

will make it fascist, the Jews will be put into a ghetto, and I shall record all these events.

Kruk's diary, written in Yiddish, is one of the most important documents relating to the Vilna ghetto. Not all of it has been saved—some pages are missing—but what survives gives an accurate description of the events in the ghetto and the lot of the Vilna Jews under Nazi occupation. The first entry in the diary is dated June 23, 1941, the evening of the German entry into Vilna; and the last, July 14, 1943, about two months before the ghetto's final liquidation. Kruk was active in the affairs of the ghetto and had a close relationship with its administration and its chairman, Jacob Gens. With a sharp eye for the developments unfolding before him, he recorded in his diary direct and undistorted information on the history of the ghetto, the deportation and extermination process, the ghetto's day-to-day life, the struggle for existence, the cultural activities, and the ghetto's underground and its relations with the Judenrat (Jewish Council). His own position faithfully reflected the Bund's attitude; at times he criticizes the Judenrat for its actions and at times he justifies it.

Kruk established and managed the ghetto library. He was also employed by Einsatzstab Rosenberg, a Nazi agency that, among other activities, collected documentary material from the Vilna headquarters of YIVO, the Yidisher Visenshaftlikher Institut (Institute for Jewish Research), for transfer to Germany. Together with other Jewish employees of the agency, Kruk managed to smuggle into the ghetto valuable documents and thereby save them from being dispatched to Germany. His diary was typewritten, in three copies, and these were placed in different hiding places. One of the copies was discovered after the war by the poet Abraham Sutzkever, who gave it to YIVO in New York, where it was published as *Tagbuch fun Vilner Geto* (1960).

When the ghetto was liquidated, in September 1943, Kruk was deported to the Klooga concentration camp in Estonia. He continued to keep his diary in the camp. Some parts written during this period were eventually brought to Israel and handed over to Moreshet, a Holocaust research institute near Hadera, and were published. The last entry in the diary was made on September 17, 1944. The following day, Kruk was killed by the Nazis in the Lagedi concentration camp in Estonia. ◆

1897	Kruk is born in Plock, Poland.
1939	Kruk flees Warsaw for Vilna.
1939	Kruk helps refugees organize their lives.
1940	Lithuania is annexed by the USSR.
1940	Kruk is prevented from going to the United States despite a visa.
1941	Kruk decides to record events in Vilna.
1943	Kruk is deported to the Klooga concentration camp.
1944	Kruk is killed by Nazis in the Lagedi concentration camp.

Kutorgiene-Buivydaité, Elena

1888–1963

ophthalmologist: an
eye doctor.

A"Righteous among the Nations." Born in Šiauliai (until 1917, Shavli) in Lithuania, Kutorgiene completed her medical studies at Moscow University in 1912 and was then employed as an **ophthalmologist** in a hospital in Moscow. In 1922 she returned to Lithuania, worked in medical institutions in Kovno, was active in the Oeuvre de Secours aux Enfants, a Jewish welfare organization for children, and established close relations with Jewish doctors.

During the German occupation of Lithuania, Kutorgiene concealed Jews in her home in Kovno and found other places of concealment for them as well. She established close ties with the underground movement of the Kovno ghetto; the meetings that both she and the local partisans held with the commander of the ghetto underground, Haim Yelin, took place in her home. Kutorgiene helped the underground to obtain arms, sought out hiding places for underground activity, and disseminated anti-Nazi literature. Her son Viktoras assisted her. She kept a diary, *Yoman Kovno* (Kovno Diary), sections of which have been published in the USSR and in Israel, in the journal *Yalkut Moreshet*. She also hid the writings of Yelin and of his brother Meir in her home in Kovno.

Following the city's liberation, in August 1944, Kutorgiene worked on the Special Government Commission for the Investigation of War Crimes. After the war she was awarded the Order of Lenin for her extensive social and medical activity, and the Medal for Work during the Great Patriotic War; in 1958 she received the honorary title of Outstanding Doctor of Lithuania. In 1982 she was awarded the title of "Righteous among the Nations" by Yad Vashem in Jerusalem. ◆

Lambert, Raymond-Raoul

1894–1943

Jewish leader in Vichy France. Born in a suburb of Paris, Lambert was raised and schooled in French culture, and received a minimal Jewish education. After serving in the French army in World War I, he entered the French civil service, where he held several minor positions, maintained some contacts with the Jewish community, and preserved his **penchant** for literary creativity. In the 1930s his involvement in Jewish affairs became more pronounced as he edited the leading French Jewish newspaper, *L'Univers Israélite*, and was active in the Comité d'Assistance aux Refugiés (CAR), which aided German Jewish refugees. Always a most patriotic Frenchman and deeply attached to French culture, Lambert was convinced that the Jews of France had successfully integrated into French society.

Released from active duty in the army with the fall of France, Lambert immediately reassumed his communal involvement in CAR-Marseilles, while he closely followed Vichy's withdrawal from the **egalitarian** principles of the French Revolution. In September 1941 he was summoned to Vichy to meet Xavier Vallat, the commissioner for Jewish affairs in the Vichy government to discuss the creation of a compulsory Jewish organization, the Union Générale des Israélites de France (UGIF). It was eventually established on November 29, 1941, and Lambert became its central personality. The UGIF functioned as an overall Judenrat (Jewish Council) in France. It had eighteen council members, nine for the occupied zone in the north and nine for the unoccupied zone (Vichy France) in the

penchant: a strong and continued inclination.

egalitarian: relating to the belief that all people are equal.

south. Throughout the war, the northern and southern councils had little to do with each other. Although Lambert was strongly criticized by leading Jewish figures in the unoccupied zone for his negotiations with Vallat, he proceeded to organize UGIF-South into a federative system in order to provide maximum autonomy for the participating welfare societies.

During the deportations from the French internment camps in the south that took place in August and September of 1942, Lambert strongly protested to the French authorities and helped arrange the relief extended to the deportees. Having a legalistic turn of mind, he directed the UGIF council into legal operations, hoping thereby to preserve the efficacy of welfare to the community. After the widescale deportations from Marseilles in late January of 1943, which included native French Jews and UGIF employees, Lambert gravitated toward supporting resistance activity, although he remained at the head of the council and refused both to put an end to the UGIF's open-door policy and to encourage the Jewish population of Marseilles to disperse.

During the last months of his activity in the UGIF, Lambert succeeded in thwarting an attempt to unify it into an authoritarian body under the northern council. He closed ranks with his former antagonists in the Consistoire Central des Israélites de France and preserved the federative character of UGIF-South. After a heated protest made in mid-August 1942 to Prime Minister Pierre Laval regarding confiscations of Jewish property, Lambert was arrested and, together with his wife and four children, was deported to Drancy and four months later to Auschwitz. His private wartime diary, published as *Carnet d'un témoin, 1940–1943* (edited by R. Cohen; Paris, 1985), provides a fascinating look into the life of an **acculturated** French Jew during the cataclysmic days of the Holocaust. ◆

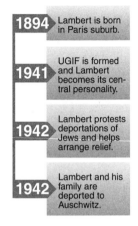

1894 Lambert is born in Paris suburb.

1941 UGIF is formed and Lambert becomes its central personality.

1942 Lambert protests deportations of Jews and helps arrange relief.

1942 Lambert and his family are deported to Auschwitz.

acculturated: having adopted the culture of another group.

Lemkin, Raphael

1901–1959

Jewish jurist. Lemkin was born into a Jewish farming family in an Eastern Galician village, and studied philosophy and law at the University of Lemberg (Lvov) and at universities in Germany, France, and Italy. He settled in Warsaw, but when World War II broke out, he fled to Vilna, and from there made his way to the United States, by way of Sweden, the USSR, Japan, and Canada. He taught law, first at Duke University and then at Yale University.

While serving as a state attorney in Warsaw, Lemkin took a special interest in crimes of mass murder and the persecution of minorities, and his preoccupation with this subject grew when Hitler came to power in Germany. In 1933 Lemkin submitted to the League of Nations Law Committee meeting in Madrid a draft proposal for an international convention on barbaric crimes and vandalism.

During his stay in Sweden, Lemkin began to collect documentation on discriminatory legislation, particularly on the racist legislation introduced by the Nazis. In 1944, by which time he had arrived in the United States, Lemkin published his book *Axis Rule in Occupied Europe, Laws of Occupation—Analysis of Government, Proposals for Redress*, and it is there that the term genocide was used for the first time. To this day the book remains the basic work for the study of racist legislation, in its general as well as its Nazi manifestations. Lemkin was appointed special counsel to the United States Economic Warfare Commission, and later served as counsel to Supreme Court Justice Robert Jackson, when the latter became United States chief counsel for the prosecution at the Nuremberg Trial of Nazi war criminals. Lemkin was also appointed counsel to the war-crimes section of the United States military headquarters in Germany, and to the prosecution in other war crimes trials conducted by the Americans at Nuremberg.

Lemkin had an important share in drafting the United Nations convention on the prevention of genocide and the punishment of the organizers of the crime of genocide. His contribution has become a cornerstone of international law, especially in its modern criminal aspect and in the protection of the human rights and liberty of peoples, religious communities, and other groups. Lemkin's other key writings include "Genocide" (in *The American*, March 1946) and "Responsibility of Persons Acting on Behalf of States in the Crime of Genocide" (in *The American*, April 1946). ◆

> Lemkin took a special interest in crimes of mass murder and the persecution of minorities, and his preoccupation with this subject grew when Hitler came to power.

1901 Lemkin is born in a Galician village.

1933 Lemkin submits a draft proposal on barbaric crimes to the League of Nations.

1944 Lemkin publishes *Axis Rule in Occupied Europe*.

1946 Lemkin publishes "Genocide."

1959 Lemkin dies.

Levi, Primo

1919–1987

> *"One wakes up at every moment, frozen with terror, shaking in every limb, under the impression of an order shouted out by a voice full of anger in a language not understood."*
>
> Primo Levi,
> *Survival in Auschwitz*

vicissitudes: regular changes in circumstances or fortune.

Italian Jewish author. Levi was born in Turin, to a family that had been living in the Piedmont region for many generations. In October 1938, when Levi was a first-year student of chemistry, the leadership of the Italian Fascist party decided to adopt a policy of racism, and by November, racial laws had been enacted in the country. Until then, being Jewish had been for Levi "a slight and insignificant difference," and this was the first time that he felt a wall of separation rising between him and the environment in which he was living. In September 1943 he earned a doctorate in chemistry, despite the difficulties he encountered as a Jew. Following Mussolini's downfall and the Pietro Badoglio government's surrender to the Allies, the Germans seized control of the greater part of Italy. Levi fled to the mountains in the north, planning to join an anti-Fascist partisan unit, but in December 1943, before his group was consolidated, he was caught by the Fascist militia. Under questioning, Levi admitted that he was Jewish, and he was imprisoned in the Fossoli transit camp; in February 1944 he was deported to Auschwitz.

Levi spent ten months as a prisoner in Auschwitz, an experience that was to leave an indelible imprint upon his view and way of life. By pure chance, he was one of the few Jews from Italy to survive Auschwitz: an Italian civilian working in the camp provided him with some extra food; Levi knew some German; and at one point he was taken on to work as a chemist in the Buna Works synthetic-rubber factory, an Auschwitz satellite camp, thanks to which he was spared many of the **vicissitudes** of camp life. In the latter part of January 1945, on the eve of the evacuation of the Auschwitz camp complex, Levi fell ill; he was not put on the death march and was liberated by the Soviet forces that entered the camp on January 27. On his release from Auschwitz, Levi did not go straight back to his home in Italy but for nine eventful and difficult months wandered through Poland, the Ukraine, and Belorussia. His account of his experiences in Auschwitz and his observations about life there were published in English as *Survival in Auschwitz: The Nazi Assault on Humanity* (1961). The book's original title was *Se questo è un uomo* (If This Is a Man).

The Survivors of the Shoah Visual History Foundation

The Survivors of the Shoah Visual History Foundation is a nonprofit organization dedicated to videotaping survivors of the Holocaust as they describe their experiences before, during, and after World War II. The foundation's goal is to preserve the memory of the Holocaust for generations to come and to promote racial, ethnic, and cultural tolerance around the world. American director Steven Spielberg created the foundation in 1994 using profits from his movie *Schindler's List*. While working on the film, Spielberg became concerned that most remaining eyewitnesses to the Holocaust had become elderly, and time was running out to record their testimonies. The foundation Spielberg subsequently established maintains headquarters in Los Angeles, with regional offices around the world. A professional staff of about 250 men and women is supported by several thousand volunteers. Staff members seek out Holocaust survivors and invite them to participate in the Shoah project. A trained interviewer and a professional camera operator videotape the survivor's testimony in the language and location chosen by the subject. Each interview is approximately two hours in length. Photographs, letters, artifacts, and family members are videotaped along with the survivor's comments. When complete, interviews are catalogued and archived using breakthrough digital technology. The testimonials are available to the public via online, interactive networks to museums and other nonprofit educational organizations, and through documentary films, books, and CD-ROMS.

When he finally returned to Turin, Levi took up his profession, working in an industrial plant. He raised a family and lived in his ancestral home. He was haunted, however, by the experience of Auschwitz; as he described it, Auschwitz "had been, first and foremost, a biological and social experiment of gigantic dimensions." Levi was one of the few survivors of the concentration camps who was intellectually equipped to observe and analyze the behavior of human beings in the reality of Auschwitz.

Survival in Auschwitz, written in 1947, was Levi's first book on his life in the camp. It was not well received, and a prominent Italian publisher had, in fact, rejected it. It took several years for Levi's talent to be appreciated: his ability to perceive the inhumane with human eyes and to present the horror authentically, in a language that avoided angry outbursts and generalizations. In 1963 he published *La tregua* (The Lull; published in English as *The Reawakening*, 1965). This is a **picaresque** story rich in detail, with colorful characters and adventures that the author had gathered in his encounters with people from many lands. Levi's pleasure at being able to communicate what he observed comes through in the book and is

"I am not even alive enough to know how to kill myself."
Primo Levi,
Survival in Auschwitz

picaresque: a story consisting of episodic adventures of a colorful main character.

> *"Today I think that if for no other reason than an Auschwitz existed, no one in our age should speak of Providence."*
>
> Primo Levi,
> *Survival in Auschwitz*

accompanied by a delicate humor; clearly, the experience of meeting with simple people of various origins was part of a rehabilitation process that enabled him to resume living.

As time went on, Levi's Jewish identity also came to be fully developed and found its expression in *Il sistema periodico* (The Periodic Table; 1984), in which the different chemical elements, which played such an important role in Levi's mind, meet with the world of his forefathers and with his own experience as a man and as a Jew.

Slowly but surely, Levi came to be widely acknowledged as an outstanding writer. His books were translated into many languages, and he was regarded as one of the great Italian writers of his time. But in April 1987 he committed suicide, without leaving behind any explanation for this step. ◆

Lévitte, Simon

1912–1970

1912 Lévitte is born in Saint Petersburg.

1929 Lévitte and his parents emigrate to France.

1939 Lévitte becomes secretary-general of the Eclaireurs.

1940 Lévitte establishes a scout leader's training institute.

1942 Lévitte forms MJS, the Zionist Youth Movement.

1943 Lévitte becomes commander of the Armée Juive.

1970 Lévitte dies.

Leader of the Eclaireurs Israélites de France (French Jewish Scouts). Born in Saint Petersburg, Lévitte emigrated in 1920 with his parents to France, where he studied agricultural engineering and joined the Eclaireurs, becoming its secretary-general in 1939. When Paris was occupied by the Germans in June 1940, Lévitte transferred the movement's headquarters to Moissac, in southern France, where he also established a scout leaders' training institute. In May 1942, in Montpellier, he formed the Mouvement de la Jeunesse Sioniste (Zionist Youth Movement; MJS); he subsequently established branches of it in all the major French cities and developed its educational functions. When the movement went underground soon after its founding, Lévitte enlisted dozens of its activists in a rescue organization, a separate network called Education Physique (Physical Training). On his initiative, Education Physique produced and distributed thousands of forged identity cards, provided clandestine lodging and means of livelihood to hundreds of families, and played a leading role in efforts to smuggle Jewish children into Switzerland. In 1943 Lévitte was appointed to the command of the Armée Juive, the French Zionist resistance movement, and he recruited to its ranks many graduates of the MJS. After the war he was appointed chief administration and supply officer of the Youth Aliya institutions in France. ◆

Lichtenberg, Bernhard

1875–1943

German Catholic priest. Lichtenberg was born in Silesia and became a priest in 1899. After World War I he served on the Berlin city council as representative of the Catholic Zentrum (Center) party. In 1938 he was appointed *Dompropst* (chief priest) of Saint Hedwig's Cathedral in Berlin.

In 1941, in a letter to Leonardo Conti, the Nazi *Reichsärzteführer* (Reich Chief of Civilian Health Services), Lichtenberg protested against the Euthanasia Program, following the lead set by the bishop of Münster, Clemens von Galen. That same year, he offered a public prayer for the Jews who were being deported to the east, calling on the congregants to observe the biblical commandment "Love thy neighbor" with regard to the Jews. Lichtenberg was denounced to the authorities and arrested, put on trial, and sentenced to two years in prison. On his release in October of 1943, when Lichtenberg was sixty-eight years old and a sick man, the Gestapo sent him to Dachau; he died on the way there. ◆

1875 Lichtenberg is born in Silesia.

1899 Lichtenberg becomes a priest.

1941 Lichtenberg protests the Nazi euthanasia program.

1941 Lichtenberg offers public prayer for Jews who are being deported.

1943 Lichtenberg is sent to Dachau, and dies en route.

Liebeskind, Aharon "Dolek"

1912–1942

Underground fighter; leader of the He-Haluts ha-Lohem group in Kraków. Born in Zabierzow, a village near Kraków, Liebeskind studied law at Kraków University. In 1938 he became secretary of the Akiva movement, which he had joined at the age of fourteen. In early 1939 he was appointed national secretary of Akiva and went to live in Warsaw, although he retained his home in Kraków and continued to lead the movement there; he also managed to complete his doctoral dissertation. His job kept him in Warsaw until the outbreak of the war.

From the onset of the German occupation of Poland, Liebeskind was convinced that the Jews would not be able to live under the occupation regime, and he did all he could to get the members of his movement out of Poland. A charismatic figure, much admired by his fellow members and disciples, he did not accept an immigration certificate to Palestine for himself, so as not to abandon his family and followers in time of trouble.

In December 1940 Liebeskind was put in charge of an agricultural and vocational training program in the Kraków area, sponsored by the Jewish Self-Help Society, which had its head offices there. He utilized his position to promote the activities of the Jewish underground in the city, which he had founded and which he led. Using the society's official stationery, he distributed leaflets and arranged money transfers to the members of the underground. Liebeskind also arranged for the financing of the Kopaliny training farm, headed by Shimshon Draenger, which served as a cover for underground operations. His post enabled him to move around and thereby to maintain and strengthen contact with fellow members in various locations.

The deportation of Jews from the Kraków ghetto in June 1942 convinced Liebeskind that the only way left was that of armed struggle, even though it did not hold out much hope of survival. He is credited with saying that "the Jewish fighters are fighting for three lines in history." He initiated the establishment of a broadly based fighting organization in Kraków, forging ties with the other leaders of the He-Haluts (pioneer) youth organizations in the city. An especially close tie existed between Liebeskind and Avraham Leibovich ("Laban") of the Dror movement, and the two became the commanders of the resistance organization, the Fighting Organization of the Pioneering Jewish Youth (He-Haluts ha-Lohem).

When the authorities began to pursue him, in November 1942, Liebeskind and the organization's headquarters moved to the "Aryan" part of the city. From there he renewed contact with the Polish Communist Workers' party (PPR)—which had been broken off in the wake of an abortive attempt made in September 1942 to leave the ghetto and take refuge in the forests—and with its Jewish unit, commanded by Heshek (Zvi) Bauminger. Liebeskind's aim was to launch a large-scale attack on the Germans inside Kraków. On December 22, 1942, He-Haluts ha-Lohem and the Jewish unit of the PPR attacked German targets in Kraków. They inflicted many casualties on the Germans, but following the attack, the headquarters and most of the members of He-Haluts ha-Lohem fell into German hands. On December 24 Liebeskind was caught in the headquarters bunker and killed in a hand-to-hand fight. ◆

> Liebeskind's aim was to launch a large-scale attack on the Germans inside Krakow.

Lipke, Janis

D. 1987

Latvian who saved many Jews from the Riga ghetto. On December 1, 1941, Lipke and his eight-year-old son witnessed a particularly brutal massacre of thousands of Jews in Riga. From then on, Lipke resolved to do everything in his power to save Jews from the Germans and their Latvian collaborators. He left his job as a dockworker and joined a Luftwaffe (German air force) civilian enterprise as an overseer, so as to be able to enter the ghetto to fetch Jews for work in various Luftwaffe installations in and around the city. He then arranged for trusted Latvian confidants to replace those Jews who failed to return to the ghetto, so that the final count would match the number of workers who left each morning. These Latvian friends entered the ghetto with Jewish badges on their coats, then removed them and left the following morning with other Latvian contractors who came to fetch Jews for work.

Lipke also arranged for Jews to escape from labor camps in the Riga vicinity. By visiting Jews inside labor camps or whispering coded messages to them across barbed-wire fences, he coordinated their escape. To some he provided jewelry and money left in his care by relatives of imprisoned Jews, so that

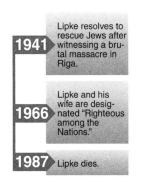

1941 Lipke resolves to rescue Jews after witnessing a brutal massacre in Riga.

1966 Lipke and his wife are designated "Righteous among the Nations."

1987 Lipke dies.

they could bribe the gate guards if necessary. Some he brought to his home, with the help of a Latvian named Karlis who transported them on his truck, hidden beneath a heap of lumber and other items. At first, Lipke kept them in a specially constructed shelter, with the help of his wife, Johanna, and their eldest son. He then devised a plan to transfer Jews across the Baltic Sea to Sweden and drew on his dockworking experience to prepare a boat that he hoped to launch for this purpose. But the plan had to be abandoned, since suspicions arose and the authorities intervened. Lipke was able to talk himself out of it and was freed. A Jewish fellow conspirator, Perl, was executed.

Lipke then arranged for fleeing Jews to be taken to a farm in Dobele, which he had purchased for this purpose. They were hidden by friendly Latvians in an underground shelter and other hiding places outside Riga. Lipke maintained close links with all those under his care for extensive periods of time; when danger threatened, he arranged their transfer to safer locations. He was active in the rescue of Jews from December 1941 up to the country's liberation by the Russians in October 1944.

In 1966 Janis and Johanna Lipke were recognized by Yad Vashem as "Righteous among the Nations." ◆

Lubetkin, Zivia

1914–1976

One of the leaders of the Jewish underground in Poland and a founder of the Żydowska Organizacja Bojowa (Jewish Fighting Organization; ŻOB). Born in Beten, in eastern Poland, Lubetkin joined Freiheit (Dror), the Zionist pioneering youth movement, and eventually became a member of He-Haluts ha-Lohem's executive council. When World War II broke out, she was caught in the Soviet-occupied part of Poland, but in 1940 she made her way back to German-occupied Warsaw to take part in her movement's underground operations.

Lubetkin was one of the outstanding figures in the underground movement in Poland. In 1942 she was one of a small group of underground members who founded the Antifascist Bloc, the first organization to be established in the Warsaw ghetto whose purpose was to offer armed resistance to the Germans. In July of that year, when the great deportation from Warsaw was in full swing, Lubetkin took part in establishing the ŻOB, and from the outset played an important role in determining its character and policy. She was a member of the Żydowski Komitet Narodowy (Jewish National Committee), the political leadership of the ŻOB, and of the Coordinating Committee, which served as an intermediary between the Jewish National Committee and the Bund.

Lubetkin participated in the first armed resistance operation launched by the ŻOB, in January 1943, and in the Warsaw ghetto uprising in April of that year. She spent the final days of the uprising in the organization's command bunker at 18 Mila Street, leaving the bunker on May 10 and, with a group of survivors, passing over to the "Aryan" side of Warsaw by way of the sewer system. Until the end of the war Lubetkin stayed in hiding in the Warsaw underground, and was in the ranks of the ŻOB units that joined the Warsaw Polish uprising from August to October of 1944.

When the war was over, Lubetkin became active in the She'erit ha-Peletah (the "surviving remnant") organization and was one of the organizers of the Beriha. In 1946 she settled in Palestine and was among the founders of Kibbutz Lohamei ha-Getta'ot (the Ghetto Fighters' Kibbutz) and of its memorial center, Bet Lohamei ha-Getta'ot. Lubetkin held various leading public positions as the representative of the kibbutz movement, Ha-Kibbutz ha-Meuhad, and was a witness in the Eichmann trial. She was married to Yitzhak Zuckerman. ◆

> *"The tomorrow did not worry us. The rejoicing amongst the Jewish fighters was great and, see the wonder and the miracle, those German heroes retreated, afraid and terrorized from Jewish bombs and hand grenades, homemade."*
> Zivia Lubetkin,
> 1943

Lublin, Lucien

1909–

Underground organizer in France. Born in Brest-Litovsk, Lublin received a degree in electrical engineering in Toulouse, France. At the outbreak of World War II he enlisted in the French army. Lublin was a Zionist

Labor Movement activist, and in January 1942, together with Abraham Polonski, he founded a Jewish military underground, the Armée Juive, and became a member of its supreme command. Lublin placed the underground under the authority of the Yishuv, the organized Jewish community in Palestine, and of the Hagana, the Yishuv's underground armed force. He obtained financial backing with the aid of the leaders of the Zionist Labor Movement in France, and recruited for the underground the cream of Zionist youth and members of the He-Haluts movement who slipped into France from the Netherlands. In late 1943 and early 1944 about three hundred members of the Armée Juive, including He-Haluts members from the Netherlands, managed to flee over the border to Spain with the aid of the Armée Juive flight network; from Spain most immigrated to Palestine. Many other members fought in the partisan battles in France. After the war, Lublin founded the Oeuvre de Protection des Enfants Juifs (Society for Protecting Jewish Children), an organization for aiding children who had survived the Holocaust and helping them immigrate to Palestine. ◆

Lutz, Carl Charles

1895–1975

Swiss diplomat who heroically rescued Jews in Hungary in 1944. Born in Switzerland, Lutz studied in the United States, and in 1935 served as head of the Swiss consulate in Tel Aviv. At the outbreak of World War II in September 1939, he interceded on behalf of the twenty-five hundred German settlers in Palestine who were being deported as enemy aliens by the British. This stood him in good stead with German authorities in Hungary years later. On January 2, 1942, he arrived in Budapest to represent the interests of the United States, the United Kingdom, and other countries that had severed relations with Miklós Horthy's Hungary, a member of the Axis nations.

During the fall of 1942, in his capacity as the representative of British interests, Lutz, in coordination with Moshe (Miklós) Krausz (who represented the Jewish Agency in Budapest), drew up lists of children and gave them certificates of immigration to Palestine. Nearly two hundred children and their adult chaperons were able to leave for Palestine before the German occupation of Hungary.

When the Germans invaded Hungary on March 19, 1944, Lutz invited Krausz to move into a Swiss office on Szabadsag Ter and continue his work from there. Under Lutz's protection, from this office and later from the Glass House at 29 Vadasz Utca, Krausz continued to promote various schemes for immigration to Palestine and related rescue projects.

The protection of Hungarian Jews with documents that certified them as foreign nationals had begun somewhat before the German occupation. The Geneva representative of the El Salvador government, George Mantello, had granted papers to thousands of Hungarian Jews that certified them as Salvadoran nationals. Lutz, who also represented Salvadoran interests in Budapest, was responsible for the distribution of these certificates. Perhaps this is what inspired Moshe Krausz to urge the Jewish Agency and the Swiss to persuade the British to declare that all bearers of Palestinian certificates of immigration were to be treated as potential British nationals. By the end of June 1944, the British had accepted the proposal. In the meantime, various diplomats in Budapest and abroad, including Lutz, pressured the Hungarian government to stop the deportations that had begun in mid-May. Early in July, Horthy ordered the deportations stopped, and soon thereafter declared his government's willingness to allow some seventy-five hundred bearers of certificates to leave for Palestine. The stage was now set to bring these Jews under Swiss protection.

With the help of Krausz, a group of fifty Jews was assembled in the Glass House to work with Lutz. Photos were collected from four thousand persons, and Lutz issued four collective passports, each with one thousand names. Each person was then

Yad Vashem

Yad Vashem, the Holocaust Martyrs' and Heroes' Remembrance Authority, is Israel's national institution of Holocaust commemoration. The idea of establishing a memorial in Palestine for the Jews who fell victim to the Holocaust was conceived during World War II, when reports were received of the mass murder of Jews in the German-occupied countries. The name "Yad Vashem" means literally "a monument and a name." The phrase comes from Isaiah 56:5: "I will give them, in my house and in my walls, a monument and a name, better than sons and daughters; I will give them an everlasting name that shall never be effaced."

Located in Jerusalem, Yad Vashem includes a library, an auditorium, an archive, a synagogue, a historical museum, an art museum, and several other monuments, all dedicated to preserving the memory of the six million Jews who died during the Holocaust. Under a program established in 1953, Yad Vashem has identified and honored close to 15,000 persons as "Righteous among the Nations." The "Righteous among the Nations" award is given to non-Jews who risked their lives to extend aid to Jews who were helpless or threatened with death or deportation to concentration camps. Many of the Righteous helped Jews during the Holocaust by sheltering them in their homes or religious institutions, helping them pass as non-Jews by providing false credentials or baptismal certificates, and helping them flee to safer locations or across the border to a safer country. Those recognized as "Righteous among the Nations" are awarded the Righteous Medal and their names are inscribed on the Wall of Honor in the Garden of the Righteous at Yad Vashem. The garden is lined with carob trees that were planted by many of the rescuers when they visited Israel as guests of the Holocaust survivors whom they saved.

issued a "protective letter" (*Schutzbrief*) guaranteeing that person's safety until his or her eventual departure for Palestine. To add as many people as possible to these *Schutzbriefe*, Lutz interpreted the permits as representing family units and not individuals. Eventually, protective letters were drawn up for fifty thousand Jews.

At the same time, Lutz instructed the recently arrived Swedish diplomat Raoul Wallenberg on the best uses of the protective passes, and gave him the names of persons in the government hierarchy with whom to negotiate. This idea served as a model for various types of protective letters issued by other neutral countries and by the International Red Cross through Friedrich Born, its representative in Budapest. In addition, after the pro-Nazi Arrow Cross Party came to power in mid-October of 1944, the Zionist youth underground manufactured and distributed tens of thousands of false documents, perhaps more than one hundred thousand, mostly in the name of Switzerland. Owing to the proliferation of false protective papers, the authorities pressured Lutz and Wallenberg to affirm the validity of the documents they had distributed. Lutz acquiesced so as to preclude the collapse of the entire rescue project. Late in November, he and his wife sorted out the bearers of legitimate passes from those holding forged papers at the assembly point in the Óbuda brickyard.

In the meantime, Lutz and other neutral diplomats, including Wallenberg and the papal nuncio, Angelo Rotta, interceded to have the new Hungarian government recognize the protective documents, using as bait the recognition of the regime by their governments. With the establishment of two ghettos, one for holders of protective passes and one for the rest of the Jews, Lutz procured twenty-five high-rise apartment buildings for concentrating the people under his protection. The Glass House and its annex also became a refuge for about three thousand Jews.

During the notorious death march of November 10 to 22, 1944, when over seventy thousand Jews were forcibly marched toward the Austrian border under the most inhumane conditions, Lutz and his fellow diplomats interceded on behalf of many Jews. Lutz made use of Salvadoran certificates still in his possession, following the deportees on their march and filling in many of their names on the documents. Those saved in this way were allowed to return to Budapest, which was already under siege by the Red Army. Ernst Kaltenbrunner, the Gestapo head, in a dispatch to the German Foreign Ministry complained about the disappearance of many Jews on this march as a result of intervention by the Swiss legation, as well as by the representatives of Sweden, Spain, Portugal, and the Vatican.

With the tightening of the Soviet siege of Budapest in December 1944, all foreign representatives were ordered to leave the beleaguered capital. Maximilian Jaeger, the head of the Swiss legation in Budapest, had already departed on November 10. But Lutz, not willing to abandon his protégés, decided to remain behind. Over thirty thousand Jews (out of a total of some one hundred thousand) with various protective passes—Swiss, Swedish, Red Cross, and Vatican—were housed in the so-called international ghetto.

Lutz later related that a German diplomat revealed to him that the Arrow Cross had received instructions not to harm the

1895 Lutz is born in Switzerland.

1935 Lutz serves as head of the Swiss consulate in Tel Aviv.

1939 Lutz's actions put him in good stead with German authorities.

1942 Lutz arrives in Budapest to represent the United States and the U.K.; helps Hungarian children immigrate to Palestine.

1944 Lutz rescues Jews in Germany.

1945 Lutz escapes from invading Russians and goes to Buda.

1965 Lutz is designated a Yad Vashem "Righteous among the Nations."

1975 Lutz dies.

protected houses so long as Lutz remained in Budapest, as a token of Germany's gratitude to him for having looked after the interests of German expatriates in Palestine in 1939 and 1940. For three months thereafter, Lutz, together with his wife and a group of Jewish refugees, lived a precarious existence in the basement of the abandoned, but bombarded, British legation, almost without food and water. When the Russians stormed the building, Lutz jumped through the window and managed to reach Buda, the section of the city occupied only in February 1945.

In 1965 Lutz was recognized by Yad Vashem as a "Righteous among the Nations." ◆

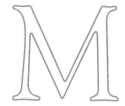

Mayer, Saly

1882–1950

Swiss Jewish leader; representative of the Joint Distribution Committee (JDC). Mayer made his living as a lace manufacturer, and retired in the 1930s. He was elected a representative of a liberal-democratic party in his native Saint Gall in 1921 and was involved in the financial sector of municipal administration until 1933. Mayer was active in the Saint Gall Jewish community, founding a modern welfare organization there, and became secretary of the Schweizerischer Israelitischer Gemeindebund (Federation of Swiss Jewish Communities; SIG). He assumed the presidency of the SIG in 1936, and held it until late in 1942.

During his presidency, the SIG joined the World Jewish Congress, and was actively involved in the negotiations regarding the **partition** of Palestine in 1937. In 1938, with the Austrian Anschluss, a stream of three thousand to four thousand Jewish refugees from that country began arriving in Switzerland. Mayer became involved in negotiations with Dr. Heinrich Rothmund, head of the Alien Police, regarding their reception; he was later criticized for the restrictive Swiss policy on Jewish immigration. It is true that Mayer accepted the **fiat** of the government without public protest. The Swiss Jewish community numbered about eighteen thousand, and they were committed to looking after the refugees already staying in the country, whose well-being hinged on this financial commitment. Public opinion supported the antirefugee stance of the government, and it may be questioned whether options were available to the Jewish leadership in these circumstances.

partition: division.

fiat: an authoritative command.

pedantic: tending to display one's knowledge.

1882 — Mayer is born.

1921 — Mayer is elected to represent the liberal-democratic party.

1936 — Mayer becomes president of SIG.

1937 — Mayer negotiates about the partition of Palestine.

1938 — Thousands of Jewish refugees begin arriving in Switzerland.

1940 — Mayer is appointed JDC's representative.

1942 — Mayer's anti-refugee stance forces him out of SIG's presidency.

1943 — Mayer seeks to provide ransom money to save Jews.

1944 — Mayer negotiates with Nazis.

1950 — Mayer dies.

Help from the JDC enabled the SIG to look after the increasing number of refugees. This brought Mayer into close contact with the JDC, and he was appointed its representative in Switzerland in 1940, on a voluntary basis. In 1942 he was forced out of the presidency of the SIG, at least partly because of the above-mentioned criticism.

At first the sums at Mayer's disposal for help to Jews in occupied Europe were small: $6,370 in 1940 and $3,030 in 1941. His main tasks were to receive information from all over occupied Europe and transmit it to the JDC European office in Lisbon, and to look after the refugees in Switzerland. A lonely, very conservative, **pedantic,** and suspicious man, Mayer had bad relationships with other Jewish organizations in Switzerland, with the exception of the He-Haluts office under Nathan Schwalb.

Mayer's role changed with the entry of the United States into the war in 1941. In order to circumvent American restrictions on transferring funds to Nazi Europe, Mayer suggested (and the JDC agreed) that money be sent to support the increasing number of Jewish refugees in Switzerland, and that equivalent sums of Swiss Jewish money, freed from the obligation to keep the refugees alive, be sent to Nazi Europe. He received $235,000 early in 1942 and $1,588,000 late in 1943, but from the spring of 1942 to the fall of 1943 no money was received, since the Swiss refused to accept philanthropic dollars to be converted into Swiss francs in Switzerland. However, despite the arrangements for refugees in Switzerland, whose numbers increased until they reached about twenty-five thousand in 1944, much of the money had to go to support them. In effect, in 1942 and 1943 Mayer had $1,127,515 to spend outside of Switzerland. In 1944 he received $6,467,000, and between January and May 1945, another $4,600,000. Of these sums he had to spend $1,913,000 in Switzerland in 1944, and about another $1 million in the first months of 1945, so that he had in fact somewhat over $4.5 million to spend in Europe in these seventeen months. This was of course much more than he had had before, and it went largely to Hungary, Romania, France, and Shanghai. In the end it was far from adequate, and each country obtained much less for saving lives than it demanded. Even so, Mayer received an increasing proportion of the total JDC budget: in 1944, 42 percent ($15,216,000 was all the JDC could obtain that year from American Jews).

In the summer of 1942, Mayer was approached by the Slovak underground Jewish leadership (Pracovná Skupina, or

Working Group) to provide ransom money to save Jewish lives. Later, in November and December, negotiations began in Slovakia for a larger ransom payment (the Europa Plan), which was supposed to save western and southeastern European Jews from deportation. Mayer at first saw these offers as simple **extortion** demands, but he changed his mind in the spring of 1943 and sought to provide the money. The Lisbon office refused to accept his views, but he nevertheless sent Swiss money through He-Haluts (illegally) to Bratislava, and intervened with the Jewish Agency to provide money from Istanbul to Slovakia.

In 1944, after the failure of the Joel Brand-Bandi Grosz mission from Hungary to Istanbul (the "Blood for Trucks" offer), the Hungarian Jewish negotiator with the Nazis, Rezső Kasztner, suggested that Mayer negotiate with the Nazis for the ransom of Hungarian Jews. Mayer was told by the United States authorities that he should negotiate but not offer either money or goods, and that he had to report to the United States legation on his moves. The Swiss gave him identical instructions, and forbade the Nazis to cross into Swiss territory. The JDC told him he was not their representative in these talks. Mayer nevertheless engaged in the negotiations between August 21, 1944, and February 5, 1945, with SS-Obersturmbannführer Kurt Becher and his representatives. Kasztner also attended most of these meetings. In the course of skillful negotiations, orders were obtained from Heinrich Himmler to abandon plans for the deportation of the Jews of Budapest, and Mayer succeeded in arranging for a meeting between Becher and the representative of the American War Refugee Board in Switzerland, Roswell D. McClelland, on November 5, 1944. To **assuage** the Nazis and keep the negotiations going, Mayer, contrary to his instructions, arranged for the supply of a number of tractors to the Nazis.

After the war, Mayer was accused of not conducting these talks in conjunction with other Jewish organizations, and of not standing up for Jewish demands strongly enough. The Hungarian Jewish negotiators accused him of not supplying the money and goods that the Nazis demanded. While it is only human that these accusations should have been leveled against Mayer, they seem to have little substance. Mayer proved to be his own **querulous** self when he turned his Hungarian Jewish colleagues into bitter enemies because he suspected them—wrongly—of financial dishonesty. Approached after the war by Becher and other Nazis to help them escape American justice, he managed to evade them.

extortion: the process of obtaining money by force or intimidation.

assuage: to calm or satisfy.

querulous: tending to complain.

Mayer continued to serve as liaison for the JDC in central Europe after the war, and he sent food parcels to Dachau and other places in south Germany immediately upon their liberation. He also intervened, not always felicitously, in the reconstitution of JDC committees in Hungary and Romania. Gradually, his role diminished, and although he was much praised by the JDC for his work, he retired. He died before he could write his memoirs. ◆

McDonald, James Grover

1886–1964

"When domestic policies threaten the demoralization of hundreds of thousands of human beings, consideration of diplomatic correctness must yield to those of common humanity."

James Grover
McDonald

League of Nations High Commissioner for Refugees from Germany. McDonald taught history and political science at the University of Indiana and in 1919 became chairman of the Foreign Policy Association in New York, serving in that capacity until 1933. He then became involved in the Jewish refugee problem, which brought him into conflict with officials of the State Department. Several visits to Nazi Germany convinced McDonald that the National Socialists were tending toward a radical solution of the "Jewish question." On April 3, 1933, following the Nazis' anti-Jewish boycott of April 1, he reacted to the events in the Reich in a speech before the Foreign Policy Association, expressing his dismay at the State Department's anti-Semitic perception of the Jewish plight.

McDonald's growing involvement with the refugee crisis placed him in contact with James Rosenberg, Felix Warburg, Mildred Wertheimer, and the Lehman brothers (Arthur and Herbert Henry). They were the financial bulwark of the private Jewish agencies in America, among which the American Jewish Committee and the Joint Distribution Committee in particular were active in behalf of German Jewry. It was partly their influence, together with that of Raymond Fosdik, president of the Rockefeller Foundation, that led to McDonald's appointment, in 1933, as head of the newly created League of Nations' office of the High Commissioner for Refugees from Germany. The problem of Jewish refugees being predominant, a department of Jewish affairs was instituted in the office, headed by the British Zionist Norman Bentwich. McDonald designed a comprehensive plan of economic, legal, and political-aid activities.

But almost from the outset, the commissioner found himself beset with problems that made his office virtually impotent. The appointment of an American commissioner to a League agency was anomalous, since America did not belong to the world organization. The commission, unlike other humanitarian efforts of the League, found little support in the State Department. The British and French foreign offices proved singularly unsupportive. Germany, which had just left the League, claimed that McDonald's activity constituted interference with an internal issue, and did not welcome the commission's activities. Because of the lack of a budget, 90 percent of the administrative expenses were assumed by the Joint Distribution Committee. In 1935, when the Nuremberg Laws added potential new refugees to the problem, McDonald decided to resign, but in a dramatic fashion, so that the refugee problem would be highlighted. His widely publicized statement of resignation, delivered on December 3, 1935, accused the German government of planning racial extermination; he condemned the members of the League for their heartless indifference to the plight of the refugees. "I cannot remain silent. ... When domestic policies threaten the demoralization of hundreds of thousands of human beings, consideration of diplomatic correctness must yield to those of common humanity." The entire document, with forty pages of supportive material, was printed in the *New York Times*.

The German annexation of Austria in March 1938 and the deteriorating refugee problem led to a change in the Roosevelt administration's policy. Thirty-two nations were invited to attend a conference on refugee problems, held at Evian in July of that year. Simultaneously, Franklin D. Roosevelt established a quasi-governmental agency, the President's Advisory Committee on Political Refugees (PAC), to serve as a link between the government and the numerous private agencies involved with refugees. McDonald was appointed its chairman, but with no budget or salary.

He soon discovered that the problems he had faced as High Commissioner were amplified on the American domestic scene. Virtually every suggestion funneled through the PAC to ease the plight of the refugees was rejected by the State Department, either on grounds of legality or practicality or, more commonly,

1886 McDonald is born.

1919 McDonald becomes chair of the Foreign Policy Association.

1933 McDonald becomes League of Nations High Commissioner for Refugees from Germany.

1935 McDonald resigns from his post in protest.

1936 McDonald makes public statement of protest in the *New York Times*.

1938 Deteriorating refugee problem leads to a change in U.S. refugee policy.

1940 McDonald clashes with the State Department over its rejection of special visas.

1945 McDonald is appointed to the Anglo-American Committee of Inquiry on Palestine.

1948 McDonald becomes first American ambassador to Israel.

1964 McDonald dies.

on the ground that the security of the United States would be compromised by admitting spies. Finally, in the fall of 1940, McDonald clashed directly with the State Department, when the PAC's requests to grant special visas to prominent European labor, political, and cultural leaders were rejected. Discouraged, he turned down a vague offer to head the American delegation to the Bermuda Conference, held in April 1943.

Particularly nettling for McDonald was the agreement between the governments of Britain and the United States to prevent large-scale immigration to the most logical haven, Palestine. Over the years, the Zionist experiment had won his grudging admiration. The fact that he was acceptable to leading American Zionists earned him a place on the Anglo-American Committee of Inquiry on Palestine, appointed by President Harry S Truman in 1945 to examine the Palestine problem. The committee's recommendation that 100,000 displaced persons—Jewish survivors—be immediately admitted to Palestine was turned down by the Mandatory power, the British government. After the establishment of Israel in May 1948, McDonald became the first American ambassador to the Jewish state, a position he held until 1951. ◆

> Particularly nettling for McDonald was the agreement between the governments of Britain and the United States to prevent large-scale immigration to Palestine.

Meiss, Léon

1896–1966

consistory: a group of counselors.

rapprochement: establishment or renewal of friendly relations.

Jewish leader in Vichy France. A distinguished lawyer, Meiss was active in communal affairs before World War II, especially in the Consistoire Central des Israélites de France (Central **Consistory** of French Jews). With the fall of France in 1940, he joined the large exodus of Jews from the north and participated in reconstituting the Consistoire in Lyons. As vice president of the organization, Meiss took an active role in determining its policy, forcefully intervening at Vichy on various occasions to protest the regime's anti-Semitic policy and maintaining relations with diverse elements in the community. He was instrumental in 1943 in bringing about a **rapprochement** between the Consistoire and the Union Générale des Israélites de France. After the arrest, in October 1943, of Jacques Helbronner, the president of the Consistoire, Meiss succeeded in prevailing on the organization to support underground activities and align itself with political and immigrant elements of all shades in the community. These negotiations eventually led to the establishment of an umbrella organization to coordinate French-Jewish resistance activity, the Conseil Représentatif des Juifs de France. After the war, Meiss played a significant role in the Jewish community's rehabilitation. ◆

Menczer, Aron

1917–1943

Youth Aliya activist. A member of the Gordonia Zionist youth movement in Vienna, Menczer worked for Youth Aliya following the Anschluss of Austria in March 1938. In March 1939 Menczer escorted a group of Youth Aliya wards to Palestine on behalf of the organization. His sense of duty toward the Jewish youth still in Austria made him return to Vienna, where he rejected a further opportunity to emigrate.

In September 1939 Menczer was appointed head of Youth Aliya in Vienna. In 1940, when exit from the country was no longer possible, he concentrated his efforts on education through the Youth Aliya school in the city, which 400 pupils attended regularly. Under his leadership the various Zionist youth movements in Austria united into one body, with Menczer as its director. He also maintained contact with activists of the pioneer youth movements in Bedzin and Sosnowiec in Poland, which he visited late in 1940, and helped them establish a pattern of regular activities.

After the closing down of the Youth Aliya institutions in Austria, Menczer was sent to a forced-labor camp near Linz, where he continued his educational efforts by correspondence. On September 14, 1942, he was taken back to Vienna, and on September 24 was transferred to Theresienstadt, where he became a youth leader and, in November, a member of the He-Haluts central council.

In August 1943 Menczer joined a team that cared for a group of twelve hundred children brought to Theresienstadt from Białystok. On October 15 of that year the children, together with Menczer and other escorts, were deported to the Birkenau camp, where they all perished. ◆

1917 Menczer is born.

1938 Menczer begins working for Youth Aliya.

1939 Menczer escorts Youth Aliya wards to Palestine; is appointed head of Youth Aliya in Vienna.

1940 Menczer unites various youth movements in Austria.

1942 Menczer is moved to Theresienstadt; becomes a youth leader.

1943 Menczer and 1,200 children under his care are deported to Birkenau, where they perish.

Mikołajczyk, Stanisław

1901–1966

1901 Mikolajczyk is born in Holsterhausen, Germany.

1931 Mikolajczyk becomes prominent leader of the People's Party.

1939 Mikolajczyk leaves Poland when Germans invade.

1940 Mikolajczyk becomes deputy chair of the Polish National Committee in Exile in London.

1943 Mikolajczyk becomes prime minister of the Polish government-in-exile.

1947 Mikolajczyk flees Communist Poland.

1966 Mikolajczyk dies.

Polish statesman. Mikołajczyk was born in Holsterhausen, in Westphalia, Germany; in his early youth he moved to Poznań, where he was active in the area's rural youth movement. From 1931 on he was one of the prominent leaders of the People's Party (Stronnictwo Ludowe) and a member of the Polish parliament, the Sejm. When the Germans invaded Poland in September 1939, Mikołajczyk left the country but remained politically active in exile. In 1940 and 1941 he was deputy chairman of the London-based Polish National Committee in Exile; from the beginning of 1942 to mid-1943 he was deputy prime minister and minister of the interior in the Polish government-in-exile. In the latter post he was in charge of all ties with occupied Poland and of the efforts to alert the free world to the Nazi terror in Poland and the events of the Holocaust.

On July 14, 1943, Mikołajczyk was elected prime minister in the Polish government-in-exile. When the war ended he returned to Poland and was appointed deputy prime minister and minister of agriculture. But before long he came to reject the new Communist regime, joining the ranks of the opposition, and in October 1947 he fled the country. Mikołajczyk settled in the United States, where he was active in Polish emigré groups. He wrote *The Rape of Poland: Pattern of Soviet Aggression* (1948). ◆

Mushkin, Eliyahu

D. 1942

Chairman of the Minsk Judenrat (Jewish Council) and a supporter of its underground and the local partisans. A native of Minsk and an engineer by profession, Mushkin was a member of the municipality staff. The Germans occupied Minsk at the end of June 1941, and shortly afterward, Mushkin was appointed Judenrat chairman because of his knowledge of German or, according to one version, because he was recommended for the post by a member of the city council.

Mushkin lost little time in establishing contact with the Minsk ghetto underground. He was helpful in aiding Jews to escape from the ghetto, and supplied the partisan units in the area with money, medicines, and equipment. Through his personal authority, Mushkin exercised a decisive influence on the attitude of the other members of the Judenrat, which for all practical purposes became the executive arm of the underground, carrying out its decisions. Mushkin was able to warn the underground of impending dangers, and the Jews respected him. His close contacts with the underground, coupled with the duties that the German authorities imposed on him, put Mushkin in a precarious situation. He had to be extremely careful, and could not afford to trust even some of his own staff.

In February 1942 Mushkin was arrested. One version has it that he was charged with attempting to bribe a Gestapo officer to release a Jewish prisoner. According to another version, he was arrested when someone informed on the Judenrat to the Gestapo, revealing that the Judenrat was providing the partisans with clothing, medicines, and equipment. A third version is that Mushkin had given refuge to a German officer who sought to avoid frontline service, and that it was this officer who gave him away. Mushkin was tortured and, a month after his arrest, he was hanged. The members of his family were killed in one of the "night *Aktionen*." ◆

His close contacts with the underground, coupled with the duties the German authorities imposed on him, put Mushkin in a precarious situation.

Nèvejean, Yvonne

D. 1987

Belgian rescuer of Jewish children during the Holocaust. Yvonne Nèvejean headed the Oeuvre Nationale de l'Enfance (National Agency for Children; ONE), a Belgian government-subsidized agency supervising children's homes throughout the country. When the deportations of Jews began in the summer of 1942, she was contacted by heads of the Comité de Défense des Juifs en Belgique (Committee for the Protection of Jews in Belgium; CDJ), the principal Jewish clandestine organization at the time. She was asked whether she was prepared to help rescue Jewish children separated from their parents (who had been deported or were hiding) by placing the children, through the ONE network, in religious and lay institutions and with private families. Without even consulting the ONE board of directors, Nèvejean committed the ONE to a vast rescue operation that eventually saved up to four thousand Jewish children (nicknamed "Yvonne's children"). They were referred to her by trusted CDJ personnel, and were then fetched by ONE nurses and social workers and provided with the necessary new identities and ration cards. After a brief stay in ONE-sponsored children's homes,

they were sent off for permanent refuge in institutions and with private families. The financing for this wide-ranging operation came initially from CDJ sources. When these proved insufficient, Yvonne Nèvejean obtained funds from banks and from the London-based government-in-exile, which were then parachuted into Belgium.

An operation of such magnitude, with the participation of untold numbers of lay and religious persons, could not go on without denunciations. Some rescuers and rescued persons were arrested, but on the whole the Gestapo failed to disrupt the ONE network. On one occasion, Nèvejean was made to accompany a suspicious German official to a children's home in Tervueren at which a third of the 250 children were Jewish. But by directing the German's attention to a non-Jewish **mulatto** child, she was able to avoid his scrutiny of the other children. In another instance, when the Gestapo broke into the Wezembeek children's home and transported its staff and the Jewish children to the Mechelen camp, Nèvejean interceded with Queen Mother Elisabeth, who, with the help of Léon Platteau of the Belgian Ministry of Justice (both later recognized as "Righteous among the Nations"), succeeded in securing the release of the children and their supervisors.

In 1965 Yvonne Nèvejean, now known as Yvonne Feyerick-Nèvejean, was awarded the Yad Vashem title of "Righteous among the Nations." ◆

mulatto: a person of mixed white and black ancestry.

Nicolini, Giuseppe

Rescuer of Jews in Assisi, in central Italy. Soon after the German invasion of Italy in September 1943, Giuseppe Nicolini, bishop of Assisi, summoned Rufino Nicacci, father guardian of the San Damiano monastery in Assisi. He charged Nicacci with finding temporary shelter for a group of fleeing Jews, mostly from the Trieste area in northern Italy, who had unexpectedly appeared in town. Nicacci arranged for some two hundred Jews to be supplied with false identities and hidden in parishioners' homes, moved out of the area, or given sanctuary in monasteries and convents. To provide for the religious needs of the Jews staying in the convent, the sisters operated a kitchen where dietary kosher laws were observed.

Also involved in this extensive rescue operation (several thousand Jews passed through the town at one point or another) was Aldo Brunacci, a professor canon at the San Rufino Cathedral of Assisi. The person formally in charge of the operation, he insisted that Jews could be hidden in cloisters as well, such as the Convent of the Stigmata. Father Brunacci was also in charge of a clandestine school for Jewish children, in which they received instruction in Judaism from their own mentors. In May 1944 Brunacci was arrested and tried by a Perugia court. He was spared only through the Vatican's intercession, on condition that he be banished from Assisi for the duration of the war.

Not a single Jew was ever betrayed in Assisi, nor was there any attempt to induce the many fleeing Jews passing through the town to convert. Father Brunacci remarked after the war: "In all, about two hundred Jews were entrusted to us by Divine Providence; with God's help, and through the intercession of Saint Francis, not one of them fell into the hands of their persecutors."

After the war, Giuseppe Nicolini, Rufino Nicacci, and Aldo Brunacci were recognized by Yad Vashem as "Righteous among the Nations." ◆

> *"In all, about two hundred Jews were entrusted to us by Divine Providence; with God's help, and through the intercession of Saint Francis, not one of them fell into the hands of their persecutors."*
>
> Aldo Brunacci

Niemöller, Martin

1892–1984

Protestant pastor and leader of the anti-Nazi Confessing Church (Bekennende Kirche). Born in Westphalia, the son of a pastor, Niemöller entered the German navy in 1910 and in World War I served as a U-boat commander, with great distinction. He was ordained in 1924, and in 1931 became pastor of the influential Berlin parish of Dahlem, where his naval fame and his preaching attracted large congregations.

Niemöller was unsympathetic to the Weimar Republic and welcomed the Nazis initially, but he soon saw the dangers of the regime. In 1934 he formed the Pfarrernotbund (Pastors' Emergency League), and in 1937 he assumed leadership of the Con-

> *"First they came for the Jews. I was silent. I was not a Jew."*
>
> Martin Niemoller

1892 Niemöller is born in Westphalia.

1924 Niemöller is ordained a pastor.

1931 Niemöller becomes pastor of an influential Berlin parish.

1934 Niemöller forms the Pastor's Emergency League.

1937 Niemöller assumes leadership of the Confessing Church.

1945 Niemöller is released from seven years in concentration camps; helps to issue the "Stuttgart Confession of Guilt."

1984 Niemöller dies.

fessing Church. He was arrested for "malicious attacks against the state," given a token sentence, and fined the modest sum of 2,000 reichsmarks. Upon his release, Niemöller was re-arrested on Hitler's order and spent the next seven years in the concentration camps of Sachsenhausen and Dachau, usually in solitary confinement. At the outbreak of World War II, moved by patriotism, he offered his services to the navy, but his offer was rejected. He was released in 1945 by Allied forces and helped to issue the "Stuttgart Confession of Guilt" (1945), which confessed the collective war guilt of the Germans.

Niemöller himself shared the guilt: "First they came for the Jews. I was silent. I was not a Jew. Then they came for the Communists. I was silent. I was not a Communist. Then they came for the trade unionists. I was silent. I was not a trade unionist. Then they came for me. There was no one left to speak for me." After the war Niemöller became a convinced pacifist, denounced nuclear weapons, and advocated a neutral, disarmed, and reunited Germany. ◆

Pechersky, Aleksandr Sasha

1909–

Leader of the Sobibór uprising. Pechersky was born in Kremenchug, in the Ukraine, and as a child moved to Rostov-on-Don, where he graduated from a music conservatory. He became a bookkeeper, but was also active in drama and music circles. He served in the Red Army, holding the rank of second lieutenant.

When the Germans attacked the Soviet Union, Pechersky was called up and posted to the front. In September 1941 he was promoted to lieutenant. He was taken prisoner the following month and contracted typhoid fever; he managed, however, to conceal his illness and turn up for the prisoners' parades, since the Germans shot all Soviet prisoners of war who fell ill. In May 1942 Pechersky escaped, together with four other prisoners, but they were all caught. Contrary to the usual German procedure, they were not shot but were sent to a **penal** camp, in Borisov. It was there, when Pechersky had to undress, that he was identified as a Jew, a fact he had previously managed to hide from the Germans. On August 20 of that year, Pechersky was transferred to an SS camp on Sheroka Street, in Minsk, in which some one hundred Soviet Jewish prisoners of war were held, together with several hundred Jewish civilians from the Minsk ghetto. He stayed there for over a year.

On September 18, 1943, the Minsk ghetto was liquidated and Pechersky was sent to the Sobibór extermination camp, together with two thousand Jews from the ghetto and the camp on Sheroka Street. They reached Sobibór on September 23.

penal: having to do with punishment.

Aleksandr Pechersky (left) with Aleksei Weizen, a survivor of Sobibór.

1909 Pechersky is born in Kremenchug, in the Ukraine.

1941 Pechersky is promoted to lieutenant in the Red Army.

1942 Pechersky is sent to a penal camp in Borisov; is transferred to an SS camp in Minsk after being identified as Jewish.

1943 Pechersky is sent to Sobibór camp, where he plans an uprising that kills most SS men in the camp.

1943 After a mass escape from the camp, Pechersky joins Soviet partisans.

1944 Pechersky is badly injured in battle.

1957 Pechersky publishes *They Fought Back*.

1963 Pechersky is the chief prosecution witness in trial of SS guards.

1967 Pechersky publishes *The Fighting Ghettos*.

Pechersky was one of eighty Jewish prisoners of war who, on arrival in the camp, were selected for construction work; the rest of the transport was sent to the gas chambers to be killed.

Shortly after Pechersky's arrival in Sobibór, he was contacted by the camp underground; as an officer, he agreed to take over the command of the underground and to lead it in an uprising. During the next three weeks Pechersky reorganized the underground, making the prisoners of war its core and planning the uprising. It took place on October 14, 1943, under Pechersky's command; in its course most of the SS men in the camp were killed and a mass escape from the camp took place. Together with a group of prisoners of war, Pechersky succeeded in crossing the Bug River, and on October 22 he made contact with Soviet partisans in the Brest area. He joined the partisans and fought in their ranks until the summer of 1944, when the Soviet army advanced into the area and the partisans joined up with the regular army units. Pechersky, now fighting in the Soviet army, was badly wounded in August 1944, and was hospitalized for four months. On recovering, he was discharged and returned to his hometown, Rostov, where he settled.

Pechersky was the chief witness for the prosecution in the trial, held in Kiev in the spring of 1963, of eleven Ukrainians who had served as guards in the Sobibór camp. His account of the Sobibór uprising was published in Yuri Suhl's *They Fought Back* (New York, 1957) and in *The Fighting Ghettos*, edited by Meyer Barkai (Philadelphia, 1967). ◆

Plotnicka, Frumka

1914–1943

A leader of the He-Haluts underground in Poland. Born in Plotnicka, near Pinsk, she was a member of the Freiheit (Dror) movement from her youth. Late in 1938 she worked at the Dror main office in Warsaw.

When World War II broke out, Plotnicka, together with most of the people in the *hakhsharot* (Zionist training farms), moved to Kovel, in Soviet-occupied eastern Poland, in the hope that there they would find a way of reaching Palestine. In 1940 she was one of a group of Dror headquarters members who were asked to return to the German-occupied area in order to reorganize Dror as an underground movement. Basing herself in Warsaw, Plotnicka endeavored from the beginning of the invasion of the Soviet Union (in June 1941) to consolidate and strengthen the He-Haluts underground movements throughout occupied Poland, even visiting near-inaccessible ghettos. In September 1942 she went to Bedzin on a mission for the Żydowska Organizacja Bojowa (Jewish Fighting Organization; ŻOB), to assist in setting up a self-defense organization there. She was in contact with several people and organizations in Switzerland and Slovakia and with the Rescue Commitee of the Jewish Agency in Turkey, to which she passed on information about the situation in occupied Poland. Plotnicka rejected opportunities to save her life and move to Slovakia, and to obtain documents as a foreign national. She fell in battle on August 3, 1943, together with the last group of fighters in Będzin. ◆

1914 Plotnicka is born in Plotnicka.

1938 Plotnicka works at the Dror main office in Warsaw.

1940 Plotnicka is asked to reorganize Dror as an underground movement.

1941 Plotnicka works to strengthen the underground throughout occupied Poland.

1942 Plotnicka goes to Bedzin on a ZOB mission.

1943 Plotnicka dies in battle.

Polonski, Abraham

1903–

F ounder of the Jewish underground in France. Born in Russia, Polonski was an electrical engineer in Toulouse, France. After the fall of the French army in June 1940, Polonski, who was a follower of the Zionist activist Vladimir

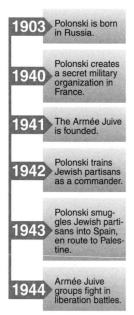

1903 Polonski is born in Russia.

1940 Polonski creates a secret military organization in France.

1941 The Armée Juive is founded.

1942 Polonski trains Jewish partisans as a commander.

1943 Polonski smuggles Jewish partisans into Spain, en route to Palestine.

1944 Armée Juive groups fight in liberation battles.

Jabotinsky, reacted by creating a secret military organization, La Main Forte (The Strong Hand), the aim of which was to recruit a fighting force throughout the world to conquer Palestine from the British. Polonski was the first French Jew who worked to create a Jewish military underground under the Nazi occupation. With the participation of Labor Movement Zionist activists, the Armée Juive was founded in January 1942, uniting the best of the forces of Zionist youth. Its command, headed by Polonski and by Lucien Lublin, trained Jewish partisans, and in 1943 and 1944 smuggled about three hundred of them into Spain, from where they continued on to Palestine. Armée Juive groups were active in the cities of Toulouse, Nice, Lyons, and Paris; they took revenge on informers who helped the Gestapo, and they fought in liberation battles of the summer of 1944. After the war Polonski participated in the "illegal" immigration from France to Palestine. ◆

Rayman, Marcel

1923–1944

French Jewish underground fighter. Born in Warsaw, Rayman emigrated with his parents to France, where he became active in the Communist Jewish Workers' Sports Club (Yidishe Arbeiter Sportishe Klub).

In June 1940, when Paris was occupied by the Germans, Rayman joined the Deuxième Détachement (Second Company), a Yiddish-speaking unit that was under the command of the Communist partisan organization the Francs-Tireurs et Partisans (Fighters and Partisans; FTP). He participated in numerous attacks on German soldiers and army installations in Paris. When his company was liquidated by the French secret service, Rayman was put into the "Manouchian Company," a Communist partisan unit led by the Armenian poet Missak Manouchian. On September 28, 1943, Rayman took part in a daring operation in which SS-Obergruppenführer Dr. Julius von Ritter, the German official in charge of enlisting French laborers for work in Germany, was killed. Rayman fell into Gestapo hands a few days later and was one of the accused in a show trial, together with Manouchian and twenty-one other fighters, most of them Jewish. All of the accused, including Rayman, were executed. ◆

1923	Rayman is born in Warsaw.
1940	Rayman joins the Deuxième Détachment.
1943	Rayman takes part in a daring operation.
1943	Rayman is arrested by the Gestapo.

Rayski, Abraham (Adam)

1914–

Jewish Communist, active in the anti-Nazi resistance in France. Born in Białystok to a traditional middle-class family, Rayski was attracted to communism at an early age. He left for Paris in 1932 and within two years became a full-time journalist on the Communist newspaper *Neie Presse*. From July 1941 until the end of World War II, he served as national secretary of the Jewish section of the French Communist party. His articles in the clandestine press, his contribution to the establishment of the Conseil Représentatif des Juifs de France, and his role in the development of the Jewish resistance played a major part in Jewish survival in France. Rayski published vivid autobiographical memoirs, *Nos illusions perdues* (Our Lost Illusions; 1985). ◆

Reik, Haviva (Emma)

1914–1944

> "Everyday that we are still alive is like a gift from heaven."
>
> Haviva Reik

World War II parachutist and emissary of the Jewish Agency's underground military organization, the Hagana. Reik was born in a small village near Banská Bystrica, Slovakia. She was a member of the Ha-Shomer ha-Tsa'ir Zionist youth movement and in 1939 settled in Palestine, where she joined Kibbutz Ma'anit. At the time of the El Alamein battle she enlisted in the Hagana's strike force, the Palmah. When her period of service was completed, Reik learned about the parachutists' unit for which volunteers were being sought and promptly joined, in the hope of being sent to Slovakia to help in the rescue of Jews in that country.

On September 21, 1944, Reik was dropped over Slovakia at a point near Banská Bystrica, which at the time was the center of the Slovak National Uprising. Her mission was to get to Bratislava and there to establish contact with the leaders of the Pracovná Skupina (Working Group), Rabbi Michael Dov Weissmandel and Gisi Fleischmann. Reik had been preceded a week earlier by three other parachutists, Rafael Reiss, Zvi Ben-Yaakov, and Chaim Hermesh (Kassaf). At the end of September

a fifth parachutist was dropped, Abba Berdiczew, who brought radio transmitters along for his colleagues. Reik and her group were unable to begin any activity on behalf of the Jews since, like their Slovak partisan friends, they were forced to fight for their lives against the Germans. They tried to set up an independent Jewish unit and succeeded in rounding up some forty Jewish partisans from among the general partisan units that were still operating against the Germans.

After the fall of Banská Bystrica, at the end of October 1944, Reik and her comrades from Palestine retreated into the Tatra Mountains, together with the Jewish partisan group. There, near the village of Bukovice, they set up a small camp, collecting weapons and trying to make the camp a stronghold. "Every day that we are still alive," Reik wrote in a letter, "is like a gift from heaven." On the sixth day of their stay in the camp, owing to inadequate security precautions, they were captured by a unit of the Ukrainian "Galicia" Waffen-SS division that was operating in the area against the Slovak rebels. Reik, Reiss, and Ben-Yaakov were among those taken prisoner, and on November 20, 1944, the Germans executed them at Kremnica. Kibbutz Lahavot Haviva, the postwar "illegal" immigration ship *Haviva Reik,* and the Israeli educational center Givat Haviva were all named after Haviva Reik. ◆

Ringelblum, Emanuel

1900–1944

Historian and Jewish public figure; founder and director of the clandestine archive Oneg Shabbat. Ringelblum was born in Buczacz, Eastern Galicia, into a middle-

class merchant family. In World War I the family suffered economic setbacks and moved to Nowy Sącz. In 1927 Ringelblum was awarded a doctorate by the University of Warsaw for his thesis on the history of the Jews of Warsaw in the Middle Ages. From an early age, Ringelblum was a member of Po'alei Zion Left and was active in public affairs. For several years he taught history in Jewish high schools. In 1930 he took on part-time employment with the Joint Distribution Committee and established close working relations and personal ties with Yitzhak Gitterman, one of its leaders in Poland, which he maintained in the war years as well. In November 1938 the Joint sent Ringelblum to the Zbąszyn camp, where six thousand Jews were gathered—Polish citizens who had been expelled from Germany at the end of October. The five weeks that Ringelblum spent there, as the person responsible for the fortunes of the refugees, left an indelible impression on him.

In his professional capacity Ringelblum belonged to the third generation of historians of the Jews of Poland, a generation educated and trained in independent Poland. In 1923 a number of these historians formed a group, with Ringelblum as one of its outstanding scholars and organizers, that eventually was associated with YIVO (Yidisher Visenshaftlikher Institut; Institute for Jewish Research). Ringelblum was one of the editors of the publications issued by the group—*Yunger Historiker* (1926–29) and *Bleter far Geschichte* (1934, 1938). In his research work Ringelblum concentrated on the history of the Jews of Warsaw, which he planned to bring up to date. Most of his writings are based on original archival material and cover a wide range of subjects; by 1939 he had published 126 scholarly articles.

During the war, Ringelblum was engaged in four spheres of activity in the Warsaw ghetto: (1) working in an institute for social

"Death lurks in every chink, every little crack. There have been cases of everyone living in an apartment being fearfully tortured because someone opened a shutter."

Emanuel Ringelblum, May 1942, *Notes from the Warsaw Ghetto* self-aid among Warsaw Jews (Żydowska Samopomoc Społeczna; also known as Jüdische Soziale Selbsthilfe); (2) working in the political underground, with emphasis on its cultural affairs sector; (3) establishing and administering the clandestine Oneg Shabbat Archive; and (4) keeping an up-to-date chronicle of events, including articles on specific subjects, concerning the life of the Jews during the German occupation of Poland, especially Warsaw, covering the period from the beginning of the war up to his own arrest, on March 7, 1944.

Ringelblum was in charge of the "public sector" in the self-aid organization. He ran a network of soup kitchens for the desperately impoverished Jewish population and organized and promoted the growth of "House Committees" (Komitety Domowe), made up of volunteers with no previous experience of public activity. These committees eventually became a dynamic instrument for dealing with the growing distress.

Ringelblum and his associates made the soup kitchens—in which tens of thousands of soup portions were dispensed every day—into clubs, under the auspices of the political underground. Together with his friend Menahem Linder, Ringelblum founded in the Warsaw ghetto a society for the promotion of Yiddish culture (Yidishe Kultur Organizatsye), which arranged lectures, observances of anniversaries of Jewish writers, and meetings with writers and scholars in the ghetto.

Ringelblum's outstanding achievement was the secret Oneg Shabbat Archive, which he launched in the first few months of the war. In the initial stage, Ringelblum and a small group of friends concentrated on collecting testimonies and reports on events by Jews who came to Warsaw from the provinces in order to solicit aid from the self-aid organization. Ringelblum was aware that there was no precedent for what was happening to the Jews under the occupation, and believed that "it was important that future historians have available to them accurate records of the events that were taking place." He attracted a large circle of friends and activists to the archive, and succeeded in gaining the support of writers and underground activists representing the various political shadings. As reported by Hirsch Wasser, the secretary of the underground archive (and the only surviving member of the team): "Every item, every article, be it long or short, had to pass through Dr. Ringelblum's hands. . . . For weeks and months he spent the nights poring over the manuscripts, adding his comments and instructions."

> *"The Gestapo men in the Pawia Street prison have to have their daily victims. Just the way a pious Jew feels bad if he misses prayers one day, the Gestapo men have to pick up a few Jews every day and break a few arms and legs."*
>
> Emanuel Ringelblum, May 1942, *Notes from the Warsaw Ghetto*

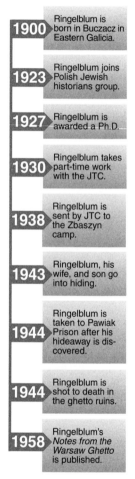

During the last stages of the ghetto's existence, Ringelblum and his associates collected every document and piece of evidence relating to the deportations and the murders and passed them on to the Polish underground, which in turn transmitted the information to London. This was how the Polish underground and London learned for the first time about the Chełmno extermination camp and came in possession of a detailed report on the deportation of 300,000 Jews from Warsaw. The archive also put out in the ghetto a bulletin, *Yediot* (News), which enabled the underground to keep abreast of events. The ghetto archive—also known as the Ringelblum Archive—is the most extensive documentary source that we have about Jews under the Nazi regime.

Ringelblum himself kept a running record of events and important items of information, at first on a daily basis (until July 1942) and then on a weekly and monthly basis. It was not a diary but rather a chronicle of events, augmented by the author's own appraisals and the historical associations that the events brought to his mind. Ringelblum's notes abound in abbreviations and allusions; he obviously regarded them as the raw material for a comprehensive work that he would write after the war. After the mass deportation, Ringelblum's method of writing underwent a change. He no longer put down information in the form of a digest, but instead dealt with the broad and pressing issues of the time, in an attempt to evaluate the events he was witnessing and fathom their meaning, and his writings convey his bitter resentment and fear. He also composed biographical notes on many of the outstanding Jewish personalities who had gone to their death in the deportations and the struggle, with details of their accomplishments and of their fate under the occupation and in the ghetto. He dealt extensively with the lives of Yitzhak Gitterman, Mordecai Anielewicz, Ignacy (Yitzhak) Schiper, Meir Balaban, and Janusz Korczak. Ringelblum continued writing up to the last months of his life, which he spent in hiding with Poles. It was in that period that he wrote his work on Jewish-Polish relations, an attempt to encompass a multifaceted subject without the help of written sources or reference materials.

The sum total of Ringelblum's writings represents the most extensive effort made by any person to transmit information on the events that were taking place and to cope with their significance. Ringelblum's works have been translated and published, in full or in part, in Yiddish, Polish, English (*Notes from the Warsaw Ghetto*; 1958), Italian, French, German, and Japanese. He was the model for the hero of John Hersey's *The Wall*.

After the great deportation Ringelblum became an advocate of armed resistance, and the archive was put under the aegis of the civilian arm of the Żydowska Organizacja Bojowa (Jewish Fighting Organization; ŻOB). In March 1943 Ringelblum accepted the invitation that he had repeatedly received from the Polish side, and with his wife and thirteen-year-old son left the ghetto and went into hiding among the Poles. On the eve of Passover 1943 he entered the ghetto on his own and walked straight into the uprising. What happened to him during the deportation and the fighting is not known, but in July 1943 he was found in the Trawniki labor camp. Two members of the Warsaw underground—a Polish man and a Jewish woman—got him out of Trawniki and took him to Warsaw, in the guise of a railway worker. Together with his family and another thirty Jews, he hid in an underground refuge—and continued writing. A Jewish team that had set itself the task of rescuing Jews who were hiding among the Poles sought to enlist Ringelblum for their operation and to utilize his non-Jewish appearance. On March 7, 1944, however, before Ringelblum had decided whether to leave the hideaway, the place was discovered and all the Jews and Polish-protected persons who had taken refuge there were taken to Warsaw's Pawiak Prison. According to one report, Jewish prisoners who were working in the prison as skilled craftsmen proposed that Ringelblum join their group, but when he came to the conclusion that there was no chance for his family to be saved, he rejected the offer. A few days later Ringelblum, his family, and the other Jews who had been with him in the hideout were shot to death among the ruins of the ghetto. ◆

> *"For long, long months, we tormented ourselves in the midst of our suffering with the questions: does the world know about our suffering? And if it knows, why is it silent?"*
>
> Emanuel Ringelblum, June 1942, *Notes from the Warsaw Ghetto*

Robota, Roza

1921–1945

Jewish underground activist in the Auschwitz-Birkenau camp. Born in Ciechanów, Poland, Robota was a member of the Ha-Shomer ha-Tsa'ir Zionist underground in the

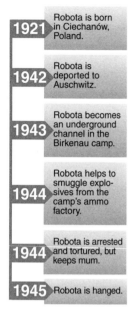

1921 Robota is born in Ciechanów, Poland.

1942 Robota is deported to Auschwitz.

1943 Robota becomes an underground channel in the Birkenau camp.

1944 Robota helps to smuggle explosives from the camp's ammo factory.

1944 Robota is arrested and tortured, but keeps mum.

1945 Robota is hanged.

town. In 1942 she was taken to Auschwitz, together with a transport from Ciechanów, and was among the first prisoners to be put into the women's camp in Birkenau. A Jewish underground group set up in Auschwitz in 1943 contacted Robota, and she became the channel through which the group was able to win support in the Birkenau women's camp.

In 1944, with Robota's help, minute quantities of explosives were smuggled out of the Union ammunition factory in the camp. They were handed over to the underground in Auschwitz I and to the Sonderkommando men employed in the Birkenau crematoria. In the wake of the investigation held after the Sonderkommando mutiny of October 1944, Robota and three other young female prisoners working in the Union factory were arrested. Robota was the only one who knew the names of the core group that ran the operations of the underground and its channels of communication, but despite the torture that she underwent, she did not reveal a single name. On January 6, 1945, just a few weeks before the camp was evacuated, Roza Robota and three comrades—Ella Gartner, Tusia, and Regina—were hanged. ◆

Rowecki, Stefan

1895–1943

Polish officer; commander of the Armia Krajowa (Home Army). In the underground, Rowecki was known by the code name Grot ("arrowhead"). During World War I he fought in the ranks of the Polish Legion, commanded by Józef Piłsudski, and after the war became an officer in the Polish army, reaching the rank of colonel.

In the fighting of September 1939 Rowecki was in command of an armored brigade. When the Polish forces in besieged Warsaw surrendered at the end of that month, Rowecki, on the orders of the Polish general Juliusz Karol Rommel, went underground to create and head a secret resistance organization engaging in anti-German actions. Subordinate to the authority of the Polish government-in-exile, it was first named Służba Zwycięstwu Polski (Service for the Victory of Poland); in 1940 it was renamed Związek Walki Zbrojnej (Union for Armed Struggle), and as of 1942 was called Armia Krajowa. It became the strongest and most important element of the Polish underground.

In 1940 the Polish government-in-exile appointed Rowecki to the rank of brigadier general. He developed the concept of restricting actual fighting against the Germans and instead worked to strengthen the underground so as to prepare it for an uprising that would take place when the German army in Poland was on the verge of collapse. This concept failed to prove itself when the test came. Rowecki decided to cooperate, within limits, with the Żydowska Organizacja Bojowa (Jewish Fighting Organization; ŻOB) in the Warsaw ghetto and to supply it with some assistance. On June 30, 1943, Rowecki was arrested in Warsaw by the Germans, taken to the Sachsenhausen concentration camp, and murdered. His memoirs, *Wspomnienia i notatki, czerwiec-wrzesień* (Recollections and Notes, June–September), were published posthumously in Warsaw, in 1957. ◆

1895 Rowecki is born.

1939 Rowecki becomes commander of an armored brigade.

1939 Rowecki creates a secret resistance group.

1940 Rowecki is named brigadier general by the Polish government-in-exile.

1943 Rowecki is arrested and executed.

1957 Rowecki's memoirs are published in Warsaw.

Rufajzen, Oswald Shmuel Rufeisen (later Brother Daniel)

1922–

Wartime activist. Rufajzen was born in Zadziele, a village in the Kraków district, and during his studies joined the Akiva youth movement. In 1939, when World War II broke out, he fled to Vilna, where he joined the *halutsim* (members of the Zionist pioneering movements) who had gathered there. In June 1941, when Vilna was occupied by the Nazis, Rufajzen succeeded in obtaining an "Aryan" document certifying that he was a Volksdeutsche (ethnic German) named Josef Oswald. He moved to Mir, where he became the interpreter of the gendarmerie commandant, gaining his complete confidence. After a while he was appointed police commander for the area.

In Mir, Rufajzen met two of the *halutsim* with whom he had become acquainted in Vilna; both were organizers of the ghetto underground. Oswald (the name by which Rufajzen now went)

1922 Rufajzen is born in Zadziele, a village near Kraków.

1939 Rufajzen flees to Vilna and joins the *halutsim.*

1941 Rufajzen obtains an "Aryan" identity document; becomes interpreter for the gendarmerie commandant.

1942 Rufajzen's advance warning enables 180 Jews to escape the ghetto.

regularly passed information on the activities of the Germans to his friends in the ghetto underground, and on more than one occasion saved those in the ghetto from falling into traps engineered by the police, such as a sham "sale" of weapons to ghetto Jews by a local farmer. Oswald's friends told him of their determination to resist a German *Aktion* by force, and asked him to supply them with arms. Over a period of time he provided the ghetto with twelve rifles, two submachine guns, eight pistols, thirty hand grenades, and thousands of rounds of ammunition. At Oswald's suggestion the underground altered its plan to escape from the ghetto in the course of the *Aktion*, by advancing the date for the escape. On August 6, 1942, he informed the ghetto underground commanders of the date that had been fixed for the liquidation of the ghetto (August 13) and the date on which he would be taking the town police on an "anti-partisan patrol" (August 9). On that day, with the town empty of police and Germans, 180 Mir Jews fled the ghetto and took refuge in the forests.

Following the flight, Oswald was arrested and interrogated by the German commander, Schulz, on suspicion of having provided the Jews with arms and helping them to flee. He managed to escape from the place where he was being held and found refuge in a monastery, where he remained for the next sixteen months. When the search for him intensified, Oswald fled once more, this time to the forest. The partisans thought he was German and placed him under arrest, but he was saved by Jewish partisans from Mir who interceded on his behalf.

When the war was over Oswald took part in the efforts to apprehend local inhabitants of Mir who had collaborated with the Germans. He then left for Kraków, where he was baptized and given the name of "Daniel, the son of Miriam." Later he went to Israel and joined the Stella Maris monastery on Mount Carmel. ◆

Safran, Alexander

1910 –

Chief Rabbi of Romania from 1940 to 1947. A native of Bacǎu, Safran studied at the rabbinical seminary in Vienna, and completed his doctorate at the University of Vienna. On his return to Romania he became rabbi in his hometown. In 1940, at the age of thirty, he was elected Chief Rabbi of Romania at a most critical moment for the country's Jews, with the Iron Guard gaining in strength and the whole country becoming **fascist.**

The body that elected Safran was composed of rabbis and Jewish community representatives of the Regat (Romania in its pre-World War I borders), with the chief rabbis of the other parts of the country (Bessarabia, Bukovina, and Transylvania) also supporting their choice. Within a short while Safran gained the recognition and respect of the Jewish and Romanian establishments. From April to August 1940 he was a member of the Romanian senate, the only public office still held by a Jew after the dissolution of all political parties and organizations by King Carol II in 1938. Safran cooperated with Wilhelm Filderman, the veteran leader of Romanian Jewry and president of the Federatia Uniunilor de Comunitati Evreesti (Union of Jewish Communities), in efforts to persuade the Romanian government to desist from, or at least to moderate, its anti-Jewish legislation.

Even under the fascist regime of the Iron Guard (September 6, 1940, to January 24, 1941), Safran remained the representative of Romanian Jewry vis-à-vis the authorities, and as their

fascist: describing a political movement with a strong central government that exalts the nation above the individual.

dedicated spiritual leader he tried to keep up the Jews' morale with his sermons and by organizing relief operations. He helped the Jewish communities to establish independent Jewish educational institutions when Jewish students were excluded from the public schools, and he saw to it that the new schools were given a Jewish and Zionist complexion. Together with Filderman, Safran tried—unsuccessfully—to prevent the deportation to Transnistria of the Jews of Bessarabia and Bukovina. In the fall of 1941 Safran lodged appeals with the country's dictator, Ion Antonescu; with the head of the Romanian church, Patriarch Nicodim; with the archbishop of Bukovina, Tit Simedria; and with Queen Mother Helena.

Following the dissolution of the Jewish communities by the authorities on December 17, 1941, Safran was one of the group that proposed the establishment of the Jewish Council, an underground leadership headed by Filderman and made up of representatives of all sectors of the Jewish population. As of the summer of 1942, Safran's home became the council's meeting place. The council was to play a role in forestalling the deportation of Romania's Jews to the extermination camps in Poland. Safran established highly important contacts with the royal court, with Romanian churchmen, and with the papal nuncio, Archbishop Andrea Cassulo, who frequently intervened on behalf of the Jews. In the summer of 1942 Safran persuaded the archbishop of Transylvania, Nicolae Balan, to intervene with Antonescu against the planned deportation of Romanian Jews to Poland. Through Cassulo, Safran transmitted to the Vatican reports on the true situation of Romanian Jewry and the threat of their extermination, and he also asked for the Vatican's intercession on behalf of the Jews of Hungary.

When Romania was liberated in August 1944, Safran was not prepared to cooperate with the Jewish Communists of the new Jewish Democratic Committee in the breakup of traditional Jewish organizations, since he would thereby be playing a part in bringing Jewish life in Romania to a standstill. As a result, in December 1947 he was dismissed from his post and forced to leave the country. He took up residence in Switzerland and became the rabbi of the Jewish community in Geneva. Safran's memoirs, *Resisting the Storm: Romania 1940–1947*, appeared in 1987. ◆

Saliège, Jules-Gérard

1870–1956

A rchbishop of Toulouse; an active opponent of anti-Jewish measures in France. Prior to World War I, Saliège came under the influence of innovative Catholic thinkers who advocated theological reassessment and deeper involvement in social and political issues. Saliège opposed racism as un-Christian in the 1930s and continued to do so with the advent of Vichy's anti-Semitic ideology in 1940. During the deportations of Jews from unoccupied France in August 1942, he composed a pastoral letter that he disseminated among all the parishes in his diocese. The letter, which had considerable impact on French public opinion and was widely reproduced, forcefully denounced the inhuman actions and demanded recognition of Jews as "brothers." Saliège's strong protest was part of the upheaval in opinion among leading Catholic figures in France on the "Jewish question," which produced widespread popular support for Jews in southern France from the summer of 1942. ◆

Jule-Gérard Saliège forcefully demanded recognition of Jews as "brothers."

Schindler, Oskar

1908–1974

P rotector of Jews during the Holocaust. Schindler was born in Svitavy (Ger., Zwittau), in the Sudetenland, and came to Kraków in late 1939, in the wake of the German invasion of Poland. There he took over two previously Jewish-owned firms dealing with the manufacture and wholesale distribution of enamel kitchenware products, one of which he operated as a trustee (*Treuhänder*) for the German occupation administration.

Schindler then established his own enamel works in Zablocie, outside Kraków, in which he employed mainly Jewish workers, thereby protecting them from deportations. When the liquidation of the Kraków ghetto began in early 1943, many

Oskar Schindler
(second from left) and a
group of his Jewish and
Polish employees in
Kraków in 1940.

Jews were sent to the Płaszów labor camp, noted for the brutality of its commandant, Amon Goeth. Schindler used his good connections with high German officials in the Armaments Administration to set up a branch of the Płaszów camp in his factory compound for some nine hundred Jewish workers, including persons unfit and unqualified for the labor production needs. In this way he spared them from the horrors of the Płaszów camp.

In October 1944, with the approach of the Russian army, Schindler was granted permission to reestablish his now-defunct firm as an armaments production company in Brünnlitz (Brnenc, Sudetenland) and take with him the Jewish workers from Zablocie. In an operation unique in the annals of Nazi-occupied Europe, he succeeded in transferring to Brünnlitz some seven hundred to eight hundred Jewish men from the Grossrosen camp, and some three hundred Jewish women from Auschwitz. In Brünnlitz, the eleven hundred Jews were given the most humane treatment possible under the circumstances: food, medical care, and religious needs. Informed that a train with evacuated Jewish detainees from the Goleszow camp was stranded at nearby Svitavy, Schindler received permission to take workers to the Svitavy railway station. There, they forced the ice-sealed train doors open and removed some one hundred Jewish men and women, nearly frozen and resembling corpses, who were then swiftly taken to the Brünnlitz factory and nourished back to life, an undertaking to which Schindler's wife, Emilie, particularly devoted herself. Those whom it was too late to save were buried with proper Jewish rites.

Schindler was devoted to the humane treatment of his Jewish workers and to their physical and psychological needs. He

"The names on the list are definite. But the circumstances encourage legends. The problem is that the list is remembered with an intensity which, by its very heat, blurs. The list is an absolute good. The list is life. All around its cramped margins lies the gulf."

Thomas Keneally,
Schindler's List,
1982

Schindler's List

One day in 1980 Australian author Thomas Keneally visited a luggage store in Beverly Hills, California, own by a man named Leopold Page. Page, whose original name was Leopold Pfefferberg, told Keneally a fantastic story about a German-Catholic businessman and war profiteer named Oskar Schindler, who had risked his life and sacrificed his fortune to save hundreds of Jews during World War II. Page himself was a "Schindlerjuden," one of the Jews saved by Oskar Schindler. Intrigued by Page's story, Keneally sought out and interviewed other Schindlerjuden; Keneally also spoke to many of Schindler's friends and associates. Keneally later visited the setting of Schindler's activities in Poland, and researched countless archival documents and testimonials about the Holocaust. In 1982 Keneally published a book entitled *Schindler's Arc*, a novelized account of Oskar Schindler's rescue efforts during World War II. *Schindler's Arc* received great acclaim, was widely read, and won Britain's prestigious Booker Prize. One of the book's admirers was American film director Steven Spielberg. In 1993 Spielberg released a powerful film adaptation of Keneally's book under the title *Schindler's List*. The movie starred Irish actor Liam Neeson as Schindler. *Schindler's List,* shot mostly on location in Poland, earned Spielberg the best reviews of his career and won seven Academy Awards, including Best Picture and Best Director. Keneally's book was later reprinted with the same title as the film.

used his good connections with the Abwehr and with friends in high government positions, as well as his jovial and good-humored disposition, to befriend and ingratiate himself with high-ranking SS commanders in Poland. This stood him in good stead when he needed their assistance in extracting valuable and crucial favors from them, such as ameliorating conditions and mitigating punishments of Jews under his care. He was imprisoned on several occasions when the Gestapo accused him of corruption, only to be released on the intervention of his connections in Berlin ministries.

In 1962 Oskar Schindler planted a tree bearing his name in the Garden of the Righteous at Yad Vashem, Jerusalem. ◆

Schiper, Ignacy Yitzhak

1884–1943

Jewish historian and public figure. Schiper was born in Tarnów, in Eastern Galicia, and studied at the universities of Kraków and Vienna, majoring in philosophy. In 1907 he was awarded the degree of doctor of jurisprudence, his thesis dealing with the economic situation of the Jews of Poland in the Middle Ages. In the pre–World War I period, Schiper was constantly on the move through the towns and cities of Galicia as a lecturer and propagandist on behalf of his party, the Poh'alei Zion Zionist Socialists. He was elected to the Sejm (the Polish parliament) in 1919 and held his seat until 1927. He left his party over differences with its leadership and joined the General Zionists, but continued to play an important role in the Polish Zionist movement and in Jewish public affairs.

Schiper was a prolific and original historian, ranked as one of the two outstanding Jewish historians in independent Poland (the other was Meir Balaban). His studies dealt with a broad range of historical periods and processes, and he advanced innovative and bold theses, not all of which were accepted by his colleagues. He regarded himself as the historian of the people, stressing the study of economic activities and the struggle for survival of the ordinary Jew, in contrast to his predecessors, who concerned themselves with learned and prominent Jews. Schiper greatly influenced the young Jewish historians who embarked on their scholarly research in the interwar period, among them Emanuel Ringelblum.

When World War II broke out in September 1939, Schiper was seriously ill, but the difficulties and dangers of that fateful moment spurred him to further activity. He had been about to leave Poland for Palestine, but was prevented from doing so by the abrupt closing of the Italian Travel Agency in Poland. During the war and the existence of the Warsaw ghetto, Schiper was active in public affairs. He often appeared at public meetings, took part in Idische Kultur Organizacje (Jewish Culture Organization) activities, and lectured in the clandestine seminars held by the He-Haluts Zionist movement. He spoke out against the positions taken by the Warsaw Judenrat (Jewish Council) and the corruption in its ranks. For a while he served on a committee appointed to suggest ways of improving the work of the Judenrat, but its attempts proved of no avail.

Even in the ghetto, Schiper continued his scholarly work. At a closed Zionist meeting held during Passover 1942, he stated that when the time came for the Jews to face deportation from the ghetto, they should rise up and fight like the Maccabees, for the sake of their honor. In the event, however, when the deportations were launched in July 1942, Schiper opposed a policy of resistance. In a statement he made at the time, he

1884 Schiper is born in Tarnów, in Eastern Galicia.

1907 Schiper is awarded the doctor of jurisprudence degree.

1919 Schiper is elected to the Polish parliament.

1927 Schiper leaves his parliament seat and joins the General Zionists.

1939 Schiper's plan to leave Poland for Palestine is foiled.

1942 Schiper tells Jews they should fight like the Maccabees, but opposes a policy of resistance.

1943 Schiper tries to escape to refuge among the Poles, but lacks the money to be smuggled to the "Aryan" side.

1943 Schiper is seized and deported to Majdanek.

1943 Schiper is killed during the general massacre of Jews.

pointed out that the Jewish people had on more than one occasion gone through difficult trials and had suffered destruction and loss of life, but by accepting partial losses they had managed to keep intact their identity as a people and had assured their continued existence.

Schiper lived through most of the deportations from the Warsaw ghetto, but after the January 1943 deportation he came to the conclusion that the fate of the Jews of Warsaw was sealed, and tried to escape to take refuge among the Poles, on their side of the city. Schiper, however, was "as poor as a church mouse" (as Ringelblum put it in a biographical sketch of him), and could not afford the cost of being smuggled over to the "Aryan" side of Warsaw and safeguarded there. He was seized during the period of the final deportation and the ghetto uprising, and was deported to Majdanek, where he was apparently killed in the course of the general massacre of Jews in the Lublin camps in November 1943. ◆

Schmid, Anton

1900–1942

German soldier who rescued Jews during the Holocaust. A sergeant in the Wehrmacht, stationed in Vilna, Schmid was responsible for collecting straggling German soldiers near the railway station and reassigning them to new units. A large group of Jews from the Vilna ghetto were assigned to different labor duties in Schmid's outfit: upholstering, tailoring, locksmithing, and shoe mending. He gained their affection and confidence. Shocked by the brutalities of the mass killings at Ponary, Schmid decided in late 1941 to do whatever he could to help Jews survive. He managed to release Jews incarcerated in the notorious Lakishki jail, rescued Jews in various ways, and surreptitiously supplied food and provisions to Jews inside the ghetto. In three houses in Vilna under his supervision, Jews were hidden in the cellars during Nazi-staged *Aktionen*. Schmid also became personally involved with leading figures in the Jewish underground, such as Mordecai Tenenbaum (Tamaroff), and cooperated with them. He helped some of them reach Warsaw and Białystok (to report on the mass

1900 Schmid is born in Germany.

1941 Schmid decides to do whatever is necessary to help Jews.

1942 Schmid is arrested and executed.

1964 Schmid is designated a Yad Vashem "Righteous among the Nations."

killings at Ponary) by transporting them over long distances in his truck. Some of these underground operatives met, planned activities, and slept in his home. He sent other Jews to ghettos that were relatively more secure at that time, those of Voronovo, Lida, and Grodno.

The circumstances of Schmid's arrest are still shrouded in mystery. It was later learned that he was arrested in January 1942 and was sentenced to death by a military tribunal. He was executed on April 13 of that year and was buried in a Vilna cemetery. In 1964 Schmid was posthumously recognized by Yad Vashem as a "Righteous among the Nations." ◆

Schonfeld, Solomon

1912–1982

English rabbi, educator, and rescue activist. Schonfeld studied at Slobodka, Lithuania, and at Nitra, in Slovakia. In Nitra he became the student and lifelong friend of Rabbi Michael Dov Weissmandel, who helped inspire his rescue work. At twenty-two, Schonfeld succeeded his father as rabbi of Adas Yisroel, a small Orthodox congregation in the Stamford Hill section of London; principal of the first Jewish Secondary School; and presiding rabbi of the Union of Orthodox Hebrew Congregations.

Schonfeld was the creator of the Chief Rabbi's Religious Emergency Council (CRREC), a rescue organization nominally under the **auspices** of Chief Rabbi Dr. Joseph Hertz, who was later to become his father-in-law. In actuality, during the CRREC's ten years of existence, Schonfeld was the prime mover behind its every act and rescue effort. The purpose of the

auspices: approval and support.

CRREC, founded in early 1938, was to bring to England Orthodox rabbis, teachers, and other religious functionaries whom the British refugee organizations did not wish to sponsor, considering them "unproductive." In the winter of 1938 Schonfeld organized two children's transports to bring to London more than 250 Orthodox children from Vienna who were being ignored by the official Jewish community there. Until he could place them, he housed them temporarily in his emptied secondary schools and in his own home. He also established a rabbinical academy, Yeshivat Ohr Torah, to bring over 120 students who were over sixteen years of age.

Although essentially a loner and an iconoclast, Schonfeld won over British public figures and government officials to his rescue schemes. He obtained entry permits that enabled him to rescue more than thirty-seven hundred Jews before and immediately after the war.

During the war, Schonfeld tried to implement a number of rescue schemes, such as obtaining 1,000 visas to Mauritius for alleged "rabbis" that served as protective papers in Nazi-occupied countries. After the war he helped rehabilitate Jewish displaced persons in the British sector of Germany, sending in five synagogue ambulances with ritual objects, kosher food, and medicine. Schonfeld made several trips to Poland and Czechoslovakia to bring children, mostly war orphans, to England. ◆

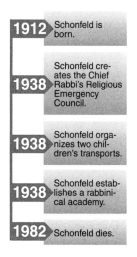

1912	Schonfeld is born.
1938	Schonfeld creates the Chief Rabbi's Religious Emergency Council.
1938	Schonfeld organizes two children's transports.
1938	Schonfeld establishes a rabbinical academy.
1982	Schonfeld dies.

Schwartz, Joseph J.

1899–1975

American Jewish leader; European director of the Joint Distribution Committee (JDC) from 1940 to 1949. Schwartz was born in the Ukraine in 1899 and was taken to the United States in 1907. He studied for the rabbinate at the Rabbi Isaac Elchanan Theological Seminary in New York City and served as rabbi of Congregation Pincus Elijah in New York from 1922 to 1925. In 1927, he received a Ph.D. from Yale University in oriental studies. He was an instructor at the American University in Cairo, Egypt, in 1930, and from 1930 to 1933 he taught at Long Island University. He then joined the Brooklyn Jewish Federation as a social worker; in 1939 he

The Voyage of the *St. Louis*

The *St. Louis* was a German ship that departed from Hamburg for Cuba on May 13, 1939, with 936 passengers, of whom 930 were Jewish refugees bearing certificates permitting them to disembark in Havana. These certificates had been arranged by the Cuban director of immigration, Manuel Benitez Gonzalez, in lieu of the usual immigration visas. Although according to Cuban law such certificates required no fee, Gonzalez sold them for personal gain, for as much as $160. The anger of Cuban government officials concerning Gonzalez's illicit wealth, combined with local sentiment against the influx of additional Jewish refugees and the Cuban government's pro-fascist leanings, led Cuban officials to invalidate the landing certificates on May 5, 1939. The *St. Louis* passengers were aware of the decree, but believed that their certificates, which were bought well before May 5, would be honored. When the *St. Louis* reached Havana on May 27, its passengers were denied entry. The American Jewish Joint Distribution Committee (JDC) attempted to negotiate on behalf of the refugees, but Cuban officials insisted that the ship leave Havana Harbor. The *St. Louis* left Havana on June 2 and traveled in circles in the waters between Florida and Cuba while negotiations continued. American immigration officials announced that the refugees would not be allowed to enter the United States. On June 5 an agreement was reached to allow them to land in Cuba for a $453,000 bond ($500 per refugee), to be deposited by the following day. The JDC could not meet the deadline, and the ship sailed for Europe on June 6. Twenty-nine passengers had been permitted to land, of whom twenty-two were Jews with valid Cuban visas. Great Britain, Belgium, France, and the Netherlands agreed to accept the refugees while the *St. Louis* was en route to Europe. Most of the passengers who took refuge in these countries were later killed by the Nazis.

became an adjunct secretary at the JDC, working with Moses A. Leavitt.

Very soon, Schwartz was sent to serve as the committee's deputy director for Europe, under Morris C. Troper, working out of Paris. By 1940 Troper had returned to the United States, and Schwartz became "Mr. Joint" for Europe. At the time of the fall of France in 1940, Schwartz moved the JDC office to Lisbon, and from there he directed rescue and aid operations throughout the Holocaust period. He was responsible for organizing the emigration from Europe of persons who could still obtain visas to countries in the Western Hemisphere, arranging for berths on Portuguese and Spanish ships. He transmitted funds to France, where his coworkers became active in rescuing and hiding adults and, mainly, some seven thousand children after 1942. Schwartz also actively supported the armed Jewish underground, much against the JDC's policy at that time in the

United States. In Switzerland he nominated Saly Mayer, president of the Federation of Swiss Jewish Communities (Schweizerischer Israelitischer Gemeindebund), as the JDC's Swiss representative. In close cooperation with Schwartz, Mayer transmitted funds to occupied Europe. Schwartz also aided "illegal" Jewish emigration to Palestine in 1940 and 1941, and established another JDC outpost in Istanbul. In conjunction with Judah L. Magnes, president of the Hebrew University, he was responsible for the upkeep of Jewish religious institutions in Palestine and for sending many thousands of parcels to the Soviet Union from Tehran. These saved the lives of thousands of Jewish refugees in the starvation-ridden areas of Soviet Central Asia.

At the end of the war, Schwartz moved back to liberated Paris, reorganized the French JDC operation, and began sending JDC teams to the newly established displaced persons' camps in Germany, fighting for Allied army recognition and entry permits, which were slow in coming. Schwartz also negotiated agreements with eastern European authorities to send JDC teams to these countries. He directed his attention especially to Hungary and Romania, where relatively large Jewish communities had survived. It would be no exaggeration to say that until about 1947 or 1948 the Jews in these countries were kept alive, in part at least, by the JDC, directed by Schwartz. In Poland, too, Schwartz managed to negotiate agreements with the local government enabling the JDC to send aid in attempts at Jewish reconstruction, for instance in the newly Polish region of Silesia. Also of vital importance was Schwartz's help in facilitating the illegal movement of Jewish refugees through Europe with the Beriḥa organization, which was directed by local Zionist-oriented and Palestinian Jewish activists.

In August 1948 Schwartz met with Israeli officials and arranged for the JDC's crucial support for mass emigration to Israel. At the same time, he negotiated an agreement establishing the Malben service for the aged in Israel, which provided care for elderly refugees immigrating there. In 1950, with the closure of the displaced persons' camps in Germany, where he had supervised the JDC's activities, Schwartz became the vice-chairman of the United Jewish Appeal in the United States, raising money for the new state of Israel. From 1955 he was executive vice president of the State of Israel Bonds Organization, until his retirement in 1970.

1899 Schwartz is born in Ukraine.

1907 Schwartz is taken to the United States.

1922 Schwartz begins serving as a rabbi in New York.

1927 Schwartz receives a Ph.D. in oriental studies from Yale University.

1930 Schwartz begins teaching at Long Island University.

1939 Schwartz becomes an adjunct secretary at the JDC.

1940 Schwartz moves the JDC office to Lisbon; begins to aid "illegal" Jewish emigration to Palestine.

1943 Schwartz's coworkers rescue some seven thousand children.

1947 Schwartz's efforts keep Hungarian and Romanian Jews alive.

1948 Schwartz arranges for JDC's support for mass emigration to Israel.

1955 Schwartz becomes vice president of the State of Israel Bonds Organization.

1975 Schwartz dies.

Schwartz was one of American Jewry's outstanding leaders. Possessing an overpowering intelligence and a great store of general Jewish knowledge, a pro-Zionist sympathizer who was very careful to remain objective as one of the heads of a nonpolitical organization, he was a man of tact and a deep understanding of the human condition, a true humanitarian. ◆

Sendler, Irena "Jolanta"

1916–

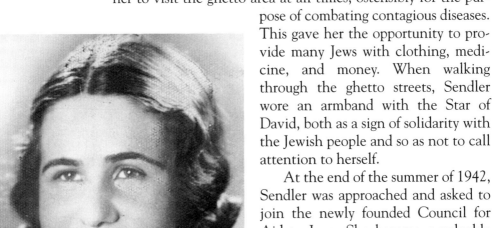

One of the most active members in the Rada Pomocy Żydom (Council for Aid to Jews), known as Zegota, a Polish underground organization in the Warsaw area. From the early days of the German occupation, Sendler worked to alleviate the suffering of many of her Jewish friends and acquaintances. Employed in the Social Welfare Department of the Warsaw municipality, she received a special permit allowing her to visit the ghetto area at all times, ostensibly for the purpose of combating contagious diseases. This gave her the opportunity to provide many Jews with clothing, medicine, and money. When walking through the ghetto streets, Sendler wore an armband with the Star of David, both as a sign of solidarity with the Jewish people and so as not to call attention to herself.

At the end of the summer of 1942, Sendler was approached and asked to join the newly founded Council for Aid to Jews. She became a valuable asset to Zegota, for she had already enlisted a large group of people in her charitable work, including her companion Irena Schulz, who had a widespread network of contacts in the ghetto and on the "Aryan" side. Irena Sendler specialized in smuggling Jewish children out of the ghetto and finding secure places for them with non-Jewish families in the War-saw region. Each of her coworkers was made responsible for several blocks of apartments where Jewish children were sheltered. She herself oversaw eight or ten apartments where Jews were hiding under her care. The sheltering families were supported by funds from Zegota.

In October 1943 Irena Sendler was arrested by the Gestapo, taken to the infamous Pawiak Prison, and brutally tortured to make her reveal information. Failing to elicit such information, her interrogators told her she was doomed. However, on the day set for her execution, she was freed, after her underground companions bribed one of the Gestapo agents. Officially she was listed on public bulletin boards as among those executed. Forced to stay out of sight for the remainder of the German occupation, Sendler continued working surreptitiously for Zegota. In 1965 she was recognized by Yad Vashem as a "Righteous among the Nations." ◆

1916 Sendler is born.

1942 Sendler joins the new Council for Aid to Jews.

1943 Sendler is arrested by the Gestapo and tortured at Pawiak prison.

1965 Sendler is designated a Yad Vashem "Righteous among the Nations."

Sereni, Enzo

1905–1944

Zionist emissary, pioneer, and thinker; one of the parachutists sent by the Palestinian Yishuv to occupied Europe. Sereni was born in Rome, of an old and distinguished family. As a youth he became a Zionist socialist and an activist among Jewish youth in Italy. He received a doctorate in philosophy in 1925. In 1927 he immigrated to Palestine, where he worked in the orchards. The following year he helped found Kibbutz Givat Brenner. In 1931 and 1932 Sereni was an emissary for Zionist Youth Movements in Germany; he was there again in 1933 and 1934, working in the Haavara and the Youth Aliya.

At the outbreak of World War II, Sereni enlisted in the British army and was employed in the antifascist campaign in Egypt. He was sent in 1941 to Iraq, where he helped to prepare the Jewish youth for underground activity and for immigration to Palestine. In 1943 he was appointed a liaison officer between the Palestinian parachutists and their British trainers, and despite his age and the opposition of all his acquaintances he

1905 Sereni is born in Rome.

1927 Sereni immigrates to Palestine and works in the orchards.

1928 Sereni helps found Kibbutz Givat Brenner.

1931 Sereni becomes an emissary for Zionist youth movements in Germany.

1941 Sereni is sent to Iraq and helps prepare the Jewish youth.

1944 Sereni is dropped into Italy and captured by Germans; he is executed at Dachau.

insisted on joining them. In May 1944 he was dropped into northern Italy, where he was captured by the Germans. He was interned in Dachau, and became a leading figure among the prisoners. Sereni was executed there in November 1944.

Sereni had a unique, multifaceted, and lively personality; he combined a broad general education and individualism with a socialist labor movement outlook and constant activity for the general interest of the community. He studied classical literature and pursued scholarly research, particularly on fascism. After his death, his widow, Ada Sereni (née Ascarelli), was one of the leaders of the "illegal" immigration movement to Palestine. ◆

Silver, Abba Hillel

1893–1963

A merican rabbi and communal leader. Born in Lithuania and brought to the United States in 1902, Silver was ordained at Hebrew Union College in 1915. He became the Rabbi of the Temple at Congregation Tifereth Israel, in Cleveland, Ohio, in 1917—a position he retained for the remainder of his career. As rabbi, Silver became active in a number of social causes, among which Zionism and his efforts at fostering Jewish education were paramount. Known for his skill as a public speaker, Silver considered himself a political Zionist in the Herzlian mold. His emphasis on political Zionism led Silver to support Chaim Weizmann in the latter's dispute with Louis Brandeis over the wisdom of continued diplomatic activity, in light of the acceptance of the British Mandate for Palestine. Considered a "radical" within American Zionism, Silver was closely identified with the Republican party, in contrast to the majority of Jewish leaders, who were Democrats.

With the rise of the Nazis, Silver returned to political activity after a hiatus of nearly a decade. His militantly anti-Nazi position catapulted him to a central role in American Jewish life. Silver was one of the organizers of the American Jewish anti-Nazi boycott, despite the advice of more moderate leaders against such "provocations." His boycott activities led him to oppose the Haavara Agreement, which he saw as breaking the unity of the Jewish anti-Nazi front. In 1938 Silver assumed the

> "We cannot truly rescue the Jews of Europe unless we have free immigration into Palestine."
>
> Abba Hillel Silver

chairmanship of the United Palestine Appeal (UPA). He did not see the UPA as a philanthropic agency, since he rejected the idea that Zionism could ever be reduced to philanthropism, but rather as an educational tool to unify American Jewry for its decisive political role.

During the 1930s Silver opposed acts designed to drive a wedge between the Zionist movement and Great Britain, such as efforts at illegal immigration into Palestine. Silver also opposed the Peel partition plan (1937), believing that Britain's reversal of its Palestine policy was only temporary. However, the war, the White Paper of 1939, and the disturbing news filtering out of Nazi-occupied Europe led to a rethinking of his position, drawing Silver into the **maximalist statist** camp of David Ben-Gurion, as opposed to the **minimalist** position of Stephen S. Wise and Chaim Weizmann.

maximalist: one who advocates immediate action to secure the whole of a program or set of goals.

Silver first articulated his statist position at the UPA annual convention of January 25–26, 1941, and the need for a Jewish state became central to all of his activities. In cooperation with Ben-Gurion, Silver organized the Extraordinary Zionist Conference, which met at the Biltmore Hotel in New York from May 9 to 11, 1942. The resulting Biltmore Resolution was seen by Silver as a declaration of the Jews' intention to establish Palestine as a Jewish commonwealth after the war. He devoted himself to turning this dream into a reality, assuming the cochairmanship, with Wise, of the American Zionist Emergency Council (AZEC). Silver's strategy was to arouse public opinion, thereby gaining the support of American politicians for Jewish and Zionist causes. He saw no efficacy in quiet diplomacy, which relied on the goodwill of leaders who had little or no interest in Jewish issues. Silver especially distrusted Franklin Delano Roosevelt, summing up his evaluation of the president by quoting the biblical verse "Put not your faith in princes."

statist: a person who advocates the formation and maintenance of a strong state.

minimalist: one who favors restricting the achievement of a set of goals to a minimum.

Silver's activism met with some success, but also with a good deal of opposition. Many Zionists, Wise included, felt uncomfortable with Silver's brash tactics and maximalist demands. Instrumental in the creation of the American Jewish Conference (1942), Silver's rhetoric kept the commonwealth plank on the agenda, helping to win the conference's overwhelming approval. The victory was short-lived, however, since the American Jewish Committee rejected the idea of Jewish statehood and withdrew from the conference. Tension between Wise and Silver broke out into an open rift in 1944 when the latter worked, against the wishes of the administration, for a congressional resolution supporting the Jewish commonwealth. Silver resigned from the AZEC in December 1944, but returned as sole chairman in June 1945 when American Zionists and many non-Zionist American Jews, shocked by the horrors of the Holocaust, realized that his call for an unrelenting public campaign on behalf of Jewish interests was justified. He played a major role in the 1947 campaign of the Jewish Agency at the United Nations to approve the plan for the partition of Palestine.

Silver has been criticized for his stubborn emphasis on Palestine as the only haven for European Jewry in its hour of need. In his passionate speech at the American Jewish Conference, he stated his credo:

> We cannot truly rescue the Jews of Europe unless we have free immigration into Palestine. We cannot have free immigration into Palestine unless our political rights are recognized there. Our political rights cannot be recognized there unless our historical connection with the country is acknowledged and our right to rebuild our national home is reaffirmed. These are inseparable links in the chain. The whole chain breaks if one of the links is missing.

Silver was approached by Peter Bergson (Hillel Kook) to head the Emergency Committee to Save the Jewish People of Europe. Seeking an establishment leader to give his organization some respectability, Bergson did not see Silver's activist policy as incompatible with his own. Silver, however, refused to cooperate, mistrusting Bergson's motives.

A respected scholar, Silver was also a gifted writer. His works include *The History of Messianic Speculation in Israel* (1927), *Where Judaism Differed* (1956), two collections of speeches: *World Crisis and Jewish Survival* (1941) and *Vision and Victory* (1941), and numerous articles. ◆

1893 Silver is born in Lithuania.

1902 Silver moves to America.

1915 Silver is ordained.

1917 Silver becomes rabbi of a temple in Cleveland.

1938 Silver becomes chair of the UPA.

1941 Silver articulates his statist position.

1942 Silver organizes the Zionist Conference.

1944 Silver resigns from the AZEC.

1947 Silver plays a major role in the campaign to partition Palestine.

1963 Silver dies.

Šimaite, Ona

1899–1970

Lithuanian librarian who helped Jews in the Vilna ghetto. A librarian at Vilna University, Šimaite was distressed at the sight of Jewish sufferings at the hands of the Germans and their Lithuanian collaborators. She later explained: "I could no longer go on with my work. I could not remain in my study. I could not eat. I was ashamed that I was not Jewish myself." Under the pretext of recovering library books loaned from the university to Jewish students, she was able to obtain permission to enter the ghetto. There she saved valuable literary and historical works entrusted to her by public institutions, such as YIVO (the Yivo Institute for Jewish Research), and private individuals, among them the Yiddish poet Abraham Sutzkever. She hid these materials in various places, including under the floor of her apartment.

Šimaite also negotiated the return of Jewish possessions, left in non-Jewish hands, that were needed by the ghetto dwellers to purchase necessary foodstuffs, and she recruited people to hide Jews outside the ghetto. On her daily visits to the ghetto she brought food and other provisions for needy Jews there. Befriending Tanya Sterntal, a lone Jewish girl in the ghetto, Šimaite decided to rescue her. Spiriting her out under the watchful eyes of the guards at the gates, Šimaite hid her in several locations, until she was accidentally discovered.

Ona Šimaite was arrested in the summer of 1944 when she adopted a ten-year-old Jewish girl, registering her as a relative from a bombed-out town that, upon inquiry, turned out to be fictitious. She was brutally tortured to elicit information on her Jewish contacts but did not divulge names or places. Because of these tortures her spine was ruptured, causing her pain for the rest of her life.

The Nazis wanted to execute Šimaite but her friends from Lithuanian academic circles bribed the Gestapo and succeeded in mitigating her sentence to imprisonment in a concentration camp. Deported to the Dachau camp, she was later transferred to southern France, where she was liberated in August 1944. Except for a brief spell in Israel, Ona continued living in France until her death.

Ona Šimaite consistently refused any honors for her deeds during the war, claiming that it was the suffering Jews who were the true heroes. In the words of Abba Kovner, the poet-fighter of the Vilna ghetto: "If there are ten Righteous among the Nations [in the world], Ona Šimaite is certainly one of them." She was recognized by Yad Vashem as a "Righteous among the Nations" in 1966. ◆

"I could no longer go on with my work. I could not remain in my study. I could not eat. I was ashamed that I was not Jewish myself."

Ona Šimaite

1899 Šimaite is born in Lithuania.

1944 Šimaite is arrested and tortured for adopting a Jewish child.

1944 Šimaite is deported to Dachau.

1944 Šimaite is transported to France and liberated.

1966 Šimaite is designated a "Righteous among the Nations."

1970 Šimaite dies.

Skobtsova, Elizaveta (Mother Maria)

1891–1945

tsarist: relating to the Russian emperor.

Nun in France who assisted Jews during the Holocaust. Skobtsova was born in Riga, Latvia, where her father, Juri Pilenko, was chief prosecutor for the **tsarist** government there. She wrote poetry in her youth, and one of her works, "Scythian Shards," was well known in literary circles in Saint Petersburg. During the Russian Revolution, Skobtsova joined the Socialist Revolutionary party. Sent to Anapa, on the Black Sea, she was arrested by the White forces. After her release, she married and bore two children. Settling in France, Skobtsova decided, after the death of her four-year-old daugh-

ter, to become a nun in the Russian Orthodox church. In 1932 she took her vows and chose the name of Maria.

Until the outbreak of World War II, Skobtsova coordinated welfare activities for Russian emigrés in France. Her church purchased for this purpose a building in Paris on Rue de Lourmel that soon became the nerve center of her extensive activities. Her immediate aide was Father Dimitri Klepinin, also a refugee from Russia.

With the onset of the persecution of Jews in France by the Germans, she decided that her Christian calling required her to come to the aid of Jews in whatever way possible. As a first step, she made the church's free kitchen available for impoverished Jews; then, she arranged temporary shelter for others. Father Klepinin issued false baptismal certificates for those needing new identities. Stunned by the German edict in June 1942 requiring Jews to wear the yellow star she penned the following poem:

> Israel—
> Two triangles, a star
> The shield of King David, our forefather,
> This is election, not offense
> The great path and not an evil.
> Once more is a term fulfilled
> Once more roars the trumpet of the end
> And the fate of a great people
> Once more is by the prophet proclaimed.
>
> Thou art persecuted again, O Israel
> But what can human ill-will mean to thee,
> Thee, who has heard the thunder from Sinai?

In July 1942 Mother Maria succeeded in penetrating the Vélodrome d'Hiver sports stadium in Paris, where thousands of Jews had been assembled on the eve of their deportation. With the connivance of garbage collectors, she smuggled out several children in garbage bins. She continued her charitable work for Jews in spite of warnings that she was being closely watched by the Gestapo. Arrested together with Klepinin on February 8, 1943, she readily admitted to the charge of helping Jews elude Nazi roundups. She was sent to the Ravensbrück concentration camp, where she died from exhaustion on March 31, 1945, days before the camp's liberation. Father Klepinin perished earlier, in February 1944, in the Doramittelbau camp.

Mother Maria and Father Klepinin were both recognized as "Righteous among the Nations" by Yad Vashem. ◆

Sousa Mendes, Aristides de

1885–1954

> *"My desire is to be with God against man, rather than with man against God."*
>
> Aristides de Sousa Mendes

Portuguese career diplomat. Sousa Mendes was consul general in Bordeaux, France, in May 1940, when the Anglo-French front collapsed in the north. A wave of refugees, among them thousands of Jews, hastened to the south of France in the hope of crossing into Spain and proceeding to Portugal, from where they hoped to escape from Europe by ship. In order to cross the Spanish frontier, the refugees needed a Portuguese entry or transit visa. However, on May 10, 1940, the Portuguese government banned the further passage of refugees through its territory and instructed its consular representatives in France not to issue visas to most persons who had no final entry goal and who were seeking temporary shelter in Portugal; no visas at all were to be issued to Jews.

The sudden halt of entry into Portugal via Spain created a 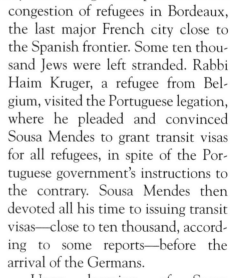 congestion of refugees in Bordeaux, the last major French city close to the Spanish frontier. Some ten thousand Jews were left stranded. Rabbi Haim Kruger, a refugee from Belgium, visited the Portuguese legation, where he pleaded and convinced Sousa Mendes to grant transit visas for all refugees, in spite of the Portuguese government's instructions to the contrary. Sousa Mendes then devoted all his time to issuing transit visas—close to ten thousand, according to some reports—before the arrival of the Germans.

Upon learning of Sousa Mendes's insubordination, the Portuguese government ordered his immediate recall and dispatched two emissaries from Lisbon to accompany him home. On their way to the Spanish border with Sousa Mendes, they stopped in Bayonne, a city that came under the jurisdiction of the Bordeaux consulate. Visiting at the local Portuguese legation, Sousa Mendes, still the formal superior of the Bayonne consul, ordered him to issue special visas to the Jewish refugees waiting outside. These visas were unique documents: slips of paper with the consulate seal and the inscription "The Portuguese government requests of the Spanish government the courtesy of allowing the bearer to pass freely through Spain. He is a refugee from the European conflict en route to Portugal."

Upon his return to Lisbon, the government, fuming at Sousa Mendes's disobedience, had him summarily dismissed from the Ministry of Foreign Affairs, with all his retirement and severance pensions suspended. Sousa Mendes countered by appealing directly to the government and the National Assembly to be reinstated, but to no avail. Burdened with the task of feeding a family that included thirteen children, and with no other means at his disposal, Sousa Mendes sank into poverty. He died in 1954, forgotten, heartbroken, and impoverished. (His wife had died earlier, in 1948.) In 1966, through the efforts of his daughter Joana in the United States, he was posthumously honored by Yad Vashem as a "Righteous among the Nations."

Sousa Mendes explained the motivation of his actions as follows: "If thousands of Jews can suffer because of one Catholic [i.e., Hitler], then surely it is permitted for one Catholic to suffer for so many Jews." On another occasion, he had stated: "My desire is to be with God against man, rather than with man against God."

In 1985 an international committee for the perpetuation of Sousa Mendes's memory was set up. Bending to foreign pressure, in 1988 the Portuguese National Assembly agreed to award him a full rehabilitation. ◆

1885 Sousa Mendes is born.

1940 Sousa Mendes issues thousands of transit visas to Jews.

1948 Sousa Mendes's wife, mother of 13, dies.

1954 Sousa Mendes dies forgotten, heartbroken, and impoverished.

1966 Sousa Mendes is designated a Yad Vashem "Righteous among the Nations."

1985 An international committee is established to remember Sousa Mendes.

1988 The Portuguese government fully restores Sousa Mendes's reputation.

Spiegel, Isaiah

1906 –

Writer, poet, and critic of Yiddish literature. Spiegel grew up in Łódź, received a traditional education, and went on to study in a public school. He taught Yiddish and Yiddish literature in the Central Yiddish Schools

Organization of the Bund. Spiegel remained in the Łódź ghetto throughout its existence, from May 1940 until its liquidation in August 1944, and was employed by the Judenrat (Jewish Council) in various departments. In August 1944 he was deported to Auschwitz-Birkenau and spent the rest of the war in several labor camps.

Spiegel first published Yiddish poems in 1922. In 1930 his first book of poetry appeared in print, *Mitn Punim tsu der Zun* (Facing the Sun). On the eve of World War II he had another book of poems ready for publication, as well as a collection of stories about the Jewish weavers in the slum quarter in which he had grown up, and a Yiddish translation of Byron's poem "Cain." All these manuscripts were lost in the war.

While in the ghetto, Spiegel wrote many short stories and poems. He was one of the most prolific and important writers among the sixty or so in the Łódź ghetto. When the ghetto was liquidated in August 1944, Spiegel hid some of his writings in a cellar and took the rest with him to Auschwitz, only to have them taken away on his arrival. After the liberation he returned to Łódź and found the manuscripts of sixteen of the stories he had hidden there; he reconstructed the rest of them from memory and published them. He also published a collection of poems that included those he had composed during the war.

Spiegel's works that were saved in manuscript form all date from the early period of the ghetto, prior to the first great deportation of January to May 1942; they refer to events that occurred no later than the spring of 1941. The original manuscript differs from the published version, the many dissimilarities and revisions reflecting the changes in the author's view as a result of the Holocaust experience that had taken place in the interval.

Spiegel's ghetto writings reflect the prevailing circumstances: the lack of contact with the world outside and the absence of an armed resistance movement in the ghetto. His stories deal with the inner life of the people imprisoned in the ghetto and the human relationships between them. No mention is made of the Judenrat chairman, Mordechai Chaim Rumkowski, of the Jüdischer Ordnungsdienst (Jewish ghetto police) chiefs, or of the Germans who were in charge of the ghetto administration. The famous story *Geto Malkhes* (The Ghetto Kingdom) does not refer to "King" Rumkowski, but to "King" Hunger. Other stories depict simple people whose lot is hunger, cold, and death. Spiegel also describes instances of alienation between individuals, Jews who were unable to stand up under the terrible pressure of life in the ghetto. In all the stories there is contrast and dramatic tension between the author's muted and moderate style and the horror that pervades the subject matter. Spiegel's talent for shocking people was notably demonstrated when one of his poems was recited at a theater performance attended by Rumkowski: the Judenrat chairman's first reaction was to state that the poem's author had to be driven out of the ghetto at once.

From 1945 to 1948 Spiegel lived in Łódź and once again taught school. He lived in Warsaw from 1948 to 1950 and was secretary of the Polish Yiddish Writers' Association. Spiegel then settled in Israel, where he writes literary criticism and composes stories dealing with Israeli themes. ◆

> *"Heaven, merciful heaven,*
> *Why do I stammer in my prayers."*
> Isaiah Spiegel,
> from the poem
> "Merciful Heaven"

Sternbuch, Recha

1905–1971

Recha Sternbuch and her husband, Isaac, were Swiss representatives of the Va'ad Ha-Hatsala rescue committee of the Orthodox rabbis in the United States. Initially active in assisting Jewish refugees coming to Switzerland as well as Jews entering there illegally from France, the Sternbuchs headed the Hilfsverein für Jüdische Flüchtlinge in Shanghai (Relief Organization for Jewish Refugees in Shanghai), established in 1941 to provide aid for rabbis and yeshiva students stranded in Shanghai. They later expanded their rescue activities, changing the name of their organization to the Hilfsverein für Jüdische Flüchtlinge im Ausland (Relief Organization for Jewish Refugees Abroad) and initiating numerous projects: sending parcels to Jews in Poland and Czechoslovakia, rescuing Jews by using Latin American passports, maintaining contact with Jewish leaders in Slovakia and Hungary, and monitoring developments throughout Nazi-occupied Europe. On September 2, 1942, the Sternbuchs informed Jewish leaders in the United States of the large-scale deportations taking place from the Warsaw ghetto and urged them to enlist the aid of American leaders. The Sternbuchs took part in negotiations that

1905 Sternbuch is born.

1941 Relief Organization for Jewish Refugees in Shanghai is established.

1942 Sternbuch and her husband inform U.S. Jews of deportations.

1945 Twelve hundred Jews are rescued due to the Sternbuchs' efforts.

1971 Sternbuch dies.

resulted in the rescue from the Theresienstadt ghetto of 1,200 Jews, who arrived in Switzerland on February 6, 1945. After World War II, Recha Sternbuch played a very active role in recovering Jewish children from non-Jewish homes, orphanages, and convents. ◆

Sugihara, Sempo

1900–1986

Japanese consul general in Kovno, Lithuania, who actively assisted Jewish refugees in 1940. In early August of that year, three weeks before the Soviet authorities intended to remove all foreign consular representatives from Kovno, Sugihara was approached by Dr. Zorah Warhaftig, a leader of the Mizraḥi religious Zionist movement and a representative of the Jewish Agency Palestine Office in Lithuania. Warhaftig asked Sugihara to grant Japanese transit visas to Polish Jewish refugees stranded in Kovno, as a means for them to obtain Soviet visas. He outlined to Sugihara a plan under which the refugees would travel to the Dutch-controlled island of Curaçao in the Caribbean, where no entry permit was necessary, by way of the USSR and Japan. The Soviets had made their approval of the plan conditional on the refugees' obtaining transit visas from Japan.

Though his government rejected the proposal, Sugihara decided to grant such visas to any Jewish refugees who requested them. During the remaining weeks before he was scheduled to leave Kovno, on August 31, Sugihara devoted most of his time to this matter. Many rabbinical students, such as those of the famed Mir academy, availed themselves of this opportunity to leave

Lithuania; after spending time in China and other countries, they eventually reached the United States and Israel. In all, it appears that at least sixteen hundred visas were issued (Sugihara estimated the figure at some thirty-five hundred).

Sugihara was reassigned to other Japanese legations in Europe. Upon his return to Tokyo in 1947, he was asked to submit his resignation for his insubordination seven years earlier. In 1984 Yad Vashem awarded him the title of "Righteous among the Nations."

Years later, recalling the dramatic and tense days of August 1940, Sugihara explained his predicament: "I really had a hard time, and was unable to sleep for two nights. I thought as follows: 'I can issue transit visas . . . by virtue of my authority as consul. I cannot allow these people to die, people who had come to me for help with death staring them in the eyes. Whatever punishment may be imposed upon me, I know I should follow my conscience'" (Ryusuke Kajiyama, in *Sankei Shinbun Yukan Tokuho*, January 24, 1985). ◆

> *"I cannot allow these people to die, people who had come to me for help with death staring them in the eyes. Whatever punishment may be imposed upon me, I know I should follow my conscience."*
>
> Sempo Sugihara

Sutzkever, Abraham

1913–

Yiddish poet and partisan fighter. Sutzkever was born in Smorgon, Belorussia. During World War I his family fled to Siberia, and in 1922 settled in Vilna, where Sutzkever attended school. In 1930 he joined the Yiddishist scout movement Bin. He wrote poetry from the age of fourteen, but it was not until 1934 that a poem of his appeared in print, in a literary magazine. In the period from 1934 to 1941 Sutzkever's poetic work grew into a unique contribution to Yiddish literature. Beginning in 1935 he was a regular contributor to *Yung-Vilne*, the organ of the modernist writers in Vilna, and to major literary journals in Warsaw and in the United States. Two volumes of poetry that he published before the Holocaust contain the poems he wrote before 1939. From June 1941 to September 1943, Sutzkever lived under the Nazi occupation in Vilna and in the Vilna ghetto. On September 12 of that year he escaped to the forest, together with his wife and Shmaryahu Kaczerginski, and joined the partisans.

> *"The earth still wheels about; and Time has still No power over lasting memory."*
>
> Abraham Sutzkever, from "Spiritual Soil"

Under the Nazi occupation Sutzkever composed over eighty poems. A substantial number of the manuscripts of these poems, or copies of them, were saved by the poet himself. It was only many years later, however, that he published, on the basis of these manuscripts, a small collection of poems from the time he spent in the Vilna ghetto and in the forest, in *Di Ershte Nacht in Geto* (The First Night in the Ghetto; Tel Aviv, 1979).

Sutzkever's ghetto poems are often written around events that he himself experienced. His life in the ghetto and the poetry he wrote there were linked to the cultural and communal life of the ghetto: some poems, for example, were devoted to theatrical performances in the ghetto; others were read in public, as a poem on the opening of an exhibition on May 1, 1943, or a eulogy for a ghetto teacher.

Sutzkever aided in selecting the material to be presented in the ghetto theater and conducted a literary youth circle in the Yugent Klub (Youth Club). While on forced labor, he had to sort for the Germans the collections of books and manuscripts in the library of the Yiddish Institute (YIVO), which was outside the ghetto. Together with Kaczerginski and others, he used the opportunity to acquire weapons and smuggle them into the ghetto. He also smuggled books, manuscripts, and works of art into the ghetto. During the time that he spent in the YIVO building he composed many of his poems, which he then read to his friends in the ghetto and to the members of the Writers' Association that had been formed there. For the dramatic chronicle *Dos Kever-Kind* (Child of the Tomb), which he read to the Writers' Association in May 1942, Sutzkever in July was awarded that year's literary prize. *Kol Nidre,* the great poem that he wrote in February 1943, is the only literary creation to describe a German *Aktion* (the liquidation of Vilna's "small ghetto" on Yom Kippur, the Day of Atonement, October 1, 1941). The dates on the manuscripts of the poems reveal that as the end of the ghetto approached Sutzkever wrote at an increasingly rapid pace. On September 12, 1943, he left the Vilna ghetto clandestinely, with a group of partisans. While serving with the Voroshilov Brigade in the Naroch Forest, Sutzkever also recorded testimonies on the crimes committed by the Nazis and on the struggle with the Nazis, and he kept a record of the partisan movement's history in the area.

On March 12, 1944, Sutzkever was flown from the Naroch Forest to Moscow. He stayed in the Soviet Union until his appearance as a witness for the Soviet prosecution in the Nuremberg Trial, in February 1946. (His appearance was the result of the Jewish Antifascist Committee's intervention with the chairman of the Lithuanian Supreme Soviet.) In 1947 Sutzkever settled in Israel. He continued to write poetry and prose, and became the editor of *Di Goldene Keyt* (The Golden Chain), a Yiddish literary and cultural quarterly that was founded in 1949.

Since 1947 the Holocaust and Israel have been the themes of Sutzkever's literary creations. English translations of some of his poems are in *Burnt Pearls: Ghetto Poems of Abraham Sutzkever* (Oakville, Ontario, 1981) and "Green Aquarium," in *Prooftexts: A Journal of Jewish Literary History* 2/1 (January 1982), pp. 95–121. ◆

Szenes, Hannah

1921–1944

Poet; one of the group of Palestinian Jews who parachuted into Nazi-occupied Europe. Szenes was born into an assimilated Budapest Jewish family that produced a number of Hungary's poets, writers, and musicians. Hannah, too, at an early age displayed remarkable talent, keeping a diary and composing poems—first in Hungarian, and later, when she became an ardent Zionist, also in Hebrew. In 1939, at the age of nineteen, she immigrated to Palestine and two years later joined Kibbutz Sedot Yam, near Caesarea.

Hannah Szenes volunteered in 1943 to parachute into occupied Europe in order to aid Jews under Nazi oppression, and she underwent training in Egypt. In March 1944, about a week before the German occupation of Hungary, Szenes was dropped into Yugoslavia, where, together with fellow parachutists from Palestine, she spent three months with Tito's partisans. She was hoping that with the partisans' help she would be able to get into Hungary. She was convinced that even if she and her comrades did not succeed in rescuing Jews, their personal sacrifice would be a symbol and inspiration to the Jews of Europe. A chance meeting with a Jewish woman partisan inspired her to compose a poem, "Ashrei ha-Gafrur" (Blessed Is the Match),

1921 Szenes is born in Budapest.

1939 Szenes immigrates to Palestine.

1941 Szenes joins Kibbutz Sedot Yam.

1943 Szenes volunteers to parachute into occupied Europe.

1944 Szenes is dropped into Yugoslavia.

1944 Szenes crosses the border into Hungary and is captured.

1944 Szenes is convicted of treason and shot to death.

the text of which she deposited with Reuven Dafni, a fellow parachutist.

At the beginning of June 1944 Szenes crossed the border into Hungary and was immediately captured, with a radio transmitter in her possession. She was taken to Szombathely, put into prison, and tortured; but no torture, and not even the threat that her mother's life was at stake, could extract from her the code for the transmitter with which she had been equipped. After five months in jail she was brought to trial, at which she forcefully and proudly defended herself. She was convicted of treason against Hungary, and shot by a firing squad.

Hannah Szenes has been the subject of novels, plays, and a motion picture; she has become a symbol of courage, steadfastness, and moral strength. Her writings have been published in many editions. In 1950 her remains were brought to Israel and interred on Mount Herzl in Jerusalem. A village, Yad Hannah, commemorates her name. ◆

Szlengel, Władysław

D. APRIL 1943

Jewish poet and songwriter who wrote in Polish. Many of Szlengel's poems were composed in the Warsaw ghetto; they deal with the distressed situation there and with the resistance offered by the Jews in the final months of the ghetto's existence.

Before the war Szlengel wrote poems and lyrics, including satiric poems for the press and stage. In the ghetto, he composed works of prose and poetry for Sztuka (Art), one of the clubs for the emerging elite and the few people of means in the ghetto. Szlengel succeeded in conveying in his writings of that period his views on the occupiers and his misgivings about the running of the ghetto's institutions. Emanuel Ringelblum reported that Szlengel's poems "were highly popular in the ghetto and reflected its moods." They passed from hand to hand and were recited at meetings.

When the deportations from the Warsaw ghetto were launched, Szlengel's mood changed. From then on his works emphasized the terror felt in the ghetto and the bitter settling of accounts between men and God (one of his poems is entitled "A Reckoning with God"). In the poem "Telephone," Szlengel complains that no one is left whom he can call in the Polish side of the city. In his last poems, which he wrote when he was working in a broom workshop, Szlengel records the decline of the ghetto and its final days. One poem titled is "The Small Station of Treblinka," and another, "A Page from the Diary of the *Aktion*." Szlengel was apparently a ghetto policeman for a time, but he resigned, as he was incapable of taking part in the roundups of ghetto inhabitants conducted by the ghetto police during the deportations. Even in the final stages of that period, Szlengel continued to recite his poems before small groups in clandestine gatherings. In these poems, Szlengel bids farewell to life (as in "Five Minutes to Twelve"), expresses his admiration for those offering resistance with weapons in their hands, and calls for revenge:

> Hear, O God of the Germans,
> the Jews praying amid the barbarians,
> an iron rod or a grenade in their hands.
> Give us, O God, a bloody fight
> and let us die a swift death!

Szlengel was killed in April 1943. He is known to have been in a bunker during the Warsaw ghetto uprising, but the circumstances and the exact date of his death are not known. Only a part of his poetry and prose writings has been preserved. A collection of his writings in Polish was published under the title *Co czytałem umarłym* (What I Read to the Dead), the name of one of his prose compositions. ◆

> Szlengel's poems were highly popular in the ghetto, where they were passed from hand to hand and were recited at meetings.

Sztehlo, Gábor

1909–1974

Evangelical minister in Budapest, Hungary, who saved many Jewish children during the Holocaust. Sztehlo represented the Protestant Good Shepherd (Jo Pasztor) Committee before international welfare and rescue organizations. Originally established as an association of Jews converted to Protestantism, this committee, under Sztehlo's leadership, dedicated itself during the second half of 1944 to the rescue of abandoned Jewish children, in coordination with the International Red Cross. In November of that year, with the increase of anti-Jewish terror in the streets of Budapest, Sztehlo decided to expand his aid services to save Jewish children. Other welcome guests included young Jewish conscripts of the Hungarian labor battalions who had deserted their units and sought shelter.

With the intensification of the Russian siege in December 1944, Sztehlo's institutions were damaged by artillery shells, and many were no longer suitable for shelter. Sztehlo then transferred thirty-three children with forged documents to the cellars of his own home. There he hid with his family for twenty feverish days, with shells exploding above them as the Germans on the upper floors of the building exchanged fire with the Russians, a block away. When Budapest was liberated, Sztehlo assembled the children and brought them to new quarters, caring for them until Jewish organizations or families came to claim them. Sensitive to the religious needs of the children, he facilitated their attendance at services in reconstituted synagogues. Survivors credit him with the rescue of hundreds of Jewish children.

In 1972 Gábor Sztehlo was recognized by Yad Vashem as a "Righteous among the Nations." ◆

Tenenbaum, Mordechai

1916–1943

One of the leaders of the Vilna, Warsaw, and Białystok undergrounds (in the last he was also in command of the uprising). Born in Warsaw, Mordechai Tenenbaum (Tamaroff) was the seventh child in a family of moderate means. He went to a Tarbut, a secular school in which Hebrew was the language of instruction. In 1936 he was accepted as a student in the Warsaw Oriental Institute; the knowledge of Semitic languages that he acquired there was to help him later in circulating in occupied Poland by posing as a Tatar. Erudite in literature, history, and philosophy, Tenenbaum was self-taught.

For a short time Tenenbaum was a member of the Ha-Shomer ha-Le'ummi (national guard) movement; in 1937 he joined the Freiheit youth organization (which was renamed Dror). He engaged in training for kibbutz life in Baranovichi and attended a course for Hebrew tutors in Vilna and a military training course organized by his movement in Zielonka. At the end of 1938, Tenenbaum was called to Warsaw to join the staff of

1916 Tenenbaum is born in Warsaw.

1936 Tenenbaum is accepted as a student in the Warsaw Oriental Institute.

1937 Tenenbaum joins the Frieheit youth organization.

1938 Tenenbaum is called to the He-Haluts headquarters in Warsaw.

1939 Tenenbaum remains in Vilna while his comrades go to Palestine.

1941 Vilna is taken by the Germans.

1942 Tenenbaum helps found the ŻOB; leaves for Bialystok to organize a resistance movement.

1943 The Germans begin deporting the Jews of Bialystock.

1943 Tenenbaum succeeds in unifying all the underground movements in the ghetto.

1943 Tenenbaum becomes commander of the Bialystok ghetto united underground.

1943 All trace of Tenenbaum is lost during the ghetto uprising.

the He-Haluts head office. He was a regular contributor to the movement's periodicals, and his ideological articles, which were to guide the movement and its *hakhshara* (agricultural training program), were remarkable for their revolutionary content and the passionate zeal that inspired them.

In September 1939, before the fall of Warsaw, Tenenbaum and his comrades in the He-Haluts head office left the city and made their way to Kovel and Vilna, their purpose being to evade the Germans and reach Palestine. The number of available immigration "certificates" to Palestine was negligible, and Tenenbaum provided his comrades with forged immigration documents; he, however, chose to stay behind in Vilna and see the struggle through.

In June 1941 Vilna was taken by the Germans, who lost no time in launching *Aktionen*. Tenenbaum tried to help his fellow members by providing them with forged work permits, but many were caught. During the lull in the *Aktionen*, Tenenbaum sent his girlfriend, Tama Schneiderman, on a mission to Warsaw. In accordance with a joint decision made by the He-Haluts leaders, he moved the survivors of the He-Haluts kibbutz from Vilna to the Białystok ghetto, which was still relatively quiet. He accomplished this thanks to the help he received from Anton Schmid, an anti-Nazi Austrian sergeant (*Feldwebel*) in the German army.

Tenenbaum took part on January 1, 1942, in a meeting of He-Haluts youth in the ghetto, who issued a call to the Jews not to permit themselves "to be led like sheep to the slaughter," to refuse to cooperate, and to resist deportation by all available means. A copy of this appeal, to which he had added a comment of his own, was hidden away by Tenenbaum and was found in the ghetto after the city was liberated. Tenenbaum left Vilna with forged documents identifying him as a Tatar by the name of Yussuf Tamaroff, and went by train to the Grodno and Białystok ghettos. Together with Zvi Mersik, he arranged a meeting of He-Haluts members in the area and conducted a regional seminar of the movement.

In March of that year, Tenenbaum returned to Warsaw and rejoined his colleagues from the He-Haluts head office. At a meeting attended by representatives of all political parties, he gave a report on the situation in Vilna and the other ghettos he had visited, trying to convince his audience that events in Vilna provided evidence that it was the Germans' policy to exterminate all the Jews under their control. Some of those present did not agree with Tenenbaum's assessment. Shortly thereafter, reports came in of the mass murder of Jews in Lublin and its vicinity and of the gassing of Jews in the Chełmno extermination camp, which the Germans had put into operation in December 1941.

The various movements decided to unite and operate as undergrounds, and Tenenbaum became one of the founders of the Antifascist Bloc (Blok Antyfaszystowski) and one of the editors of its organ, *Der Ruf* (The Call). He visited branches of the movement in the Kraków, Częstochowa, and Będzin ghettos, gathering information and guiding and encouraging the underground activities. Together with Yitzhak Zuckerman, Tenenbaum edited *Yediot*, the underground organ of the Dror movement in the Warsaw ghetto, writing the paper's editorials and contributing articles, thereby reinforcing the fighting spirit of Jewish youth and their determination to resist the Germans. By hiding copies of the paper in safe places, Tenenbaum preserved them for posterity. Tenenbaum was one of the founders of the Żydowska Organizacja Bojowa (Jewish Fighting Organization; ŻOB) in July 1942, and was active in acquiring arms from outside the ghetto and training the movement's members in their use. In November 1942, by decision of the ŻOB and the Żydowski Komitet Narodowy (Jewish National Committee), Tenenbaum left for Białystok in order to organize and lead a resistance movement there. When he arrived, he found the ghetto sealed and surrounded by Germans to prevent the entry of Jews from neighboring communities that were being liquidated. Tenenbaum attempted to reach Grodno, but was stopped on the way by Germans, who discovered that his papers were false. Though shot in the leg, he escaped, and after many vicissitudes managed to reach the one Grodno ghetto that was still in existence (the other having been destroyed).

After recovering from his wounds, Tenenbaum traveled to Białystok, the only other ghetto in the area that was still intact. He sought to unify all the underground movements in the ghetto, to acquire arms, and to manufacture explosive devices. He succeeded in gaining the support of the Judenrat (Jewish Council) chairman, Efraim Barasz, and through him obtained the money needed for his operations. Tenenbaum then assumed yet another task, the establishment of an underground archive. He collected German documents; evidence concern-

> *"Let us fall as heroes, and though we die, yet we shall live."*
> Mordechai Tenenbaum

> Tenenbaum sought to unify all the underground movements in the ghetto, to acquire arms, and to manufacture explosive devices.

manifesto: a written declaration of the views,
intentions, and motives of
a person or group.

ing Białystok, Grodno, and other towns in the area; the minutes of Judenrat meetings and copies of the announcements it had made; and folklore items and songs composed in the ghetto. He also kept a diary and urged others to do so, and wrote articles, letters, and **manifestos.** All this he preserved as a memorial to the Jews, their sufferings, and their struggle against their murderers, and as a means to indict the Germans before history for their unspeakable crimes. He made a firm demand to the Polish underground to supply the ghetto fighters with weapons, and turned with a last-minute appeal to the civilized world to save the remnants of Polish Jewry. His writings are marked by honesty and human warmth as well as by accuracy and clear analysis, and they represent an extraordinary testimony of the era, unparalleled among underground leaders. Only Emanuel Ringelblum's archive can be compared with the record that Tenenbaum bequeathed to posterity.

In January 1943 Tenenbaum sent Tama Shneiderman, his friend and liaison officer, to the Warsaw ghetto, and Bronka Winicki, a young girl from Grodno, to the "Aryan" part of Białystok. Schneiderman took money and reports with her to deliver to the ŻOB. She failed to return from her mission, and her disappearance during the first Warsaw ghetto uprising, which took place that month, ended the contact between Białystok and Warsaw.

At the beginning of February 1943, the Germans began the deportation of the Jews of Białystok. Because of the scarcity of weapons in the underground's possession, Tenenbaum decided to keep his forces intact and hold back, but to intensify efforts to obtain more arms and train his men. He also sent emissaries into the forests to make contact with the partisans and to search for arms. The Jews employed in German factories were instructed to sabotage the products on which they were working. Weapons were stolen from the Germans, food was stockpiled, and, in the large bunker that the Dror underground had built at 7 Chmielna Street, its members listened to foreign broadcasts. Tenenbaum drew up a call for resistance: "Let us fall as heroes, and though we die, yet we shall live." He moderated a heated discussion in Kibbutz Dror in which the issue was whether to fight in the ghetto or to join the partisans in the forest; his position, which prevailed, was that the underground should first fight in the ghetto and only then continue the struggle in the forest. The minutes of that historic meeting have been preserved in the underground's archive. In July 1943 Tenenbaum succeeded in unifying all the underground movements in the ghetto—only a few weeks before the ghetto's liquidation. He became commander of the Białystok ghetto united underground, with Daniel Moszkowicz, a Communist, as his deputy.

On August 16, 1943, anticipating the liquidation of the ghetto by the Germans, Tenenbaum gave the signal for the uprising. His plan was to break the German blockade of the ghetto and thereby to enable many of its inhabitants to escape to the forests and continue the fighting from there. But the German forces surrounding the ghetto were too strong; masses of Jews, who were crowded into a single street, were seized with panic and despair and did not join the fight that the underground had launched. The wooden houses in the ghetto failed to provide any cover for the fighters. Nevertheless, some groups of fighters held out for a month and even harassed the German forces at night; some small groups that had been caught jumped from the trains that were rushing them to their death or fought their way through the German lines and joined the partisans.

On the day of the uprising, Tenenbaum displayed superb self-control and leadership. All trace of him was lost during the fight, and it is not known when or where he fell. Rumor had it that he and his deputy committed suicide. After the liberation the Polish government gave Tenenbaum, posthumously, the award of Virtuti Militari. Most of Tenenbaum's archive is kept by Yad Vashem; a small part is preserved by the Żydowski Instytut Historyczny (Jewish Historical Institute) in Warsaw, and another part by Bet Loḥamei Ha-Getta'ot. ◆

> **All trace of Mordechai Tenebaum was lost during the ghetto uprising, and it is not known when and where he fell.**

van der Voort, Hanna

Dutch rescuer of Jewish children. Hanna van der Voort came from Tienray, in the Limburg province in the southern Netherlands. Together with Nico Dohmen, she helped find hiding places for 123 Jewish children in the southern Netherlands. Receiving these children through an extensive underground network with which they were affiliated, they sought out and arranged temporary and permanent places of refuge with private families, transferring children from place to place as circumstances warranted. The money for the upkeep by the host families originated with an underground organization. Dohmen, as a courier between the sheltering families and the underground, maintained close contact with the children and devoted much time and effort to counseling his wards and lifting up their spirits. They were given special courses on how to behave as Catholic children, but no one tried to convert them.

One account of the help received through Dohmen relates:

> Day and night he was at work to find placement with farmers who had many children of their own and who were willing to feed one more mouth. Nico usually had to speak to the local priest, who in turn convinced the farming family that it was a good deed to save a child. Nico was himself a Catholic and had an easy dialogue with the clergy. Nico played the role of "ersatz father" to dozens of children. In addition, he had to supply food coupons to the family for the child. These had to be stolen from the Germans by another division of the underground.

Day and night [Dohmen] was at work to find placement with farmers who had many children of their own and who were willing to feed one more.

Hanna van der Voort was eventually arrested and tortured by the Germans, who failed to elicit information from her. Her sufferings in jail caused permanent damage to her health. Both Hanna van der Voort and Nico Dohmen were recognized by Yad Vashem as "Righteous among the Nations." ◆

Visser, Lodewijk Ernst

1871–1942

1871 Visser is born in the Netherlands.

1915 Visser becomes a member of the Dutch Supreme Court.

1933 Visser joins the Committee for Special Jewish Affairs.

1939 Visser becomes Dutch Chief Justice.

1940 Visser is suspended from the court after the Germans occupy the Netherlands; becomes chairman of Jewish Coordinating Committee.

1941 Germans dissolve Visser's committee.

1942 Visser dies of a heart attack.

Dutch jurist active in Jewish affairs. Visser held various posts in the Dutch legal system and in 1915 was appointed to the Dutch Supreme Court, becoming Chief Justice in 1939. He was active in the work of Jewish charitable organizations, especially those handling Jewish refugees. In 1933 he joined the Committee for Special Jewish Affairs (headed by Abraham Asscher), which had been founded in the wake of the Nazi rise to power in Germany. After the occupation of the Netherlands by the Germans in May 1940, Visser was suspended from his supreme court post (as were all Jews in government service), and the supreme court, by a vote of 12 to 5, decided not to oppose his suspension.

In December 1940 the major Jewish organizations in the Netherlands established the Joodse Coördinatiecommissie (Jewish Coordinating Committee) as the central organ for confronting the Germans' anti-Jewish policy. Visser became its chairman and in that capacity strongly criticized the action of Asscher and David Cohen in agreeing to set up the Joodse Raad (Jewish Council), as required by the Germans. Visser had profound differences of opinion with the leadership of the Joodse Raad over its policies; in October 1941, however, the Germans dissolved Visser's coordinating committee and made the Amsterdam Joodse Raad the sole representative body of Netherlands Jewry. Visser and Cohen had an animated and important exchange of letters, in which they aired their differing views on the policy to be pursued by Dutch Jewry. Cohen argued that the Jews had to cooperate with the Germans, since they ruled the country, while Visser stated his belief that the far-reaching concessions made by the Joodse Raad to the Germans were quite unjustified and only led to a deterioration in the situation.

Visser firmly believed that the Dutch administration should not be relieved of its constitutional obligation to protect the Jews, as Dutch citizens with equal rights. When he learned that, in retaliation for clashes between Jews and Dutch Nazis, Jewish youngsters had been deported to the Mauthausen camp, to perish there within a short while, Visser addressed passionate appeals to the secretaries-general of the Dutch government departments, calling on them to resist the German anti-Jewish measures. Later he protested against the evacuation of the Jews from various places. He was warned to desist from this campaign, at the risk of being put into a concentration camp. Three days after receiving a warning letter to this effect, Visser suffered a heart attack and died. ◆

Wallenberg, Raoul

1912–?

Swedish diplomat who saved the lives of tens of thousands of Jews in Budapest. Wallenberg was born into a distinguished family of bankers, diplomats, and officers; his father, who died before he was born, was an officer in the Swedish navy. Wallenberg grew up in the house of his stepfather, Frederik von Dardell. He studied architecture in the United States, but then took up banking and international trade, which brought him to Haifa in 1936 for a six months' stay. On the recommendation of the Swedish branch of the World Jewish Congress and with the support of the American War Refugee Board, the Swedish Foreign Ministry, in July 1944, sent Wallenberg to Budapest, in order to help protect over 200,000 Jews who were left in the Hungarian capital after the deportation of 437,000 Hungarian Jews to Auschwitz.

The Swedish legation in Budapest initiated its operation on behalf of the persecuted Jews a short while after the German occupation of Hungary, on March 19, 1944. At that time, Adolf Eichmann and a special detachment under him, together with the Hungarian authorities, began organizing the deportation of the Jews to

Raoul Wallenberg Street

Raoul Wallenberg, the Swedish diplomat who saved tens of thousands of Jews by issuing them special Swedish passports, has become legendary for his heroic rescue efforts. Among the many memorials established in Wallenberg's honor since he disappeared in 1945 is the large number of streets, parks, and plazas named for him around the world. There is a Raoul Wallenberg Square in Stockholm, Sweden, and a Raoul Wallenberg Memorial Park in Budapest, Hungary. Several cities in Israel, including Jerusalem, Haifa, and Tel Aviv, have streets named after Wallenberg. Charleston, South Carolina, has a Raoul Wallenberg Boulevard. In Washington, D.C., the street bordering the United States Holocaust Memorial Museum, formerly 15th street, was renamed Raoul Wallenberg Place by an Act of Congress in 1986. A plaque embedded in the sidewalk along Washington's Raoul Wallenberg Place reads in part: "A shining light in a dark and depraved world, he proved that one person who has the courage to care can make a difference."

"Since my last report the situation regarding the Hungarian Jews has deteriorated considerably. The new government intends to draft the Jewish population to work in the countryside and on the defense of Budapest, and then expel them after the end of the war. The first few have already been taken away."
Raoul Wallenberg, dispatch to the Swedish Foreign Ministry, 1944

their death. The Swedish foreign minister, Ivar Danielsson, had proposed giving provisional Swedish passports to Hungarian Jews who had family ties or commercial connections with Swedish citizens. By the time Wallenberg arrived in Budapest, several hundred such "protective passports" had been issued. His arrival, on July 9, 1944, coincided with the stoppage of the deportations, a decision taken by the Hungarian government as a result of international pressure, including intervention by King Gustav V of Sweden.

The protective operation carried out by the Swedish legation, in conjunction with other diplomatic missions, was nevertheless maintained, and Wallenberg, the new legation attaché, was put in charge of a section created expressly for this purpose. Before taking up his post he had been given special authority, at his request, for certain arrangements to be left in his hands, such as the transmission of funds by means of the War Refugee Board (which in turn received the money from Jewish organizations in the United States).

The summer of 1944 was relatively quiet, but this quiet came to an end when the coup d'état of October 15 took place and the anti-Semitic fascist Arrow Cross Party, headed by Ferenc Szálasi, seized power in the country. The Jews of Budapest now faced mortal danger, both from the Arrow Cross murder actions and from Eichmann's deportations. From that moment on, Wallenberg displayed his courage and heroism in the rescue actions he undertook. Over the course of three months he issued thousands of "protective passports." Most of the time, both the Hungarian authorities and the Germans honored the signature of the Swedish legation, and the protective documents afforded protection for many Jews.

When Eichmann organized the death marches of thousands of Jews to the Austrian border, Wallenberg pursued the convoy in his car and managed to secure the release of hundreds of bearers of such passports and take them back to Budapest. His impressive and self-assured manner enabled him even to remove persons from the trains in which they were about to be sent to Auschwitz, or to release them from the Munkaszolgálat (Labor Service System), into which they had been drafted.

The Jews were also in danger of being killed by Arrow Cross men, and to prevent this, Wallenberg set up special hostels accommodating fifteen thousand persons—an operation in which other diplomatic missions were also involved by issuing protective documents of their own. There were thirty-one protected houses, which together formed the "international ghetto," a separate entity, quite apart from Budapest's main ghetto. The management of these houses posed many complicated problems, since it involved the provision of food as well as sanitation and health services, all requiring much money; as many as six hundred Jewish employees were engaged in the administration and maintenance of the houses.

Both the "international ghetto" and the main ghetto were situated in Pest, which was the first part of Budapest to be occupied by the Soviets. Wallenberg made efforts to negotiate with the Soviets and to ensure proper care for the liberated Jews. The Soviets were highly suspicious of the Swedish mission and charged its staff with spying for the Germans. The large number of Swedish documents in circulation also raised doubt in their minds. When the Soviets requested him to report to their army headquarters in Debrecen, Wallenberg must have believed that he would be protected by his diplomatic immunity, especially since the Swedish legation had represented Soviet interests vis-à-vis the Germans, and he made his way to the Soviet headquarters. He returned to Budapest on January 17, 1945, escorted by two Soviet soldiers, and was overheard saying that he did not know whether he was a guest of the Soviets or their prisoner. Thereafter, all trace of him, and of his driver, Vilmos Langfelder, was lost. The other staff members of the Swedish legation were also held by the Soviets, but within a few months they all returned to Stockholm, via Bucharest and Moscow.

"A civil servant in a position to provide an overall view of the transports describes them as horrible and unspeakably brutal. Food often consists of one loaf of bread per car, sometimes of a pound of bread and 8 ounces of marmalade. One bucket of water is allotted to each car. The journey generally takes five days. There are many deaths."
Raoul Wallenberg, dispatch to the Swedish Foreign Ministry, 1944

In the first few years following Wallenberg's disappearance, the Soviets claimed that they had no knowledge of a person named Wallenberg and were not aware that a person of that name was being held in any of their prisons. German prisoners of war, however, coming back from Soviet imprisonment, testified that they had met Wallenberg in prisons and camps in various parts of the Soviet Union. In the mid-1950s, on the basis of these accounts, Sweden submitted a strong demand to the Soviets for information on Wallenberg, to which the Soviets replied, in 1956, that they had discovered a report of Wallenberg's death in 1947 in a Soviet prison. Wallenberg's family, and especially his mother, did not accept this claim, which conflicted with testimonies from other sources.

As the years went by, public opinion, in Sweden and all over the world, became increasingly critical of the manner in which the Swedish government had handled the issue. The subject of Wallenberg came up time and again, and with even greater force after the death of his mother in 1979. Books were published about Wallenberg and public committees were set up to deal with the case, especially in Britain, the United States, and Israel. The reports that were published revealed that in the final days preceding Budapest's liberation, Wallenberg, with the help of Hungarians and the Zsidó Tanács (Jewish Council), was able to foil a joint SS and Arrow Cross plan to blow up the ghettos before the city's impending liberation. Through this act—the only one of its kind in the Holocaust—some 100,000 Jews were saved in the two ghettos. In recognition of this rescue action on Wallenberg's part, the United States Congress awarded Wallenberg honorary American citizenship. Memorial institutions were created in his honor, streets were named after him, and films were produced about his work in Budapest. Wallenberg's name and reputation as a "Righteous among the Nations" have become a legend. ◆

> *"Since the last report the situation of the Hungarian Jews has further deteriorated. Probably in the vicinity of 40,000 Jews, of whom 15,000 men from the Labor Service and 25,000 of both sexes seized in their homes or in the street, have been forced to march on foot to Germany. It is a distance of 240 kilometers."*
>
> Raoul Wallenberg, dispatch to the Swedish Foreign Ministry, 1944

Warhaftig, Zorah

1906–

Jurist and political figure. Warhaftig was born in Volkovysk, in western Belorussia, and studied law at the University of Warsaw. He was active in Jewish public life in Warsaw, especially in the religious Zionist Mizraḥi movement. Warhaftig was chairman of the head office of He-Haluts ha-Mizraḥi (Mizraḥi Pioneers) and vice-chairman of the Palestine Office. In the summer of 1939 he was a delegate to the Twenty-first Zionist Congress, which took place in Geneva, and returned to Warsaw a few days before World War II broke out.

Having served as vice-chairman of the Boycott of Nazi Germany Committee, Warhaftig had to flee and went to Lithuania. There he headed the Palestine Committee for Polish Refugees and devoted his time to the refugees' welfare and their settlement in Palestine. When Lithuania was occupied by the soviets in 1941, Warhaftig made his way to Japan, where he kept up his work on behalf of the refugees, with special emphasis on the rescue of rabbinical students. In 1942 he went to the United States and was elected to the executive board of the World Jewish Congress.

In 1947 Warhaftig settled in Palestine. He was put in charge of the Va'ad Le'ummi (National Council of the Jews in Palestine) legal department and in 1948 became a member of the Provisional State Council. From 1949 to 1981 he was a Knesset (parliament) member, representing Ha-Po'el ha-Mizraḥi (Mizraḥi Workers) and the National Religious party. He was deputy minister of religious affairs from 1952 to 1962, and minister of religious affairs from 1962 to 1974. Warhaftig was an expert on Jewish laws and published important research papers on law and the administration of justice in the state of Israel.

Warhaftig published a memoir about his activities during the Holocaust, *Refugee and Survivor* (1988). ◆

1906 Warhaftig is born in Volkovysk, Belorussia.

1939 Warhaftig becomes a delegate to the 21st Zionist Congress.

1941 Warhaftig travels to Japan to work on behalf of Jewish refugees.

1942 Warhaftig moves to America and joins the World Jewish Congress.

1947 Warhaftig settles in Palestine.

1949 Warhaftig becomes a member of the Knesset.

1962 Warhaftig becomes Israel's deputy minister of religious affairs.

1988 Warhaftig publishes his memoirs.

Wdowinski, David

1895–1970

One of the founders and leaders of the Żydowski Związek Wojskowy (Jewish Military Union; ŻZW) in the Warsaw ghetto. Wdowinski was born in Będzin, and at the end of World War I was active in a Jewish self-defense organization in Lvov. He studied at the universities of Vienna, Brno, and Warsaw, and became a psychiatrist. At the request of Vladimir Jabotinsky, the leader of the Zionist Revisionist movement, Wdowinski gave up his professional practice and devoted all his time to working in the leadership of the Revisionist movement in Poland.

1895 Wdowinski is born in Bedzin.

1942 Wdowinski helps found the ŻZW.

1961 Wdowinski is a witness at the Eichmann trial in Jerusalem.

1963 Wdowinski publishes memoirs, *And We Are Not Saved.*

1970 Wdowinski dies of a heart attack during a memorial meeting.

Wdowinski was an active member of the Warsaw ghetto underground and represented his movement in the advisory body of the Żydowskie Towarzystwo Opieki Społecznej (Jewish Mutual Aid Society). In the summer of 1942 he helped found the ŻZW, which was headed by members of Betar (the youth wing of the Revisionist movement), and he was apparently responsible for formulating the ŻZW's policy lines. Following the Warsaw ghetto uprising, Wdowinski was imprisoned in concentration camps. After the war he emigrated to the United States. He published a book of memoirs, *And We Are Not Saved* (1963), which recounted his activities and those of the Betar movement in the Warsaw ghetto. Wdowinski was a witness at the Eichmann Trial in Jerusalem in 1961. He died of a heart attack during a memorial meeting for the Warsaw ghetto uprising, in Tel Aviv in 1970. ◆

Weill, Joseph

1902–1988

Weill's underground organization smuggled over one thousand children to Switzerland; not one of them was lost.

French activist in the underground and in welfare organizations. Born in Bouxwiller, Alsace, Weill was the son of Rabbi Ernest Weill, a leading French scholar. Weill was a physician, and before the war he directed a private hospital in Strasbourg. At the outbreak of World War II he was recruited into the army and was responsible for health services for the inhabitants of the French region bordering on Germany, who had been dispersed throughout central France. The temporary resettlement had been carried out by the French authorities in order to protect these civilians.

When France fell, in June 1940, Weill was the medical adviser of the Jewish organization Oeuvre de Secours aux Enfants (Children's Aid Society; OSE). Thanks to his extensive connections in government circles, he was allowed access to the detention camps in the south of France, where the Vichy government had assembled tens of thousands of Jews with their families in degrading conditions of distress and malnutrition. The detailed and exact reports that Weill circulated on the condition of these detainees alerted Swiss and American humanitarian organizations to the need for assistance. As a direct consequence, the French authorities released from the camps hundreds of old people and thousands of children, a process involving many months of negotiations and not completed until the spring of 1941. Most of those released were taken into OSE institutions.

When deportations from France to eastern Europe began, Weill and his helpers rescued hundreds of Jewish children from the hands of the police. Weill showed his aides how to prepare forged identity cards for these children in order to hide their Jewish identity. He created an underground organization, the Réseau Garel (Garel Network), which placed the children with Christian and nonreligious families and institutions involved in saving Jews.

Activists in the Réseau Garel kept in constant touch with each child and paid his or her monthly maintenance. They worked to bolster the children's spirits and helped them to maintain their attachment to Judaism. In all, the Réseau Garel cared for four thousand children, and smuggled over one thousand of them into Switzerland. Not one of the children entrusted to this organization was lost.

In May 1943, with the Gestapo on his trail, Weill was compelled to flee to Switzerland. There, he dealt with the absorption of the Jewish children smuggled out of France and, with the aid of the smuggling network, was responsible for transferring Joint Distribution Committee funds to Jewish underground workers in France. On Weill's initiative, extension courses in local medical schools were authorized in the first half of 1944 for about two hundred Jewish doctors interned in refugee camps in Switzerland. Weill also brought about sixty young people from these camps into an abridged social-work course taught by Dr. Paul Baerwald, in an effort to prepare a professional labor force to care for survivors of the Nazi camps.

After the war, Weill served as president of the Consistoire Israélite, the umbrella organization of the Jewish communities of Alsace. His autobiography, titled *Déjà . . . Essai autobiographique*, was published in 1983. ◆

1902 Weill is born in Bouxwiller, France.

1940 Weill is medical advisor of the Jewish group OSE.

1941 Weill's negotiations help release thousands from detention camps.

1943 Weill is compelled to flee to Switzerland.

1944 Weill gets medical schools to offer courses to refugee doctors.

1963 Weill's autobiography is published.

1988 Weill dies.

Weissmandel, Michael Dov

1903–1956

Rabbi; one of the leaders of the Pracovná Skupina (Working Group), a Jewish underground organization in Slovakia. Born in Debrecen, Hungary, Weissmandel attended rabbinical academies in Trnava and Nitra in Slovakia. In 1935 he accompanied his teacher Rabbi Samuel David Ungar (who was also his father-in-law) on a trip to Palestine, together with an ultra-orthodox Agudat Israel delegation headed by Unger.

In October 1940 a Judenrat, the Ústredňa Židov (Jewish Center), was established in Slovakia. Between March and October 1942, 40,000 of Slovakia's 90,000 Jews were deported to the Lublin reservation in Poland, and 18,000 to the Auschwitz extermination camp. The Pracovná Skupina was set up at the height of the deportations, and it became the central agency for rescuing Jews, aiding deportees in Polish camps, gathering and disseminating information on the extermination of Jews in Poland, and establishing links to Jewish and non-Jewish organizations abroad.

Together with Gisi Fleischmann, the head of the Pracovná Skupina, Weissmandel tirelessly sought ways of rescuing Jews, and he pleaded for help from every possible source, in Slovakia and abroad. In his letters to Jewish organizations and individuals, written in rabbinic Hebrew, he voiced harsh criticism of their failure to respond without delay to his demands.

In the summer of 1942, Weissmandel favored the proposal of some activists within the Ústredňa Židov to pay a ransom to Dieter Wisliceny, Adolf Eichmann's deputy in Slovakia, in exchange for the cessation of deportations from Slovakia to extermination camps; a sum between $40,000 and $50,000 was in fact paid, in two installments. Weissmandel and the other members of the Pracovná Skupina believed that it was these payments that stopped the deportations from Slovakia. After the Holocaust, others claimed that the cause of the stoppage was opposition from Slovak cabinet ministers and influential persons, together with pressure brought to bear by the Catholic church and public opinion.

Basing themselves on their experience with Wisliceny, the members of the Pracovná Skupina believed that negotiations for the rescue of Jews from all parts of occupied Europe in exchange for money stood a chance of succeeding. This program came to be known as the Europa Plan. When the group failed in its efforts to come up with a down payment of $200,000 toward the total sum of $2 million to $3 million, as demanded by Wisliceny, Weissmandel sought to gain time by deception. Using official stationery that he had obtained from Switzerland, he produced fictitious letters containing positive replies to his requests for money, signing them "Ferdinand Roth," supposedly a "representative of world Jewry."

On March 19, 1944, Weissmandel wrote to friends in Budapest to inform them of his contacts with Wisliceny, who had been posted there following the Nazi seizure of Hungary. But by the time the deportations of Hungary's Jews were launched, in May of that year, Weissmandel had changed his mind regarding contacts with the Nazis, and he advised these same friends to "beware of deceit and trickery"—to try to escape and offer resistance, but under no circumstances to enter the ghettos.

On April 7, 1944, two Jews from Slovakia, Walter Rosenberg (Rudolf Vrba) and Alfred Wetzler, managed to escape from Auschwitz. They reported to the Pracovná Skupina on the death factory in operation there, and also produced a precise sketch of the camp layout. A few weeks later, on May 27, two more Jews, Czesław Mordowicz and Arnost Rosin, escaped from Auschwitz, confirmed the evidence given by Rosenberg and Wetzler, and reported on the destruction of Hungarian Jewry. This information was passed on to Jewish organizations abroad, as well as to the government of Slovakia and to the Catholic church in that country. Gisi Fleischmann and Weissmandel took the lead in organizing this information campaign. Weiss-

1903 Weissmandel is born in Debrecen, Hungary.

1935 Weissmandel accompanies his teacher to Palestine.

1940 A Judenrat is established in Slovakia.

1942 40,000 of Slovakia's 90,000 Jews are deported.

1942 Weissmandel tirelessly seeks ways of rescuing Jews; favors paying an anti-deportation ransom to Eichmann's deputy.

1944 Weissmandel changes his mind regarding contact with the Nazis.

1944 Weissmandel helps lead an information campaign about Auschwitz.

1944 Weissmandel's demands that Auschwitz be bombed are in vain.

1944 Deportations from Slovakia resume.

1944 Weissmandel is put on a train but jumps off and escapes.

1956 Weissmandel dies.

1960 Weissmandel's memoirs are published.

mandel repeatedly demanded that the Allies bomb Auschwitz—the camp, the railway lines leading to it, and the bridges and tunnels en route. These efforts were in vain.

The deportations from Slovakia were resumed in the fall of 1944, following the suppression of the Slovak National Uprising and the occupation of the country by the Germans. Weissmandel and his family were put on a train to Auschwitz. He managed to jump off during the journey, went into hiding in the Bratislava area, and eventually left Slovakia in a train, organized by Rezső (Rudolf) Kasztner, that took him and other Jews to Switzerland. From there he left for the United States.

In Mount Kisco, New York, Weissmandel reestablished the Nitra *yeshiva*, and it was from there that he issued a manifesto in which he virulently denounced Zionism and the premature establishment of a Jewish state, "before the Almighty willed it and sent the Messiah." His book *Min ha-Metzar (From the Depths)*, containing his memoirs and views, was published posthumously in 1960. ◆

Weizmann, Chaim

1874–1952

Statesman and scientist; first president of the state of Israel. Born in Motol, in the Pale of Settlement in Russia, Weizmann moved at the age of eleven to nearby Pinsk. In 1892 he went to Germany, and for two years, in 1892 and 1893, studied at the Darmstadt Polytechnic. He then (until 1897) studied dye chemistry at the Charlottenburg Polytechnic in Berlin. In 1897 Weizmann entered Fribourg University in Switzerland, from which he received his Ph.D. in chemistry in 1899. He settled in Manchester, England, in 1904, and by 1913 had risen at the University of Manchester to the rank of reader in biochemistry; he had also assumed key roles within the World Zionist Organization and the English Zionist Federation.

Following the entry of Turkey into World War I, Weizmann decided that the cause of Zionism had to be tied to Great Britain. He made an outstanding and unique contribution to the British war effort with his **fermentation** process yielding acetone, a solvent necessary in arms production. Weizmann was

fermentation: a chemical change in an organic substance.

the key Zionist negotiator in the attainment, on November 2, 1917, of the Balfour Declaration, which offered British support for the creation of a Jewish national home in Palestine. In 1920 he was elected president of the World Zionist Organization, and he initiated the establishment of an enlarged Jewish Agency in 1929.

In August 1933 the Zionist Congress nominated Weizmann, then out of office, to head the Jewish Agency's Department for the Settlement of German Refugees. Weizmann's first action was to try to coordinate all Jewish relief activities and to streamline the strategies of the Jewish organizations involved in such work. His efforts met with little success, since the differences in the philosophies and orientations of the various Jewish groups were too deep to be bridged within a brief period. Weizmann opposed mere philanthropy; he always wished to bring about an organized, carefully controlled immigration of German Jews and other refugees to Palestine, to the extent that the country could absorb them. Nevertheless, in light of the increased persecution of German Jews, he did not adopt a rigid policy. On the contrary, he hoped that a large influx of immigrants would greatly enhance the Zionist enterprise in Palestine. He felt that the young Jews, who had no future in Germany, should be given preference and that as much of their property as was possible to save ought to be transferred to Palestine. Although he was not personally involved in the details of the Haavara Agreement, he supported it. Weizmann also expended much effort in trying to persuade outstanding scientists to emigrate to Palestine; besides wishing to save their lives, he wanted to establish Palestine as an international center of scientific research.

Returning to office as president of the World Zionist Organization in 1935, Weizmann used his diplomatic connections to try to blunt the racial persecution of Jews in Germany and elsewhere. Shortly after Hitler assumed the chancellorship in 1933, Weizmann had met with Ramsay MacDonald, the prime minister of Great Britain, and other British ministers. He also turned repeatedly for help to Benito Mussolini, with whom he met, to Jan Christian Smuts, the prime minister of South Africa, and to French diplomats. To all of them, as well as in various international forums, he protested against the racial, civil, and economic discrimination against Jews.

On the eve of World War II, Weizmann pledged full Jewish cooperation against Hitler to the British prime minister, Neville

1874 Weizmann is born in Motol in Russia.

1892 Weizmann goes to Germany to study at the Darmstadt Polytechnic.

1897 Weizmann enters Fribourg University in Switzerland.

1899 Weizmann receives his Ph.D. in chemistry.

1904 Weizmann settles in Manchester, England.

1913 Weizmann becomes a reader in biochemistry.

1917 Weizmann is a key negotiator in attaining the Balfour Declaration.

1920 Weizmann is elected president of the World Zionist Organization.

1933 Weizmann is named to head the Jewish Agency's Department for the Settlement of German Refugees.

1939 Weizmann pleads for the suspension of regulations limiting Jewish immigration to Palestine.

1946 Weizmann is removed from the presidency of the World Zionist Organization.

1949 Weizmann publishes an autobiography.

1952 Weizmann dies.

Chamberlain, and he proposed the establishment of a Jewish fighting division under its own flag within the British military forces. As the Nazi destruction of European Jewry proceeded, Weizmann was involved in trying to organize desperate rescue efforts, all declined by Great Britain. An example was his plea, in September 1939, for the suspension of the White Paper regulations severely limiting Jewish immigration to Palestine during this period of emergency, so that European Jews might find refuge there. In February 1943 Great Britain also rejected a proposal, probably emanating from the Romanian government, asking for $3.5 million—$50 per person—as "security" in exchange for transferring 70,000 Jews to a place of refuge, preferably Palestine.

In May 1944 Joel Brand, a Zionist official in Budapest, brought a report to Palestine that the Germans were prepared to halt the wholesale murder of European Jewry and to evacuate one million Jews in return for 10,000 trucks and quantities of tea, coffee, cocoa, and soap. The British detained Brand on a trumped-up charge of being a Nazi agent. In July of that year, Weizmann met with British foreign secretary Anthony Eden and pleaded for a positive response to the Brand mission, if only to gain time. His plea did not result in any action being taken. He also requested the bombing of the extermination camps. The British replied that technical difficulties made this unfeasible.

After the war, Weizmann, ill and half-blind, was shunted to the periphery of the Zionist movement by David Ben-Gurion and Abba Hillel Silver. In December of 1946 he was removed from the presidency of the World Zionist Organization. Nevertheless, he continued to perform indispensable services for the movement, and when the state of Israel was established he was appointed its first president. In 1949 he published his autobiography, *Trial and Error*. ◆

> *"If we had money we could buy all the land we want and many more things, Commission or no Commission. But I am distressed to see that Jews don't take the warning which history is giving them, they are smitten with blindness."*
> Chaim Weizmann, in a letter to Abraham Goldberg, 1938

Westerweel, Joop

1899–1944

Dutch Christian rescuer of Jews. Westerweel took part in Christian Socialist movements as a young man and engaged in the antifascist struggle. He taught in a modernist school in Bilthoven that absorbed many German refugee children in the 1930s.

In the early stages of the deportations of Dutch Jews to Poland, Westerweel became acquainted with Joachim ("Schuschu") Simon (1919–43), one of the counselors of a group of *halutsim* (Zionist pioneers) living on a farm near his school. Together they created an underground movement for concealing the *halutsim* from the two principal farms in the Netherlands, Loosdrecht and Gouda. From August 10 to 16, 1942, hiding places were found for sixty pioneers, forty-eight of them from the Loosdrecht training farm. Subsequently, Westerweel and "Schuschu" began to organize an escape route for the *halutsim* over the border and into neutral Switzerland and Spain.

In October and November 1942, "Schuschu" traveled to France to establish contacts with the Jewish underground there, and between December 1942 and January 1943 the first *halutsim* were smuggled into France through Belgium, prior to transferral to Spain. After taking three pioneers to Switzerland, "Schuschu" returned to organize further escapes. Several young pioneers were introduced as workers in the Organisation Todt, which built fortifications in western France. In May 1943 the first "workers" arrived in France, maintaining contact with the heads of the group. On one of his many journeys into France to organize escapes into Spain and Switzerland, "Schuschu" was arrested in the south of the Netherlands (January 24, 1943) while in possession of material that might jeopardize his colleagues. After succeeding in informing them of his arrest, "Schuschu" committed suicide in prison. His work was carried on by his comrades, and the Westerweel group expanded to twenty members. In a memorable farewell speech delivered to a group of *halutsim* in the Pyrenees in February 1944, Westerweel urged that on their arrival in Palestine they remember their comrades who had fallen on the way.

On March 11 Westerweel and a friend were captured by the Germans while attempting to transfer two young girls to the Belgian border crossing. Westerweel was taken to the Vught camp where, despite severe torture, he refused to betray his group. He was executed on August 11, 1944. His group continued its activities, smuggling a total of 150 to 200 Jews into France, including about 70 *halutsim*. A Westerweel Forest was planted in Israel in 1954. ◆

Wiesel, Elie Eliezer

1928 –

Writer; 1986 Nobel Peace Prize laureate. Raised in a religious home in Sighet Marmaţiei, Transylvania, Wiesel tenuously held on to his faith in God after being deported to Auschwitz with his family in 1944. Liberated from Buchenwald, he later took up studies at the Sorbonne in Paris, and became a foreign correspondent for the Israeli daily newspaper *Yediot Aharonot*. In his memoir *Un di Velt Hot Geshvigen* (1956), written in Yiddish and adapted and translated into eighteen languages (Fr., *La Nuit*; Eng., *Night*), Wiesel epitomizes the experience of a concentration camp inmate in a unique style and syntactic structure that have provided a verbal resource for discourse about the Holocaust. He has written twenty-five novels whose underlying artistic *modus operandi* is to bring to life pictures drawn from the Jewish annals, transforming them into vibrant human experiences.

"Oh, it is not death that frightens me, but the impossibility of imparting some meaning to my past."

Elie Wiesel, *The Testament*, 1981

While his novels and discursive prose deal with the fragility of the human condition, the anguished memories of his ordeals, woven into the text of the story, express the collective loss of a seared generation. Always mindful of the suffering of the other victims, Wiesel has nevertheless continuously pointed out the uniqueness of the Jewish experience, stated in a memorable formulation: "While not all victims were Jews, all Jews were victims."

On accepting the Congressional Medal from President Ronald Reagan in 1985, Wiesel appealed to the president not to visit the cemetery in Bitburg, Germany, in which forty-seven SS men are buried. "Your place, Mr. President, is with the victims," he declared. This impulse to boldly jolt the conscience of

Elie Wiesel, whose face is visible on the far right of the center bunk, at Buchenwald in 1945.

society earned Wiesel the Nobel Peace Prize. In his presentation address, Egil Aarvik, the chairman of the Norwegian Nobel Committee, summed up Wiesel's message to humanity: "Do not forget, do not sink into a new blind indifference, but involve yourselves in truth and justice, in human dignity, freedom, and atonement."

In his tenure as chairman of the U.S. Holocaust Memorial Council between 1980 and 1986, Wiesel instituted national Days of Remembrance in the United States, and his leadership inspired the introduction of Holocaust curricula in numerous states, cities, and counties. In his words and deeds, Wiesel has helped to bring the Holocaust to the frontiers of American consciousness. He is a professor in the humanities at Boston University. ◆

"The impact of the Holocaust on believers as well as unbelievers, on Jews as well as Christians, has not yet been evaluated. Not deeply, not enough."
Elie Wiesel,
Legends of Our Times, 1968

Wiesenthal, Simon

1908 –

Investigator of Nazi war criminals. Born in Buchach (Pol., Buczacz), Galicia, Wiesenthal studied architecture at the Prague Technical University and was living in Lvov, Poland, when World War II began. He was arrested by Ukrain-

ian police and spent most of the war in concentration and forced-labor camps, among them Janówska (Lvov), Płaszów, Gross-Rosen, and Buchenwald. He was liberated in Mauthausen on May 5, 1945, by the United States Army.

After the war Wiesenthal devoted himself to the investigation of Nazi war criminals. He worked initially for the War Crimes section of the United States Army in Austria, and in 1947 established the Jewish Historical Documentation Center in Linz. Public interest in Nazi war criminals waned, and Wiesenthal therefore closed his Linz center in 1954. He resumed his work in Vienna in 1961 in the wake of

The Simon Wiesenthal Center

The Simon Wiesenthal Center, named for the Viennese Nazi-hunter Simon Wiesenthal, was established in Los Angeles in 1977 by its founder and dean, Rabbi Marvin Hier. In 1979 the center opened a museum developed by Holocaust historian Efraim Zuroff. A year earlier, the center launched a national outreach project to provide educational programs from high school students. Since it's establishment, the Wiesenthal Center has focused on political issues related to the Holocaust and has specialized in the use of mass media to educate the public about the events of World War II. Among its major campaigns were the efforts to cancel the statute of limitations on war crimes in West Germany, and attempts to force South American governments such as those of Paraguay and Chile to surrender leading Nazi criminals who had fled there. The center has also played a key role in uncovering hundreds of Nazi collaborators of eastern European origin who escaped after World War II to Western democracies, and in convincing the governments of Great Britain, Australia, and Canada to investigate this issue and prosecute the criminals found in those countries. In 1982 the Wiesenthal Center's documentary *Genocide* was awarded an Academy Award as the best documentary film of the previous year. A year earlier the center began producing *Page One,* a weekly radio program on Jewish affairs broadcast by dozens of stations and the National Public Radio satellite throughout North America. The center also helped produce a documentary on the life and fate of Raoul Wallenberg, and it has videotaped more than four hundred hours of testimony by Holocaust survivors and liberators. In addition, the Wiesenthal Center has produced and published a variety of books, journals, and exhibitions relating to the Holocaust.

the Eichmann trial, which generated renewed interest in the prosecution of Nazi war criminals.

Among the most prominent Nazis whom Wiesenthal helped discover and/or bring to justice were Franz Stangl, commandant of the Treblinka and Sobibór extermination camps; Gustav Wagner, deputy commandant of Sobibór; Franz Mürer, commandant of the Vilna ghetto; and Karl Silberbauer, the policeman who arrested Anne Frank. In 1977 the Simon Wiesenthal Center for Holocaust Studies was established at the Yeshiva University of Los Angeles in honor of Wiesenthal's life's work. Besides his efforts to prosecute Nazi war criminals, Wiesenthal has played an important role in commemorating the victims of the Holocaust. His works on the Holocaust include *The Murderers among Us; Sunflower; Max and Helen;* and *Every Day Remembrance Day: A Chronicle of Jewish Martyrdom.* ◆

> *"Hatred can be nurtured anywhere, idealism can be perverted into sadism anywhere. If hatred and sadism combine with modern technology the inferno could erupt anew anywhere."*
> Simon Wiesenthal, *Justice Not Vengeance,* 1989

Wilner, Arie

1917–1943

One of the founders of the Żydowska Organizacja Bojowa (Jewish Fighting Organization; ŻOB) in his native Warsaw, and the ŻOB's liaison officer with the Poles. When World War II broke out, Wilner was a member of the Zionist youth movement Ha-Shomer ha-Tsa'ir in Warsaw, and his plan to emigrate to Palestine was postponed because of the training assignments he was given. In September 1939 he was among those who escaped from Warsaw and made their way to Vilna, which had been occupied by the Soviet Union and became part of Lithuania. Wilner was active in Vilna until its conquest by the Germans in June 1941. He returned to Warsaw and was one of the first to warn of the significance of the massacres that were being carried out in the east.

Wilner became involved in underground activities, and his Polish appearance enabled him to travel and make frequent visits to the ghettos in occupied Poland. In June 1942 he was among the founders of the ŻOB and became its representative on the "Aryan" side of the city. He established contact with the main Polish underground organization, the Armia Krajowa

Arie Wilner's Polish appearance enabled him to travel and make frequent visits to the ghettos in occupied Poland.

(Home Army), and obtained from it recognition of the ŻOB. A close relationship developed between Wilner and Henryk Wolinski, who was in charge of the Jewish section in the Armia Krajowa; but Wilner also kept in touch with the Communist underground, the Armia Ludowa, and used every means available to acquire arms and bring them into the ghetto. Although the center of Wilner's activities lay outside the ghetto, he participated in the major decision making of its underground and in resistance operations. After the crisis experienced by the ŻOB in September 1942, Wilner contributed to its reconsolidation, and in January 1943 he took part in an armed uprising.

On March 6, 1943, Wilner was arrested by the Germans during a search of his apartment on the "Aryan" side, in which he was found to be in possession of arms. The Germans thought

Żydowska Organizacja Bojowa

The Żydowski Organizacja Bojowa (Jewish Fighting Organization) or ŻOB was a Jewish armed group established in Warsaw, Poland, on July 28, 1942. At this time, mass deportations of Jews from the Warsaw ghetto to concentration and extermination camps were in full swing, and ŻOB members hoped to enable Jews to defend themselves and offer armed resistance to the Nazi enemy. From the very beginning, the ŻOB made efforts to spread the concept of resistance to the provinces and to other cities and to unify the various opposition forces operating in Poland. One of the first actions undertaken by the ŻOB was to purge the Warsaw ghetto of people who were assisting the Germans, especially the Jewish ghetto police commanders and agents who reported to the Germans on developments in the ghetto. Even before the first ghetto uprising, which occurred in January 1943, the acting chief of the Jewish police at the time of the deportations, Jacob Lejkin, was executed. Later, in the wake of the uprising, such activity was extended. It reached, among others, Dr. Alfred Nossig, a man of great talent and a noteworthy past as an active Zionist, who in his last days in the Warsaw ghetto had become a Nazi informer. The ŻOB's original aim had been simply to take revenge, but in the event their punitive actions also struck fear into the hearts of Nazi collaborators and neutralized them.

he was a member of the Polish underground; they interrogated and tortured him, but he gave no one away. His arrest, however, led to tension between the Armia Krajowa and the ŻOB, and contact between the two was broken off for a short time. The Germans discovered that Wilner was a Jew, and sent him to a nearby concentration camp, from which he was rescued in a daring operation led by Henryk Grabowski, a member of the Polish Catholic Scout movement. When the Warsaw ghetto uprising broke out, Wilner was suffering from a wounded leg, but he later took an active part in the fighting. Wilner was in the ŻOB command bunker when it was discovered; according to eyewitnesses, he called on the fighters to commit suicide, and he himself was among those who perished in the bunker. His parents and sisters were hidden with Poles in Warsaw and were saved. ◆

Wittenberg, Yitzhak Leo Itzig

1907–1943

The first commander of the Fareynegte Partizaner Organizatsye (United Partisan Organization; FPO) in Vilna. Born into a working family, Wittenberg was a tailor and, from an early age, a member of the Communist party. During the short-lived Soviet regime in Lithuania (June 1940 to June 1941), he made a name for himself as a Communist activist. Under the German occupation and in the Vilna ghetto, Wittenberg became a leader of the Communist underground. He was one of the sponsors of the FPO, and his willingness to join with Zionists in a united organization—which included the anticommunist Zionist Revisionists—is an indication of his personality and his strong ties with the Jewish population. In January 1942, when the FPO came into being, Wittenberg was elected its commander, on the basis of his personal qualities, his experience in underground operations, and his ties with Communist circles outside the ghetto. He soon won the respect of all the elements of the organization.

One of the Vilna Communists, who lived outside the ghetto, gave Wittenberg away when he himself was imprisoned by the Germans, although the latter were apparently unaware of the existence of the FPO and Wittenberg's role in it. The Judenrat (Jewish Council) was asked to surrender Wittenberg, and its chairman, Jacob Gens, had a sharp confrontation on the issue with the FPO. Wittenberg was arrested by the Lithuanian police, only to be set free by armed FPO members, and he went into hiding in the ghetto. The incident threatened to develop into an open struggle for power. Gens appealed to the ghetto population, claiming that the FPO's attitude was jeopardizing all the Jews, and as a result many Jews turned against the FPO and its commanders. This exposure to mass pressure, and the recognition that the time was not ripe for a general uprising, persuaded the FPO command to decide on the difficult step of surrendering Wittenberg to the Judenrat.

Wittenberg accepted the decision when he learned that it had the support of the underground Communist party leadership in the ghetto. "Wittenberg Day" in the Vilna ghetto—July 16, 1943, a day that had a far-reaching impact on the FPO—ended with Wittenberg surrendering to the Jewish police. He apparently committed suicide in prison, by taking poison. ◆

Wolinski, Henryk

1901–1986

P olish jurist. Prior to World War II, Wolinski was employed in central government institutions in Warsaw. In February 1942 he became a member of the Armia Krajowa (Home Army; AK), under the code names Wacław and Zakrzewski, heading the section for Jewish affairs in the operational command of the AK's Information and Propaganda Office. Wolinski prepared reports on German policy for the extermination of the Jews. These reports were intended for the AK command and for the Polish government-in-exile in London. In the fall of 1942 the Jewish Fighting Organization (Żydowska Organizacja Bojowa; ŻOB) contacted Wolinski, subsequently maintaining this contact for the AK command through Arie (Jurek) Wilner and Yitzhak (Antek) Zuckerman. Wolinski fervently pleaded the Jewish cause before the AK commanders and participated in the Rada Pomocy Żydom (Council for Aid to Jews), known as Zegota, subsequently creating a council cell in the AK operational command that aided many Jews in hiding. After the war Wolinski was a legal adviser and attorney in Katowice.

In 1974 he was accorded the title "Righteous among the Nations" by Yad Vashem. ◆

Wurm, Theophil

1868–1953

Evangelical theologian who was appointed bishop of Württemberg in 1933. At the time of the Nazi rise to power, Wurm supported the German Christians (Deutsche Christen), a fraction that supported the Nazis. Late in 1933, however, when the Nazis wanted to enforce the *Gleichschaltung* (coordination under Nazism) law—that is, to subject the church institutions to Nazi ideology and organization—Wurm went into the opposition. He joined the Confessing Church (Bekennende Kirche) and violently opposed the appointment of Ludwig Müller as Reich bishop of the Evangelical Church (Evangelische Kirche), an appointment made to ensure support of the Nazis by the Protestant church and opposition to the Confessing Church. Because of his position, Wurm was placed under house arrest in 1934. Following a public protest, Wurm, like Bernhard Lichtenberg and Clemens August Graf von Galen, violently attacked the Euthanasia Program and the persecution of the Jews.

After the war, in 1945, Wurm was chairman of the Evangelical Church Council in Germany and one of the authors of the "Stuttgart Confession," which acknowledged that church clergy had not done enough in the struggle against the Nazis. ◆

Theophil Wurm was one of the authors of the "Stuttgart Confession," which acknowledged that church clergy had not done enough in the struggle against the Nazis.

Yelin, Haim

1913–1944

Writer and anti-Nazi fighter. Yelin was born in the town of Vilkija, Lithuania. At the end of World War I his family settled in Kovno and earned its livelihood by importing Yiddish books and managing the Libhober fun Vissen (Pursuers of Wisdom) library. In 1932 Yelin graduated from the Hebrew *Realgymnasium* in Kovno. He was found physically unfit for military service. For a short while he was active in No'ar Tsiyyoni Halutsi (Zionist Pioneering Youth; NETSAH), but left it when he became attracted to the Communist party (which was illegal), during his studies in the faculty of economics at Kovno University (1934–38). He was a regular contributor to the Communist daily *Folksblat* and the monthly *Shtrala*.

After the incorporation of Lithuania into the Soviet Union in July 1940, Yelin was appointed to a senior post in the government printing office. During the first few days of the German invasion, in June of 1941, he and his family tried to escape into the Soviet interior, but they failed and on their return were put into the Kovno ghetto. For a time Yelin lived under an assumed name in the ghetto, and he also changed his appearance, out of fear that if recognized he would be charged with the Communist activities he had engaged in under the Soviet regime.

At the end of 1941, together with some of his friends who were also veteran Communist sympathizers, Yelin established a group that called itself the Antifascist Struggle Organization; he was elected its commander. His duties included managing the group's internal affairs, and liaison with elements outside the

1913 Yelin is born in Valkija, Lithuania.

1932 Yelin graduates from the Hebrew *Realgymnasium* in Kovno.

1934 Yelin begins studying economics at Kovno University.

1940 Yelin takes a senior post in the government printing office.

1941 Yelin and his family try to escape into the Soviet interior, but fail.

1943 Yelin establishes contact with partisans.

1944 Yelin is ambushed by Gestapo agents and executed.

ghetto. Disguised as a peasant or a railway worker, he would leave the ghetto, seeking to establish contact with remnants of the Communist party, as well as with the Soviet partisans who were becoming active in the area.

It was not until the summer of 1943 that Yelin succeeded in establishing permanent contact with the partisans. He became a member of the Communist party and was permitted to enter the partisans' base in the Rudninkai Forest, 90 miles (145 km) east of Kovno. As a result of his efforts a united front was formed of all the underground groups in the ghetto, including the Zionists, with the aim of enabling Jewish youths to join the partisan units in the forests. Yelin himself accompanied the first few groups who left the ghetto for this purpose. The operation, which enabled 350 young Jews to join the partisans, made Yelin a leading figure in the Kovno underground. On April 6, 1944, while on a mission outside the ghetto, he was ambushed by Gestapo agents, and later executed. ◆

Zabinski, Jan

B. 1897

Polish agricultural engineer and zoologist who saved many Jews in Warsaw. On the eve of the German occupation, Dr. Zabinski was director of the Warsaw zoo. The Germans appointed him superintendent of the city's public parks as well. Availing himself of the opportunity to visit the Warsaw ghetto, ostensibly to inspect the state of the flora within the ghetto walls, Zabinski maintained contact with prewar Jewish colleagues and friends and helped them escape and find shelter on the "Aryan" side of the city.

Many cages in the zoo had been emptied of animals during the September 1939 air assault on Warsaw, and Zabinski decided to utilize them as hiding places for fleeing Jews. Over the course of three years, hundreds of Jews found temporary shelter in these abandoned animal cells, located on the western bank of the Vistula River, until they were able to relocate to permanent places of refuge elsewhere. In addition, close to a dozen Jews were sheltered in Zabinski's two-story private home on the zoo's grounds. In this dangerous undertaking he was helped by his wife, Antonina, a recognized author, and their young son, Ryszard, who nourished and looked after the needs of the many distraught Jews in their care. At first, Zabinski paid from his own funds to subsidize the maintenance costs; then money was received through the Jewish Committee, headed by Dr. Adolf Berman, Jerzy Zemian, and Rachel Auerbach.

An active member of the Polish underground Armia Krajowa (Home Army), Zabinski participated in the Warsaw Polish uprising of August and September 1944. Upon its suppression,

Many cages in the Warsaw zoo had been emptied of animals during the September 1939 air assault, and Zabinski decided to utilize them as hiding places for fleeing Jews.

Jan Zabinski (fourth from right) at Yad Vashem in 1968 with some of the people he saved.

he was taken as a prisoner to Germany. His wife continued his work, looking after the needs of some of the Jews left behind in the ruins of the city.

In 1965 Jan and Antonina Zabinski were recognized by Yad Vashem as "Righteous among the Nations." ◆

Zagan, Shakhne

1892–1942

Zionist leader and one of the prime movers in the creation of the Warsaw ghetto underground. Born in Kraków, Zagan in his youth was active in the Zionist Socialist movement and in 1920 became a leader of the radical wing in the Po'alei Zion party headquarters in Warsaw. He involved himself in editing periodicals and in party organization and propaganda. Zagan was one of the few party leaders who did not join the mass exodus from Warsaw in September 1939, and was among those who took the lead in organizing welfare and mutual aid activities for refugees and establishing soup kitchens for the needy. He was a member of the Żydowskie Towarzystwo

Opieki Społecznej (Jewish Mutual Aid Society), a political advisory council.

In the ghetto underground, Zagan devoted himself to educational affairs and to the publication of underground newspapers. Po'alei Zion Left distinguished itself with multifaceted activities in the underground, and Zagan led his comrades in most of the initiatives and operations they launched. He was one of the founders and leaders of the Antifascist Bloc, the first armed organization set up in Warsaw. In the summer of 1942, when the mass deportation of Jews from Warsaw was launched, Zagan was inclined to support organized resistance, but he did not take a resolute and consistent stand. In early August of that year, when the deportation was in full swing, Zagan and his family were seized and taken to the Treblinka extermination camp. ◆

Zeitlin, Hillel

1871–1942

Religious thinker, journalist, scholar, and writer. Born in Korma, in the Mogilev district of Belorussia, Zeitlin moved in 1907 to Warsaw, where he was among the founders of the two major Yiddish dailies, *Haynt* and *Der Moment*, and a contributor to both. A student of kabbala and Hasidism, Zeitlin sought to attract his contemporaries to the sources of Judaism and Jewish thought, and wrote (in both Hebrew and Yiddish) about problems of religious belief; in his own attitude he passed from fervent and ecstatic faith to heresy and back again to religious faith. He was the outstanding figure among a group of pre–World War II writers—including Uri Zvi Greenberg, H. Leivick, Itzhak Katzenelson, and his own son, Aaron Zeitlin—who foretold the approaching end of European Jewry.

For Zeitlin, the anticipation of the Holocaust emerged from his religiosity. He criticized modern attempts to interpret life and based his view of the world on traditional Jewish sources, expressing in his works a sense of guilt and a clear feeling of an impending catastrophe. After 1917 he wrote descriptions of his dreams and visions, interpreting them as forewarnings of coming events. A dream of his own death and another of a sinking

> *"Have I witnessed any positive moments in the Ghetto? Unfortunately, I have only seen negative ones: hunger, epidemics, mass-mortality."*
> Hillel Zeitlin, 1942

1871 Zeitlin is born in Korma in Belorussia.

1907 Zeitlin moves to Warsaw.

1917 Zeitlin begins writing of his visionary dreams, interpreting them as forewarnings.

1931 Zeitlin gives a lecture in which he describes a dream of Jews aboard a sinking ship.

1939 Zeitlin describes a vision of total destruction of the Jewish world.

1942 Zeitlin disappears when the Warsaw ghetto is liquidated.

ship, with the Jews aboard dying as martyrs, were described in his writings and also in a lecture he gave in 1931 ("Why Is the Ship of Salvation Unable to Reach the Shore?"). Yet another dream he described involved a deportation train with Jews aboard. In July 1939, a few weeks before the war broke out, Zeitlin gave a detailed account of a vision of total destruction that he had experienced—of the Nazi enemy going from city to city, from town to town, from one Jewish community to the other, destroying the Jews of Poland, brutally attacking the old and the young, and leaving no remnant. He related this vision to a group of friends and disciples, and the account was then published in *Der Nayer Ruf,* a periodical dedicated to religious revival and national unity.

The little that is known about Zeitlin's life and work in the Holocaust years is culled from diaries and memoirs written by others. Up until the mass deportation from Warsaw at the end of July 1942, he lived in his apartment in the "small ghetto" there, writing voluminously and translating the Book of Psalms into Yiddish, but he took no part in public life and did not publish his writings. The latter were all lost when he was forced to leave his house without prior notice. For a while he stayed in the Jewish hospital, until the Jewish New Year (September 12 in 1942), when that institution was liquidated. Zeitlin is said to have been shot to death on the Umschlagplatz. ◆

Zimetbaum, Mala

1922–1944

Escapee from Auschwitz. Zimetbaum was born in Poland and as a child moved with her family to Belgium. In September 1942 she arrived in Auschwitz with a transport of Belgian Jews and, following a *Selektion,* was put into a women's camp in Birkenau. Because of her fluency in several languages she became an interpreter in the camp, gaining the confidence of the SS women in charge. Despite the advantages and the status that went with the position she held, Zimetbaum went to great lengths to help rank-and-file prisoners and was one of the few prisoners holding official appointments to gain general sympathy among the inmates.

In the camp Zimetbaum met Adek Galinski, a young Polish prisoner who had come to Auschwitz with the first transport. Galinski was in contact with the underground and was preparing his escape from the camp. In June 1944 Zimetbaum and Galinski escaped from Auschwitz; she was the first woman to do so. Because of the position she had held, her escape had a great impact on the prisoners. The two escapees reached the Slovak border, but were apprehended there and within a few weeks were sent back to the camp. Both were sentenced to be hanged— Zimetbaum in the women's camp and Galinski in the men's camp—but both committed suicide while being

taken to the gallows. Mala Zimetbaum had a concealed razor blade, and she cut an artery on one of her wrists. When the SS man holding her tried to wrest the blade away she slapped his face with her bleeding hand. ◆

Zorin, Shalom

1902–1974

Jewish partisan commander. Born in Minsk, Zorin was a carpenter by trade. Between 1917 and 1920 he fought in the Civil War as a Communist partisan. After Minsk was occupied by the Germans in late June of 1941, Zorin lived in the Minsk ghetto and worked in the local prisoner-of-war camp, where he made the acquaintance of a captured Soviet officer, Semyon Ganzenko. In late 1941 they both escaped to the forests in the Staroe Selo area, about 19 miles (30 km) southwest of Minsk. With others they formed a legion of partisans called Parkhomenko, with 150 members, many of whom were Jews.

As the number of Jews in the unit increased, anti-Semitism intensified and there were many clashes between Jews and non-

Jews. Zorin defended the Jews, and consequently Ganzenko, who was the commander of the brigade, charged him with forming a Jewish partisan unit, "Unit 106" (subsequently called the "Zorin Unit"), to absorb Jews who escaped from the ghettos. Unit 106 began with sixty men and fifteen guns. With the passage of time the unit grew to eight hundred men. After successive attacks by the Belorussian police units and the Germans in the Staroe Selo region, the Zorin Unit transferred its base to the Naliboki Forest, close to the bases of many partisan units. Zorin's chief of staff was Anatoly Wertheim; his commissar was Chaim Fogelman; and the head of the special department charged with internal security was a partisan named Melzer. The contact with the Minsk ghetto was maintained through eleven- to fifteen-year-old boys, who also brought to the forest large groups of Jews who had escaped from the ghetto.

The Zorin Unit had a Jewish civilian camp, with artisans who established workshops in the forest and served the partisan units throughout the area. They provided a sewing workshop, a shoemaker's workshop, a bakery, a sausage factory, a workshop for repair of arms and bomb production, a flour mill, and a large

Partisans

Partisans are resistance fighters who work underground in enemy-occupied territory during wartime. Partisan personnel are civilians who do not belong to a regular army, but they usually operate in an organized manner under the orders of a commander. In some cases the partisan commander is a member of the regular military forces. During World War II, partisans in Nazi-occupied Europe operated primarily in eastern Europe and in the Balkan states. Partisans achieved their goals through propaganda operations, circulation of underground newspapers, organized strikes, and sabotage acts. During the latter stages of the war, partisan units also engaged in guerrilla warfare, armed struggle, and rescue missions.

hospital with doctors from Minsk. Soviet and Jewish holidays (including Passover and Hanukkah) were celebrated in the camp, and a school was created, with seventy pupils of different ages. There were about one hundred men in the combat unit. Zorin was outstanding in his fatherly concern for all the members in his unit, and he believed the saving of Jewish lives to be his principal task.

In a battle fought in July 1944 with a retreating German unit, seven of Zorin's men were killed and Zorin received a leg wound. He immigrated to Israel in 1971. ◆

Zuckerman, Yitzhak Antek

1915–1981

One of the founders and leaders of the Żydowska Oganizacja Bojowa (Jewish Fighting Organization; ŻOB) in Warsaw. Zuckerman was born in Vilna, the son of an observant family. On graduating from the Hebrew high school in Vilna, he joined the Zionist youth movements He-Haluts and He-Haluts ha-Tsa'ir. In 1936 he was invited to join the He-Haluts head office in Warsaw, and in 1938, when the united youth movement Dror—He-Haluts was formed, Zuckerman became one of its two secretaries-general. He took an interest in Yiddish and Hebrew literature, and in education in the spirit of pioneering Zionism and socialism. Zuckerman toured Jewish communities in towns and cities, especially in eastern Poland, organizing branches of the movement and youth groups, and offering them guidance for their activities.

When World War II broke out in September 1939, Zuckerman, together with his comrades—activists in He-Haluts and in the youth movements—left Warsaw for the east, the parts of Poland that had been occupied by the Soviet Union. There he engaged in organizing underground branches of the movement. In April 1940 he crossed back into the German-occupied territory, on instructions from his movement, in order to promote underground activities there. He became one of the outstanding underground leaders in Warsaw and indeed in all of Poland; he helped to found and edit the underground press, organized clandestine seminars and conferences, and set up the Dror high school. Zuckerman also established the pattern of his move-

"From the beginning of the ghetto, we called on them: 'Jews, save your wives and children, hide them!' And on the other hand, we called 'Stand up and fight!' These two things weren't contradictory."
Yitzhak Zuckerman, A Surplus of Memory, published posthumously in 1991

Yitzhak Zuckerman (center, the tallest) and members of the Warsaw "Kibbutz I" at a memorial for their comrades in 1945. The sign, in Polish, translates as "Honor to the Fallen Heroes."

"We thought that uprising and rescue went together. We thought so all along the way, from the time of the Jewish Fighting Organization in the ghetto."
Yitzhak Zuckerman, A *Surplus of Memory*, published posthumously in 1991

ment's activities in underground conditions, making secret visits to ghettos in German-occupied territory. He took part in organizing and guiding the branches and cells of the movement in the provincial towns, and in setting up surreptitious *hakhsharot* (agricultural training farms). He helped create frameworks for coordinating activities with other youth movements operating illegally, especially the Zionist-Marxist Ha-Shomer ha-Tsa'ir. It was in this period that Zuckerman became close to Zivia Lubetkin; the two underground leaders eventually married and became partners in various undertakings and in the great struggle.

In his memoirs, *Chapters from the Legacy,* Zuckerman records that when the reports reached Warsaw in the fall of 1941 concerning the mass murders being carried out by the Einsatzgruppen in the areas that the Germans had taken from the Soviets, underground educational activities no longer seemed to be worthwhile or important. "There was no point to them . . . unless such activities went hand in hand with an armed Jewish resistance force." He was among those who initiated contacts with the various Jewish underground factions in Warsaw, in early 1942, for the creation of a unified military resistance movement. These efforts, however, failed at this time.

Zuckerman joined the Antifascist Bloc, established in the spring of 1942, and was one of its activists. The organization did not last long, however, and had no achievements to record.

When the mass deportation of Jews from Warsaw was launched, on July 22, 1942, a group of public figures in the ghetto held an emergency meeting. Zuckerman demanded on behalf of He-Haluts that the seizure of the Jews be resisted by force. His proposal was turned down, and no agreement was reached on any other issue. On July 28 Zuckerman took part in a meeting attended only by the leaders of the three pioneering movements, Ha-Shomer ha-Tsa'ir, Dror, and Akiva. It was at this meeting that the decision was taken to set up the ŻOB, and Zuckerman became a member of its staff headquarters. The new organization was not able to carry out large-scale resistance operations in the ghetto while the deportations were taking place, but it kept together a nucleus of determined activists and spread the ideas of armed resistance and appropriate preparation to other ghettos besides Warsaw. In December 1942 the ŻOB sent Zuckerman on a mission to Kraków, to discuss with the resistance movement there possible avenues for its operations. On the night of December 22, following a military action by the Kraków organization, Zuckerman was wounded in the leg, and managed only with great difficulty to make his way back to Warsaw.

On January 18, 1943, when the second phase of deportations from the ghetto was launched, a group of fighters, with Zuckerman at their head, barricaded themselves in a building in the ghetto and opened fire on the Germans. As a member of the enlarged ŻOB staff Zuckerman participated in the intensive preparations for a revolt that continued from the end of January to April 1943, and was appointed commanding officer of one of the three main fighting sectors into which the ghetto was divided. As the time for the revolt drew close, Zuckerman was ordered to cross over to the Polish side of Warsaw, as the authorized representative of the ŻOB and as its liaison officer with the fighting organizations belonging to the Polish underground. At the time when the Warsaw ghetto uprising was in full swing, Zuckerman made efforts to supply arms to the fighters, and in the final days of the revolt he and other members of the organization formed a rescue team that made its way through the sewers into the ghetto, which was now going up in flames.

After the revolt, Zuckerman, together with some other survivors, was active in the Żydowski Komitet Narodowy (Jewish

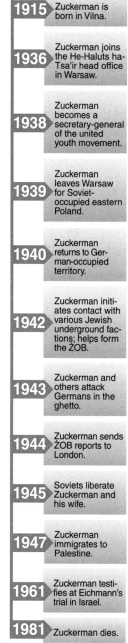

1915 Zuckerman is born in Vilna.

1936 Zuckerman joins the He-Haluts ha-Tsa'ir head office in Warsaw.

1938 Zuckerman becomes a secretary-general of the united youth movement.

1939 Zuckerman leaves Warsaw for Soviet-occupied eastern Poland.

1940 Zuckerman returns to German-occupied territory.

1942 Zuckerman initiates contact with various Jewish underground factions; helps form the ŻOB.

1943 Zuckerman and others attack Germans in the ghetto.

1944 Zuckerman sends ŻOB reports to London.

1945 Soviets liberate Zuckerman and his wife.

1947 Zuckerman immigrates to Palestine.

1961 Zuckerman testifies at Eichmann's trial in Israel.

1981 Zuckerman dies.

National Committee), which gave aid to Jews in hiding and maintained contact with Jews in some of the forced-labor camps and Jewish partisan units based in the forests in central Poland. In March 1944 Zuckerman drew up a summary report on the establishment of the ŻOB and its record; that May, the report was transmitted to London, through the channels of the Polish underground. Zuckerman and other Jewish leaders who were in hiding with the Poles were the signatories of appeals for help and of situation reports concerning the remnants of Polish Jewry. In the last two years of the war these were forwarded to London and to authoritative Jewish organizations, by way of the Polish underground. During the Warsaw Polish uprising of August 1944, Zuckerman was in command of a group of Jewish fighters, remnants of the underground and the ŻOB.

In January 1945, Zuckerman and his wife, Zivia, were liberated by the Soviet forces, and he at once applied himself to relief work among the surviving remnants of Polish Jewry. He took part in the restoration of the He-Haluts movement and the mass exodus of Jews from Poland in 1946 and 1947, known as the Beriḥa.

Zuckerman left for Palestine in early 1947. He was one of the founders of Kibbutz Lohamei ha-Getta'ot (the Ghetto Fighters' Kibbutz) in western Galilee and one of the sponsors of Bet Loḥamei Ha-Getta'Ot (the Ghetto Fighters' Museum), established to perpetuate the memory of the fighters and the study of the Holocaust. For the rest of his life he kept a loving eye on the development of the latter project. Appearing as a witness in the Eichmann trial in 1961, Zuckerman read to the court the last letter he had received from Mordecai Anielewicz, the commander of the Warsaw ghetto revolt, on April 23, 1943, when the fighting was at its height. ◆

> *"The January uprising gave us wings, elevated us in the eyes of the Jews, and enhanced our image as fighters, giving us a good name. Every Jew in the ghetto knew about the January uprising."*
>
> Yitzhak Zuckerman, A *Surplus of Memory*, published posthumously in 1991

Zygelbojm, Samuel Artur

1895–1943

A leader of the Polish Bund. Zygelbojm was born in Borowice, a village in the Lublin district, into a family of ten children; his father was a teacher and his mother a seamstress. At the age of eleven Zygelbojm had to give up school in order to help provide for the family. After World War I and the establishment of independent Poland, Zygelbojm moved to Warsaw, where he became the Bund-appointed secretary of the Union of Metal Workers. From 1924 he was a member of the Bund central committee and secretary of the Central Council of Jewish Trade Unions. As of 1930 he also edited *Arbeter Fragen* (Workers' Issues), the trade unions' journal. In 1936 he was transferred to Łódź to run the Bund branch there, and in 1938 he was elected to the Łódź city council.

When World War II broke out, Zygelbojm returned to Warsaw. He was one of the two Jews among the twelve hostages that the Germans took in Warsaw at the beginning of the occupation (the other was Abraham Gepner). After his release he was among the group of Bund members who organized an underground center of the party, and he was delegated by the Bund to represent it in the first Judenrat (Jewish Council) set up in Warsaw. At the end of December 1939, when he was in danger of being arrested, Zygelbojm left the country in a semilegal way and went to Belgium. There he gave a report to a Socialist International meeting on the persecution of the Jews in the early stage of the Nazi occupation of Poland. When Belgium fell into German hands, Zygelbojm fled to France, and in September 1940 he left France for New York. In March 1942 he was sent to London as a member of the National Council of the Polish government-in-exile, which now became the central arena of his activities.

Zygelbojm adhered to the hard line of his party, and his uncompromising anti-Zionist position did not make it easier for the other Jewish member of the council, the Zionist Ignacy Isaac Schwarzbart, to cooperate with Zygelbojm. In the meetings of the National Council, Zygelbojm stressed his belief in a free Poland in which an **egalitarian** and just society would rid

egalitarian: relating to the belief that all people are equal.

"May my death be a resounding cry of protest, against the indifference with which the world looks at the destruction of the Jewish world, looks on and does nothing to stop it."

Samuel Artur Zygelbojm, 1943

itself of the evil of anti-Semitism. When, however, more and more reports came in of the murder campaign that was being conducted in Poland, Zygelbojm, with tremendous zeal and devotion, took up the task of letting the world know what was happening. He mobilized aid for the persecuted Jews and, with the help of the Polish government-in-exile, appealed to public opinion in the free countries, and especially to the organized Socialist movement, to provide aid and effective means of rescue. Zygelbojm maintained close ties with Socialists in the government-in-exile and its institutions, and as a result he sometimes received information that had been withheld from Schwarzbart.

In May 1942 a report reached Zygelbojm from the Bund in Warsaw on the mass murder of Jews in Poland. This report, which had been passed on to London by the Polish underground, was one of the first sources of information concerning the mass slaughter and its dimensions. It contained a list of the places in which *Aktionen* had been carried out, identified the sites of the extermination camps, and gave an estimate of the number of Jews who had by then been killed—seven hundred thousand. In public appearances Zygelbojm made constant efforts to draw attention to what was taking place in Poland and to appeal to the conscience of the world. In an address broadcast by the BBC, on June 2, 1942, Zygelbojm spoke of "the Jews in the ghettos who day by day see their relatives being dragged away en masse to their death, knowing only too well that their own turn will come." "It will be a disgrace to go on living," Zygelbojm said in that speech, "to belong to the human race, unless immediate steps are taken to put a stop to this crime, the greatest that history has known." In another speech, in September 1942, Zygelbojm disclosed that reports were reaching the Polish government in London of seven thousand Jews being deported daily from Warsaw.

In October 1942 Zygelbojm met with Jan Karski, the liaison officer between the Polish underground and the government-in-exile. Karski had just come from Poland, and before leaving had seen one of the camps and visited the Warsaw ghetto. (He believed that he had seen the Bełżec camp, but many years after the war it became clear that he had been to some other camp in the Lublin area.) Karski was the bearer of a message from two Jewish representatives with the underground on the Polish side of Warsaw, one of them Leon Feiner, a member of the Bund, and the other, apparently, Arie Wilner. Feiner, so Karski said, had asked him to report:

> We are full of hate for all those who saved themselves and are now there, because they are not helping us . . . are not doing enough. We know that over there, in the free world, they cannot believe what is going on here; so something must be done to force the world to believe. . . . We here are all dying, so let them die there too; let them besiege the Churchill government and the other governments, declare a hunger strike and die on the doorstep of these governments, and refuse to move from there until the governments believe what is going on here and take steps to save the remnants that are still alive.

As Karski reported it, Zygelbojm's reaction was: "But that's impossible! If I do that, they'll send two policemen to arrest me for breaking the peace; I am sure they would take me to some institution for a psychiatric examination. That's just impossible."

Zygelbojm, at an increasing rate and with an ever-growing sense of urgency, kept on making appeals. The statements he made at the time were each an SOS. He felt that he was racing against time, and became increasingly aware of his helplessness and his failure to communicate to his interlocutors the tempest raging in his own soul. He appealed to Churchill and Roosevelt and made sharp accusations in meetings of the Polish National Council. In a speech on the BBC in December 1942, Zygelbojm declared: "If Polish Jewry's call for help goes unheeded, Hitler will have achieved one of his war aims—to destroy the Jews of Europe irrespective of the final military outcome of the war."

Zygelbojm's last letters, to the Polish Bund's office in the United States and to his brother in Australia, speak with despair of the futility of his rescue efforts; he states in them that he "belongs to those who are over there." On May 12, 1943, when word came of the liquidation of the last Jews of Warsaw—among them his wife, Manya, and his sixteen-year-old son, Tuvia—Zygelbojm put an end to his life. In farewell letters addressed to the president of the Polish republic, Władysław Raczkiewicz, and to the prime minister of the Polish government-in-exile, Władysław Sikorski, Zygelbojm wrote:

> Responsibility for the murder of the entire Jewish population of Poland lies primarily with the murderers themselves, but indi-

1895 Zygelbojm is born in Borowice in Poland.

1924 Zygelbojm becomes a member of the Bund central committee.

1930 Zygelbojm begins editing the journal *Workers' Issues*.

1938 Zygelbojm is elected to the Łódź city council.

1939 Zygelbojm flees to Belgium.

1940 Zygelbojm flees to New York.

1942 Zygelbojm becomes a member of the Polish government-in-exile; begins appealing to the world to help Polish Jews.

1943 Zygelbojm, in despair, commits suicide.

> *"I cannot keep quiet, I cannot live, while the remnants of the Jewish people in Poland, who sent me here, are being destroyed."*
>
> Samuel Artur Zygelbojm, 1943

rectly humanity as a whole is responsible, all the Allied nations and their governments who to date have done nothing to stop the crime from going on. . . . The Polish government did much to rouse world opinion, but it was not convincing enough. . . . I cannot keep quiet, I cannot live, while the remnants of the Jewish people in Poland, who sent me here, are being destroyed. My comrades in the Warsaw ghetto have died a hero's death in the final battle, with a weapon in their hands. I did not have the honor to fall like them. But I belong to them and to their grave—their mass grave. May my death be a resounding cry of protest, against the indifference with which the world looks at the destruction of the Jewish world, looks on and does nothing to stop it. I know that a human life is of little value nowadays, but since I did not succeed in accomplishing anything while I was alive, I hope that my death will shock those who have been indifferent, shock them into action in this very moment, which may be the last moment for the remnants of Polish Jewry. ◆

Blobel, Paul

1894–1951

S officer. Born into a Protestant family, Blobel attended a vocational school, where he learned construction and carpentry. In World War I he volunteered for the army and served in the engineering corps. After the war he resumed his studies, became an architect, and settled in Solingen. In the depression he lost his job and could not find any other employment. He joined the Nazi party in October 1931, and in January 1932 enlisted in the SS. In March 1933 he entered service with the Staatspolizei (Stapo) in Düsseldorf, and on June 1, 1934, he transferred to the SD (Sicherheitsdienst; Security Service) with the rank of *Untersturmführer* and was appointed SD officer for the Düsseldorf area. He advanced rapidly in the SS hierarchy and became a *Standartenführer* on January 30, 1941.

At the beginning of June 1942, Blobel was summoned to Pretzsch, a town on the Elbe northeast of Leipzig, where candidates for service in the Einsatzgruppen were being assembled to be deployed in German-occupied territory in the Soviet Union. Blobel was appointed commanding officer of Sonderkommando 4a of Einsatzgruppe C, which was assigned to the Ukraine. At the head of this unit Blobel went from Sokal to Kiev by way of Volhynia, engaging in *Aktionen* along the route, in Lutsk, Dubno, Zhitomir, Berdichev, and other places. When Kiev fell, he entered the city and with his unit organized and carried out the murder of Kiev's Jews at Babi Yar, on September 29 and 30, 1941. His last *Aktion* in that area took place in Kharkov, where his unit murdered 21,685 Jews in Drobitski Yar at the end of December 1941.

On January 13, 1942, Blobel was released from his post for reasons of health—he suffered from a liver ailment that was aggravated by his excessive drinking. When he recovered he was called to the Reichssicherheitshauptamt (Reich Security Main Office; RSHA) and put in charge of *Aktion* 1005, an operation whose goal was to obliterate the traces of the mass murders committed by the Germans. Blobel established his headquarters in Łódź; his direct superior was the Gestapo chief, Heinrich Müller, in Berlin.

Until the fall of 1943, the method Blobel used was to cremate the bodies on huge pyres. The first experiments to employ this method were carried out in Chełmno. The permanent camps, such as Auschwitz, were later equipped with crematoria. In the fall of 1943 Blobel set up special units, the Sonderkommandos 1005, for the specific task of disinterring and cremating the bodies from the mass graves in the German-occupied parts of the Soviet Union. These units were manned by Jewish and other prisoners who were killed when their work in a given place was done. Some of these prisoners, especially the Jews among them, succeeded in escaping, notably in Babi Yar, Janówska, the Ninth Fort in Kovno, Ponary, and Grabowka, near Białystok. At the end of October 1944, when their tasks were completed, the German personnel who had served in the Sonderkommandos 1005—men of the SD, Sicherheitspolizei (Security Police), and Ordnungspolizei (German regular police)—all joined Einsatzgruppe "Iltis," a new unit commanded by Blobel. It was posted to Carinthia, on the Austro-Yugoslav border, to take part in fighting against the Yugoslav partisans.

Blobel was arrested after the war and was one of the principal defendants in the *Einsatzgruppen* case (Trial 9) at the subsequent Nuremberg proceedings. He was sentenced to death in 1948 and hanged at the Landsberg prison in Bavaria on June 8, 1951. ◆

Bormann, Martin

1900–1945?

Nazi leader and close aide of Adolf Hitler. Bormann was born in Halberstadt into the family of a postal worker. Toward the end of World War I he interrupted his high school studies to enlist in the artillery, but the war ended before he reached the front. At the end of the war Bormann joined the Deutsche Freikorps, which carried out acts of violence along the Latvian border after Latvia declared itself independent. Subsequently, Bormann was active in the underground, paramilitary nationalist Frontbann organization, created by Ernst Röhm, and participated in one of its political assassinations (*Fememorde*). In 1923 he was arrested for this, and sentenced to a year's imprisonment. In prison he became acquainted with Rudolf Höss, future commandant of the Auschwitz extermination camp. After Bormann's release in 1925, he joined the Nazi party and the SA (Sturmabteilung; Storm Troopers) in Thuringia, and in 1926 was appointed head of Nazi press affairs and deputy SA commander of the region. In 1928 he rose to the rank of *Gauleiter* of Thuringia. Known in the Nazi party as an active fund-raiser, he was appointed treasurer at the party center in Munich.

With the Nazi rise to power in 1933, Bormann was elected to the Reichstag and became head of the office of Rudolf Hess, Hitler's deputy in the party. From this time Bormann remained at the center of Nazi power around Hitler and was responsible for all financial and administrative affairs. He was always in the shadow of the Führer, excelling as a planner and a behind-the-scenes man, but not as a public speaker.

After Hess's strange flight to Scotland in 1941, Bormann's power increased. In 1942 he was appointed head of the party secretariat and of the party staff, with the rank of *Reichsminister*, and in 1943 he became Hitler's secretary. In this capacity, Bormann also controlled Hitler's appointments calendar, sometimes preventing important figures such as Hermann Göring, Joseph Goebbels, Heinrich Himmler, and Albert Speer from approaching the leader. He took notes on Hitler's speeches and monologues at luncheons with his favorites, the material known as Hitler's "table talks."

As the war continued and became Hitler's principal occupation, Bormann's status grew, since he was charged in Hitler's name not only with party affairs but with the domestic affairs of Germany. In particular, Bormann was active in fields such as the Euthanasia Program, the war against the church, the pillage of art objects in the occupied countries of eastern Europe, and the expansion of forced-labor programs throughout Europe. Above all, Bormann, who was completely amoral, was the zealous executor of the racist plan of National Socialism and in particular of the persecution and extermination of the Jews. He signed the series of anti-Jewish edicts ordering the deportation of the Jews to the east, the concentration of power in Jewish affairs in the hands of the SS, and the concealment of the massacre as the "transfer of the Jews to labor in the east."

Bormann was appointed commander of the People's Army (Volkssturm), created toward the end of the war, in October 1944. His desire for greater personal power did not cease even after Hitler entered his bunker in Berlin. In the last stage of Nazi rule, Bormann tried to have Göring executed, was a witness to Hitler's marriage to Eva Braun a day before their suicide, and observed the suicide of Goebbels and his family. Before the surrender, it was Bormann who informed Admiral Karl Dönitz that Dönitz had been appointed the Führer's successor.

After Hitler's death, Bormann allegedly tried to conduct negotiations with the Soviets, but after becoming convinced that these were hopeless he gave the order to escape from the bunker. With that his trace vanished. On October 29, 1945, Bormann was indicted *in absentia* with the other Nazi leaders by the International Military Tribunal at Nuremberg, and on October 1, 1946, he was sentenced to death *in absentia*.

Bormann's fate is uncertain. According to unreliable testimony, he was killed by a Soviet shell or committed suicide, and according to rumors that spread in the 1960s he escaped to South America, perhaps to Paraguay. In early 1973 a West German forensic expert determined that one of two skeletons discovered in West Berlin during excavations in 1972 was almost certainly that of Bormann. On the basis of this determination, Bormann was officially declared dead. ◆

Clauberg, Carl

1898–1957

SS physician infamous for his experiments in sterilizing Jewish women at the Auschwitz extermination camp during World War II. Clauberg was born at Wupperhof and served in the infantry during World War I. He later studied medicine at the universities of Kiel, Hamburg, and Graz, qualifying as a doctor in 1925. He had a successful medical career and in 1937 was appointed professor of gynecology and obstetrics at the University of Königsberg. At the same time he was chief doctor at a women's clinic in Upper Silesia and published numerous papers in his specialty. Clauberg was an enthusiastic Nazi, joining the party in 1933 and rising to the rank of *Brigade-führer* in the SS.

The sterilization program was initiated in 1941, and in 1942 Heinrich Himmler entrusted Clauberg with its experimental implementation at Auschwitz. He had the cooperation of internee doctors there (including the Polish camp doctor, Władysław Dering, whose experiments were later the subject of a famous libel case in England in 1964). The experiments at Auschwitz lasted until 1944; they involved sterilization by means of injections into the womb, which caused unimaginable suffering to the victims, Jewish and Gypsy women. Clauberg conducted similar experiments in the women's concentration camp of Ravensbrück in 1945.

Arrested by the Russians at the end of the war, Clauberg was tried in 1948 for his role in the "mass extermination of Soviet citizens." He was sentenced to twenty-five years' imprisonment, but was released in 1955 under the German-Soviet prisoner repatriation agreement. Clauberg showed no regrets for his experiments, and even boasted of his "scientific achievements." At the initiative of the Central Council of Jews in Germany, an action to prosecute Clauberg was undertaken in the West German courts. The council accused Clauberg of "having caused severe bodily harm" to Jewish women. The Kiel police put him under arrest, but he died in a hospital shortly before the date of the trial. ◆

Eichmann, Adolf

1906–1962

Nazi official who played a central role in organizing the anti-Jewish policies culminating in the "Final Solution." Eichmann was born in Solingen, in the Rhineland; his father was an accountant. His mother died when he was eight years old, and the family—the father and five children—moved to Linz, Austria. Eichmann did not complete secondary school, nor did he finish the course in mechanics at the vocational school that he attended for two years. After holding

several different jobs he became a traveling salesman for an American oil company, Vacuum Oil; using a motorcycle for his rounds, he had an accident in which he was seriously injured. In 1933 he was dismissed from his job. The previous year an acquaintance, Ernst Kaltenbrunner, had persuaded Eichmann to join the Austrian National Socialist party, and eventually also the SS. When the latter was outlawed in Austria in 1933, Eichmann, now unemployed, moved to Germany. There he enlisted in the Austrian unit of the SS, where he also went through military training. He then served for a while in the Dachau concentration camp.

In October 1934 Eichmann volunteered to work in the central office of the SD (Sicherheitsdienst; Security Service), then headed by Reinhard Heydrich, and moved to Berlin. At the time, Heinrich Himmler was chief of police in the SD. Eichmann first worked in the section that dealt with the Freemasons, and in 1935 he was moved to a new intelligence section, the Jewish section, then under Herbert Hagen. Henceforth Eichmann regarded the solution of the "Jewish question" in the Third Reich as his life mission.

Eichmann was now one of the chief planners of the anti-Jewish operations undertaken by the SS; before long, he was also responsible for their execution. At this time the SD and the Gestapo joined in an effort designed to speed up the emigration of the Jews from Germany, as part of which Hagen and Eichmann were sent in 1937 to Palestine and Egypt on a fact-finding mission. Eichmann's conclusion was that increased immigration of Jews into Palestine was not desirable, since the establishment of a Jewish state was not in the interest of the Third Reich.

Following the annexation of Austria to Germany in March 1938, Eichmann was sent to Vienna to organize the emigration of the Jews. It was here that he first revealed his organizational talent and his ability to put the anti-Jewish aims of the Nazis into practice. It was Eichmann who evolved a method of forced emigration, consisting of three elements: undermining the economic condition of the Jews by confiscation of their property; putting fear into their hearts by the use of terror; seizing control of Jewish communal institutions and forcing their leaders to cooperate (a foretaste of the Judenrat). In August 1938, in order to streamline the Jewish emigration process, Eichmann set up the Zentralstelle für Jüdische Auswanderung (Central Office for Jewish Emigration), whose purpose was to strip the Jews of all their belongings and leave them with no option but to seek emigration to some other country and to get there with the help of some Jewish organization (mainly the Joint Distribution Committee). Eichmann also took direct action to expel Jews, by pushing some of them into a no-man's-land across the Austrian border. Contrary to his previous reservations concerning Jewish immigration into Palestine, he now cooperated with the Jewish organizations that were running Aliya Bet ("illegal" immigration). When the Germans seized control of Bohemia and Moravia, Eichmann introduced the system of forced emigration to Prague, and, in the summer of 1939, he established in the Czech capital a Central Office for Jewish Emigration, on the model of the Vienna office. The pattern established by Eichmann had been adopted by the Reich leaders even earlier, in the wake of *Kristallnacht,* and on January 24, 1939, on Hermann Göring's order, the Reichszentrale für Jüdische Auswanderung (Reich Central Office for Jewish Emigration) was set up in Germany under Heydrich in the Ministry of the Interior.

During 1938 and 1939 Eichmann's authority over Jewish policies grew rapidly; when war broke out, his area of operations was greatly widened and his own position strengthened. Following Himmler's creation in September 1939 of the Reichssicherheitshauptamt (Reich Security Main Office; RSHA), under Heydrich, Eichmann was appointed head of the Jewish section in the Gestapo, whose chief at the time was Heinrich Müller. Eichmann's authority exceeded that of a section chief. In practice he came directly under Heydrich, but from time to time he was also called in by Himmler. In 1939 and 1940 Eichmann played the central role in the expulsion of Poles and Jews from the Polish areas that had been incorporated into the Reich. By that time Eichmann had already established, in coordination with Müller, the pattern for the mass expulsion of Jews in an operation in which Jews from Vienna and Czechoslovakia were deported to Nisko. On the basis of this pattern, the methods were developed for mass deportations throughout the Nazi period. The Nisko operation served as a precedent for the attempt to concentrate all the Jews of the Reich in the Lublin Reservation—the first phase in the Nazi leaders' search for a total solution to the "Jewish question." After Nisko, further attempts were made, under Eichmann's supervision, to expel Jews from several places in Germany itself, but they met with opposition in Germany and elsewhere, and the Lublin Reservation plan was rescinded.

In October 1940 Eichmann in person led the expulsion of 6,500 Jews from Baden-Pfalz and the Saar district to the south of France. The operation may have been connected with the Madagascar Plan; while this plan was being prepared by the German Foreign Ministry, Eichmann was working out his own detailed program for the creation of a huge police-controlled ghetto on that tropical island off the coast of Africa. Eichmann was, by this time, in undisputed control of the Jewish populations of Germany, the Ostmark (Austria), and the Protectorate of Bohemia and Moravia. From time to time he summoned the leaders of these Jewish populations to his office in Berlin to give them his orders, especially concerning the issue of forced emigration—orders that were then carried out under the watchful eye of Eichmann's representatives in the respective capitals. He had a network of officials in most of the German-occupied countries and in the satellite states, where they served as "advisers" to the governments, their task being to promote the implementation of anti-Jewish policies. The more prominent of these representatives were Alois Brunner, Theodor Dannecker, Dieter Wisliceny, and Rolf Günther (Eichmann's deputy).

A significant change in Eichmann's activities came with the decision to execute the "final solution of the Jewish question," together with the war against the Soviet Union. The final form of the Jewish section in the RSHA had been laid down in March 1941, and henceforth the section bore the designation IV B 4. Eichmann now gave orders on various occasions prohibiting the emigration of Jews from the European continent, and he ceased cooperating with the organizers of the "illegal" immigration into Palestine. His operations reached their full extent after Himmler's order of October 1941 prohibiting the emigration of Jews, which coincided with the start of transports of Jews from Germany to the east. Preparations for mass murder had begun even earlier, in the summer of 1941, at which time Eichmann, on Himmler's order, held talks with Rudolf Höss, the commandant of Auschwitz, on the practical details of the mass murder.

In October 1941 Eichmann took part in more discussions on the subject, conducted by those charged with the implementation of the "Final Solution." At this point, he was promoted to *Obersturmbannführer* (lieutenant colonel). Since Eichmann was the officer in charge of transporting the Jews of Europe to the extermination sites, Heydrich asked him to prepare the Wannsee Conference, where the implementation of the operation was outlined, with the participation of all government bodies that had a part in the "Final Solution." It was Eichmann who sent the invitations to the various officials, drafted Heydrich's address to the conference, and took down the minutes. Following the conference, he called in his representatives from the various countries to plan the operation. In 1942 and 1943, the years in which Jews from all over Europe were being deported to the extermination camps in Poland, it was from Eichmann's office that the orders went out for the time and place of departure of the transports, the number of deportees, and so on. The schedules were coordinated with the railway authorities in each country; Eichmann was also in close contact with Martin Luther of the German Foreign Ministry. Rules were laid down on rounding up the Jews, seizing their homes, and confiscating their property; Eichmann saw to it that in Germany itself, his section would benefit from the booty.

Eichmann made every effort to solve problems in a way that ensured the maintenance of a regular timetable for the deportation trains going to the extermination camps. He made several visits to the camps and was well versed in the murder procedure. Eichmann was not directly involved in the extermination actions in Poland or the areas that had belonged to the Soviet Union, nor did he take any part in the Einsatzgruppen operations, but through his representatives, he was active in all the other European countries from which Jews were being sent to their death. Only the Scandinavian countries—Denmark, Norway, and Finland—had no Eichmann representatives. One of the problems that confronted Eichmann and his associates was the treatment of the partners of mixed marriages and their progeny; there were many discussions on the subject, but the issue was never completely resolved.

A special place in Eichmann's actions was held by the Theresienstadt ghetto, which served first as a concentration camp for Jews from Czechoslovakia and Vienna, and later also for Jews of privileged status (mainly from Germany) and those over sixty, of whom it could not be said that they were being sent to the east to work. In practice, the "ghetto for the aged" was no more than a transit camp, from which a great many trains left for the extermination camps. Eichmann also tried to project Theresienstadt as a "model ghetto" by showing it to Red Cross commissions—after first altering its appearance with temporary improvements—in order to refute published reports of the atrocities that the Nazis were committing.

Only in Hungary was Eichmann personally in charge of the deportations. Immediately after the occupation of the country by German forces on March 19, 1944, Eichmann arrived in Hungary, accompanied by a large team of aides, which he had assembled at the Mauthausen camp in preparation for the invasion. In Hungary, Eichmann put to full use all the experience he had gained; within a short period—from May to early July—he succeeded in deporting some 440,000 Jews from all the provinces that were then part of Hungary. This was made possible by the cooperation of the Hungarian authorities. Even after the Hungarians stopped the deportations in early July, Eichmann tried, by deceptive tactics, to have additional thousands of Jews deported from Budapest. But it was only in October 1944, following the Arrow Cross Party coup d'état in Hungary, that he was able to resume his murderous operations. By now it was no longer possible to send the Jews to Auschwitz by train, since the murders in the gas chambers there had stopped and the eastern front had drawn near. Eichmann's answer was to put 76,000 Jews on death marches to Austria, from where they were to be sent to forced-labor camps in Germany.

In Hungary, Eichmann encountered various efforts to rescue the Jews; among these was the rescue work carried out by Raoul Wallenberg, in conjunction with other representatives of neutral countries, which persisted despite all that Eichmann tried to do to thwart it. Eichmann played a major role in the "Blood for Goods" plan, which led to the Joel Brand mission to Istanbul, with a proposal to set Jews free in exchange for a supply of trucks and other goods needed by the Germans. He was also involved in the Europa Plan conceived in Slovakia, according to which Jews were to be released in return for a large payment in United States dollars. On various occasions Eichmann intervened in order to foil opportunities that presented themselves for saving Jews and removing them from German control, as in negotiations with Bulgaria and Romania. In two instances Eichmann was forced to agree to the liberation of some Jews: in the "Repatriation" plan, which primarily affected Jews of Spanish origin trapped in Greece, and in the program for the exchange of Jews and Germans.

When the war ended, Eichmann went into hiding and then, like other SS men, fled to Argentina with the help of the Vatican. He lived there with his family until May 1960, when he was captured by the Israeli Security Service and brought to Israel. In April 1961 he was put on trial before the district court in Jerusalem. He was found guilty and sentenced to death; the Israeli Supreme Court, sitting as a court of appeals, upheld the sentence, and on June 1, 1962, Eichmann was executed by hanging. His body was cremated and the ashes scattered over the sea.

The trial engendered a debate about Eichmann's character. Some, headed by Hannah Arendt, argued that Eichmann was a very ordinary individual, who was not motivated by any special hatred of Jews, and that all he did—as he himself claimed—was to carry out the orders received from his superiors, within the general framework of Nazi bureaucracy. Others believe that Eichmann was the personification of the spirit of inhumanity in Nazism, the regime that nurtured the rise of destructive drives and created the conditions for mass murder and the execution of the "Final Solution." What cannot be doubted is that Eichmann served the Nazi program for exterminating the Jewish people with zeal and efficiency. ◆

Frank, Hans

1900–1946

Jurist and Nazi official; governor-general of Poland from 1939 to 1945. When Hitler's Germany conquered Poland in September 1939, the eastern third of the country was occupied by the Soviet Union (in accordance with the secret terms of the Nazi-Soviet Pact), the western third was annexed to the Third Reich, and the central region became a German-occupied territory known as the Generalgouvernement. Appointed governor-general was the legal expert of the Nazi party and Hitler's personal lawyer, Hans Frank, who henceforth played a major, albeit vacillating, role in implementing the racial policies that the Nazis pursued so relentlessly in eastern Europe.

Hans Frank graduated from a Munich *Gymnasium* in 1918. The young Frank displayed his commitment to militant nationalist and right-wing politics by joining the Epp Freikorps (a paramilitary group commanded by Ritter von Epp in 1919 while he was pursuing the study of law at the universities of Kiel and Munich. In 1923 he passed his first-level exams, joined the SA (Sturmabteilung; Storm Troopers) and Nazi party, and took part in Hitler's ill-fated Beer-Hall Putsch in Munich. He fled briefly to Austria, then returned to Germany to finish his doctorate at the University of Kiel in 1924.

In 1926 Frank left the Nazi party in protest against Hitler's renunciation of German claims over the South Tyrol, only to rejoin a year later. His career in the party then flourished as he undertook the legal defense of various party members, most prominently in Hitler's many libel cases and in the 1930 Leipzig trial of three Nazi army officers. He also handled the very delicate matter of researching Hitler's family tree for possible Jewish ancestors.

After Hitler took power, Frank's usefulness rapidly diminished. He was given numerous honorific but powerless positions that helped to make plausible the charade of Hitler's "legal revolution." In 1933 he was appointed minister of justice for the state of Bavaria, and in 1934, minister without portfolio. From 1934 to 1941 he was president of the Academy for German Law, with the self-assigned task of reformulating German law on the basis of National Socialist principles. A middle-class intellectual who was never admitted to the inner circle of Nazi leaders, Frank remained oblivious to Hitler's open aversion to law, lawyers, and any procedures that threatened to curtail his own freedom of action. He came to prominence when Hitler appointed him head of the Generalgouvernement in October 1939.

Frank's ambitions in the Generalgouvernement, both to build up a strong power base for himself and to retain Hitler's favor, encountered almost constant frustration. Hitler's practice of presiding over a chaotic system of "institutional Darwinism"—leaving his various vassals to engage in a constant internal struggle for power and jurisdiction and keeping for himself the role of indispensable arbiter and pacesetter—was incompatible with Frank's mania for "unity of administration." While Frank managed to curtail the influence of the military and to reach an agreement for close cooperation with Hermann Göring concerning the economic exploitation of the Generalgouvernement, his efforts to control the activities of Heinrich Himmler's SS and police were totally futile.

As a result, Frank was torn between two opposing tactics. In his desire to build up his own domain, he inclined toward a pragmatic policy of economic stabilization, less arbitrary and oppressive treatment of the Poles, and their closer integration into the Third Reich. However, in response to contrary hints periodically emanating from Hitler, or in order to outbid his rival Himmler, Frank often veered suddenly to support policies of radical brutality and destructiveness, usually accompanied by bombastic pronouncements delivered with great rhetorical flourish. Thus, Frank vacillated between opposing and supporting the influx of Poles and Jews expelled from the "incorporated territories," between approving the self-sufficiency and rational exploitation of ghetto economies and encouraging the starvation and then mass murder of the Jews, between a genocidal repression of Polish culture and national consciousness and recruitment of Polish collaboration through assuring the Poles a place in the New Order.

Ultimately, Frank's loyalty to Hitler and his own ambition could not be reconciled. He saw himself as the head of the model "crusader kingdom" of Germany's *Drang nach Osten* (drive to the east), while Hitler saw the Generalgouvernement as the racial dumping ground, the slave-labor reservoir, and finally the slaughter yard of the Third Reich. Since Himmler's views more closely approximated those of Hitler, Frank's defeat was inevitable. On March 5, 1942, the hapless Frank was summoned before a tribunal consisting of Himmler, Hans Heinrich Lammers, and Martin Bormann, and stripped of all jurisdiction over racial and police matters. These were now to be the exclusive domain of Himmler's *Höherer SS- und Polizeiführer* (Higher SS and Police Leader), Friedrich Wilhelm Krüger.

Perhaps feeling himself free to play the fool, or hoping to force Hitler to relieve him from his humiliating position, Frank delivered a series of lectures at four German universities in the summer of 1942, denouncing the emasculation of German justice by the police state. He also sent Hitler a long memorandum criticizing SS policies in Poland. "You should not slaughter the cow you want to milk," he concluded. Hitler relieved Frank of all his party positions and forbade him to speak publicly within the Reich, but refused to accept his numerous letters of resignation. Thus Frank remained as governor-general until he fled before the Russian advance; he took with him the many volumes of his official diary that have since become a major source for historians of the Third Reich and an important document for the Nuremberg Military Tribunals. Frank was tried among the major war criminals in the Nuremberg Trial, and hanged at Nuremberg. ◆

Goebbels, Joseph

1897–1945

Nazi leader. Goebbels was born in Rheydt, in the Rhine district, into a poor and pious Catholic family. Born with a clubfoot, he did not serve in the army in World War I; instead, he studied at the University of Heidelberg and earned a doctorate in literature and philosophy. After failing in his attempts to become a writer, Goebbels found ample room for his talents as a propagandist and speaker for the Nazi party, which he joined in 1924. At first he worked together with Gregor Strasser, a rival of Adolf Hitler, but before long he became one of Hitler's most ardent admirers and in 1926 was appointed *Gauleiter* of Berlin, his assignment being to win over the capital for the party. In 1928 he was elected to the Reichstag. Two years later he was also appointed the party's chief of propaganda, and it was he who ran the Nazis' stormy election campaigns from 1930 to 1933.

On March 13, 1933, soon after Hitler's accession to power, Goebbels was appointed minister of propaganda and public information. He imposed Nazification upon the country's artistic and cultural life, working through the branches of the ministry that he headed. He controlled the media (although he had to contend with some rivals in that regard), and it was at his prompting that "un-German" books were burned on May 10, 1933. Goebbels was also one of the creators of the "Führer" myth, an important element in the Nazis' successful bid for the support of the masses.

By the time the Nazi regime was firmly established, Goebbels's position was weakened and he also lost some of his standing in Hitler's eyes. Once the political forces that had opposed the Nazis were destroyed, Goebbels no longer had an "enemy" to fight (except for the Jewish "enemy"), and Hitler was angered by the frequent crises in Goebbels's marital life, fearing that they might cause damage to the party's image.

When the war broke out, Goebbels assumed a key role in psychological warfare (although in that field, too, he had rivals), and when the situation on the fronts took a turn for the worse, he again played a central part in the leadership. His ties with Hitler resumed their closeness, although the feelers that he put out to bring the war to a "political end" were disregarded, as, for a long while, was his demand for the "totalization" of the war. It was only in July 1944 that he was appointed to the coveted task of having responsibility for the total mobilization of the population for the war effort.

When Hitler put an end to his life in the besieged capital, Goebbels refused to accept the post of Reich chancellor, to which he was appointed in Hitler's will. On May 1, 1945, on the morrow of Hitler's suicide, Goebbels and his wife, Magda, followed Hitler's example and also committed suicide in the Führer bunker, after first ordering the killing of their six children, aged four to twelve.

Goebbels was the father of modern propaganda in a totalitarian state (a term that he coined), in which he made use of every available means. The propaganda he spread was remarkably replete with defamations, libels, and lies; he was convinced that people would believe the lies if only they were repeated often enough, and the bigger the lie, the better chance it had of being believed. Goebbels's propaganda always incited hate against some enemy. He was a radical and fanatic anti-Semite, but his hatred of Jews was also based on utilitarian considerations of exploiting anti-Semitism for the furthering of his propaganda aims.

Goebbels was relentless in depicting "the Jew" as an abominable creature and the principal enemy of the German people. It was Goebbels who conceived the idea of the *Kristallnacht* pogroms in November 1938, and it was he who gave the event its flippant designation. Following these pogroms, he drastically reduced organized Jewish activities and freedom of movement in the sphere that he controlled. Once the war had broken out, the ministry he headed launched a concerted effort designed to aggravate living conditions for the Jews of Berlin. The first deportations of Berlin Jews to the Łódź ghetto, in October 1941, were carried out to fulfill an express promise that Goebbels had given to Hitler, to make Berlin *judenrein* ("cleansed of Jews") as soon as possible. In pursuit of this aim, Goebbels always kept in touch with Hitler and with the Reichssicherheitshauptamt (Reich Security Main Office; RSHA). His diary contains specific mention of the destruction of the Jews; in an entry that he made in May 1943, when the extermination operation in Poland was at its height, Goebbels stated: "The nations that were the first to reveal the true face of the Jew will be the ones that will take the Jew's place in ruling the world." ◆

Göring, Hermann

1893–1946

Nazi leader. Göring was born in Rosenheim, Bavaria, the son of a wealthy family. In World War I he distinguished himself as a fighter pilot and commander of a renowned fighter squadron. He joined the Nazi party in 1922, was appointed commander of the SA (Sturmabteilung; Storm Troopers), and in November 1923 took part in the abortive Nazi putsch in Munich, in which he was wounded. In 1928 Göring was elected to the Reichstag on the Nazi ticket; he was elected Reichstag speaker in 1932. When Adolf Hitler came to power, Göring was appointed minister without portfolio, and then commissioner of aviation and Prussian minister of the interior. In April 1933 he became prime minister of Prussia and was one of the men responsible for the creation of the Gestapo. In the minds of many people, Göring was regarded as being behind the plot to burn down the Reichstag, in February 1933. In June 1934 he played a major role, together with Heinrich Himmler, in the liquidation of the SA leader Ernst Röhm and his cohorts. Göring was appointed commander of the German air force (the Luftwaffe) in January 1935; this was followed by his promotion to *Reichsmarschall*. In 1936 he was put in charge of the Four-Year Plan and given dictatorial powers in the economic sphere. From August 1939 Göring chaired the ministerial Reich Defense Council (Reichsverteidigungsrat), and on September 1, 1939, when war broke out, Hitler appointed him to be his successor.

As the person in charge of the country's economy, Göring was responsible for the confiscation of Jewish property in 1937. Following the *Kristallnacht* pogroms, Hitler put him in charge of the "Jewish question," and Göring lost no time in accelerating the plundering of the Jews, imposing on them a collective fine of a billion reichsmarks. On January 24, 1939, he issued orders for the establishment of the Zentralstelle für Jüdische Auswanderung (Central Office for Jewish Emigration), on the model of Eichmann's operations in this sphere in Vienna. When Poland was occupied, Göring became involved in the expulsion of Jews from the western parts of Poland that were annexed to the Reich, and he set up the Haupttreuhandstelle Ost (Main Trusteeship Office East), to take charge of and administer confiscated Jewish property. On July 31, 1941, Göring ordered Reinhard Heydrich to "carry out all necessary preparations with regard to the Jewish question in the German sphere of influence in Europe." In the opinion of many scholars, this order was the first important document that set the "Final Solution" in motion, and it establishes Göring's share in the responsibility for the extermination of the Jews of Europe.

As a result of the failures of the Luftwaffe in the Battle of Britain (1940–41), its weak performance on the Soviet front, and its inability to defend Germany's skies, relations between

Hitler and Göring soured. In the last few days of the Nazi regime, Göring lost whatever standing he had left, and was dismissed from all his posts and from the party; Hitler appointed Admiral Karl Dönitz in his place.

Göring was arrested by the Allies and was one of the defendants in the trial of major war criminals by the International Military Tribunal (the Nuremberg Trial). He was sentenced to death, but on October 15, 1946, the eve of his scheduled execution, he poisoned himself in his prison cell. ◆

Greiser, Arthur

1897–1946

Prominent figure in the Nazi party and the Third Reich administration. Greiser was born in the town of Środa, in the Poznań (Ger., Posen) province; his father was a government official. In World War I Greiser served as an air force officer. After the war he spent some time in the Freikorps and then tried his hand at business, without much success. In 1924 Greiser was one of the founders of Stahlhelm (Steel Helmet), a nationalist association of former servicemen, in Danzig. In 1928 he joined the Nazi party, and then the SA (Sturmabteilung; Storm Troopers); after a while, he switched to the SS. Greiser held various Nazi party posts in Danzig, was elected to the city senate, and was appointed its president in 1934, replacing Hermann Rauschning. (Between the two world wars Danzig had the status of a free city, under international trusteeship.)

During the Polish campaign in September 1939, Greiser was appointed head of the civilian administration of Poznań. In October and November he became *Gauleiter* and *Reichsstatthalter* (governor) of the Warthegau, the large Polish territory (which included the city of Łódź) that was incorporated into the Reich. Unlike the other governors of the Polish territorial units, Greiser was able to gain the support of persons with influence in the Reich Chancellery in Berlin and to maintain good relations with Heinrich Himmler. In 1942 he was appointed an SS-*Gruppenführer*. Greiser was determined to uproot the Polish population from the area under his administration, in order to speed up its "Germanization." His fanatic anti-Polish policy expressed itself in various forms, such as confiscating Polish property, restricting educational and cultural activities, "Germanizing" Polish orphans, and persecuting the Catholic church and the Polish clergy. His most severe action, however, was the expulsion of Poles and Jews from the territory. In the period from 1939 to 1945, some 630,000 Poles and Jews were removed or expelled from the Warthegau, and 537 Volksdeutsche (ethnic Germans) were brought in from areas in the Baltic states, southeastern Poland, Romania, and the Soviet Union.

In 1945 Greiser was captured by the Americans in the Alps and extradited to Poland. During the trial of Hans Biebow in 1946, the former German commissar of the Łódź ghetto testified that Greiser had rejected appeals to improve the food rations of the Jews in the ghetto, and that his radical anti-Jewish attitude had served as a model to his subordinates. Greiser had praised the men of the German unit that from December 1941 operated the Chełmno extermination camp in the area under his administration, the first of its kind in occupied Poland. Upon the conclusion of a *Sonderbehandlung* ("special treatment," that is, extermination) operation in which one hundred thousand Jews from the Warthegau had been killed, Greiser wrote a letter to Himmler proposing that the same treatment be meted out to Poles afflicted with tuberculosis, because they were endangering the health of the German population.

Greiser was tried in June and July 1946 by a Polish national tribunal and was sentenced to death. He was hanged in front of the house in Poznań that had served as his residence when he was governor of the Warthegau. ◆

Hess, Rudolf

1894–1987

Nazi leader; a close aide of Adolf Hitler. In World War I, Hess volunteered for service in the German army, serving first as an infantry officer and later as a pilot. Hess was among the first to join the Nazi party, in 1920. He took part in the abortive November 1923 putsch, when Hitler

tried to overthrow the Bavarian government, and was imprisoned in the Landsberg prison with Hitler, whom he helped to compose *Mein Kampf*. When the two were released in 1925, Hess became Hitler's personal aide and private secretary, a position he held until the Nazi rise to power, in January 1933. In April of that year, Hitler appointed Hess deputy leader of the Nazi party, and in December he was also named minister without portfolio; henceforth all the laws issued by the Nazi regime bore Hess's signature. A member of Hitler's inner circle, Hess was entrusted in 1938 with important missions relating to Germany's takeover of Austria and the Sudeten region of Czechoslovakia.

On the eve of World War II, Hess was a member of the Geheime Kabinetsrat (Secret Cabinet Council) and the Ministerrat für die Reichsverteidigung (Reich Ministerial Defense Council), two bodies with little influence. Hess's belief that he had been removed from the decision-making process, coupled with Hitler's intention to attack the Soviet Union, seem to have been among the factors that gave him the bold idea of flying to Britain. In May 1941 Hess took that step, in the hope that the impending invasion of Russia would persuade the British to make peace with Germany. No authoritative information has ever emerged as to whether Hess undertook his daring mission entirely on his own initiative, or whether he was inspired to do so by Hitler, directly or indirectly.

In the event, Hitler repudiated the attempt as soon as its failure was known. Hess was arrested when he landed in Britain and was held there until the end of the war. After the war he was one of the defendants at the main Nuremberg Trial, together with the other leaders of the Nazi regime. In October 1946 Hess was acquitted of war crimes and crimes against humanity, but was found guilty of crimes against the peace; he was sentenced to life imprisonment. The Soviet judge in the trial had demanded that he be condemned to death.

From that time on Hess was held in the Spandau Prison in West Berlin, under the joint control of the United States, Great

Britain, the Soviet Union, and France. At no time would the Soviets agree to his release, and for many years, until his death by suicide in August 1987, Hess was the sole inmate of the huge prison. ◆

Heydrich, Reinhard

1904–1942

Head of the Nazi Sicherheitspolizei (Security Police; Sipo), the SD (Sicherheitsdienst; Security Service), and, later, the Reichssicherheitshauptamt (Reich Security Main Office; RSHA); key person in planning and executing the anti-Jewish policies of the Third Reich.

Heydrich was born in Halle, a provincial Saxon town, to a family of musicians. His father was an opera singer and the director of a conservatory. In his youth Heydrich was exposed to his father's cult of Richard Wagner, his mother's stern discipline, and the worship of the authority of the state and its rulers. He was also exposed to a (false) suspicion that he was partly of Jewish origin.

Commissioned as an ensign and trained as a signal officer, Oberleutnant zur See Heydrich was discharged from the navy in April 1931. A naval court of honor found him guilty of misconduct toward a female friend, whom he mistreated and whose reputation he further blemished during the court proceedings.

Frustrated by the rules of civil society, Heydrich, who initially had regarded the Nazi party with contempt, was introduced by a family friend to Heinrich Himmler. Himmler made him an intelligence officer and entrusted him in 1931 with the organization of the SS espionage and surveillance apparatus, the SD. Freed from the restraints of navy discipline and the civil code of behavior, and benefiting from his threatening mien and "Aryan" look, Heydrich gave full rein to his ruthlessness, cynicism, and ambition, combining them with loyalty to his new masters. Inquiry into his alleged Jewish ancestry showed the rumor to be false, but his superiors capitalized on the suspicion, which guaranteed his loyalty. As SD chief, Heydrich was entrusted with the information gathering, blackmail, and intrigue needed to establish Himmler's control over the secret state police (Gestapo) during the first years of the Nazi regime. He was assisted by able administrators such as Carl Albrecht Oberg.

At the same time, Heydrich became executive director of the Bavarian political police, the nucleus of the Gestapo system under Himmler. The SD, together with the Gestapo, of which he later became executive director, was instrumental in establishing the Nazi terror apparatus and executing the leaders of the SA (Sturmabteilung; Storm Troopers) on June 30, 1934.

Heydrich played a role in purging the army high command in 1938, and also helped plant the false information that led to Stalin's purge of the Red Army's high command. Reflecting Himmler's fanatical race ideology, the SD developed into a political network of espionage and warfare, both ideological and practical, while suggesting increasingly radical solutions to the "Jewish question," such as pogroms and forced emigration. In 1936 Heydrich was made chief of the Gestapo and the Kriminalpolizei (Kripo), retaining separate control over the SD.

As Gestapo chief, Heydrich had unlimited power to confine to concentration camps "enemies of the Reich," among them Jews. He encouraged competition between the SD and the Gestapo, which under his aegis vied with each other to execute Hitler's Jewish policies. They also competed with other party elements, under Joseph Goebbels's influence, and with the SA. SD functionaries such as Adolf Eichmann were encouraged to implement "solutions" to the "Jewish question," such as the assembly-line deportation organized primarily for Jews in Austria and Czechoslovakia.

In *Kristallnacht*, the Goebbels-instigated pogrom of November 9 and 10, 1938, the SA and the Nazi party took the lead. Heydrich, however, assisted by Heinrich Müller and using prepared lists, saw to it that thousands of Jews were arrested by the Gestapo and SS. On January 24, 1939, Hermann Göring established the Reich's Zentralstelle für Jüdische Auswanderung (Central Office for Jewish Emigration), appointing Heydrich's subordinate Müller as its executive director. This transferred the implementation of the Reich's Jewish policy to the SS; from then on, Heydrich was the chief executor of this policy.

When war broke out in 1939, Heydrich was in charge of the Einsatzgruppen. In a special ordinance of September 21, 1939, he ordered them to carry out the ghettoization and concentration of Polish Jews and the establishment of Judenräte (Jewish councils). He then unified the Gestapo and SD within the framework of the newly established RSHA, giving ruthless SD functionaries such as Eichmann complete executive power in their anti-Jewish actions. Heydrich was instrumental in such schemes as the Nisko and Lublin Plan and the proposed mass deportations to Madagascar. In 1941, prior to Hitler's assault on the Soviet Union, Heydrich concluded, apparently on Hitler's order, an agreement with the army high command securing military assistance for the Einsatzgruppen in Russia. Heydrich ordered the latter to implement the "special tasks" of immediate annihilation of the Jews and Soviet officials in the Russian areas soon to be occupied.

On July 31 of that year, Göring, possibly on Heydrich's initiative, charged him with the "final solution of the Jewish question" in the entire German sphere of influence in Europe. To carry out this task, Heydrich required the cooperation of the Reich's ministerial agencies, and to this end he convened a meeting of top officials at Wannsee, a Berlin suburb, on January 20, 1942, to confirm the program for the planned extermination. Heydrich enjoyed direct access to Hitler and steadily increasing power, but it is debated to what extent he initiated the rationale and the methods adopted for the "Final Solution."

Late in 1941 Heydrich was rewarded for his anti-Jewish terror and extermination campaign by being appointed acting governor of the Protectorate of Bohemia and Moravia. Attacked by Czech resistance fighters in an ambush near Prague, Heydrich died of his wounds on June 4, 1942. In retaliation, five days later the Germans destroyed the Czech village of Lidice and killed all its male inhabitants. ◆

Himmler, Heinrich

1900–1945

Reich Leader (*Reichsführer*) of the SS, head of the Gestapo and the Waffen-SS, minister of the interior from 1943 to 1945, and, next to Adolf Hitler, the most powerful man in Nazi Germany. Himmler was born in Munich into a middle-class Catholic family; his father was a schoolteacher with authoritarian views. Educated at a secondary school in Landshut, Himmler joined the army in 1917 as an officer cadet, but he never saw service at the front. Later he studied agriculture and economics at the Munich School of Technology. He worked briefly as a salesman and as a chicken

farmer in the 1920s. During this period he developed a close contact with the embryonic Nazi party. Himmler took part in the Hitler putsch of 1923 at the side of Ernst Röhm, joined Röhm's terrorist organization, the Reichskriegsflagge (Reich War Flag), and held various positions in the *Gau* (region) of Bavaria.

In 1926 Himmler became assistant propaganda leader of the Nazi party. He joined the SS in 1925 and in 1929 became its head. This personal bodyguard of Hitler, which at that time numbered some two hundred men, became under Himmler's leadership a key element in the power structure of the Nazi state. Himmler was elected a Nazi Reichstag deputy in 1930, and immediately after the Nazi seizure of power in January 1933 was appointed police president in Munich and head of the political police throughout Bavaria. This gave him the power base to extend SS membership, organize the SD (Sicherheitsdienst; Security Service) under Reinhard Heydrich, and secure their independence from Röhm's SA (Sturmabteilung; Storm Troopers).

In September 1933 Himmler was appointed commander of all the political police units throughout the Reich (except Prussia). The following year, Hermann Göring appointed him deputy head of the Gestapo in Prussia. Himmler was instrumental in crushing the abortive SA putsch of June 1934, which eliminated Röhm and the SA as potential rivals for power and opened the way to the emergence of the SS as an independent force. The next stage in Himmler's ascendancy came in 1936, when he won control of the entire police force throughout the Third Reich, with the title of *Reichsführer-SS* and Head of the German Police. He created a state within a state, using his power to terrorize all opponents of the regime as well as his personal enemies. Himmler established the first concentration camp at Dachau in 1933, and the further organization and administration of the camps continued to be the work of the SS.

Himmler was inspired by a combination of fanatic racism and a belief in occult forces. His concern for "racial purity" led to the encouragement of special marriage laws that would further the systematic procreation of children of perfect "Aryan" couples, and also to the establishment of the Lebensborn (Fountain of Life) institutions at which girls would couple with SS men, both selected for their perfect Nordic qualities. Himmler aimed to create an aristocracy of the "master race," based on the traditional virtues of honor, obedience, and courage. By recruiting "Aryans" of different nationalities into the Waffen-SS, he would establish a pan-European order of knighthood, owing allegiance to Hitler alone. These fantasies went hand in hand with Himmler's efficiency, utter lack of scruples, and competence in administration. He suffered, however, from psychosomatic illnesses that took the form of intestinal cramps and severe headaches. Himmler was squeamish, and on one occasion he almost fainted at the spectacle of a hundred Jews, including women, being shot to death on the Russian front. This helped lead to the introduction of poison gas as "a more humane means" of execution.

The war gave Himmler the opportunity to implement the other side of his program, that is, the elimination of Jews and Slavs as "subhumans." This made Himmler one of the greatest mass murderers in history. In October 1939 he was appointed *Reichskommissar für die Festigung des deutschen Volkstums* (Reich Commissar for the Strengthening of German Nationhood) and was also given absolute authority in the newly annexed part of Poland. This entailed responsibility for the replacement of Poles and Jews by Volksdeutsche (ethnic Germans) from the Baltic states. By the time of the invasion of the Soviet Union in 1941, Himmler controlled all the organs of police and intelligence power, and through the SS he dominated the concentration and extermination camps in Poland. His Waffen-SS with its thirty-five divisions almost constituted a rival army to the Wehrmacht. He also controlled the political administration in the occupied territories. When he was made minister of the interior in 1943, Himmler gained jurisdiction over the courts and the civil service as well. He used these powers to exploit Jews and Slavs as slave laborers, to gas millions of Jews, and to institute pseudo-medical experiments on "asocial individuals" (Jews, Gypsies, and criminals), to determine their resistance to extremes of cold and decompression.

The killing of the Jews represented for Himmler the fulfillment of a mission. The "Final Solution" was the means to achieve the racial supremacy of the "Aryan" and purify the world of contamination by subhumans. His four Einsatzgruppen in the east were the agencies of extermination when the SS established the extermination camps of Bełżec, Sobibór, and Treblinka in the spring of 1942. After the July 1944 bomb plot on Hitler's life, Himmler received even further advancement, as commander in chief of the Reserve Army and commander of Army Group Vistula.

Toward the end of the war, aware of the inevitable German defeat, Himmler made a number of gestures, apparently hoping to ingratiate himself with the Allies. He sanctioned negotiations in Budapest that would have allowed the release of Hungarian Jews in return for trucks supplied by the Allies. In November 1944 he tried to conceal the evidence of mass murder in the extermination camps and permitted the transfer of several hundred camp prisoners to Sweden. He also tried to initiate peace negotiations with the Allies through Count Folke Bernadotte, head of the Swedish Red Cross. Himmler ordered a cessation of the mass murder of Jews at this time, and proposed surrendering to General Dwight D. Eisenhower in the west while continuing the struggle in the east. This proposal infuriated Hitler, who stripped Himmler of all his offices. Even Admiral Karl Dönitz, who succeeded Hitler in the last days of the war as head of the German government, spurned Himmler's services. After the German surrender, Himmler assumed a false identity and tried to escape, but he was captured by British troops. He committed suicide on May 23, 1945, before he could be brought to trial as one of the major war criminals. ◆

Hitler, Adolf

1889–1945

Führer (leader) of the Third German Reich. Born in Braunau, Austria, the son of a customs official from a smallholder family, Hitler spent his youth in the country of his birth. From 1900 to 1905 he attended the intermediate grades of the *Realschule* (secondary school), which concluded his formal education. Hitler's father died in 1903. In 1907 Hitler took the entrance test for the Vienna Academy of Art's School of Painting, and failed. His mother died that year, of breast cancer;

the doctor who treated her was a Jew named Eduard Bloch. In 1908 Hitler made Vienna his home, living on the orphan's stipend that he received. Anti-Semitism was rife in Vienna at the time. In Hitler's own words, the Vienna period of his life was formative and decisive in shaping his views, and especially his concept of the Jews; but it is not certain whether by then he was already an anti-Semite.

In 1913 Hitler moved to Munich. When World War I broke out in 1914, he volunteered for the Bavarian army. He served as a dispatch runner in Belgium and France, was promoted to private first class (lance corporal), and was awarded medals for bravery, one of them the Iron Cross, First Class, in 1918. That October he was temporarily blinded in a British gas attack, and in the military hospital at Pasewalk he learned of Germany's collapse. It was then and there, by his own admission, that Hitler decided to enter politics, in order to fight the Jews.

On his return to Munich, Hitler stated, in his first political document (written on September 19, 1919), that the final goal of anti-Semitism must be "the total removal of the Jews." He served as a political spokesman and agent for the Bavarian army, and in 1919 joined a small anti-Semitic party that in 1920 took the name Nationalsozialistische Deutsche Arbeiterpartei (National Socialist Workers' Party, or NSDAP). The party's 1920 platform called for all the Jews of Germany to be deprived of their civil rights and for some of them to be expelled. Hitler gained attention as a public speaker, and in 1921 became the party chairman, with unlimited powers. In November 1923 he headed an attempt to bring the government down by an armed putsch, known as the Munich (Beer-Hall) Putsch, for which he was sentenced in 1924 to five years' imprisonment in a fortress.

During his imprisonment in Landsberg, Hitler dictated the first volume of his book *Mein Kampf* (My Struggle). He was released after only nine months. In 1925 he reestablished the National Socialist party and created the Schutzstaffel (Protection Squad; SS) to serve as the party's fighting force. Several of the German states prohibited his appearance as a public speaker.

The second volume of *Mein Kampf* was published in 1926, a year after the first. Another book, written in 1928 but not published in his lifetime, appeared in 1961 as *Hitler's Second Book*. It contains Hitler's grounds for his anti-Semitism, based on the race theory. In the book, Hitler now promoted his anti-Semitism as the central aspect of his personal and political career.

Hitler aimed to use constitutional means to gain a parliamentary majority in order to destroy the constitution by due process. In 1928 the National Socialist party ran in the Reichstag elections for the first time, receiving only 2.8 percent of the votes. The party began its rise in 1929, and in the 1930 elections it won 18.3 percent of the total vote. In 1932 Hitler was granted German citizenship, which enabled him to run in the presidential elections. He lost, against Paul von Hindenburg, but received 36.8 percent of the vote. In the Reichstag elections of July 1932, the National Socialist party received 37.3 percent, the highest it ever obtained in free elections, and it became the largest political party represented in the Reichstag. But in the elections held in November of that same year, the party received only 33.1 percent of the vote, and Hitler failed in his attempt to seize control of the government.

On January 30, 1933, Hitler was appointed chancellor of a minority government. The conservative opponents of the Weimar Republic hoped to use him as a means to gain mass support while controlling him and his radical movement, but it was he who took control of the state apparatus and later the state power to establish a regime of terror.

Although his party held only three out of the eleven ministries, Hitler managed to set up a dictatorship. Following the Reichstag fire of February 27, basic civil rights were suspended and, after elections held on March 5, parliamentary rule was abolished by the *Ermächtigungsgesetz* (Enabling Law). This law transferred all legislative power from the Reichstag to the cabinet, where the conservatives held a solid majority. Eventually, by outmaneuvering them, Hitler became all-powerful. Anti-Semitic riots took place in March, culminating in the boycott of April 1, 1933, and in a law, passed on April 7, that inaugurated the Jews' elimination from public life in Germany. On July 14, after the dissolution of the trade unions and the other political parties, the NSDAP became the only recognized party in the land.

After Hindenburg's death, on August 2, 1934, Hitler also became head of state and commander in chief of the Wehrmacht, and assumed the title of *Führer und Reichskanzler* (Leader and Reich Chancellor). He was now the dictator of Germany. The rearmament of the country was accelerated, as was the persecution of the Jews. The Nuremberg Laws were adopted on September 15, 1935, and many other decrees issued by Hitler or in his name led to the exclusion of the Jews from German society. By the end of 1937 about 150,000 Jews had left Germany, approximately one-third of the country's Jewish population.

After the Anschluss of Austria on March 13, 1938, nearly 200,000 Jews were added to the Reich. Although a quarter of them left the country within six months, at the end of 1938 Germany again had the same number of Jews that it had had in 1933. In October 1938 some 17,000 Jews of Polish nationality were expelled from Germany to Poland. This was soon to be followed by the November *Kristallnacht* pogrom.

Hitler's radical racial *Weltanschauung* was combined with a Social Darwinism that saw the Jew as a source of danger to Germany and humanity, and as a central factor in the dynamic development of hostile ideological trends such as democracy, liberalism, and socialism. Even the Christian sources of ethnic political thinking in Western society were perceived by Hitler as manifestations of the infiltration of the Jewish spirit into western European civilization.

As early as the 1920s, in *Mein Kampf*, Hitler presented the Jews, or rather "international Jewry," as the world's foremost enemy:

> [The National Socialist movement] must open the eyes of the people concerning foreign nations and must over and over again recall who is the real enemy of our present world. In place of the insane hatred for Aryans . . . it must condemn to general wrath the evil enemy of humanity as the true creator of all suffering. . . . It must see to it that, at least in our country, the most deadly enemy is recognized and that the struggle against him, like an illuminating sign of a brighter epoch, also shows to the other nations the road of salvation of a struggling Aryan humanity.

On January 30, 1939, Hitler declared in the Reichstag that a new world war would lead to the destruction of the Jewish race in Europe. When the war began in Poland, on September 1 of the same year, the Germans embarked upon the destruction of

Jews in that country, although for a while this was done in a haphazard rather than a methodical way. It was also at about this time that the systematic killing of the mentally ill with toxic gas was undertaken, on Hitler's orders.

In September 1939 Reinhard Heydrich told his assistants that Hitler had agreed to the expulsion of the Jews from Germany into the Polish territories annexed by the Reich. Hitler informed Alfred Rosenberg that he wished to concentrate all the Jews from the territories under German rule in an area between the Vistula and Bug rivers. He told Hans Frank, on June 19, 1941 (three days before the attack on the Soviet Union), that the Jews would be dispatched from the General-gouvernement, which would then serve only as a kind of Jewish transit camp.

The systematic killing of Jews (the "Final Solution") began after the German invasion of the Soviet Union on June 22, 1941. According to Hitler's world view and his political strategy, the goal of the territorial expansion—to gain Lebensraum ("living space") in the east—and the destruction of the Jewish people as the central ideological enemy were connected and were the focal point of the whole struggle.

The first massacres of Jews in the Soviet Union were carried out by the Einsatzgruppen in June 1941; the killing was then extended to include the rest of the Jews of Europe. On several occasions Hitler reminded the public about his prophecy concerning the destruction of the Jews, and on April 2, 1945, he boasted that he had "exterminated the Jews of Germany and central Europe." His political testament of April 29, 1945, ended with a call for "merciless resistance to the universal poisoner of all nations—international Jewry." The following day he committed suicide in Berlin.

Decision Making and Jewish Policy

A fundamental tenet of Nazi ideology with regard to decision making was the so-called *Führerprinzip* ("leadership principle"), which called for the exercise of absolute authority from above and absolute obedience from below. The iron discipline and maximum efficiency implied in this conception of decision making, the Nazis assumed, set them apart from the divisiveness and inefficiency of their supposedly chaotic predecessors, the democrats and liberals of the Weimar Republic. After 1933 many German institutions, including schools and universities, adopted the *Führerprinzip* to emphasize their allegiance to the new regime. Hitler was glorified by the principle because it made him the fount of all wisdom and the universal giver of orders. When historians and social scientists after the war were called upon to explain the functioning of the Nazi system, they found variations of the *Führerprinzip* a congenial component for their models of totalitarianism.

Scholars have subsequently discovered the decision-making process of the Third Reich to have been considerably more chaotic than the *Führerprinzip* would suggest. Hitler's work habits alone were too unsystematic to allow him to run a smoothly functioning decision-making apparatus. His interests, moreover, were not sufficiently broad for him to perform the role of a universal giver of orders. Only in matters of foreign policy, rearmament (and, after 1939, war), and the architectural reconstruction of Berlin was he able to concentrate his attention consistently and effectively.

Hitler's erratic work habits have long been known by scholars, but have not always been taken sufficiently into account in their analyses of the Nazi system. To be sure, Hitler was at times capable of working for weeks at a pace that left his aides exhausted, but these bouts of frenzied activity would be followed by weeks of lethargy. During these periods of lethargy, aides had difficulty prevailing on him to perform even the necessary routines of his office, let alone make important decisions. Albert Speer's memoirs provide the most accessible evidence of Hitler's work habits, but they were already attested to by his private secretaries in interrogations conducted shortly after the war ended.

Hitler was not an effective delegator of responsibility. He did not generally assign subordinates to take responsibility for policy areas that, for whatever reason, he chose not to supervise himself. The result was often a competitive free-for-all among ambitious subordinates eager to demonstrate their competence to the Führer as well as to assure for themselves a position in the top ranks of the Nazi hierarchy. To secure these positions they had to be able to overcome rival claimants who sought the same powers and status. Those most successful in this fight for survival, such as Hermann Göring and Heinrich Himmler, wound up in charge of vast empires; those less able or less ambitious, like Alfred Rosenberg or Wilhelm Frick, had to be satisfied with occupying a less prestigious rung on the Nazi ladder.

Hitler's authority over these empire builders rested largely upon his unique personal qualities, the wellspring of his charismatic powers, and less upon his legal position at the top of a bureaucratic hierarchy. Although he rarely did so, Hitler could at any time intervene authoritatively in any of the innumerable disputes between his ambitious underlings. This was learned by Ernst Röhm and the SA (Sturmabteilung; Storm Troopers) leadership during the June 1934 "Night of the Long Knives," in which Röhm and others were murdered on Hitler's orders. Hitler's powers, though not always exercised, have been called permanently potential: they could be exercised with unexpected and brutal swiftness. Indeed, the relationship of Hitler to his subordinates has been compared to the feudal relationship between lord and vassal.

Controversies about the Nazi decision-making process and Hitler's role in it have been particularly prevalent among scholars of the Holocaust. As it became clear to them during the 1960s that the *Führerprinzip*, at least as it was defined by the Nazis, did not reflect how most major decisions on Jewish policy in the Third Reich were actually made, an interpretive school arose. This school suggested that the rivalries between would-be claimants for control over Jewish policy were themselves an important radicalizing element in the persecutions of the Jews, propelling them from the Arierparagraph ("Aryan clause") legislation of 1933 to the Nuremberg Laws of 1935, the "Aryanization" (Arisierung) of Jewish-owned properties, and the Deportations of 1938 and 1939.

Ultimately, in this view, it was the most radical claimants, Heinrich Himmler and the SS, who managed to outmaneuver their rivals and establish themselves, after the war broke out, as chief executors of a policy of mass murder. This interpretation suggests that the "Final Solution" and the Auschwitz extermination camp that has become its symbol were the result of a radicalization process that, in the wake of the extraordinary Nazi military successes against the Soviet Union in the summer of 1941, was freed of all external constraints. Because they focus their analysis on how the Nazi system functioned in practice, these scholars have come to be called "functionalists." They see Hitler primarily as the legitimizer of the process of persecution, a process in which he only occasionally played a directing role, but one that he heartily endorsed and encouraged.

The "intentionalists," on the other hand, suggest that Nazi Jewish policy was from its beginning the product of long-term Nazi intentions. They point to utterances made by Hitler from the 1920s about the killing of Jews as evidence of his early intention to solve "the Jewish problem" by physical annihilation. Hitler and his minions, in their view, hid their ultimately murderous intentions until time and circumstances in 1941 were ripe for the "Final Solution" to be implemented. The escalation of the persecution of German Jewry during the years after 1933 was, accordingly, part of a clearly conceived design whose incremental unfoldings were realized only as circumstances allowed.

Neither the fundamentalists nor the intentionalists have managed to prevail in the debate, partly because the documentation that might allow either side to prove its argument is lacking, either because it was destroyed or because it never existed. Abundantly clear to both sides, however, is the fact that Hitler paid less attention to the details of Jewish policy than he did to foreign policy, rearmament, or war.

Although, as far as is known, Hitler never devoted one of his bouts of frenzied activity to the making of Jewish policy, it is instructive to observe his role at several critical turning points in the making of that policy. The notorious Nuremberg Laws of September 1935 and the infamous *Kristallnacht* pogrom of November 1938, both milestones in the escalating persecution of Jews, came about—at least in their timing—not as a result of long-range planning but by the accident of circumstance. In the case of the Nuremberg Laws, the underlying racist logic that Aryans and Jews should no longer be allowed to marry or have sexual relations was so much a part of Nazi ideology that civil servants in the Interior Ministry had long before prepared drafts of legislation to prevent such race mixing. However, Hitler's sudden decision at the 1935 Nuremberg party rally to present to his puppet Reichstag a law governing such mixing was the product of his need to fill an unexpected hiatus in the rally's agenda. The officials suddenly called upon to draft the concrete legislation were caught off guard, and had to improvise without the extensive files back at their offices in Berlin.

The circumstances leading to the *Kristallnacht* pogrom in November 1938, although different from those surrounding the creation of the Nuremberg Laws, demonstrate a similar inclination on Hitler's part to act impulsively. On November 7 a Jewish youth, seeking revenge for the deportation of his parents from Germany, shot and killed a German diplomat in Paris. This inspired Propaganda Minister Joseph Goebbels, eager to ingratiate himself with the Führer and to gain additional influence in Jewish policy, to propose to Hitler that the SA be set free all across Germany to wreak vengeance against the "Jewish crime in Paris." The result was a brutal night of murder, rioting, and looting. The decrees issued two days later served to complete the process of excluding Jews from German economic and cultural life. The Nazis announced those decrees as punishment, but in fact they had been ready for some time beforehand. Nevertheless, their sudden implementation was the result of Hitler's impulse. Thus was a significantly new stage in Nazi Jewish policy inaugurated.

Against this background it may be possible to understand more fully the decision in 1941 to implement the "Final Solution" by means of extermination camps established in eastern Europe. No single document with Hitler's signature calling for the mass murder of Jews has ever been found. This lack has sometimes been attributed to the chaotic way in which the Nazi system functioned, suggesting that the order could have been delivered orally, or even that by 1941 the system no longer required an order from Hitler to set the machinery of murder in action. Another possibility is that Hitler and the Nazi leaders deliberately tried to keep the order secret, either by delivering it orally or marking it "Destroy after reading." Alternatively, such a document might have been destroyed by an act or accident of war. There is no debate among scholars, however, about Hitler's responsibility for the decision to implement the "Final Solution," even if its execution was carried out largely by the elaborate SS machinery under the command of Himmler. ◆

Höss, Rudolf

1900–1947

Camp commandant of Auschwitz. Höss was born in Baden-Baden; his father was an officer in the German colonial army in southeast Africa. When World War I broke out Höss volunteered for service, even though he was underage. On his return to Germany after the war he joined the

Freikorps in East Prussia, then the Rossbach Freikorps in the Baltic states, and later participated in terrorist actions against the French occupation forces in the Ruhr and against the Poles in the struggle for Silesia (1921).

In November 1922, Höss joined the Nazi party while attending a reunion of members of the Rossbach Freikorps in Munich. In June 1923 he was arrested in the Ruhr district and sentenced to a ten-year prison term, for participating in the murder by a Freikorps underground group of a German teacher who had collaborated with the French. By 1928 Höss was pardoned, and as soon as he was released he joined the Artamanen society, a nationalist-*völkisch* group that advocated work on the land and settlement in the east, on Polish territory. Höss and his wife, Hedwig, who was also a member of Artamanen, worked for various groups of the society's *Arbeitsdienst* (labor service), which was a device for recruiting members for militant Nazi organizations, mainly the SS.

In 1933, on instructions from the Nazi party and local estate owners, Höss formed an SS cavalry unit that was based on the Sullentin estate in Pomerania. In June 1934 he joined the SS for active service, at the suggestion of Heinrich Himmler, who was one of the leaders of the Artamanen Society. From December 1934 until May 1938 Höss held various appointments in the administration of the Dachau concentration camp, where he trained under Theodor Eicke, the first commandant of the camp. In May 1940 Höss was posted to Auschwitz, appointed *Obersturmbannführer,* and became the actual founder of the camp and its first organizer and commandant. In the summer of 1941, Höss began readying the camp under his command for the extermination of masses of human beings, and as of January 1942 he was at the helm of the killing operation in the installations set up for this purpose in Auschwitz-Birkenau.

A report on the extermination in Auschwitz that Höss wrote while under investigation after the war in a Kraków jail opens with the following words:

> In the summer of 1941—I cannot state the precise date—I was summoned by the adjutant's office to Berlin, to report to Reichsführer-SS [Chief of the SS] Himmler. Without his aide-de-camp present—contrary to his usual practice—Himmler said to me: "The Führer has ordered the 'Final Solution of the Jewish Question.' We, the SS, are charged with the execution of this

task. I have chosen the Auschwitz camp for this purpose, because of its convenient location as regards transportation and because in that area it is easy to isolate and camouflage the camp. I first thought to appoint one of the senior SS officers to this task, but then I changed my mind because of the problems of the division of authority that such an appointment would run into. I am herewith charging you with this task. This is a strenuous and difficult assignment that calls for total dedication, regardless of the difficulties that will arise. Further practical details will be conveyed to you by Sturmbannführer Adolf Eichmann of the Reichssicherheitshauptamt, who will soon get in touch with you. The offices concerned will hear from him at the appropriate time. You must keep this order absolutely secret, even from your own superiors. After you talk with Eichmann let me know what arrangements you propose to be made."

On December 1, 1943, Höss was appointed chief of Section 1D of the SS Wirtschaftsverwaltungshauptamt (Economic-Administrative Main Office; WVHA). In late June of 1944 he was sent back to Auschwitz, on a temporary assignment, to preside over the murder of the Jews of Hungry. In that operation—*Aktion* Höss, as it was named—430,000 Jews were brought to Auschwitz in fifty-six days, to be annihilated there. In recognition of his "outstanding service" in the concentration camps, Höss was awarded war crosses classes I and II, with swords. After the fall of the Reich, Höss assumed the name Franz Lang; he was released from a prisoner-of-war collection point and put to work in agriculture.

In March 1946 Höss was recognized, arrested, and handed over to the Polish authorities, in keeping with the agreement on the Extradition of War Criminals. He was taken to Warsaw and from there to Kraków, where his case was investigated. In the Kraków jail where he was held in 1946 and 1947, Höss wrote an autobiography and a series of notes about the SS commanders in the concentration camp and those who were in charge of putting the "Final Solution" into effect, including a profile of Eichmann (published in English as *Commandant of Auschwitz: The Autobiography of Rudolf Hoess;* 1960). The supreme court in Warsaw sentenced Höss to death, and he was hanged in Auschwitz on April 16, 1947. ◆

Kaltenbrunner, Ernst

1903–1946

Nazi politician. Born in Ried im Innkreis (Upper Austria), Kaltenbrunner attended school in Linz. After studying chemistry and law in Prague and elsewhere, he practiced as a lawyer. He joined the National Socialist party and the SS in 1932. In 1934 and 1935, Kaltenbrunner was imprisoned in Austria on a charge of high treason. He headed the SS in that country from 1935 until 1938.

After the Anschluss, Kaltenbrunner, now an SS-*Gruppenführer*, was promoted to the post of under secretary of state for public security in the Ostmark (as Austria was renamed by the Nazis). He remained there until 1941, and at the same time was a member of the Reichstag. Together with Gauleiter Josef Bürckel, Kaltenbrunner was responsible for the Zentralstelle für Jüdische Auswanderung (Central Office for Jewish Emigration) in Vienna, headed by Adolf Eichmann. Up until Eichmann's transfer to Prague in April 1939, 150,000 Jews emigrated from Austria. After the attempt on Reinhard Heydrich's life on May 27, 1942, Kaltenbrunner was appointed head of the Reichssicherheitshauptamt (Reich Security Main Office; RSHA). Heydrich died on June 4, and Kaltenbrunner was formally named his successor as chief of the Sicherheitspolizei and the SD (Sicherheitsdienst; Security Service) on January 30, 1943.

In addition to Heinrich Himmler, Kaltenbrunner was one of the main initiators of *Aktion Reinhard* and bore much of the responsibility for the implementation of the "Final Solution" from 1942 to 1945, although few contemporary documents record his activities in this connection. The same holds true for his participation in the Euthanasia Program. This may be partly attributed to Himmler's growing tendency to reserve the credit for himself. There exists evidence, however, of Kaltenbrunner's role as instigator of the deportation from Theresienstadt in the spring of 1943 of Jews unfit for work, and of Bulgarian Jews in the summer of 1943. In 1945 Kaltenbrunner took as his personal adjutant an SS officer who in 1941 had been responsible for the murder of at least sixty thousand Jewish men, women, and children in Lithuania.

Because of Kaltenbrunner's personal reserve, many of his department heads appeared to be more important than they actually were in the power structure of the RSHA. This may have been connected with Kaltenbrunner's belief that, in contrast to many of his subordinates, he had a very real chance to survive after the end of the war. Even at Nuremberg, he attempted to play the part of someone who "had absolutely no idea." Nevertheless, on October 9, 1946, the International Military Tribunal sentenced him to death by hanging, and the sentence was carried out on October 16.

The so-called Kaltenbrunner reports are a collection of reports on the Gestapo interrogations conducted after the attempt on Hitler's life of July 20, 1944. They were drawn up for Martin Bormann, on Kaltenbrunner's orders, by an ad hoc RSHA unit headed by SS-Obersturmbannführer Walter von Kielpinski. According to the historian Hans-Adolf Jacobsen, they were the result of "thousands of investigations" carried out by some four hundred RSHA officials operating in eleven groups—the Sonderkommandos 20 Juli—who took part in suppressing the attempted coup. ◆

Koch, Karl Otto

1897–1945

Commandant of concentration camps. Koch was born in Darmstadt, where he attended a commercial secondary school and became a bank clerk. Toward the end of World War I he was wounded and captured by the British, and was a prisoner of war until October 1919. In 1930 he became a member of the Nazi party and a year later joined the SS. He held senior command posts in the Sachsenburg, Esterwegen, and Lichtenburg (Prettin) concentration camps in 1934, and the following year was appointed commandant of the notorious Columbia Haus, a prison in Berlin. In 1936 Koch was commandant of the Esterwegen and Sachsenhausen concentration camps; in May 1937 he married Dresden-born Ilse Köhler (1906–67). On August 1 of that year Koch was appointed commandant of the newly established Buchenwald camp, and promoted to SS-*Standartenführer*. His wife was made an SS-*Aufseherin* (overseer) in the camp commanded by her husband. Before long she became notorious for her extreme cruelty to the prisoners and for her nymphomania, which she vented on the SS guards in the camp.

In September 1941 Karl Otto Koch was appointed commandant of Majdanek, then a Soviet prisoner-of-war camp run by the Waffen-SS in Lublin. Under his tenure the camp was greatly enlarged, and civilian prisoners, including Jews, were brought in. Crematoria were constructed, and there was an enormous rise in the number of prisoners killed. In July 1942, after a mass outbreak from the camp, Koch was suspended and put on trial before an SS and police court in Berlin, but was acquitted in February 1943. He then held administrative posts in postal-service security units, only to be arrested again in August of that year on charges of embezzlement, forgery, making threats to officials, and "other charges." The last apparently referred to murders for which he was responsible that went beyond existing orders, and to his hobby of collecting patches of tattooed human skin and shrunken human skulls; Ilse was also arrested as an accomplice to her husband. It was she who selected the living prisoners whose skin she wanted, after they were killed, for her own collection and for use in making lampshades. In early 1945 Karl Otto Koch was sentenced by the Supreme Court of the SS (*Oberste SS- und Polizeigericht*) in Munich, and in April of that year he was executed.

Ilse Koch was acquitted and went to Ludwigsburg to live with her two children and her husband's stepsister. She was arrested by the Americans on June 30, 1945, tried in 1947, and sentenced to life imprisonment. In 1949 she was released under a pardon granted by General Lucius D. Clay, the military governor of the American zone in Germany. Under pressure arising out of hearings held by a United States Senate committee, she was immediately rearrested upon her release, and in January 1951 was again sentenced to life imprisonment, by the *Landesgericht* (State Court) in Augsburg. In September 1967 she committed suicide in her prison cell. ◆

Mengele, Josef

1911–1978?

Doctor and SS officer. Mengele was born in Günzburg, Germany; in 1935 he was awarded a D.Phil. degree by the University of Munich, and in 1938 an M.D. degree from the University of Frankfurt. He was a member of Stahlhelm, an extreme right-wing and anti-Semitic organization, from 1931 to 1934; he joined the Nazi party in 1937 and the SS in 1938. From June 1940 he served in the Waffen-SS medical corps, and in August of that year he was appointed an *Untersturmführer*. In May 1943 he was promoted to *Hauptsturmführer* and was posted to the Auschwitz extermination camp, where he remained until its evacuation on January 18, 1945. Mengele spent much of his time on pseudoscientific medical experiments and also on the *Selektionen* of Jews who were brought to the camp. In the course of these *Selektionen*, most of the Jews were immediately sent to their death in the gas chambers; the rest were put on forced labor in concentration camps.

Mengele's pseudoscientific experiments, in which he used human beings as guinea pigs, dealt primarily with infants and young twins, and with dwarfs. The experiments involved the maltreatment of the prisoners in various ways, such as the excision of their genital organs and a variety of harmful injections into the veins or directly into the heart.

When Auschwitz was evacuated, Mengele was transferred to the Mauthausen concentration camp; when that camp was liberated on May 5, 1945, all trace of him was lost. In mid-1949 he turned up in Argentina, where he was given asylum. Mengele's criminal actions were documented at the Nuremberg Trial and in the trials of the Nazi criminals who had functioned at Auschwitz. In 1959 the West German authorities issued a warrant for his arrest, and in 1960 the West German Foreign Ministry asked Argentina for his extradition, but Mengele succeeded in escaping to Brazil and from there made his way to Paraguay. According to one version, he was drowned in December 1978, in Brazil, but this has been questioned.

In February 1985 a public trial of Mengele, *in absentia,* was held at Yad Vashem in Jerusalem, with the participation of Auschwitz survivors on whom Mengele had carried out his experiments. ◆

Müller, Heinrich

1900–?

Chief of the Gestapo. After attending elementary school, Müller was apprenticed to the Bavarian Aircraft Works in Munich. In 1917 he volunteered for the air force, became a fighter pilot on the western front in April 1918, and was awarded several distinguished-service medals. In June 1919 he was discharged as a noncommissioned officer. He began working at the Munich police headquarters in December 1919. In the spring of 1929 he passed with distinction the examination for the intermediate level of the police force, and became the Munich police headquarters expert in the fight against "leftist movements," especially Communism. Müller was a hard and ambitious worker who on occasion disregarded the law, according to evidence given by the Nazi party district administration in 1936. Under the Weimar Republic, his political affiliation fluctuated between the German National Popular Party and the Bavarian People's Party; rumor had it that in 1933 he and some of his colleagues opposed handing over the Munich police administration to the SA (Sturmabteilung; Storm Troopers) and the SS.

Before long, however, Müller became one of the most important aides to Reinhard Heydrich, the new Bavarian police chief. This was a result of his intimate knowledge of the Communist party and of the German section of the Comintern (the Third Communist International), and his familiarity with Soviet police methods. Müller's reports also gained Heinrich Himmler's attention; this won him promotion to the rank of senior police secretary, on May 1, 1933, and, on November 16,

1933, to senior secretary of the criminal police. In 1935, he was appointed controller of the criminal police. To ensure that no problems arose in the relations between the Bavarian political police and the Gestapo and SS, Müller, who was not a party member, was in 1936 appointed a member of the SD (Sicherheitsdienst; Security Service), with the rank of *Untersturmführer*.

Soon afterward, Heydrich was appointed Gestapo chief, and he took Müller along with him, together with his former superior, Gerhard Flesch, appointing them joint directors of subsection II 1 (suppression of hostile elements). Flesch and Müller were in charge of the following subdivisions: II 1 A (Communism and Marxism, including all organizations fully or partially associated with these ideologies, as well as the trade unions); II 1 B (religious organizations, Jews, Freemasons, emigrants); II 1 C (reactionaries, supporters of the opposition, Austrian affairs); II 1 D (protective-custody and concentration camps); II 1 E (economic, agricultural, and social policy; nonpolitical organizations); II 1 F (card index, good-conduct certificates, file registry); II 1 G (identification service); II 1 H (Nazi party and its affiliated organizations); II 1 W (security of weapons and explosives); and II 1 Special (special duties—surveillance and assassinations). Flesch and Müller, for their part, brought along experienced associates from Munich, such as Josef Meisinger, Franz Josef Huber, and at a later date, Friedrich Panzinger.

Müller's phenomenal rise, however, began after the suppression of the so-called Röhm putsch on June 30, 1934, the "Night of the Long Knives." Four days later Müller was promoted to SS-*Obersturmführer* and put in charge of senior officials. On January 30, 1935, Müller rose to the rank of SS-*Hauptsturmführer*; on April 20, 1936, to SS-*Sturmbannführer*; and on January 30, 1937, to SS-*Standartenführer*. It was only in June of that year, however, that he was given the rank of senior administrative councillor and criminal police councillor, against the recommendation of the Munich–Upper Bavaria Police District Administration, although by then he had been in charge of the Gestapo office for a year. From September 1939 to the end of the war, Müller was head of Section IV (Gestapo) of the Reichssicherheitshauptamt (Reich Main Security Office; RSHA) and deputy commander of the Security Police and the SD. He was responsible to Heydrich and, after Heydrich's assassination, to his successor, Ernst Kaltenbrunner.

Müller was one of the most powerful men in the Nazi state terror system, but he stayed out of the limelight. On April 20, 1939, he became an SS-*Oberführer;* and on December 14, 1940, an SS-*Brigadeführer;* two days later he was also promoted to *Generalmajor* of the police. On November 9 Müller, together with Arthur Nebe, was appointed an SS-*Gruppenführer* and to the equivalent rank in the police.

Müller remained loyal to Adolf Hitler to the end in the bunker where Hitler spent his last weeks. On October 15, 1944, Müller, the ex-pilot, was awarded the Knight's Cross with crossed swords (the highest German award in World War II) for excellence, in recognition of his services in the merciless pursuit of the participants in the July 20, 1944, plot against Hitler. These included some of Müller's friends, such as Count Wolf Heinrich von Helldorf, Arthur Nebe, Hans Gisevius, and Friedrich Werner von der Schulenburg.

All trace of Müller was lost on April 29, 1945. There exists no confirmation of the rumors that he defected to the Soviet secret service, or that he escaped to the Middle East or Latin America, or that he remained alive. ◆

Ribbentrop, Joachim von

1893–1946

Foreign minister of Germany from 1938 to 1945. Ribbentrop spent four years working in Canada before returning to Germany in 1914. After World War I he became an exporter of wines and spirits. He also secured use of the noble prefix "von" before his name by paying a lifelong annuity to a relative who had no male heirs.

Ribbentrop was introduced to Hitler in August 1932 when the latter expressed interest in someone able to read the foreign press. Ribbentrop made his Dahlem villa available for some of the meetings in January 1933 that led to Hitler's appointment as chancellor. He quickly gained a position as Hitler's foreign-policy adviser, and was appointed ambassador to England in 1936 and foreign minister in February 1938.

An early advocate of a pro-British foreign-policy orientation, Ribbentrop shared and encouraged his master's growing anti-British attitude in the late 1930s. He reached the apogee of his career with the signing of the Nazi-Soviet Pact in August 1939. His influence and importance rapidly diminished thereafter, as war and conquest replaced diplomacy. Ribbentrop's preference for a "continental policy" in continued alliance with the Soviets did not sway Hitler from his invasion of the USSR in 1941.

Ribbentrop was notoriously incompetent and excessively vain, and was despised by the other Nazi leaders (with the partial exception of Heinrich Himmler, who found him a useful ally), but he was not a fanatical anti-Semite. It was only in late 1942 and early 1943 that he fully perceived the importance that Hitler attached to "solving the Jewish question." Only then did Ribbentrop throw himself into personal diplomacy on behalf of the "Final Solution," most notoriously when he told the regent of Hungary, Admiral Miklós Horthy, in April 1943 that "the Jews must either be exterminated or taken to concentration camps. There is no other possibility." For crimes against peace as well as crimes against humanity, Ribbentrop was condemned to death by hanging at the Nuremberg Trial. ◆

Rosenberg, Alfred

1893–1946

Nazi ideologist and head of the Nazi party's foreign-policy department. Born in Revel (now Tallinn) in Estonia, Rosenberg came from a family of Baltic Germans. He studied architecture at the universities of Riga and Moscow. Fleeing to Germany in 1918, he settled in Munich, where he associated with White Russian reactionary emigré circles and joined the ultranationalist and semi-occult Thule Society. He was already becoming known for his anti-Semitic and anti-Bolshevik views through such works as *Die Spur der Juden im Wandel der Zeiten* (The Track of the Jews through the Ages) and *Unmoral im Talmud* (Immorality in the Talmud), both published in 1919.

Rosenberg joined the German Workers' party in the wake of Adolf Hitler, whom he impressed with his theories of a Judeo-Bolshevik-Masonic conspiracy constantly engaged in "undermining the foundations of our existence." In 1921 he became chief editor of the party newspaper, the *Völkischer Beobachter*, and was one of the principal disseminators of the Protocols of the Elders of Zion, a forgery of the tsarist police that appealed to Rosenberg's belief in the active working of occult powers to subvert civilization. He participated in the abortive Munich beer-hall putsch of November 1923 and was protected by Hitler from the attacks of other leading Nazis, who were affronted by Rosenberg's Baltic origins and his intellectual arrogance.

Rosenberg's role as chief Nazi ideologist was enhanced by his founding, in 1929, of the Kampfbund für Deutsche Kultur (Fighting League for German Culture) and, above all, by his major work, *Der Mythus des 20. Jahrhunderts* (The Myth of the Twentieth Century; 1930). As an expression of Nazi philosophy this book had an influence comparable to that of Hitler's *Mein Kampf*. It was enormously popular, and by 1942 had sold over a million copies. The book incorporated the racial theories of Joseph-Arthur de Gobineau and Houston Steward Chamberlain, proclaiming that race was the decisive factor determining art, science, culture, and the course of world history. The Teutons represented the "master race" of "Aryans," whose task it was to subdue Europe. This belief was combined with denunciation of Judaism and Christianity, whose ideals of compassion and charity must yield to the neo-pagan Teutonic sense of honor. The swastika was the symbol of blood and soil, and denoted the worship of Wotan and the ancient Norse gods. The Jews had subverted the ideal of race with their internationalism and a religion of humanity destructive of the Teutonic spirit. With doctrines such as these, Rosenberg's *Mythus* sought to systematize Nazi ideology.

In 1930 Rosenberg was elected to the Reichstag as Nazi deputy for Hesse-Darmstadt, and he made a rapid ascent to positions of influence after 1933. In 1934 Hitler appointed him the "Führer's delegate for the supervision of the whole intellectual and philosophical education and training of the National Socialist party." From 1933 to 1945 he also headed the party's foreign-affairs department, which gave him access especially to fascist parties in eastern Europe and the Balkans. In 1939 he established in Frankfurt the Institut zur Erforschung der Judenfrage (Institute for the Investigation of the Jewish Question). Rosenberg declared in his inaugural address there that the "Jewish question" would be considered solved "only after the last Jew has left the Greater German living space." The institute's principal task was to ransack the libraries, archives, and art galleries of European Jewry in order to promote its "research." After the fall of France, Einsatzstab Rosenberg (Operational Staff Rosenberg) seized French art treasures and sent them to Germany.

In November 1941 Rosenberg was appointed *Reichsminister für die Besetzten Ostgebiete* (Reich Minister for the Occupied Eastern Territories), where his policy differed in detail but not in principle from the extermination policy perpetrated by Heinrich Himmler, Reinhard Heydrich, and the Reichssicherheitshauptamt (Reich Security Main Office; RSHA). Although he had always regarded the Slavs as subhuman, Rosenberg regretted the policy of Germanization, believing it politically harmful; however, he found no support for this view. Condemned to death at Nuremberg as a major war criminal, he was hanged in 1946. ◆

Speer, Albert

1905–1981

Hitler's architect; German minister of armaments from 1942 to 1945. Born in Mannheim, Speer was the son of a wealthy architect. In 1930, while still an architect's assistant, he heard Hitler speak for the first time and was overwhelmed by the Nazi leader's power of persuasion. In January 1931 he joined the National Socialist party.

Shortly after the Nazis' rise to power, Speer was awarded his first large party contracts, redesigning Joseph Goebbels's official residence and planning the May 1 celebrations in Berlin. His work on these two projects attracted Hitler's attention; in the Goebbels job Speer demonstrated organizational skill, and in the May 1 pageant he produced for the first time the basic elements of the overwhelming spectacle that was to become the model for all subsequent party conventions and celebrations.

Hitler personally gave Speer assignments, and while working together the two developed close ties of friendship. Apparently seeing in the talented young man the incarnation of the unfulfilled dreams of his own youth, Hitler admitted Speer to his inner circle, opened up intoxicating new fields of action for him, and in the course of time allowed him a measure of freedom that no other member of Hitler's entourage ever enjoyed. Speer, in turn, gave Hitler outstanding service and complete loyalty.

In 1934 Speer succeeded Paul Ludwig Troost, who had died early that year, as Hitler's architect. He was given two tasks to perform: to draw up a plan for Berlin, and to create a permanent installation for party conventions and party pageantry in Nuremberg. On both of these projects, Hitler and Speer jointly developed megalomanic building plans that were to express the might and durability of the Reich and its regime.

In 1937 Speer was officially appointed inspector general of construction of the Reich's capital. This meant, among other things, that his department took charge of the apartments from which Berlin Jews were evicted in 1939. The apartments were put at the disposal of non-Jewish residents of buildings that were to be demolished to make room for Speer's construction programs and, at a later stage, of those whose dwellings were destroyed by air attacks. After deportations of Berlin's Jews to the east began in the fall of 1941, Speer's office had more apartments to allocate.

When Fritz Todt was killed in an air accident in February 1942, Speer was appointed to succeed him as minister of armaments, and in September 1943 he was named minister of armaments and war production. In this capacity he was able, by using millions of forced laborers, to raise armaments production to a remarkable degree, at the very time that Allied air attacks were growing in intensity. Hitler's backing also helped Speer in his struggles with old-time party members and in the jungle of ill-defined spheres of authority that characterized the Nazi elite.

Toward the end of the war Speer's relations with Hitler deteriorated, but it was only in the final weeks that a real change took place. In violation of an explicit order by Hitler, Speer did not permit the destruction of industry and essential installations in the areas of Germany that were about to fall into Allied hands. He later claimed that he also planned Hitler's assassination, but it is unlikely that he really meant to carry it out.

After the war, Speer was put on trial for war crimes by the International Military Tribunal at Nuremberg, charged with employing forced laborers and concentration camp prisoners. Unusual in the trial was his admission of responsibility for the actions of the Nazi regime, including actions of which he claimed he had had no knowledge. He was found guilty on two counts, war crimes and crimes against humanity, and was sentenced to twenty years' imprisonment.

Following his release, Speer published his memoirs, *Inside the Third Reich* (1970), which gained a great deal of attention. In his book, Speer describes himself as an apolitical technician, but he again accepts responsibility for the actions of the regime and expresses repentance for his role, even for those actions of which he was not aware. He also repeats his earlier statement that his greatest guilt was for his acquiescence in the murder of the Jews.

Many scholars dealing with the Nazi era have accepted the authenticity of this self-portrait. Some, like Hugh R. Trevor-Roper, have seen in Speer, the man who ignored the political implications of the regime and served it with absolute loyalty, "the real criminal of the Nazi regime." Others believe he was far more involved in the regime's actions than he admitted. ◆

Stangl, Franz

1908–1971

Nazi police officer. Stangl was born in Altmünster, Austria, the son of a former soldier in the dragoons, who brutalized him throughout his childhood. Initially a master weaver, Stangl joined the Austrian police in 1931. His talent for organization soon became evident, and he was shortly appointed *Kriminalbeamter* (criminal investigation officer) in the political division, which at that time was charged with investigating antigovernmental activities of the Right and Left.

In November 1940 Stangl became police superintendent of the Euthanasia Institute at the Hartheim castle, near Linz. In March 1942 he became commandant of the Sobibór extermination camp in Poland, and from early September 1942 to August 1943 he was the commandant of Treblinka. In less than a year there, he supervised the mass killing of at least 900,000 Jews.

In September 1943, after the inmates' revolt in Treblinka, Stangl and most of his staff were transferred to Trieste. There, aside from a brief stint at the dreaded San Sabba concentration camp, he was largely employed in organizing antipartisan measures for Odilo Globocnik, the *Höherer SS- und Polizeiführer* (Higher SS and Police Leader) of the Adriatic seaboard area.

At the end of the war Stangl made his way back to Austria, where he was eventually interned by the Americans for belonging to the SS, although they knew nothing of his association with the extermination program. In the late summer of 1947 the Austrians, while investigating the Euthanasia Program at the Hartheim castle, learned of Stangl's presence in an American prisoner-of-war camp, and he was transferred to an open civilian prison in Linz. In May 1948, about to be charged, he escaped and made his way to Rome.

With assistance from Bishop Alois Hudal, rector of Santa Maria del Anima, Stangl obtained a Red Cross *laissez-passer* (pass), money, and a job as an engineer in Damascus, Syria, where he was soon joined by his family. In 1951 the family moved on to Brazil, where, registering under their own names at the Austrian consulate, they were soon established in the city of São Bernardo do Campo, near São Paulo, where Stangl worked at the Volkswagen factory.

Sixteen years later, Stangl's presence in Brazil became known. He was arrested on February 28, 1967, and extradited to Germany that June. His trial in Düsseldorf lasted one year; in December 1970 he was sentenced to life imprisonment for joint responsibility in the murder of 900,000 people during his tenure as commandant of Treblinka. He died in prison on June 28, 1971. ◆

Streicher, Julius

1885–1946

Nazi politician specializing in anti-Semitic incitement. Born in Augsburg, Bavaria, Streicher became an elementary school teacher. In World War I he was awarded several medals for distinguished service. Streicher was one of the founders of the German Socialist party in 1919, but shortly thereafter he merged it with the Nazi party. From 1928 to 1940 he was the *Gauleiter* of Franconia; he was a member of the Bavarian provincial legislature from 1924 to 1932, and then became a member of the Reichstag. He also held the rank of *Obergruppenführer* (general) in the SA (Sturmabteilung; Storm Troopers).

Streicher was one of the most rabid anti-Semites in the Nazi party. He founded the newspaper *Der Stürmer* (The Attacker) in Nuremberg in 1923, becoming its editor and, as of 1935, its owner as well. It was he who gave the newspaper its special anti-Semitic-pornographic character. The Nazi authorities had to dissociate themselves at times from the articles it published and even closed it down in Nuremberg, Streicher's stronghold. Streicher used his influence to bar Jews from restaurants and cafés, and he tried to persuade all the municipalities in Franconia to establish ghettos. Shortly after the Nazi rise to power, he was appointed chairman of the Zentralkomitee zur Abwehr der Jüdischen Greuel- und Boykotthetze (Central Defense Committee against Jewish Atrocity and Boycott Propaganda); he was also the organizer of the anti-Jewish boycott of April 1, 1933. Streicher was one of the instigators and authors of the Nuremberg Laws, and as early as 1938, in an article entitled "War against the World enemy," he called for the total destruction of the Jewish people.

In March 1940 Streicher was suspended from his post as *Gauleiter* of Franconia, following an investigation by the supreme court of the Nazi party concerning his involvement in bribery related to the "Aryanization" of plants and enterprises. Even so, Streicher remained one of the leading protagonists of militant anti-Semitism.

When the war ended, Streicher tried to hide under a different identify. Disguised as a house painter, he was recognized and taken prisoner by American soldiers on May 23, 1945. He was among the major Nazi criminals tried by the International Military Tribunal at Nuremberg. In its judgment, the tribunal said of Streicher: "For twenty-five years he incited to hatred of the Jews, in speeches and in writing, and became widely known as the 'Number 1 enemy of the Jews.' " In an article from his own pen that he published on December 25, 1941, Streicher stated: "If one really wants to put an end to the continued prospering of this curse from heaven that is the Jewish blood, there is only one way to do it: to eradicate this people, this Satan's son, root and branch." The tribunal sentenced Streicher to death; he was executed by hanging, on October 16, 1946. ◆

Stroop, Jürgen

1895–1951

S and police chief who crushed the Warsaw Ghetto Uprising and destroyed the Warsaw ghetto. Josef Stroop (he changed his first name to the more "Aryan"-sounding Jürgen in 1941) was born in Detmold, in central Germany, into the family of a Catholic policeman from the lower middle class. He was educated in a nationalist and militarist spirit. Volunteering for the army in World War I, he was wounded three times, and in 1918 was promoted to the rank of captain. After the war Stroop was employed in the Detmold municipal administration. In 1932 he joined the Nazi party and the SS, because of both his nationalist views and his attraction to the uniforms. He quickly rose in the ranks of the SS and by 1939 was an SS-*Oberführer* and commander of a police unit.

Upon the outbreak of war between Germany and the Soviet Union in June 1941, Stroop was sent, at his own request, to the front. After being wounded he was transferred to police functions in the occupied Soviet territories, where he specialized in persecuting the population and harassing local partisans. On April 17, 1943, on the eve of the liquidation of the Warsaw ghetto, he was summoned by the *Höherer SS- und Polizeiführer* (Higher SS and Police Leader) of the Generalgouvernement, Friedrich Wilhelm Krüger. The SS and police chiefs apparently rushed Stroop to Warsaw, doubting the ability of the local police commander, Ferdinand Sammern-Frankenegg, to carry out the liquidation of the ghetto. With the commencement of this action and the outbreak of the ghetto uprising on April 19, 1943, when Sammern-Frankenegg's helplessness became apparent, Stroop assumed command.

Stroop conducted the action against the insurgent ghetto as a military campaign; the methods he employed consisted of unrestrained and indiscriminate killing and destruction. He had under his command about two thousand men from different units, equipped like frontline troops. Stroop sent daily reports on the campaign in the ghetto to Kraków, the capital of the Generalgouvernement. His concluding report at the end of the campaign, which he called the "Great Operation" (*Grossaktion*), included the following statements:

> After the first days it was clear that the Jews would not think of being deported of their own free will, but had definitely decided to defend themselves in all possible ways and with the arms in their possession. . . . The number of Jews taken from their homes in the first days and captured was relatively small. The Jews were apparently hiding in the sewers and in specially prepared bunkers. . . . Twenty- to thirty-member combat units, made up of Jewish youths eighteen to twenty-five years old, with a certain number of women, spread the revolt and renewed it periodically. These combat units had been ordered to defend themselves with arms to the end, and when necessary to commit suicide rather than be taken alive. . . . In this armed revolt there were women in the combat units, armed like men, some of them members of the He-Haluts movement. The women often fired from guns in both hands. . . . The Jewish opposition and rebels could be broken only by the energetic and constant use of strike forces day and night. On April 23, 1943, the order was given by the SS-*Reichsführer* [Heinrich Himmler], through Wilhelm Krüger, to effect the evacuation of the Warsaw ghetto with the greatest rigor and unrelenting diligence. . . . The Great Operation terminated on May 16, 1943, at 8:15 P.M., with the blowing up of the Warsaw synagogue. There is no longer any activity in the former Jewish residential quarter . . . all the buildings and everything else have been destroyed; only the Dzielna [Pawiak] security prison was spared.

In his last daily report, dated April 16, Stroop reported that out of 56,065 Jews caught, 13,929 were exterminated and about 5,000 to 6,000 were killed in the shelling and burning.

After putting down the uprising, Stroop continued to serve as SS and Police Leader in the Warsaw district. In September 1943 he was appointed Higher SS and Police Leader in Greece, with promotion to the rank of SS-*Gruppenführer*. That November, Stroop was transferred to serve in the same capacity in the Twelfth Army District in the Reich, which included the areas of Wiesbaden, Darmstadt, and Luxembourg. He remained in this post until the end of the war.

Soon afterward, Stroop was discovered, while attempting to change his identity, in the Wiesbaden area, which was in the hands of the United States army. In a search conducted in his home, an elegantly organized album was found, containing his reports from the Warsaw ghetto campaign and a series of photographs taken by the Germans during the uprising. In January 1947 Stroop was tried by the American military court in Dachau (Trial No. 12-3188, *United States* v. *Stroop*) and charged with responsibility for war crimes perpetrated in the Twelfth Army District. Out of the twenty-two accused in this trial, which concluded in March, thirteen were sentenced to death, including Stroop. The verdict was not carried out, and Stroop was extradited to Poland as a war criminal wanted in the Polish People's Republic.

The photographs, together with parts of Stroop's reports, were presented by the prosecution at the Nuremberg Trial of the principal Nazi criminals, and constituted one of the most shocking and condemning documents in the entire trial. During his interrogation in a Polish prison, Stroop provided clarifications and supplementary information to the reports he had written during the Warsaw ghetto uprising in April and May 1943. He was held in prison in Warsaw with a member of the Polish underground Armia Krajowa (Home Army), Kazimierz Moczarski, and held lengthy conversations with him. These conversations were later the subject of the book *Gespräche mit dem Henker* (Conversations with the Hangman).

In July 1951 Stroop was tried at the Warsaw district court. He was executed by hanging that September in Warsaw. ◆

Appendix B

Time Line
of the Holocaust

February 24, 1920	The Nazi party platform is written.
November 9, 1923	In Munich the Nazis, headed by Adolf Hitler, unsuccessfully try to take over the Bavarian government, in what becomes known as the Beer-Hall Putsch.
September 14, 1930	The Nazis receive over 18 percent of the vote in a Reichstag election.
July 31, 1932	The Nazis receive over 37 percent of the vote in a Reichstag election.

1933

January 30	Hitler becomes chancellor of Germany after a Reichstag election in which the Nazis receive approximately 33 percent of the vote.
February 27	The German Reichstag building is set on fire; the next day, a national emergency is declared.
March 20	A concentration camp is established at Dachau, and the first prisoners arrive the next day.
March 24	The Enabling Law (*Ermächtigungsgesetz*) is passed by the Reichstag and is used by Hitler to help establish his dictatorship.
April 1	A one-day nationwide boycott of Jewish businesses is carried out in Germany.
April 7	Quotas are applied in Germany to the number of Jewish students allowed in institutions of higher education, and laws prohibiting Jews from working in government offices are promulgated.
April 21	Ritual slaughter is outlawed in Germany.
May 10	Books are publicly burned throughout Germany.
May 17	The Bernheim petition, against Nazi anti-Jewish legislation in German Upper Silesia, is presented to the League of Nations in Geneva. On June 1, 1933, the petition is granted.

August 25	The Haavara (transfer) agreement is signed between Jewish leaders from Palestine and the Nazi authorities.
September 22	In Germany, Jews are removed from the fields of literature, music, art, broadcasting, theater, and the press.

1934

January 26	Germany and Poland sign a ten-year nonaggression pact.
June 30	Hitler orders the SS, under Heinrich Himmler, to purge the SA leadership. Many are murdered, including Ernst Röhm, in what becomes known as the "Night of the Long Knives."
July 25	Chancellor Engelbert Dollfuss is killed when the Nazis unsuccessfully try to seize power in Austria.
August 2	The German president, Paul von Hindenburg, dies, leaving the way open for Hitler to establish a dictatorship.

1935

January 13	The Saarland is retaken by Germany.
March 16	In violation of the Versailles Treaty, conscription is resumed in Germany.
September 15	The Nuremberg Laws are decreed at a Nazi party rally, defining who may be a citizen of Germany and banning marriage and other forms of contact between Jews and Germans.
October 3	Italy attacks Ethiopia.
December 31	Jews are dismissed from the civil service in Germany.

1936

March 7	German forces enter the Rhineland.
May 5	Ethiopia surrenders to Italy.
October 25	The Rome-Berlin Axis agreement is signed.

1937

March 21	Pope Pius XI issues the encyclical *Mit brennender Sorge*, a statement against racism and nationalism.
July 16	A concentration camp is established at Buchenwald.
November 25	Germany and Japan sign a military and political pact.

1938

March 13	German forces occupy Austria in what becomes known as the Anschluss.
March 23	The Jewish community organizations in Germany lose their official status and are no longer recognized by the government.
April 24	A decree calling for the registration of all Jewish property is promulgated in Germany.
April 26	Directives for the expropriation of Jewish property are issued in Austria.
May 16	In Austria, the first group of inmates begins work in the Mauthausen quarries.
May 29	The First Anti-Jewish Law is promulgated in Hungary, restricting the Jewish role in the economy to 20 percent.
June 15	Fifteen hundred German Jews are put into concentration camps.
June 25	German Jewish physicians are permitted to treat only Jewish patients.
July 6–15	A conference is held at Evian-les-Bains during which representatives from thirty-two nations discuss the refugee problem but take little action toward solving it.
July 8	On Nazi orders, the Great Synagogue in Munich is torn down.
August 17	All Jewish men in Germany are required to add "Israel" to their name, and all Jewish women, "Sarah."
August 26	In Vienna, the Central Office for Jewish Emigration (Zentralstelle für Jüdische Auswanderung) is set up under Adolf Eichmann.
September 27	Jews are barred from practicing law in Germany.
September 29	The Munich agreement is signed.
October 5	The passports of German Jews are marked with the letter *J*, for *Jude*.
October 6	As a result of the Munich agreement, the Sudetenland is annexed by Germany and the Czechoslovak Republic is established, with autonomy for Slovakia.
October 8	The Hlinka Guard is established in Slovakia.
October 28	Between 15,000 and 17,000 stateless Jews are expelled from Germany to Poland; most are interned in Zbąszyń.

November 2	Under the provisions of the first Vienna Award, parts of Slovakia and the Transcarpathian Ukraine are annexed by Hungary.
November 9–10	Following the assassination of Ernst vom Rath, a secretary at the German legation in Paris, by a Jewish youth, Herschel Grynszpan, the *Kristallnacht* pogrom takes place in Germany and Austria; some 30,000 Jews are interned in concentration camps.
November 12	In the wake of the *Kristallnacht* pogrom, a fine of 1 billion reichsmarks is levied on the Jews of Germany.

1939

January 1	The Measure for the Elimination of Jews from the German Economy is invoked, banning Jews from working with Germans.
March 2	Eugenio Pacelli becomes Pope Pius XII.
March 11	A law permitting the establishment of the Hungarian Labor Service System (Munkaszolgálat) is enacted.
March 14	Slovakia is declared independent.
March 15	German forces enter Prague; *Aktion Gitter* (Operation Bars) is launched in the Protectorate of Bohemia and Moravia, and Jews, German emigrés, and Czech intellectuals are arrested.
March 22	Germany annexes Klaipėda (Memel), Lithuania.
April 7	Italy invades Albania.
May 5	The Second Anti-Jewish Law is promulgated in Hungary, defining who is a Jew and restricting Jewish participation in the economy to 6 percent.
May 15	The Ravensbrück concentration camp for women is established in Germany.
May 17	The MacDonald White Paper, severely restricting Jewish immigration to Palestine, is issued by the British government.
July 4	The Reichsvereinigung der Juden in Deutschland (Reich Association of Jews in Germany) replaces the Reichsvertretung der Juden in Deutschland (Reich Representation of Jews in Germany).
August 23	The Nazi-Soviet Pact is signed.
September 1	A curfew is imposed on Jews throughout Germany, forbidding them to be out of doors after 8:00 P.M.
	German forces invade Poland.
September 2	In Poland, Stutthof is established as a camp for "civilian prisoners of war."
September 3	France and Great Britain declare war on Germany.

September 6	Kraków is occupied by the Germans.
September 8	German forces occupy Łódź, Radom, and Tarnów.
September 14	German forces occupy Przemyśl.
September 17	Parts of eastern Poland are annexed by the USSR.
September 18	Economic sanctions are promulgated against the Jews in Łódź.
September 21	Reinhard Heydrich meets with Einsatzgruppen commanders and Adolf Eichmann. He orders the establishment of Judenräte (Jewish councils) in Poland, the concentration of Polish Jews and a census of them, and a survey of the Jewish workforce and Jewish property throughout Poland.
September 27	The Reichssicherheitshauptamt (Reich Security Main Office; RSHA) is established.
September 28	Poland is partitioned by Germany and the USSR; German forces occupy Warsaw.
October 1	The Polish government-in-exile is formed in France (it later moves to London).
October 8	The first ghetto established by the Nazis is set up, in Piotrków Trybunalski (Poland).
October 16	Kraków is designated the capital of the Generalgouvernement.
October 18–27	Fourteen hundred Jews from Mährisch Ostrau, 1,875 from Katowice, and 1,584 from Vienna are deported to the Lublin area.
November 9	Łódź is annexed to the German Reich.
November 12	The deportation of Jews from Łódź to other parts of Poland begins.
November 15–17	All the synagogues of Łódź are destroyed by the German authorities.
November 23	Hans Frank, the governor-general of the Generalgouvernement, orders that all Jews in the Generalgouvernement must wear the yellow badge by December 1, 1939.
November 28	A regulation establishing Judenräte in the Generalgouvernement is promulgated.
November 30–March 13, 1940	Invasion of Finland by the USSR, followed by the Winter War.
December 5–6	Jewish property in Poland is seized by the German authorities.

1940

February 8	The establishment of a ghetto in Łódź is ordered.

April 9	German forces invade Denmark and Norway.
April 12	Hans Frank declares that Kraków must be *judenfrei* ("free of Jews") by November. By March 1941, 40,000 out of 60,000 Jews have been deported from Kraków.
April 27	Himmler orders the establishment of a concentration camp at Auschwitz. Early in June the first prisoners, mostly Poles, are brought there.
April 30	The Łódź ghetto is sealed.
May 10	The German offensive in Belgium, Luxembourg, and the Netherlands begins.
	Neville Chamberlain resigns as British prime minister and Winston Churchill assumes the post.
May 12	German forces cross the French border.
May 14	The Luftwaffe bombs Rotterdam heavily; the Dutch surrender to the Germans.
May 16	In France, German forces break through the French lines at Sedan.
	Hans Frank orders the launching of the AB-*Aktion*, in which thousands of Polish intellectuals and leaders are killed.
May 17	German forces occupy Brussels.
May 25	Himmler sends a memorandum to Hitler suggesting that the Jews in the eastern occupied areas be sent to Africa.
May 26–June 4	British forces retreat across the English Channel to Great Britain.
May 28	Belgium surrenders to Germany.
June 10	Italy enters the war on Germany's side, declaring war on Great Britain and France, and invading France.
June 14	German forces occupy Paris.
June 15	The USSR occupies the Baltic states.
June 22	Germany and France sign an armistice.
June 24	Italy and France sign an armistice.
June 27	Romania cedes Bessarabia and Bukovina to the USSR.
June 30	Two hundred Jews in Dorohoi are killed by a Romanian infantry battalion.
July 9	The German blitz (bombing) of London begins.
July 16	The expulsion of Jews from Alsace and Lorraine to southern France is initiated.
July 19	Telephones are confiscated from Jews in Germany.

August 2	A civilian administration under Gauleiter Gustav Simon is installed in Luxembourg.
August 3	Northern Transylvania is annexed by Hungary.
September 6	King Carol II flees Romania, his son Michael I becomes king, and a National Legionary Government is set up under Ion Antonescu.
September 7	Romania cedes southern Dobruja to Bulgaria.
September 20	The first prisoners arrive at the Breendonck camp in Belgium.
September 26	The Ústredňa Židov (Jewish Center) is established in Bratislava.
September 27	Germany, Italy, and Japan sign the ten-year Tripartite Pact, also known as the Pact of Berlin.
October 3	The first *Statut des Juifs* is promulgated in Vichy France.
October 5	Legislation for the confiscation of Jewish property is passed by the Romanian government.
October 7	The Law for the Protection of Nations is issued in Bulgaria, curbing the rights of Jews.
October 22	Jewish businesses are registered throughout the Netherlands.
October 22–25	The Jews of Baden, the Palatinate, and Württemberg are sent to the Gurs camp in France during *Aktion Burckel*.
October 28	Italy invades Greece.
November 4	Jewish civil servants are dismissed throughout the Netherlands.
November 15	The Warsaw ghetto is sealed.
November 20–25	Hungary, Romania, and Slovakia become members of the Tripartite Pact.
December 19	In North Africa, British forces begin a battle that will end in their capture of Cyrenaica.

1941

January 10	All the Jews of the Netherlands are registered.
January 21–23	The Iron Guard unsuccessfully attempts a coup in Romania, accompanied by riots against the Jews.
February 5	The Law for the Protection of the State is passed in Romania, making Romanian Jews subject to double the punishment meted out to other Romanians for crimes committed.

February 13	The Joodse Raad (Jewish Council) meets for the first time in Amsterdam.
February 17	Ion Antonescu abolishes the National Legionary Government in Romania.
February 22	A total of 389 Jewish males from the Jewish quarter of Amsterdam are sent to Buchenwald.
February 25	A general anti-Nazi strike is held in Amsterdam.
March 1	Bulgaria joins the Tripartite Pact.
	Himmler orders the construction of a camp at Birkenau (Auschwitz II). Construction begins in October 1941 and continues until March 1942.
March 3–20	A ghetto in Kraków is decreed, established, and sealed.
March 11	The United States government approves the Lend-Lease Act.
March 25	Yugoslavia joins the Axis.
March 27	A pro-Allied coup is carried out in Yugoslavia.
April 1	A pro-Nazi government is established in Iraq by Rashid Ali al-Gaylani.
April 6	German forces invade Greece and Yugloslavia.
April 7	The 30,000 Jews of Radom are placed in two ghettos.
April 9	German forces occupy Salonika.
April 10	Riots break out in Antwerp against Jews.
	The Croatian state is set up by the Germans and Italians.
April 13	The governments of Japan and the USSR sign a neutrality pact.
	German forces occupy Belgrade.
April 14	More anti-Jewish riots break out in Antwerp.
April 18	Yugoslavia capitulates to the Germans.
April 24	The Lublin ghetto is sealed.
May 11	Rudolf Hess, Hitler's deputy, lands in Glasgow on what he terms "a private peace mission."
May 15	A law is passed in Romania permitting Jews to be drafted for forced labor.
May 19	A pogrom against the Jews of Baghdad takes place.
May 30	Baghdad is taken by the British.
June 1	British forces withdraw from Crete.
June 2	The second *Statut des Juifs* is promulgated in Vichy France.

June 6	The *Kommissarbefehl* (Commissar Order) is issued in preparation for the invasion of the USSR. It states that political officers in the Soviet army must be singled out and killed.
June 8	British forces invade Vichy-controlled Syria.
June 18	Turkey and Germany sign a friendship treaty.
June 21	In Romania, Jews are expelled from the towns and villages of southern Bukovina.
June 22	The Germans launch Operation "Barbarossa," invading the USSR. They take Kishinev and Kovno, among other places.
	Zagreb Jews are arrested and sent to the Pag and Jadovno concentration camps.
June 23	The Einsatzgruppen begin their killings in the USSR, and submit reports of their activities almost daily.
June 24	German forces occupy Vilna.
June 25	About 15,000 Jews are killed in Iaşi in a pogrom.
June 26	German forces occupy Dvinsk (Daugavpils).
June 27	Hungary enters the war on the side of the Axis powers.
	The Germans occupy Białystok and kill 2,000 Jews.
June 28	German forces occupy Minsk and Rovno and reoccupy Przemyśl.
June 29	Several thousand Jews are shot in the courtyard of the Iaşi police headquarters. This day becomes known as "Black Sunday."
June 29–July 2	All Jewish males from sixteen to sixty years old are arrested in Dvinsk.
June 30	German forces occupy Lvov.
July 1	German forces occupy Riga.
July 1–August 31	Einsatzgruppe D, Wehrmacht forces, and Escalon Special, a Romanian unit, kill between 150,000 and 160,000 Jews in Bessarabia.
July 2	German forces occupy Ternopol; in Lvov, local Ukrainians commit atrocities against Jews.
July 3	German forces occupy Novogrudok.
July 4	German forces occupy Pinsk.
	Latvians serving in German units set fire to the central synagogue in Riga.
	A Judenrat is established in Vilna. About 5,000 Vilna Jews are killed during the month of July by Einsatzkommando 9 and local collaborators.

July 4–11	Five thousand Ternopol Jews are killed in a pogrom.
July 9	German forces occupy Zhitomir.
July 10	Vichy French forces surrender to the British in Syria.
	Latvia is cleared of Soviet troops.
July 13–August 9	A total of 9,012 Jews from Dvinsk are killed.
July 16	Up to this date, 2,700 Jews have been shot outside Riga.
July 16–29	The Germans and Soviets fight at Smolensk, with the Germans eventually victorious.
July 20	A ghetto is established in Minsk.
July 21	Hermann Göring signs an order giving Heydrich the authority to prepare a "total solution" to the "Jewish question" in Europe.
	Romanian forces occupy Bessarabia.
July 24	A ghetto is established in Kishinev; some 10,000 Kishinev Jews have already been killed.
July 25–27	Local Ukrainians rampage against the Jews in Lvov in a pogrom that becomes known as the Petliura Days.
July 26	After twenty-five days of fighting, Mogilev, in Belorussia, falls to German forces.
August 1	The Białystok ghetto is established.
August 4–5	A Jewish Council is established in Kovno under Elchanan Elkes and told by the German authorities that it is responsible for the transfer of the Jews to the ghetto.
August 5	Eight thousand Jewish men from Pinsk are killed.
August 7	Between 2,500 and 3,000 Pinsk Jews are murdered.
August 14	Roosevelt and Churchill sign the Atlantic Charter, an eight-point declaration of peace aims and terms.
	Smolensk is occupied by German forces.
August 17	Thirteen thousand Jews are interned in the Vertujeni camp.
August 19	Einsatzkommando 8 and local collaborators in Mogilev kill 3,726 Jews.
August 21	Four thousand more Jews are interned in the Vertujeni camp.
August 21–August 17, 1944	Seventy thousand Jews pass through the Drancy transit camp.
August 25	Soviet and British forces enter Iran.
August 27–28	At Kamenets-Podolski, 23,600 Jews are massacred by German forces under Friedrich Jeckeln; at least 14,000 of them had recently been deported from Hungary.

August 31– September 3	Eight thousand Vilna Jews are killed in Ponary.
September 1	The Euthanasia Program is officially ended; between 70,000 and 93,000 people have been killed in the German Reich during the course of the program.
September 3	The first experimental gassing at Auschwitz is carried out on Soviet prisoners of war.
September 3–6	Two ghettos are established in Vilna.
September 4	Fifteen hundred young Jews from Berdichev are shot just outside of town.
September 9	The *Židovsky Kodex* (Jewish Code) is invoked in Slovakia, defining who is a Jew.
September 10	The Vertujeni camp inmates are deported on foot to Transnistria.
September 15	In the Netherlands, laws are invoked banning Jews from many public places.
	Approximately 18,600 Jews are killed outside Berdichev.
September 15– October 13, 1942	At least 150,000 Jews from Bessarabia and Bukovina are deported to Transnistria, and some 90,000 die there.
September 19	The Jews in the Reich are required to wear the yellow badge in public.
	Kiev is captured by Germans; 10,000 Jews have been killed in Zhitomir.
September 27	Heydrich arrives in Prague as *Reichsprotektor*.
September 29–30	At Babi Yar, 33,771 Kiev Jews are killed by Einsatzkommando 4a.
October 1– December 22	In *Aktionen* in Vilna, 33,500 Jews are killed.
October 6– March 16, 1945	A total of 46,067 Prague Jews are deported to the "east" and to Theresienstadt.
October 8	The Vitebsk ghetto is liquidated and more than 16,000 Jews are killed.
October 11	A ghetto is established in Chernovtsy.
October 12	German forces reach the outskirts of Moscow, and the city is partly evacuated.
	Obersturmbannführer Martin Sandberger of Sonderkommando 1a reports that Jewish men over the age of sixteen are being killed by his Sonderkommando in Estonia; by the beginning of 1942, 936 Jews have been killed.

	Three thousand Jews are killed at Sheparovtse, near Kolomyia.
October 13	Twenty thousand Jews in Dnepropetrovsk are killed.
October 15	Jews are deported from Austria and Germany to Kovno, Łódź, Minsk, and Riga.
October 16	German forces occupy Odessa.
October 19	Jews are murdered in Belgrade.
October 19–September 28, 1943	Luxembourg Jews are deported to Łódź in eight transports.
October 23	Further Jewish emigration from Germany is prohibited.
	Nineteen thousand Jews are killed in Odessa.
October 24	German forces occupy Kharkov.
October 28	Nine thousand Jews are killed in an *Aktion* outside Kovno at the Ninth Fort; 17,412 Jews remain in the Kovno ghetto.
October 30	Four thousand of the 4,500 Jews of Nesvizh are killed, and the remaining Jews are put into a ghetto.
November 1	In Poland, the construction of an extermination center at Bełżec begins.
November 7	Twelve thousand Jews of Minsk are killed at Tuchinka.
November 7–8	Twenty-one thousand Jews are killed in the Sosenki pine grove outside Rovno.
November 7–9	More than three thousand Jews are killed in Pogulanka, outside Dvinsk.
November 8	The establishment of a ghetto in Lvov is ordered.
November 10	The Nazis finalize their plans for Theresienstadt.
November 15–July 2, 1942	After a battle lasting seven months, Sevastopol falls to the Germans.
November 20	Twenty thousand Minsk Jews are killed at Tuchinka.
November 20–December 7	Thirty thousand Jews are killed in the Rumbula Forest outside Riga, during the so-called *Jeckeln Aktion*.
November 24–April 20, 1945	A total of 140,937 Jews of Bohemia and Moravia are deported to Theresienstadt; 33,539 die and 88,196 are deported farther.
November 25	The Association des Juifs en Belgique (Association of Jews in Belgium) is established.
	The deportation of Polish Jews from Breslau begins, continuing intermittently until April 1944.
November 29	The Union Générale des Israélites de France (Union of French Jews), the organization of French Jewry, is formed.

December 6	Great Britain declares war on Romania.
	A Soviet counteroffensive begins outside Moscow.
December 7	Hitler issues the *Nacht-und-Nebel-Erlass* (Night and Fog Decree) for the suppression of anti-Nazi resistance in occupied western Europe.
	Japanese forces attack the American naval base at Pearl Harbor.
December 8	Malaya and Thailand are invaded by the Japanese.
	The first transport of Jews arrives at the Chełmno extermination camp, and transports continue to arrive until March 1943. The camp reopened for operation in April 1944. About 320,000 Jews were killed at Chełmno.
	Four thousand Jews of Novogrudok are killed.
December 10	Germany and Italy declare war on the United States, and the United States declares war on them.
December 13	Bulgaria and Hungary declare war on the United States.
December 21–31	Fifty-four thousand Jews are killed in the Bogdanovka camp, and 200 are left alive.
December 22	The Japanese invade the Philippines.
	Churchill arrives in Washington for a conference with Roosevelt.
December 23	In Kolomyia 1,200 Jews, holders of foreign passports, are arrested and subsequently killed at Sheparovtse.
December 25	Hong Kong capitulates to the Japanese.

1942

January 10–11	The Japanese invade the Netherlands East Indies.
January 14	The concentration of the Dutch Jews in Amsterdam begins. First to arrive are the Jews of Zaandam.
January 16	Deportations from Łódź to Chełmno begin, and continue until September 1942.
January 20	In the Berlin suburb of Wannsee a conference, presided over by Heydrich and attended by top Nazi officials, is held to coordinate the "Final Solution" (the extermination of the Jews).
January 21	The Germans begin a counteroffensive in North Africa.
	The Fareynegte Partizaner Organizatsye (United Partisan Organization) is created by Jews in Vilna.
January 24	Four hundred Jewish intellectuals are arrested and subsequently killed in Kolomyia.

February 1	The SS Wirtschafts-Verwaltungshauptamt (Economic-Administrative Main Office; WVHA) is established, under Oswald Pohl.
	A nationalist government is formed in Norway under Vidkun Quisling.
February 8	The first transport of Jews from Salonika is sent to Auschwitz.
February 15	The British surrender Singapore to the Japanese.
February 23	The *Struma,* a ship loaded with Jewish refugees refused entry to Palestine, sinks off the coast of Turkey; 768 passengers drown and 1 survives.
March 1	In Poland, construction of the Sobibór extermination camp begins. Jews are first killed there early in May 1942.
March 2	Five thousand Jews from Minsk are killed.
March 3	Jews in Belgium are drafted for forced labor.
March 7	The British evacuate Rangoon.
March 12–April 20	Thirty thousand Jews are deported from Lublin to Bełżec.
March 17	Killings begin at the Bełżec extermination camp, the first of the *Aktion Reinhard* camps to be put into operation.
March 19	The *Intelligenz Aktion* is carried out in Kraków; fifty Jewish intellectuals are killed.
March 19–end of March	Fifteen thousand Jews are deported from Lvov to Bełżec.
March 25	A ghetto is established in Kolomyia, containing about 18,000 Jews.
March 26	The first transport of Jews sent by Adolf Eichmann's office goes to Auschwitz.
March 26–October 20	More than 57,000 Slovak Jews are deported.
March 28	The first transport of French Jews is sent to Auschwitz.
April 3	A total of 383 Jews from Munich are deported to Piaski, near Lublin.
April 3–4	Five thousand Jews from Kolomyia are deported to Bełżec, and 250 are killed in the Kolomyia ghetto itself.
April 6	More than 600 Jews attempt to flee from Diatlovo (Zhetl) to the forest during the final *Aktion.*
April 9	American forces surrender to the Japanese at Bataan.
April 18	In Warsaw, fifty-two Jews are murdered in what becomes known as the "Bloody Night."

April 27–28	Seventy Jewish men are shot in Radom and 100 are deported to Auschwitz.
April 29	The Jews of the Netherlands are ordered to wear the yellow badge.
April 30	The Jews of Pinsk are ordered to establish a ghetto within one day. About 20,000 Jews move into it.
	Twelve hundred Jews are killed in Diatlovo during an *Aktion*. The Jews offer armed resistance but to no avail.
May 1	The Dvinsk ghetto is virtually liquidated, with only 450 Jews remaining. They are transferred to Kaiserwald late in October 1943.
May 7	In the Battle of the Coral Sea, the Allies sink over 100,000 tons of Japanese shipping.
May 10	Fifteen hundred Jews are deported from Sosnowiec to Auschwitz.
May 27	In Belgium, the wearing of the yellow badge is decreed. The decree goes into effect on June 3.
	Heydrich is severely wounded in Prague by the "Anthropoid" team. He dies of his wounds on June 4.
May 28–June 8	Six thousand Kraków Jews are deported to Bełżec and 300 are killed in the city itself.
June 4	The United States declares war on Romania.
June 4–7	United States forces defeat the Japanese at Midway, in the Pacific.
June 7	The Jews in occupied France are required to wear the yellow badge.
June 10	In reprisal for the assassination of Heydrich, the village of Lidice, in Czechoslovakia, is razed. All 192 of the men from the village are killed, as are 71 women; the rest of the women are sent to Ravensbrück.
June 11	Eichmann's office orders that the deportation of Jews from the Netherlands, Belgium, and France begin in a few weeks.
	Thirty-five hundred Jews are deported from Tarnów to Bełżec.
June 15–18	Ten thousand more Tarnów Jews are deported to Bełżec, and many Jews are murdered in the vicinity of Tarnów.
June 18	One thousand Jewish men are deported from Przemyśl to the Janówska camp in Lvov.
June 20–October 9	From Vienna, 13,776 Jews are deported to Theresienstadt.

June 21	German forces take Tobruk from the British.
June 22	The first transport from the Drancy camp in France leaves for Auschwitz.
June 25	Churchill and Roosevelt confer in Washington.
June 26	A transport from Brussels is sent to the Organisation Todt labor camps in northern France.
	In the Netherlands, an active schedule of deportations to Westerbork begins, and from Westerbork to Auschwitz.
July 1	The Sicherheitspolizei takes over the Westerbork internment camp.
July 8	Seven thousand Lvov Jews are interned in the Janówska camp.
July 11	Nine thousand Jewish males from Salonika between the ages of eighteen and forty-five are drafted into the Organisation Todt labor battalions in Greece.
July 13–14	Jews are deported from Antwerp to northern France for forced labor.
July 14	The systematic transfer of Dutch Jewry to the Westerbork camp begins.
	A closed ghetto is set up in Przemyśl.
July 15	The first transport leaves Westerbork for Auschwitz.
July 16–17	A total of 12,887 Jews of Paris are rounded up and sent to Drancy; in all, about 42,500 Jews are sent to Drancy from all over France during this *Aktion*.
July 19	Himmler orders that the extermination of the Jews of the Generalgouvernement be completed by the end of the year.
July 20	An armed Jewish uprising takes place in Nesvizh.
July 22	The Treblinka extermination center is completed; by August 1943 some 870,000 Jews have been killed there.
July 22–September 12	During the mass deportation from Warsaw, some 300,000 Jews are deported, 265,000 of them to Treblinka. About 60,000 Jews remain in the Warsaw ghetto.
July 23	Adam Czerniaków, the head of the Warsaw Judenrat, commits suicide rather than assist the Nazis in deporting the Warsaw Jews.
July 24	In Derechin an *Aktion* against the Jews takes place.
July 27, 31; August 3	On three separate days, more than 10,500 Przemyśl Jews are deported to Bełżec. The first day of the *Aktion*, Wehrmacht

	lieutenant Dr. Alfred Battel rescues Jews in the employ of the Wehrmacht.
July 28	The Żydowska Organizacja Bojowa (Jewish Fighting Organization; ŻOB) is formed in Warsaw.
July 28–31	Thirty thousand German Jews who had been sent to Minsk are murdered at Maly Trostinets.
August 5	The smaller ghetto in Radom is liquidated and 6,000 Jews are sent to Treblinka. Two thousand more are sent from the larger ghetto.
August 6–December 29, 1943	Jewish inmates from the Gurs camp in France are deported to Auschwitz and Sobibór by way of Drancy.
August 8	In Geneva, Gerhart Riegner cables Rabbi Stephen S. Wise in New York and Sidney Silverman in London about Nazi plans for the extermination of European Jewry. The United States Department of State holds up delivery of the message to Wise, who finally receives it from Silverman on August 28.
	Twenty-five hundred Jews of Novogrudok are killed.
August 9	During the liquidation of the Mir ghetto, Jews offer armed resistance. Over the next three days, some 10,000 Jews from Będzin, Sosnowiec, and Dąbrowa are selected and deported.
August 10	The Yeheskel Atlas Jewish partisan brigade attacks a German garrison in Derechin.
August 10–23	Fifty thousand Jews are deported from Lvov to Bełzec.
August 11	Two thousand Jews are killed in Rostov-on-Don.
August 12	Churchill, Stalin, and Averell Harriman meet in Moscow and affirm their goal of destroying Nazism.
August 12–18	Five thousand Jews from Będzin and 8,000 from Sosnowiec are deported to Auschwitz.
August 13–14	Jews lacking Belgian nationality are seized in Antwerp and sent to the Malines camp.
August 13–20	The majority of Croatian Jews are deported to Auschwitz.
August 15	Jews from Antwerp are deported to northern France for forced labor.
August 16–18	The large Radom ghetto is liquidated. Eighteen thousand Jews are deported to Treblinka and 1,500 who resist deportations are shot on the spot. Four thousand Jews are put into a special labor ghetto in Radom.

August 20–24	Eighteen thousand of the 20,000 Jews of Kielce are deported to Treblinka.
August 27–30	Three thousand Jews are sent from Ternopol to Bełżec.
September 2	The Lachva ghetto is surrounded by German forces and an uprising breaks out. Six thousand Jews flee, but most are caught and quickly killed.
September 3–4	The last transports of Belgian nationals are sent from Antwerp to the Malines camp.
September 4	The Jews of Macedonia are required to wear the yellow badge.
September 7	Seven thousand Jews from Kolomyia are deported to Bełżec and 1,000 are killed in the Kolomyia ghetto itself.
September 8	Eight thousand Jews are deported from Tarnów to Bełżec; about six weeks later another 2,500 are sent there.
September 9	Two thousand Lublin Jews are deported to Majdanek.
September 10–12	Jews not of Belgian nationality are seized in Antwerp. They are sent to the Malines camp and to perform forced labor in northern France.
September 12	The German Sixth Army and Fourth Panzer Army reach the suburbs of Stalingrad; the Battle of Stalingrad begins.
September 24–26	An uprising breaks out in Tuchin when the Germans move to liquidate the ghetto. Most of the Jews escape, but they are subsequently found and killed.
September 30	The Ternopol Judenrat is ordered to hand over 1,000 Jews to the Nazis, and refuses. The Nazis and their helpers arrest Jews and deport 800 of them to Bełżec.
October 2	The deportation of Dutch Jewry is intensified.
October 9	The Italian racial laws are enforced in Libya.
October 13–21	Twenty thousand Jews from Piotrków Trybunalski are deported to Treblinka and 500 escape to the forest. In July 1944 the ghetto is liquidated, and the Jews are sent to labor camps or to Auschwitz.
October 16	Over 1,000 Jews are arrested by the Nazis in Rome and deported to Auschwitz.
October 24	A total of 252 friends and relatives of persons from Lidice are murdered in Mauthausen in reprisal for the assassination of Heydrich.
October 25	Eighteen hundred Lublin Jews are deported to Majdanek.
October 27–28	Seven thousand Kraków Jews are deported to Bełżec, and 600 are shot in Kraków.

October 29– November 1	Almost all the Jews of Pinsk are murdered.
November 1	The deportation of Jews from the Białystok district to Treblinka begins.
November 2	British forces take El Alamein from the Germans.
November 8	American and British forces invade North Africa; Operation "Torch" is under way.
November 9	German and Italian forces occupy Tunisia.
November 11	Southern France is occupied by the Germans and Italians.
	Four thousand Jews are deported from Kolomyia to Bełżec.
November 18	The Germans order 8,000 Przemyśl Jews to gather for deportation, but only 3,500 do so; 500 more are found hiding. All told, 4,000 Jews are deported to Bełżec.
November 18– January 12, 1943	Some 15,000 Jews are killed in the Lvov ghetto, which becomes a Julag (*Judenlager*, or camp for Jews) in January 1943.
November 19	Soviet forces begin a counterattack near Stalingrad.
November 20	Nine hundred and eighty Jews from Munich are deported to Riga.
November 24	Rabbi Stephen S. Wise releases to the press the news contained in the Riegner cable.
December 4	Zegota (the Council for Aid to Jews) is established in Poland.
December 6	The German authorities order the Jewish leadership of Tunisia to recruit 2,000 Jews for forced labor. Eventually, 5,000 are placed in labor camps.
December 10	The Polish government-in-exile asks the Allies to retaliate for the Nazi killing of civilians, especially Jews.
December 16	A ghetto is established in Kharkov. Three weeks later approximately 15,000 Jews are killed in the Drobitski Ravine.
December 17	An Allied declaration is made condemning the Nazis' "bestial policy of cold-blooded extermination."
December 23	The last Jews in Pinsk are killed.

1943

January 1	Dutch Jews are no longer permitted to have private bank accounts, and all Jewish money is put into a central account.
January 13	Fifteen hundred Jews are deported from Radom to Treblinka.

January 14–24	Roosevelt and Churchill meet at Casablanca and declare the unconditional surrender of Germany to be a central war aim.
January 18–22	More than 5,000 Jews are deported from Warsaw and are killed. The first Warsaw ghetto uprising breaks out.
January 23	In Libya, British forces liberate Tripoli.
February 2	Ninety-one thousand German soldiers under Field Marshal Friedrich von Paulus surrender to the Soviet army at Stalingrad.
February 5–12	In Białystok, 2,000 Jews are killed and 10,000 deported to Treblinka; Jews offer armed resistance.
February 13	In Tunisia, the Jews of Djerba are forced to pay 10 million francs to the German authorities.
February 24	A ghetto is established in Salonika.
February 26	The first transport of Gypsies reaches Auschwitz. They are placed in a special section of the camp called the Gypsy Camp.
February 29	The Kolomyia ghetto is liquidated and 2,000 Jews are killed.
March 4–9	Nearly all the 4,000 Jews of Bulgarian Thrace are arrested and sent to Treblinka.
March 11	A total of 7,341 Macedonian Jews are concentrated in Skopje. Most are subsequently deported to Treblinka.
March 13	Ostindustrie GmbH is founded by the SS to exploit Jewish labor in the Generalgouvernement.
	Two thousand Jews are deported from Kraków to Płaszów.
March 14	Twenty-three hundred Kraków Jews are deported to Auschwitz and 700 are shot in Kraków.
March 17	Fifteen hundred Lvov Jews are killed and 800 are deported to Auschwitz.
March 20– August 18	Transports from Salonika arrive at Auschwitz.
April 8–9	One thousand Jews are murdered near Ternopol.
April 13	Mass graves are discovered at Katyn, Poland, the site of a massacre of Polish officers by the Soviets.
April 19–30	British and American representatives confer in Bermuda about rescue options and fail to come up with significant rescue proposals.
April 19–May 16	The Warsaw ghetto uprising takes place and the Warsaw ghetto is destroyed.

May 5–10	The last two transports of Jews are sent from Croatia to Auschwitz.
May 7	An *Aktion* takes place in Novogrudok, after which only 233 Jews of the original 7,000 remain alive. Three weeks later, 100 of the remaining Jews successfully escape and join partisan units.
May 8	Mordecai Anielewicz and other leaders of the Warsaw ghetto uprising are killed in a bunker at 18 Mila Street during the fighting.
May 11–27	Churchill and Roosevelt confer in Washington.
May 12	Samuel Zygelbojm, a Jewish representative of the Polish government-in-exile in London, commits suicide as an expression of solidarity with the Jewish fighters in Warsaw, and in protest against the world's silence regarding the fate of the Jews in Nazi-occupied Europe.
May 13	Tunisia is liberated by the Allies.
June 1	The final liquidation of the Lvov ghetto begins. When the Jews resist, 3,000 are killed. Seven thousand are sent to Janówska.
June 20	Except for a handful of workers, the Ternopol ghetto is liquidated and Jews are killed in and around the city.
June 25	Jews in Częstochowa resist the Germans with arms.
July 5	Himmler orders that Sobibór, an extermination camp, be made a concentration camp.
July 9–10	Allied forces invade Sicily.
July 20	Seventeen hundred Jews are transported from Rhodes to Athens.
July 21	Himmler orders the liquidation of the Reichskommissariat Ostland ghettos by sending the Jewish workers to labor camps and killing the rest of the Jews.
July 22– early August	The remaining Jewish workers from Ternopol are killed.
July 25	Mussolini falls from power and Pietro Badoglio forms a new government in Italy.
August 1	The final liquidation of the Będzin and Sosnowiec ghettos is begun and most of the Jews are deported to Auschwitz; Jews offer armed resistance.
August 2	The uprising at Treblinka takes place.
August 4– September 4	Seven thousand Jews are deported from Vilna to Estonia for forced labor.

August 15–20	Nazi forces under Odilo Globocnik surround the Białystok ghetto, and its 30,000 remaining Jews are ordered to appear for evacuation. A Jewish uprising breaks out in the ghetto.
August 17	By way of Athens, 120 Jews of Rhodes arrive in Auschwitz.
August 18–21	The final deportation of Białystok Jewry takes place.
September 1	An uprising is attempted in the Vilna ghetto but is aborted. During the rest of September the fighters escape to the partisans.
September 2–3	Thirty-five hundred Jews are deported from Przemyśl to Auschwitz.
September 2	The final liquidation of the Tarnów ghetto is launched. Seven thousand Jews are deported to Auschwitz and 3,000 to Płaszów. The 300 workers who remain are deported to Płaszów at the end of the year. The Jews offer armed resistance.
September 3–4	The last Jews of Belgium are deported as part of Operation "Iltis."
September 3	The Allies invade southern Italy.
September 8	German forces occupy Athens; Italian forces capitulate to the Germans in Rhodes.
	The Badoglio government in Italy signs an armistice with the Allies.
September 11	One thousand Jews discovered hiding in Przemyśl are murdered.
September 11–14	The Minsk ghetto is liquidated and almost all of its Jews are killed.
September 20	A Judenrat is set up in Athens under Moses Sciaki.
September 23–24	The Vilna ghetto is liquidated. Thirty-seven hundred Jews are sent to labor camps in Estonia and 4,000 are deported to Sobibór.
September 28	The Jews of Rome deliver a levy of 50 kilograms of gold to the Gestapo.
September 29	The last 2,000 Amsterdam Jews are sent to Westerbork.
October 1–2	In Denmark, German police begin rounding up Jews for deportation. The Danish population begins the rescue of 7,200 Danish Jews.
October 2–3	Throughout the Netherlands the families of Jewish men drafted for forced labor are sent to Westerbork.
October 13	Italy declares war on Germany.
October 14	The Sobibór uprising takes place.

October 16	Mass arrests of Jews begin in Rome.
October 18	In Rome, 1,035 Jews are deported to Auschwitz.
October 21	During the final *Aktion* in Minsk, 2,000 Jews are killed at Maly Trostinets.
October 25	Dnepropetrovsk is liberated.
October 26	Twenty-eight hundred Kovno Jews are sent to German labor camps.
November 3	Jews are arrested in Genoa, Italy.
	Aktion "Erntefest" (Operation "Harvest Festival") is launched, liquidating the Poniatowa and Trawniki camps and the remaining Jews in the Majdanek camp. Other Jews brought to Majdanek from the Lublin area are killed as well. In all, between 42,000 and 43,000 Jews are killed during the operation.
November 6–9	Jews are arrested in Florence, Milan, and Venice.
November 9	The United Nations Relief and Rehabilitation Agency (UNRRA) is founded.
November 14	Jews are arrested in Ferrara, Italy.
November 19	The Sonderkommando 1005 prisoners in the Janówska camp revolt. Several dozen escape and the rest are killed.
November 28–December 1	Churchill, Roosevelt, and Stalin confer in Tehran.
November 30	The authorities order the concentration of all Italian Jews in camps.

1944

January 15	Berdichev is liberated by Soviet forces.
January 25	The Allies carry out a successful air attack on the Schweinfurt ball-bearing factory, causing great damage to the German war effort.
March 15	Soviet forces begin the liberation of Transnistria, crossing the Bug River and reaching the Dniester on March 20.
March 17	A group of 99 prisoners breaks out of the Koldichevo camp. Twenty-four are recaptured and 75 reach partisan units, primarily the Bielski unit.
March 19	German forces occupy Hungary after an Hungarian attempt to pull forces back from the eastern front.
March 27	Eighteen hundred Kovno Jews, mostly elderly people and children, are killed.

April 5	Jews in Hungary begin wearing the yellow badge.
April 7	Alfred Wetzler and Rudolf Vrba escape from Auschwitz and reach Slovakia, bearing detailed information about the killing of Jews in Auschwitz. Their report, which reaches the free world in June, becomes known as the Auschwitz Protocols.
April 15	During an escape attempt from Ponary, where they had been employed burning corpses, fifteen prisoners succeed in escaping and sixty-five others are killed.
April 16	In Hungary, the concentration of the Jews of the Transcarpathian Ukraine begins.
May 2	The first transport of Jews from Hungary arrives at Auschwitz.
May 2–9	Two ghettos are established in Oradea.
May 9	Twenty-five hundred men in Oradea are assembled for forced labor.
May 15	Between May 15 and July 9, 437,000 Hungarian Jews are deported, primarily to Auschwitz. Most of those sent to Auschwitz are gassed soon after their arrival.
May 23	An Allied offensive begins at Anzio, in Italy.
May 24–June 3	The Jews of Oradea are deported, mainly to Auschwitz.
June 4	Rome is captured by the American Fifth Army.
June 6	D-Day. Allied forces land in Normandy with the largest seaborne force in history.
	Eighteen hundred Jews from Corfu are arrested and sent to Auschwitz.
June 17–24	The Jews of Budapest are confined to specially marked "Jewish buildings."
June 23–July 14	Transports from Łódź reach Chełmno.
July 8	The Kovno ghetto is liquidated. Two thousand Jews are killed and 4,000 are marched to Germany.
July 9	The Hungarian regent, Miklós Horthy, orders an end to the deportations from Hungary. Two days later they cease.
July 10	From Bergen-Belsen, 222 Jews with immigration certificates reach Haifa.
July 13	Vilna is liberated by Soviet forces.
July 20	An unsuccessful attempt is made to kill Hitler.
	Two thousand Jews from Rhodes are sent to Auschwitz.
July 21–25	Children's homes in France operated by the Union Générale des Israélites de France are raided. Three hundred Jewish chil-

dren, in addition to adult staff, are sent to Drancy and from there to Auschwitz.

July 23	A delegation of the International Red Cross visits Theresienstadt.
July 25	Lublin is liberated by the Soviet army.
July 26	The remaining Jews of Radom are sent to Auschwitz.
July 27	Dvinsk is liberated by Soviet forces. Twenty Jews remain in the city.
July 28	The first major death march begins, with the evacuation of the Gesia Street camp in Warsaw. Thirty-six hundred prisoners set out on foot for Kutno; 1,000 are killed on the journey of 81 miles (130 km).
July 31	American forces break through German lines in France. By the end of August, France is liberated.
August 1	The Polish rebellion begins in Warsaw.
	Kovno is liberated by the Soviet army.
August 7–30	Deportations from Łódź to Auschwitz take place.
August 11	American forces take Guam from the Japanese.
August 12	Allied forces occupy Florence.
August 23	Paris is liberated.
August 23	The regime of Ion Antonescu is overthrown and Romania joins the Allies.
August 28–29 to October 27	The Slovak national uprising takes place and is suppressed by the SS.
September 3	The last transport of Jews leaves Westerbork.
September 4	Antwerp is liberated.
September 5	The USSR declares war on Bulgaria.
September 9	Churchill and Roosevelt confer in Quebec.
September 12	Soviet forces begin their attack on Budapest.
September 16	Bulgaria surrenders to the USSR.
September 18–19	Twenty-nine hundred Jewish inmates and 100 Soviet prisoners of war from the Klooga camp are shot at Lagedi.
September 28	The Klooga camp is liberated by Soviet forces. Eighty-five prisoners are found alive, having survived in hiding.
October 2	The Warsaw Polish uprising is quashed.
October 6–7	In the Sonderkommando uprising at Auschwitz, one of the gas chambers is destroyed before the uprising is quelled.

October 13	Soviet forces liberate Riga.
October 15	Ferenc Szálasi and his Arrow Cross Party come to power in Hungary.
October 17	Soviet forces liberate Oradea.
November 8	Deportations from Budapest are resumed.
November 13	A ghetto is established in Budapest for Jews without international protection.
December 16	German forces launch an offensive, the Battle of the Bulge, in the Ardennes forest.
December 26	The Soviet encirclement of Budapest that began on September 12, 1944, is complete.

1945

January 9	American forces land in Luzon.
January 16	Soviet forces liberate Kielce; twenty-five Jews are in the city at the time.
January 17	The SS is ordered to evacuate Auschwitz, and on the following day begin leaving. Sixty-six thousand prisoners are marched on foot toward Wodzisław, to be sent from there to other camps, and 15,000 die on the way. Forty-eight thousand men and 18,000 women prisoners are still in Auschwitz and its satellite camps at this time.
	Soviet forces liberate Warsaw.
	Raoul Wallenberg is arrested by the Soviets.
January 18	The Soviets take Pest.
January 19	Łódź is liberated by the Soviet army.
January 25	Four thousand Jews are evacuated by foot from the Blechhammer camp toward the Gross-Rosen camp; 1,000 die on the way.
	From Bergen-Belsen, 136 Jews with South American passports reach Switzerland.
January 25–April 25	Fifty thousand Jews are evacuated by foot from the Stutthof camp and its satellites; 26,000 of them perish.
January 27	Soviet forces enter Auschwitz and find 7,650 prisoners there.
February 3	American forces invade Manila.
February 4–12	Churchill, Roosevelt, and Stalin meet at Yalta.
February 5	Twelve hundred Jews from the Protectorate of Bohemia and Moravia are transferred to Switzerland with the help of the International Red Cross.

February 13	Buda is taken by the Soviets.
February 19	Iwo Jima is invaded by American marines.
March 7	American forces cross the Rhine.
April 1	American forces invade Okinawa.
April 4	All German forces are expelled from Hungary.
April 5–6	More than 28,250 inmates are evacuated from Buchenwald, and from 7,000 to 8,000 others are killed.
April 9	The evacuation of Mauthausen begins.
April 11	The Buchenwald concentration camp is liberated by American forces.
April 12	Roosevelt dies and Harry S Truman succeeds him as president.
April 15	With the help of the International Red Cross, 413 Danish Jews in the Protectorate are transferred to Sweden.
	Bergen-Belsen is liberated by British forces, who find the inmates in the midst of a typhus epidemic.
April 21	Except for the sick and their caretakers, all the inmates of the Ravensbrück camp have been evacuated.
April 25	The United Nations meets in San Francisco.
April 28	Mussolini is shot by Italian partisans while trying to escape to Switzerland.
April 29	Dachau is liberated by the American Seventh Army.
	Slovakia is occupied by the USSR.
April 29–30	Ravensbrück is liberated. In the camp are 3,500 sick women.
April 30	Hitler and Eva Braun commit suicide in Hitler's bunker in Berlin.
May 2	Soviet forces take Berlin.
	German forces in Italy surrender to the Allies.
May 3	The Nazis hand over Theresienstadt, with 17,247 Jewish inmates, to the International Red Cross.
May 4	The SS leave Mauthausen.
May 7	The Germans surrender to the Allies.
May 8	VE-Day. The war in Europe is officially over.
June 26	The United Nations charter is signed in San Francisco; it goes into effect on October 24, 1945.
August 6	The United States drops the first nuclear bomb, on Hiroshima.
August 8	The USSR declares war on Japan.

August 9	The second nuclear bomb is dropped by the United States, on Nagasaki.
August 14	Japan accepts the Allied surrender terms. World War II is over.
September 2	The Japanese sign the American and British surrender terms in the Tokyo harbor, aboard the USS *Missouri*.
September 9	Japan signs the Chinese surrender terms.

1948

May 14	The new state of Israel, the Jewish national homeland, is established.

Article Sources

The biographies in *Rescue and Resistance: Portraits of the Holocaust* were extracted from the *Encyclopedia of the Holocaust*, edited by Israel Gutman and published by Macmillan Library Reference in 1990. Extracted articles were written by:

ARTICLE	AUTHOR
Abegg, Elizabeth	Mordecai Paldiel
Abugov, Alexander	Shmuel Spector
Adamowicz, Irena	Dov Levin
André, Joseph	Mordecai Paldiel
Anielewicz, Mordecai	Israel Gutman
Atlas, Yeheskel	Shalom Cholawski
Baeck, Leo	Joseph Walk
Barth, Karl	John S. Conway
Bartoszewski, Wladyslaw	Elisheva Shaul
Baublys, Patras	Mordecai Paldiel
Bauminger, Heshek	Arie Leon Bauminger
Baur, André	Richard Cohen
Beccari, Arrigo	Mordecai Paldiel
Ben-Gurion, David	Dina Porat
Benoît, Marie	Mordecai Paldiel
Berman, Adolf Abraham	Israel Gutman
Bernadotte, Folke	Elisheva Shaul
Biberstein, Marek	Aharon Weiss
Bielski, Tuvia	Yitzchak Alperowitz
Blobel, Paul	Shmuel Spector
Blum, Abraham	Israel Gutman
Bogaard, Johannes	Mordecai Paldiel
Bonhoeffer, Dietrich	John S. Conway
Bormann, Martin	Tvsi Raanan
Bor-Komorowski, Tadeusz	Shmuel Krakowski
Borkowska, Anna	Mordecai Paldiel
Brand, Joel	Randolph L. Braham
Brodetsky, Selig	Nana Sagi
Choms, Waldyslawa	Mordecai Paldiel
Clauberg, Carl	Lionel Kochan
Cohn, Marianne	Mordecai Paldiel
Deffaught, Jean	Mordecai Paldiel

ARTICLE	AUTHOR
Spiegel, Isaiah	Yehiel Szeintuch
Stangl, Franz	Gitta Sereny
Sternbuch, Recha	Efraim Zuroff
Streicher, Julius	Hans-Heinrich Wilhelm
Stroop, Jurgen	Israel Gutman
Sugihara, Sempo	Mordecai Paldiel
Sutzkever, Abraham	Yehiel Szeintuch
Szenes, Hannah	Dina Porat
Szlengel, Wladyslaw	Israel Gutman
Sztehlo, Gábor	Mordecai Paldiel
Tenebaum, Mordechai	Bronia Klibanski
van der Voort, Hanna	Mordecai Paldiel
Visser, Lodewijk Ernst	Jozeph Michman
Wallenberg, Raoul	Leni Yahil
Warhaftig, Zorah	Joseph Walk
Wdowinski, David	Israel Gutman
Weill, Joseph	Lucien Lazare
Weissmandel, Michael Dov	Shlomo Kless
Weizmann, Chaim	Jehuda Reinharz
Westerweel, Joop	Jozeph Michman
Wiesel, Elie	Eli Pfefferkorn
Wiesenthal Simon	Efraim Zuroff
Wilner, Arie	Israel Gutman
Wittenberg, Yitzhak	Israel Gutman
Wolinski, Henryk	Teresa Prekerowa
Wurm, Theophil	Zvi Bacharach
Yelin, Haim	Dov Levin
Zabinski, Jan	Mordecai Paldiel
Zagan, Shakhne	Israel Gutman
Zeitlin, Hillel	Yehiel Szeintuch
Zimetbaum, Mala	Israel Gutman
Zorin, Shalom	Shalom Cholawski
Zuckerman, Yitzhak	Israel Gutman
Zygelbojm, Samuel Artur	Israel Gutman

The following sidebars in *Rescue and Resistance: Portraits of the Holocaust* were adapted from articles in the *Encyclopedia of the Holocaust*:

Ghetto (page 6) was adapted from an article by Israel Gutman.
The Museum of Jewish Heritage (page 114) was adapted from an article by David Altshuler.

Auschwitz (page 131) was adapted from an article by Jozef Buszko and Shmuel Krakowski.

The Words "Holocaust" and "Shoah" (page 139) was adapted from an article by Uriel Tal.

Judenrat (page 89) was adapted from an article by Aharon Weiss.

The United States Holocaust Memorial Museum (page 99) was adapted from an article by Michael Bernbaum.

Yad Vashem (page 164) was adapted from an article by Shmuel Spector.

The Voyage of the *St. Louis* (page 204) was adapted from an article by David Silberklang.

The Simon Wiesenthal Center (page 250) was adapted from an article by Abraham Cooper.

Photo Credits

All photographs in *Rescue and Resistance: Portraits of the Holocaust*, except those listed below, were provided by the archives of Yad Vashem, the Holocaust Martyrs' and Heroes' Remembrance Authority, in Jerusalem.

Albert Einstein: CORBIS/Austrian Archives
Adolf Eichmann: CORBIS/Bettmann
David Ben-Gurion: CORBIS/David Rubinger
Elie Wiesel: CORBIS/Bettmann
Heinrich Himmler : CORBIS/Bettmann
Josef Mengele: CORBIS/Bettmann
Paul Goebels: CORBIS/Bettmann
Adolf Hitler: CORBIS/Bettmann
Anne Frank: CORBIS/Bettmann
Herman Goering: CORBIS/Bettmann
Raoul Wallenberg: CORBIS/Bettmann

Suggested Reading

JOSEPH ANDRÉ
Friedman, P. *Their Brother's Keepers*. 1957.

LEO BAECK
Baker, L. *Days of Sorrow and Pain: Leo Baeck and the Berlin Jews*. 1978.

Friedlander, A. H. *Leo Baeck: Teacher of Theresienstadt*. 1968.

WŁADYSŁAW BARTOSZEWSKI
Bartoszewski, Władysław. *The Convent at Auschwitz*. George Braziller, 1991.

Bartoszewski, Władysław. *The Warsaw Ghetto: A Christian's Testimony*. Beacon Press, 1988.

ARRIGO BECCARI
Zuccotti, S. *The Italians and the Holocaust*. 1987.

DAVID BEN-GURION
Teveth, Shabtai. *Ben-Gurion and the Holocaust*. Harcourt Brace, 1996.

TUVIA BIELSKI
Ainsztein, R. *Jewish Resistance in Nazi-occupied Eastern Europe*. 1974.

DIETRICH BONHOEFFER
Bonhoeffer, Dietrich. *Letters and Papers from Prison*. Macmillan Publishing, 1997.

Bonhoeffer, Dietrich. *A Testament to Freedom: The Essential Writings of Dietrich Bonhoeffer*. Harper San Francisco, 1995.

Wind, Renate, and John Bowden. *Dietrich Bonhoeffer: A Spoke in the Wind*. William B. Eerdmans Publishing Company, 1992.

TADEUSZ BOR-KOMOROWSKI
Zawodny, J. K. *Nothing But Honor: The Story of the Warsaw Uprising, 1944*. Stanford University Press, 1978.

JOEL BRAND
Brand, J., and A. Weissberg. *Desperate Mission: Joel Brand's Story*. 1958.

MARIANNE COHN
Latour, A. *The Jewish Resistance in France, 1940-1944*. 1981.

SHIMSHON DRAENGER

Dawidson, Gusta (Tova Draenger), Rodlyn Hirsch, and David H. Hirsch, trans. *Justyna's Narrative.* University of Massachusetts Press, 1978.

TOVA DRAENGER

Dawidson, Gusta (Tova Draenger), Rodlyn Hirsch, and David H. Hirsch, trans. *Justyna's Narrative.* University of Massachusetts Press, 1978.

MAREK EDELMAN

Krall, H. *Sheilding the Flame: An Intimate Conversation With Dr. Marek Edelman, the Last Surviving Leader of the Warsaw Ghetto Uprising.* 1986.

SIMON DUBNOW

Dubnow, Sophie Erlich. *Life and Work of S. M. Dubnow: Diaspora, Nationalism, and Jewish History.* Indiana University Press, 1991.

Steinberg, A. *Simon Dubnow: The Man and His Work.* 1963.

ILYA GRIGORYEVICH EHRENBURG

Goldberg, A. *Ilya Ehrenburg—Revolutionary, Novelist, Poet, War Correspondent, Propagandist: The Extraordinary Epic of a Russian Survivor.* 1984.

GISI FLEISCHMANN

Campion, Joan. *In the Lion's Mouth: Gisi Fleischmann and the Jewish Fight for Survival.* 1987.

Neumann, Y. O. *Gisi Fleischmann: The Story of a Heroic Woman.* 1970.

ANNE FRANK

Amdur, Richard. *Anne Frank.* Chelsea House Publishing, 1993.

Brown, Gene. *Anne Frank: Child of the Holocaust.* Blackbirch Marketing, 1997.

Frank, Anne. *The Diary of a Young Girl: The Definitive Edition.* Doubleday, 1995.

Gies, Miep, and Alison Leslie Gold. *Anne Frank Remembered: The Story of the Woman Who Helped to Hide the Frank Family.* Simon & Schuster, 1988.

Katz, Sandor. *Anne Frank.* Chelsea House Publishing, 1995.

Lindwer, Willy. *The Last Seven Months of Anne Frank.* Pantheon, 1991.

Wilson, Cara, and Otto Frank. *Love, Otto: The Legacy of Anne Frank.* Andrews & McMeel, 1995.

MOSHE GILDENMAN

Suhl, Y. *Uncle Misha's Partisans.* 1973.

NAHUM GOLDMANN

Patai, Raphael. *Nahum Goldmann: His Missions to the Gentiles.* The University of Alabama Press, 1987.

HAIKA GROSMAN

Chaika (Haika) Grosman. *The Underground Army: Fighter of the Białystok Ghetto*. Holocaust Library, 1987.

PAUL GRUNINGER

Hasler, A. A. *The Lifeboat is Full: Switzerland and the Refugees, 1933-1945*. 1969.

SHMARYAHU KACZERGINSKI

Kalisch, S. *Yes, We Sang: Songs of the Ghetto and Concentration Camps*. 1985.

CHAIM AARON KAPLAN

Kaplain, Chaim, and Abraham Katsh, trans. and ed. *The Warsaw Diary of Chaim A. Kaplan*. Collier Books, 1973.

MAXIMILIAN KOLBE

Frossard, Andre. *Forget Not Love: The Passion of Maximilian Kolbe*. Ignatius Press, 1991.

Romb, Anselm W. *Maximilian Kolbe: Authentic Franciscan*. Prow Books, 1990.

Stone, Ellen Murray. *Maximilian Kolbe: Saint of Auschwitz*. Paulist Press, 1997.

JANUSZ KORCZAK

Cohen, Adir. *The Gate of Light: Janusz Korczak, the Educator and Writer Who Overcame the Holocaust*. Fairleigh Dickinson University Press, 1994.

Korczak, Janusz. *Ghetto Diary*. Holocaust Library, 1978.

Korczak, Janusz. *When I Am Little and the Child's Right to Respect*. University Press of America, reissue 1991.

Lifton, Betty Jean. *The King of Children: A Biography of Janusz Korczak*. Random House, 1989.

PRIMO LEVI

Levi, Primo. *The Drown and the Saved*. Vintage Books, 1989.

Levi, Primo. *Moments of Reprieve*. Penguin USA, 1995.

Levi, Primo. *The Periodic Table*. Random House, 1996.

Levi, Primo. *The Reawakening*. Collier Books, 1996.

Levi, Primo. *Survival in Auschwitz: The Nazi Assault on Humanity*. Collier Books, 1995.

Patruno, Nicholas. *Understanding Primo Levi*. University of South Carolina Press, 1995.

AHARON LIEBESKIND

Dawidson, Gusta (Tova Draenger), Rodlyn Hirsch, and David H. Hirsch, trans. *Justyna's Narrative*. University of Massachusetts Press, 1978.

SALY MAYER

Mendelsohn, John. *Rescue to Switzerland: The Musy and Saly Mayer Affairs*. Garland Publishing, 1982.

MARTIN NIEMÖLLER

Davidson, Clarissa S. *God's Man: The Story of Pastor Niemoller*. Greenwood Publishing Group, 1979.

EMANUEL RINGELBLUM

Kermish, Joseph, ed. *To Live With Honor and Die With Horror: Selected Documents from the Warsaw Ghetto Underground Archives*. Yad Vashem, 1986.

Ringelblum, Emanuel, and Joseph Sloan, trans. and ed. *Notes from the Warsaw Ghetto: The Journal of Emanuel Ringelblum*. McGraw-Hill, 1958.

OSKAR SCHINDLER

Brecher, Elinor J. *Schindler's Legacy: True Stories of the List Survivors*. Plume, 1994.

Fensch, Thomas. *Oskar Schindler and His List: The Man, the Book, the Film, the Holocaust, and Its Survivors*. Paul Eriksson, 1995.

Keneally, Thomas. *Schindler's Arc*. Simon & Schuster, 1982.

Roberts, Jack L. *The Importance of Oskar Schindler*. Lucent Books, 1996.

JOSEPH J. SCHWARTZ

Bauer, Yehuda. *My Brother's Keeper: A History of the American Joint Distribution Committee, 1929-1939*. The Jewish Publications Society of America, 1974.

ELIZAVETA SKOBTSOVA

Hackel, Sergei. *Pearl of Great Price: The Life of Mother Maria Skobtsova, 1989-1945*. St. Vladimir's Seminary Press, 1981.

SEMPO SUGIHARA

Levine, Hillel. *In Search of Sugihara: The Elusive Japanese Diplomat Who Risked His Life to Rescue 10,000 Jews from the Holocaust*. Free Press, 1996.

Sugihara, Yukiko. *Visas For Life*. 1995

HANNAH SZENES

Atkinson, Linda. *In Kindling Flame: The Story of Hannah Senesh, 1921-1944*. Beech Tree Books, 1992.

Masters, A. *The Summer That Bled: The Biography of Hanna Senesh*. 1972.

RAOUL WALLENBERG

Bierman, John. *Righteous Gentile: The Story of Raoul Wallenberg, Missing Hero of the Holocaust*. Penguin USA, 1996.

Larsen, Anita. *Raoul Wallenberg: Missing Diplomat.* Crestwood House, 1992.

Lennea, Sharon. *Raoul Wallenberg: The Man Who Stopped Death.* Jewish Publication Society, 1994.

Marton, Kari. *Wallenberg: Missing Hero.* Arcade Publishing, 1995.

Skoglund, Elizabeth, and Tom Lantos. *A Quiet Courage: Per Anger, Wallenberg's Co-Liberator of Hungarian Jews.* Baker Book House, 1997.

Wallenberg, Raoul, and Kjersti Board, trans. *Letters and Dispatches 1924-1945.* Arcade Publishing, 1995.

Werbell, Frederick E., and Thurston Clarke. *Lost Hero: The Mystery of Raoul Wallenberg.* McGraw-Hill, 1982.

CHAIM WEIZMANN

Litvinoff, Barnet (editor). *The Essential Chaim Weizmann: The Man, the Statesman, the Scientist.* Holmes & Meier Publishing, Inc., 1983.

Reinharz, Jehuda. *Chaim Weizmann: The Making of a Stateman.* Oxford University Press, 1993.

ELIE WIESEL

Pariser, Michael. *Elie Wiesel: Bearing Witness.* Millbrook Press, 1994.

Stern, Ellen Norman. *Elie Wiesel: A Voice for Humanity.* Jewish Publication Society, 1996.

Wiesel, Elie. *All Rivers Run to the Sea: Memoires.* Knopf, 1995.

Wiesel, Elie. *A Begger in Jerusalem.* Schocken Books, reissue 1997.

Wiesel, Elie. *The Fifth Son.* Schocken Books, 1998.

Wiesel, Elie. *From the Kingdom of Memory: Reminiscences.* Schocken Books, reissue 1995.

Wiesel, Elie. *The Night Trilogy: Night, Dawn, and The Accident.* Noonday Press, 1994.

Wiesel, Elie. *Twilight: A Novel.* Random House, 1995.

SIMON WIESENTHAL

Jeffrey, Laura S. *Simon Wiesenthal: Tracking Down Nazi Criminals.* Enslow Publishers, Inc., 1997.

Pick, Hella. *Simon Wiesenthal: A Life in Search of Justice.* Northeastern University Press, 1996.

Wiesenthal, Simon. *Justice Not Vengeance.* Grove, 1990.

Wiesenthal, Simon. *The Murderers Among Us: The Simon Wiesenthal Memoirs.* McGraw Hill, 1967.

Wiesenthal, Simon, and Harry James Cargas. *The Sunflower: On the Possibilities and Limits of Forgiveness.* Schocken Books, 1997.

YITZHAK ZUCKERMAN

Zuckerman, Yitzhak, and Barbara Harshav, trans. *A Surplus of Memory: Chronicle of the Warsaw Ghetto Uprising.* University of California Press, reissue 1993.

BOOKS ABOUT RESCUE AND RESISTANCE DURING THE HOLOCUAST

Bachrach, Deborah. *The Resistance*. Lucent Books, 1998.

Bar-Zohar, Michael. *Beyond Hilter's Grasp: The Heroic Rescue of Bulgaria's Jews*. Adams Media Corporation, 1996.

Block, Gay. *Rescuers: Portraits of Moral Courage in the Holocaust*. Holmes & Meier Publishing, 1992.

Flender, Harold. *Rescue in Denmark*. Simon & Schuster, 1995.

Fogelman. *Conscience & Courage: Rescuers of Jews During the Holocaust*. Anchor, 1995.

Freeman, David K. *The Holocaust Heroes*. Enslow Publishing, Inc., 1998.

Gelman, Charles. *Do Not Go Gentle: A Memoir of Jewish Resistance in Poland, 1941-1945*. Archon, 1989.

Gutman, Israel. *Resistance: The Warsaw Ghetto Uprising*. Chapters Publishing Limited, reissue 1998.

Halter, Marek. *Stories of Deliverance: Speaking With Men and Women Who Rescued Jews from the Holocaust*. Open Court Publishing Company, 1998.

Kallen, Stuart A. *The Faces of Resistance*. Abdo & Daughters, 1994.

Kowalsky, Isaac. *Anthology on Armed Jewish Resistance, 1939-1945*. Jewish Combatants Publishing House, 1986.

Krakowski, Shmuel. *The War of the Doomed: Jewish Armed Resistance in Poland, 1942-1944*. Holmes & Meier Publishing, Inc., 1984.

Kurek, Ewa. *Your Life is Worth Mine: How Polish Nuns Saved Hundreds of Jewish Children in German-Occupied Poland, 1939-1945*. Hippocrene Books, 1998.

Kurzman, Dan. *The Bravest Battle: The Twenty-Eight Days of the Warsaw Ghetto Uprising*. Da Capo Press, 1993.

Langbein, Hermann. *Against All Hope: Resistance in the Nazi Concentration Camps, 1938-1945*. Paragon House, 1994.

Lazare, Lucien. *Rescue as Resistance: How Jewish Organizations Fought the Holocaust in France*. Columbia University Press, 1996.

Meltzer, Milton. *The Rescue: The Story of How Gentiles Saved Jews in the Holocaust*. HarperCollins, 1988.

Mendelsohn, John. *Relief and Rescue of Jews from Nazi Oppression, 1943-1945*. Garland Publishing, 1982.

Paldiel, Mordechai. *Sheltering the Jews: Stories of Holocaust Rescuers*. Fortress Press, 1998.

Pettit, Jayne. *A Place to Hide: True Stories of Holocaust Rescues*. Demco Media, 1993.

Ramati, Alexander. *The Assisi Underground: The Priests Who Rescued Jews*. Stein & Day, 1978.

Rautkallio, Hannau. *Finland and the Holocaust: the Rescue of Finland's Jews*. U. S. Holocaust Memorial Museum, 1988.

Rittner, Carol. *The Courage to Care: Rescuers of Jews During the Holocaust*. New York University Press, 1989.

Rosenberg, Maxine. *Hiding to Survive: Stories of Jewish Children Rescued from the Holocaust.* Clarion Books, 1994.

Rudavsky, Joseph. *To Live With Hope, to Die With Dignity: Spiritual Resistance in the Ghettos and Camps.* Jason Aronson, 1997.

Sherrow, Victoria. *The Righteous Gentiles.* Lucent Books, 1998.

Silver, Eric. *The Book of the Just: The Unsung Heroes Who Saved Jews from Hitler.* Weidenfeld & Nicolson, 1992.

Stradtler, Bea. *The Holocaust: A History of Courage and Resistance.* Behrman House, 1973.

Tec, Nechama. *Defiance: The Bielski Partisans.* Oxford University Press, 1994.

Tec, Nechama. *When Light Pierced the Darkness: Christian Rescue of Jews in Nazi-occupied Poland.* Oxford University Press, 1987.

Warhaftig, Zorach. *Refugee and Survivor: Rescue Efforts During the Holocaust.* Phillip Feldheim, 1996.

Werner, Harold. *Fighting Back: A Memoir of Jewish Resistance in World War II.* Columbia University Press, 1994.

Wyman, David S. *The Struggle for Rescue Action.* Garland Press, 1990.

BOOKS ABOUT GENERAL HOLOCAUST HISTORY

Abells, Chana Byers. *The Children We Remember: Photographs from the Archives of Yad Vashem, the Holocaust Martyrs' and Heroes Remembrance Authority, Jerusalem, Israel.* Greenwillow, 1986.

Adler, David A. *Hilde and Eli: Children of the Holocaust.* Holiday House, 1994.

Altshuler, David A., and Lucy S. Dawidowicz. *Hitler's War Against the Jews: A Young Reader's Version of the War Against the Jews, 1933-1945.* Behrman House, 1996.

Arad, Yitzhak, ed. *The Pictorial Atlas of the Holocaust.* Macmillan, 1990.

Ayer, Eleanor H. *The United States Holocaust Memorial Museum: America Keeps the Memory Alive.* Dillon Press, 1995.

Ayer, Eleanor H., Helen Waterford, and Alfons Heck. *Parallel Journey.* Athenuem, 1995.

Bachrach, Susan D. *Tell Them We Remember: The Story of the Holocaust.* Little Brown & Company, 1994.

Berenbaum, Michael. *The World Must Know: The History of the Holocaust as Told in the United States Holocaust Memorial Museum.* Little, Brown, and Company, 1993.

Birger, Trudi, and Jeffrey M. Green. *A Daughter's Gift of Love: A Holocaust Memoir.* Jewish Publication Society, 1992.

Bitten-Jackon, Livia. *I Have Lived A Thousand Years: Growing Up in the Holocaust.* Simon & Schuster, 1997.

Boas, Jacob. *We Are Witnesses: Five Diaries of Teenagers Who Died in the Holocaust.* Scholastic Paperbacks, 1996.

Dwork, Deborah. *Children With a Star: Jewish Youth in Nazi Europe.* Yale University Press, reissue 1993.

Finkelstein, Norman H., and Lois Hokanson. *Remember Not to Forget: A Memory of the Holocaust.* Mulberry Books, 1993.

Gilberry, Martin. *Atlas of the Holocaust.* William Morrow & Company, 1993.

Grant, R. G. *The Holocaust.* Raintree/Steck Vaughn, 1998.

Gutman, Israel (editor). *Encyclopedia of the Holocaust.* Macmillan Library Reference, 1995.

Gutman, Israel, and Michael Berenbaum, eds. *Anatomy of the Auschwitz Death Camp.* Indiana University Press, 1998.

Hander, Andrew. *Young People Speak: Surviving the Holocaust in Hungary.* Franklin Watts, Inc., 1993.

Hass, Aaron. *The Aftermath: Living With the Holocaust.* Cambridge University Press, 1995.

Kallen, Stuart A. *The Nazis Seize Power, 1933-1941.* Abdo & Daughters, 1994.

Landau, Elaine. *We Survived the Holocaust.* Franklin Watts, Inc., 1991.

Lawrence L. Langer, ed. *Art from the Ashes: A Holocaust Anthology.* Oxford University Press, 1995.

Matas, Carol. *Daniel's Story.* Scholastic Paperbacks, 1993.

Meltzer, Milton. *Never to Forget: The Jews of the Holocaust.* HarperCollins, 1991.

Novac, Ana. *The Beautiful Days of My Youth: My Six Months in Auschwitz and Plaszow.* Henry Holt & Company, 1997.

Rochman, Hazel. *Bearing Witness: Stories of the Holocaust.* Orchard Books, 1995.

Rogasky, Barbara. *Smoke and Ashes: The Story of the Holocaust.* Holiday House, 1991.

Rossel, Seymour. *The Holocaust: The World and the Jews, 1933-1945.* Behrman House, 1992.

Strahinich, Helen. *The Holocaust: Understanding and Remembering.* Enslow Publishers, Inc., 1996.

United States Holocaust Memorial Museum. *Historical Atlas of the Holocaust.* Macmillan, 1995.

Wolman, Ruth E., ed. *Crossing Over: An Oral History of Refugees from Hitler's Reich.* Twayne, 1996.

Yahil, Leni. *The Holocaust: The Fate of European Jewry, 1932-1945.* Oxford University Press, 1987.

Abwehr   The intelligence service of the German armed forces' high command.

activist   A person involved in activities or action, often militant, that support or oppose a social or political goal.

aegis   Sponsorship or patronage. Also used to refer to a kind of protection offered by a more powerful person, business, or political entity.

Agudat Israel   (Union of Israel)   Orthodox worldwide Jewish movement and political party founded in 1912 in Katowice, Upper Silesia.

Aktion   Raids against Jews, often in a ghetto, primarily to gather victims for extermination.

Aliya   Jewish immigration to Palestine and, later, to the state of Israel.

Aliya Bet   Organized "illegal" immigration to Palestine.

Allied powers; also **Allied forces**. The collective term for the coalition of nations allied against the Axis Powers in World War II, primarily used to refer to the United States, Great Britain, and the Soviet Union.

Altestenrat   (Council of Elders)   Another name for **Judenrat**. The Altestenrate existed primarily in Theresienstadt, in Kovno, and in the territories incorporated into the Reich.

Altreich   (Old Reich)   Nazi term for Germany before 1938.

ameliorism   The act or process of making something better, or improving it.

American Jewish Congress   An organization, founded by Stephen Wise in 1914–15, that seeks, among other goals, to "protect fundamental constitutional freedoms," "advance the security and posterity of the State of Israel," "remain vigilant against anti-Semitism," and "invigorate and enhance Jewish religious, institutional, communal and cultural life . . . and seek creative ways to express Jewish identity, ethics and values."

Angriff, Der   (The Attack)   Nazi newspaper published and edited by Joseph Goebbels in Berlin from 1928 to 1945.

annals   A chronological record of events, or history.

annex   To take over something, and add it to a larger thing.

annexation   The process of adding on to or joining various elements into a larger single unit.

annihilation   The complete destruction of something or someone. Often used to refer to the complete defeat of an enemy.

Anschluss   The annexation of Austria by Germany on March 13, 1938.

anthem   Most often used to refer to a song or hymn of loyalty, often to a country, as in "the National Anthem."

Anti-Comintern Pact   Agreement signed in Berlin on November 25, 1936, by Germany and Japan. They were joined in 1937 by Italy, and later by Bulgaria, Hungary, Romania, Spain, and other countries. The signatories agreed to fight the Communist International (Comintern), that is, the Soviet Union.

anti-Semitism   The hostility, hatred, or practice of discrimination against Jews.

apostolic   A term used to refer to material relating to the teachings of the twelve Apostles of Jesus, or to the Apostles themselves.

Armee Juive (Jewish Army)   The French Zionist resistance movement.

armistice   A truce, or temporary stop to fighting, agreed on by both parties involved.

Arrow Cross Party   A Hungarian fascist party.

Aryan   The name, used by Nazis and others, of the "race" of people speaking languages thought to be derived from Sanskrit. Aryans were viewed by the Nazis as a superior race.

Aryanization   The expropriation of Jewish businesses by the German authorities.

Ashkenazim   Yiddish-speaking Jews from northern France and western Germany who migrated to eastern Europe in the fifteenth and sixteenth centuries.

assimilation   A sociological term referring to the process by which individuals or groups are brought and absorbed into a new and dominant culture.

asylum   A place of safety. The term is also used to refer to political protection granted by a government to a refugee from another government or country.

attache   A person assigned, or "attached," to a diplomatic mission to serve in a specific capacity or area of expertise.

Auschwitz   The largest concentration camp and death camp operated by the Nazis during World War II, located near the town of Oswiecim in southern Poland.

Auschwitz I   The main Auschwitz camp.

Auschwitz II   Birkenau, the extermination center at Auschwitz.

Auschwitz III   Buna-Monowitz and 45 subcamps for forced labor.

Aussenpolitisches Amt (Foreign Policy Office)   Branch of the Nazi party.

autonomy   From the Greek word *autonomos*, meaning self-ruling, autonomy is a lack of control by others, or self-governing.

Axis; also **Axis Powers**   The alliance, consisting of Germany, Italy, and Japan, that signed a pact in Berlin on September 27, 1940, to divide the world into their spheres of respective political interest. They were later joined by Bulgaria, Croatia, Hungary, Romania, and Slovakia.

badge; also **yellow badge**   Badge worn by Jews in the occupied countries, on Nazi orders in order to distinguish them from the rest of the population. Most commonly, it was a yellow Star of David with or without the word "Jew" in the local language. It was usually worn both on the chest and on the back.

Barbarossa   Code name for the German attack against the Soviet Union, which began on June 22, 1941.

battalion   A military unit, usually consisting of a headquarters and two or more companies.

beatification   Literally meaning to make blessedly happy, the term is most often used in the Roman Catholic Church to mean the proclamation of a deceased person as one of the blessed.

Beer-Hall Putsch (also called the Hitler Putsch or the Munich Putsch)   A failed attempt by Hitler and the Nazis to take over the Bavarian government on November 9, 1923.

Befehlshaber der Ordnungspolizei (BdO)   Commander of the Ordnungspolizei, or German regular police; also, the commander's office.

Befehlshaber der Sicherheirspolizei (BdS)   Commander of the Sicherheitspolizei, or Security Police; also, the office of the commander.

Beriḥa   Hebrew term meaning "flight," Beriha refers to the "illegal" emigration movement (1944–48) from eastern Europe into central and southern Europe, with the ultimate aim of immigration into Palestine.

Bermuda Conference   A conference convened by the United States and Great Britain in 1943, originally to find solutions for wartime refugees. The conference became the most effective meeting among the officials to find an effective way to rescue European Jewry. The conference was held in Bermuda due to the island's inaccessibility during the war by the Germans, the press, and social organizations. Historians believe, however, that the location may have suggested a lack of urgency on the part of the United States and Great Britain to rescue European Jews.

Bernheim petition   A petition against Nazi anti-Jewish legislation that was presented to the League of Nations in May of 1933. The League of Nations allowed citizens who felt their civil rights were being violated to petition the council and in this case a group of Jewish activists from Upper Silesia, headed by Franz Bernheim, did so.

Betar movement   A Jewish youth movement formed in 1923 by Ze'ev Jabotinsky. In 1926 it became the official youth organization of the World Union of Revisionist Zionists. Many of its original members, including Menachem Begin, received military training, and went on to play important roles during and after the establishment of the state of Israel.

blood libel   The accusation that Jews kill gentiles to obtain their blood for Jewish rituals.

boycott   A form of protest in which a person or group refuses to buy products from or support companies, individuals, nations, or other groups with which they disagree.

brigade   A military unit consisting of a varying number of combat units, along with their supporting units and services.

Bund Jewish socialist, non-Zionist organization founded in Vilna in 1897 and active mainly in Poland between the two world wars.

Bund Deutscher Madel (German Girls' League; BDM) The Nazi organization for girls, parallel to the Hitlerjugend.

Calvinism A form of Christian belief or theology, a Protestant offshoot of the Catholic church, led by French reformer John Calvin (1509–64). It is characterized by belief in the absolute sovereignty of God, in predestination, and the absence of free will.

canon A religious term referring to a code or law that is established by a church council. The term also refers to a norm established for standards or judgments.

canonize To declare a deceased person a saint.

CENTOS (Centralne Towarzystwo Opieki nad Sierotami, or Central Agency for Care of Orphans), Jewish welfare agency in Poland.

Central Museum of the Extinguished Jewish Race Projected Nazi museum in Czechoslovakia.

clandestine Something kept secret or done secretly.

cloister A structure that is devoted to the study of religion, such as a monastery. In architectural terms, a covered walkway, open on one side, that runs along the outside of a building.

cohorts A group or band of people associated with a dominant leader.

collaboration Cooperation between citizens of a country and its occupiers.

commonwealth A nation or state governed by its people, or a union of self-governing states. The term is also used to refer to the people of a nation or state.

commune A collective living arrangement or community, in which individual members contribute resources and labor to the group as a whole.

concentration camp A place where groups of people are confined, usually for political reasons, and often under inhumane conditions. Prisoners are held without regard to legal rights, or have been deprived of their right of due process. The most historically well-known use of concentration camps was during the Nazi reign in German from 1933 to 1945, when millions of people were deprived of their rights, imprisoned, and many were killed.

consulate The residence or official workplace of a consul.

D-Day Code name of the Allied invasion of France on June 6, 1944.

Dachau One of the first Nazi concentration camps, located in the town Dachau, 10 miles outside Munich, it received its first prisoners on March 22, 1933. Although Dachau was not an extermination camp, 206,206 prisoners were held there over the 12 years that the camp was operated, and were subjected to medical experiments that included euthanasia. The total number of deaths at the camp is known to be at least 31,591, but it is estimated to be much higher.

death marches   Forced marches of concentration camp inmates (usually Jews) during the German retreat near the end of World War II.

DEGESCH (Deutsche Gesellschaft für Schadlingsbekampfung, mbH, or German Vermin-combating Corporation)   German firm that oversaw the distribution of Zyklon B gas.

Delasem (Delegazione Assistenza Emigrant Ebrei)   Italian organization aiding Kewisj refugees in the occupied area of Italy.

delegate   A representative for another person.

Delegatura   The underground committee of the Polish government-in-exile that received representation in Poland from 1940 to 1945. During the first 3 years of the committee, there was not a focus on the Jewish population, although in 1943 the group did establish an organization dedicated to the Jewish population in Poland.

deportation   The act of expelling a person from a country. Deportation is often used in the cases of criminals or illegal aliens.

Deutsche Ausrustungswerke (German Armaments Industry)   SS branch that exploited forced labor from concentration camps.

dialectic   The process of arriving at the truth through the exchange of logical arguments and debates.

dictator   Originally the title of a magistrate in ancient Rome, appointed by the Senate in times of emergency, in modern times the term has come to refer to an individual who assumes sole and often absolute power over a country.

diplomat   A person who is skilled in the practice of conducting international business or relations.

displaced persons (DPs)   Persons driven out of their countries of origin during World War II.

disseminate   To spread out or diffuse.

dissertation   A written work usually produced as a doctoral thesis as a means of achieving a doctorate degree.

dragnet   A system of procedures followed to apprehend a criminal.

Drancy   A detention and assembly camp for the Jews of France, established in August 1941. At least 65,000 Jews were transported from Drancy to both the Auschwitz and Sobibór extermination camps. The majority of those transported were Polish Jews, but also included French and German Jews. Within Drancy, the Jewish faith was practiced and holidays were recognized despite difficult conditions created by the Nazis.

Drang nach Osten (drive to the east)   Expression of German foreign policy and actions with regard to eastern Europe and the Soviet Union. The term originated in the first half of the nineteenth century.

Drobitski Yar (Drobitski Ravine)   Site, near Kharkov, of massacres of Jews.

Durschgangslager (Dulag)   Transit camp.

edict   A proclamation, with the force of a law, that is issued by an authority.

egalitarian   The affirmation or one who affirms political, economic, and social equality for all people.

Einsatzgruppen ("action squads")   Mobile units of the SS and SD. The Einsatzgruppen accompanied the advancing German army into Poland in September 1939 and into the Soviet Union from June 22, 1941. Their official tasks were to wipe out political opponents and seize state documents. In the Soviet Union in particular, they carried out mass murders, primarily of Jews.

emigrate   To leave one's country of origin to settle in another.

emigres   People who have left their native country, usually for political reasons.

emissary   A person who is sent to another country to act as a representative of his or her native land.

environs   The area surrounding another. The term is often used to describe the area just outside a city.

eulogy   A speech or writing used as a tribute to praise someone who has died.

Europa Plan   A plan devised by the Working Group in Slovakia for saving European Jews from extermination by paying a ransom. Amounts ranging from $40,000 to $3 million were proposed but in August 1943 negotiations between the Working Group and Germany ended with no success.

euthanasia   The act of ending someone's life through a painless means for reasons of mercy.

excise   A tax placed on the production, sale, or consumption of clothing, food, or other necessity within a country.

expatriate   A person who has left his or her native country, usually through banishment or exile, to live in another country.

extermination camps   Nazi camps in occupied Poland where, in an attempt to completely exterminate the Jewish race in Europe, a huge number of Jews were killed. Extermination camps differed from concentration camps in that all prisoners were put to death whereas concentration camps selectively killed prisoners.

extortion   To obtain something, often money or other material goods, by the use of force, coercion, or intimidation.

extremist   A person or organization whose views are considered extreme. Most often used to refer to political views or parties.

fascism   A system of government that follows the principles of a centralized authority under a dictator, strict economic controls, censorship, and the use of terror to suppress opposition.

fascist   A person who believes in or supports the political system of fascism, a 20th-century form of totalitarian government based on the premise that a viable society can be created by strict governmental regulation of national and individual lives.

fiat   A sanction or decree.

Final Solution   Nazi code name for the physical extermination of European Jewry.

flora   The plants and vegetation that are native to a particular region or era.

free professions   Professions requiring university-level training, such as medicine, the law, engineering, and university teaching.

Freemason   Also called a Mason, a member of the largest and most widely established fraternal order in the world. Freemasonry began in Europe as guilds originally restricted to stonecutters. In the 17th century they began to admit men of wealth, power, or social status, and over the years the guilds became more like societies, or clubs, devoted to general principles and ideals, such as fraternity, equality, religious toleration, and peace.

Freikorps   Volunteer armies organized beginning in 1918 by former army officers in Germany after its defeat in World War I. Their goals were to protect Germany's eastern borders and crush revolutions at home. The Freikorps dissolved in 1921.

Freiwillige (volunteers)   Non-German collaborators who joined the waffen-SS.

Führer (Leader)   Adolf Hitler's title in Nazi Germany.

functionalist   Someone who believes all possessions should be designed for, or adapted to, a particular purpose.

Galicia   Region in Southeastern Poland and the northwestern Ukraine; former Austrian crown land. Now divided between Poland and the Ukraine.

garrison   A military term for a permanent post of troops within an area.

Gau (district)   Main territorial unit in the Reich during the Nazi period.

Gauleiter   Nazi party head of a Gau.

Gebietskommissar   German head of a Gebiet or territory.

Gebietskommissariat (District Commissariat)   Lowest level in the occupied territories of the Soviet Union.

Gendarmerie   Regional or rural police.

Generalbezirk   German term meaning General Commissariat, an intermediate level of the German civil administration in the occupied territories of the Soviet Union.

Generalgouvernement   The Germans' name for the administrative unit comprising those parts of occupied Poland that were not incorporated into the Reich. It included five districts: Galicia, Kraków, Lublin, Radom, and Warsaw.

gentile   A term used to describe someone who is not a Jew, usually referring to Christians.

Gestapo   From the term Geheime Staatspolizei, meaning Secret State Police, the common name for the political police of the Nazi regime in Germany from 1933 to 1945. Founded by Hermann Göring, the Gestapo's purpose was to persecute all political opponents of the Nazi regime. It was noted for its terrorist methods.

ghetto   An area of a city, often populated by a minority group who live there for social or economic reasons, often mandated by law.

Gleichschaltung   Coordination; that is, elimination of opposition and the Nazifying of the German state.

Great Patriotic War   A term used by the Russians to describe their war with Germany and its allies. The term is interchangeable with World War II.

gynecology   The medical study of the female reproductive organs.

Haavara   Trade company established in Germany for the transfer of Jewish capital to Palestine in the form of goods.

Hagana   The underground military organization, founded in 1920, of the Yishuv, the Jewish community in Palestine.

hakhshara   The organized agricultural training of young people prior to immigration to Palestine.

haluts   A pioneer in Palestine.

Heeres Kraftfahrpark   In German, literally Army Motor Vehicle Depot. The term refers to the German maintenance services for military vehicles.

Herrenvolk   German term meaning master race. The Nazis' racial definition of the German people.

hierarchy   Most often used to refer to the structure of authority in a group or organization, ranked by authority or ability.

Hilfswillige   Soviet prisoners of war and civilians in Nazi-occupied territories who volunteered for or were drafted into the German army.

hinterlands   A geographic term referring to land that is adjacent to or just inland from a coast.

Hitlerjugend   Literally Hitler Youth, the Nazi youth organization for boys, founded in 1922.

Hlinka Guard   SS-influenced armed militia of the Slovak People's Party, named after Andrej Hlinka, Slovak nationalist leader.

Holocaust   The widespread persecution and murder of the Jews in Europe by Nazi Germany in the 1930s and 1940s. Hermann Göring, second only to Adolf Hitler in the German hierarchy, was ordered to organize "a final solution to the Jewish question" in all of German-dominated Europe. By 1941 German Jews were forced to wear badges or armbands marked with a yellow star; in the following months, thousands were deported to ghettos in Poland and elsewhere; and camps equipped with facilities for gassing people were set up in occupied Poland.

Horst Wessel Song   Nazi party anthem written in 1929 by Horst Wessel, an SA member who was killed in a private quarrel by a Communist. The Nazis elevated him to the status of hero.

humanitarian   Someone who is devoted to the promotion of the well-being of humans.

iconoclastic   A term used to describe an attack made as an attempt to overthrow traditional or popular ideas or institutions.

idealism   The philosophy or practice of envisioning things in an ideal or perfect or most desirable form. The term is often used to describe the subject of a piece of artwork or literature.

ideology   The collective term for the body of ideas and principles reflecting the social needs and aspirations of an individual, group, or culture.

immigration   The process entering and settling into a country or region that is not one's native land.

in absentia   A Latin term meaning absent or not present.

incarcerate   To imprison someone, or confine them to jail.

indoctrination   A teaching that presents a strong partisan or sectarian point of view.

insubordination   A term used to describe an act against authority.

inter   To bury or place in a grave.

interlocutor   An official who participates in a conversation or dialogue.

Iron Guard   The Romanian fascist movement.

Jewish Fighting Organization (ŻOB)   A Jewish armed group whose goal was to provide Jews with the ability to fight Nazis. The group was formed in Warsaw in 1942 when deportations from the ghettos were in full swing. The Jewish Fighting Organization was successful in ridding the ghettos of German troops and received strong backing from Jewish citizens who sought to avoid imprisonment.

Joint Distribution Committee (JDC)   Also known as the American Jewish Joint Distribution Committee was founded in 1914 and, with the rise of the Nazi party, focused on emigrating as many Jews from Germany as possible. The committee was funded by Jewish Americans but by 1942 it could no longer get relief into German Jews. Funds were used to aid French, Polish, and Romanian Jews and ceased refugee assistance in 1957 when the last displaced persons camp, Fohrenwald, was liberated.

judenfrei; also **judenrein**. A German term meaning "free" (or "cleansed") of Jews, used by the Nazis to describe an area with no Jewish residents as a result of deportation or extermination.

Judenrat   A Council of Jewish leaders, established by Nazi orders in an occupied place.

Judischer Ordnungsdienst   The Jewish ghetto police.

Julag   From the German word "Judenlager," meaning a Jewish camp.

jurisprudence   The scientific study of law.

Kapo   The supervisor of inmate laborers in a concentration camp.

kibbutz   A term used to describe a farm or settlement in modern Israel.

Kriminalpolizei   The German criminal police.

Kristallnacht   The German word, meaning "Night of Broken Glass," that refers to November 9, 1938, on which the Nazis killed more than ninety Jews at random in the streets, looted stores, and set fire to synagogues.

Lebensborn   An SS association established in 1936 to facilitate the adoption of "racially appropriate" children by childless SS couples, and to encourage the birth of "racially sound" children.

Lebensraum   Meaning "living space," a principle of Nazi philosophy and ideology expressed as the drive for the conquest of territory.

leftist   A term used to describe someone who follows the beliefs of socialist-oriented politics, including government-provided welfare, social equality for all, and protection from arbitrary authority.

legation   A diplomatic position, below that of an embassy, in a foreign country.

Lend-Lease   The American program that supplied military goods to the Allies during World War II.

libel   The legal term for a written, published, or pictorial statement that maliciously damages another person's reputation.

liquidation   The process of eliminating, ending, or killing all people or objects of the same kind.

Luftwaffe   The German air force.

Madagascar Plan   A Nazi plan, formulated in the spring of 1940, for the expulsion of Jews to the island of Madagascar. It was abandoned later the same year.

manifesto   A plan, often political in nature, that describes the intentions or principles of a specific group.

martyr   Generally used to refer to a person who dies rather than renounce his religious principles, or one who makes great sacrifices for a cause.

Mein Kampf   Meaning "My Struggle," the book written by Adolf Hitler that outlined his ideology. It was published in two volumes in 1925 and 1926.

mentor   A teacher or counselor whose trust and wisdom are conveyed to the student.

militia   The term used to describe an army made up of ordinary citizens rather than professional or career soldiers. A militia would be intended to function as a reserve or contingent force, available to be called on in case of emergency.

mischlinge   A Nazi term for a person having one or two Jewish grandparents.

Mit brennender Sorge ("With Burning Concern")   The encyclical issued by Pope Pius XI in 1937 assailing racism and the cult of the state in Germany.

modernism   A state of being characterized by modern thought, character, or standards.

modus operandi A Latin term meaning a method of operating or functioning.

monographic A term referring to a written essay or book that is specific in length, often limited to one subject.

Mosad le-Aliya Bet (Organization for "Illegal" Immigration) The immigration branch of the Yishuv's underground organization.

mother superior The highest ranking position within a convent, held by one of the nuns, who is in charge of the community.

mulatto A term used to describe someone with one white parent and one Black parent.

municipal A term referring to an area that is locally self-governed, rather than reliant on another city or town for government rule.

Muselmann A concentration camp term for an inmate on the verge of death from starvation and exhaustion.

Nacht und Nebl (Night and Fog) A Nazi codename used for the rounding-up of suspected members of the anti-Nazi resistance in occupied western Europe.

Naczelna Rada Opiekuncza (Main Welfare Council) An organization within the administrative sect of the government that coordinated Polish, Jewish, and Ukranian welfare activities under the auspices of the Nazi authorities.

National Legionary Government A government that was established in Romania in 1940 by Ion Antonescu and Horia Sima—the chief of the Iron Guard. The goal of the government was to draw close to Germany and Italy.

nationalist Someone who is devoted to the interests, culture, and residents of a specific country.

Nazi A member of the Nazi Party, or proponent of Nazism. Also called National Socialism, Nazism is a political movement that began in Germany in 1920 with the organization of the National Socialist Workers' Party, which was also called the Nazi Party. It culminated in the establishment of the Third Reich, the totalitarian state led by Adolf Hitler, which came to an end with Germany's surrender in 1945. Similar in some respects to fascism, Nazism was heavily influenced by various aspects of German culture, including a tradition of military authoritarianism, expansion, and racism.

Nazi-Soviet Pact Two agreements signed by Germany and the Soviet Union on August 19 and 23, 1939, that dealt with economic and political issues. A secret protocol divided Nazi and Soviet spheres of interest in the Baltic states and Poland.

Neolog One of the three sects of Judaism in Hungary, similar to Reform Judaism.

neutral A term referring to a person, group, or country that does not support either side of a war or dispute.

Night and Fog Decree   Issued by Adolf Hitler in 1941, the decree outlined ways of suppressing resistance movements in western European countries. The decree was issued in an attempt to put an end to underground activity in occupied France, stating that such activity was punishable by death. A special court was formed to try underground activists who had been imprisoned for their "crimes." The last prisoners were liberated in 1945.

nom de guerre   A pseudonym, or fictitious name, often used by writers to hide their identity.

numerous clausus   The quota of Jews permitted within a specific institution, as in a university.

Nuremberg Laws   Two laws issued in 1935 to further the legal exclusion of Jews from German life. The first removed the Jews' citizenship; the second defined the Jews racially and prohibited them from engaging in marital and other relations with Germans. The laws were proclaimed at the annual Nazi party rally in Nuremberg on September 15, 1935.

Nuremberg Trial   The trial of twenty-two major Nazi figures in Nuremberg in 1945 and 1946. They were tried by the International Military Tribunal.

Obercommando der Heeres (OKH)   Army High Command.

Oberkommando der Wehrmacht (OKW)   Armed Forces High Command; eventually, the high command of all the German armed forces.

Oblast (district)   The administrative unit of the Soviet Union.

occupation   The invasion, conquest, and control of a nation by armed forces.

Odessa (Organization of SS Member)   One of the groups that helped engineer the escape of Nazis from Germany after World War II.

Old Kingdom (also called Old Romania or the Regat)   Romania in its pre-1918 borders.

Organisation Todt   A semimilitarized agency that made use of forced labor. It was headed by Dr. Fritz Todt beginning in 1933 and was named after him upon his death in 1942.

ORT   An international organization, founded in Russia in 1880, for developing skilled trades and agriculture among Jews through vocational training.

Ostarbeiter (eastern worker)   A slave laborer from the eastern occupied territories.

Ostbataillone   German army units made up of Soviet collaborators (prisoners of war and Soviet citizens). They numbered about a million men.

Ostjuden   Jews from eastern Europe who had settled in Germany.

Ostland   The eastern European territories occupied by the Nazis, consisting of the Baltic states (Estonia, Latvia, and Lithuania) and the western half of Byelorussia.

pacifism   A belief that opposes any kind of war or violence as a way of resolving disputes.

Palastina-Amt (Palestine Office)   Office of the Jewish agency that dealt with immigration to Palestine.

Pale of Settlement   Area in the western part of the Russian empire in which Russian Jews were confined from 1835 to 1917.

papal nuncio   A political position, held by a member of the Catholic priesthood, who is permanently assigned the highest ranking position over a civil government.

partisans   Guerrilla fighters.

pastoral   Most often used to refer to a lifestyle or setting that is simple, serene, or idyllic, usually possessing elements of rural life.

patriot   Someone who loves, supports, and defends his country.

patriotism   Devotion to one's country.

penal camp   A jail or other holding, where prisoners are kept.

phenol   A caustic, poisonous compound used in manufacturing plastics, insecticides, dyes, and detergents.

philanthropy   In business, a term used to describe the ongoing practice or philosophy, usually of an individual, of giving to or establishing charitable or humanistic causes or foundations.

philosophy   In general terms, a speculative inquiry into the source and nature of human knowledge, or the system and ideas based on such thinking.

piety   The demonstration of devotion and reverence to God or family.

pillage   The act of stealing or robbing by means of force.

platform   In politics, the collection of principles and policies agreed to and supported by all candidates of a party.

pogrom   An organized massacre of a minority group. These massacres were frequently committed by the Nazis during World War II against the Jews.

Ponary masacres   A mass extermination site in Lithuania, Ponary had originally been a resort. Prisoners were led into narrow passages that opened into pits where the prisoners were shot. An estimated seventy to one hundred prisoners were killed at Ponary.

Potsdam Conference   A meeting held by Winston Churchill, Joseph Stalin, and Harry S Truman from July 17 to August 2, 1945, in Potsdam, Germany. Its purpose was to discuss the political and economic problems arising after Germany's surrender.

precursor   An event, object, or person that precedes or announces another.

progeny   The offspring or descendant of a group.

propaganda   Material distributed by the advocates of a specific cause to aid in influencing others to join their beliefs.

Protectorate   The relationship between two countries, in which the stronger of the two guarantees protection to the weaker country. This relationship is usually established by a treaty, and maintains that no matter how much involvement the stronger country has, the weaker one remains independent as a nation.

protégé   A person who is provided for, and trained in a specific career by an influential person within that field.

psychosomatic   The process of possessing the symptoms and characteristics of a physical illness that originate from mental or emotional causes.

punitive   A term referring to inflicting or an intent to inflict punishment.

putsch   A German term referring to an attempt to overthrow a government.

Quaker   A member of the Society of Friends, a Christian denomination of the mid-17th century, that rejected formal sacraments, creeds, priesthood, and violence.

quisling   A term meaning traitor. It was taken from the name of Vidkun Quisling, the pro-Nazi Norwegian leader. It usually refers to the leader of an enemy-sponsored regime.

rabbi   The highest ranking position within a Jewish congregation, similar to a minister in Christian religions.

rabbinate   A term used to describe the office and functions of a rabbi.

racist   Someone who discriminates against others based solely on their race.

radical   A political term used to describe those who believe in extreme and revolutionary changes within a society or government.

rampa   A Polish term for the railway platform for arriving trains at a concentration or extermination camp.

Rasse- und siedlungshauptamt   Literally the "Race and Resettlement Main Office." This term refers to the Nazi office that supervised the racial purity of SS members, as well as the colonization of SS settlers in the eastern occupied territories.

Rassenschande   Literally translated to racial defilement, this term was used by Nazis for sexual contact between an Aryan and a Jew.

ration cards   Vouchers provided to citizens of a country, often while at war, that allot the people a specific amount of food, clothing, or other necessities. Ration cards are used to avoid a shortage of necessities and provide an equal share to all.

Razzia   A Nazi term meaning a roundup of Jews.

rector   The head of an institution, often religious is nature.

Red Army   The official name of the Soviet army until June 1945, when it was changed to the Soviet Army.

Red Cross   An international humanitarian organization that focuses on providing aid to people afflicted by wars, epidemics, and natural disasters. The Red Cross was first conceived, in the 19th century, by Swiss philanthropist, Jean Henri Dunant, who was appalled by the lack of care being provided for wounded soldiers. In 1864 official delegates from 12 nations signed the first Geneva Convention, at which time the group adopted their symbol of a red cross on a white flag.

refugee A person who has fled, or been expelled, from his or her country due to natural catastrophe, war, or political or racial prosecution.

regime A government or administration in power.

rehabilitation The use of therapy and education to restore someone's mental or physical health in an attempt to reacclimate them to society.

Reichsbahn German term for the German state railways.

Reichsfluchtsteuer An emigration tax that Jews had to pay before leaving Germany.

Reichskommissariat Literally translated to Reich commissariat, the term defines the major territorial division of the German civil administration in the occupied areas of the Soviet Union.

reichsmark The German monetary unit from 1924 to 1948.

Reichssippenamt The Reich Genealogical Office.

Reichstag A term originally referring to a government body established during the time of the Holy Roman Empire. It is most commonly used to refer to the legislature in Germany whose power was taken over by Adolf Hitler in the 1930s.

Reichszentrale für Judische Auswanderung Translated meaning Reich Central Office for Jewish Emigration, the term refers to the Nazis' central agency for matters relating to Jewish emigration. Its original functions ceased in October 1941, when further emigration of Jews was prohibited.

reparation Most often used to refer to monetary compensation required from a nation defeated in war to allay or offset some of the costs of repairing the war damage.

repatriation The process of returning someone to his or her native country.

Reseau Garel Literally the "Garel Network," the term refers to the underground organization in France that placed Jewish children with Christian families and with institutions involved in saving Jews.

Restgetto The residual ghetto after an *Aktion*.

restitution The process of restoring an item to its rightful owner. Often the term refers to compensation for losses, damages, and injury following a war by the defeated side.

Revisionists Members of the New Zionist Organization, founded by Vladimir Jabotinsky in 1925.

"Righteous among the Nations" The title, given by Yad Vashem to non-Jews who risked their lives to save Jews in Nazi-occupied Europe.

SA In English translated to "Storm Troopers," the term refers to shock units founded by the Nazi party in 1921.

sabotage A destructive action taken by an enemy intended to force its opponent to surrender.

SD In English translated to "Security Service," the term refers to the SS security and intelligence service, established in 1932 under Reinhard Heydrich.

secretariat   The governmental position of secretary.

selektion   The process of selecting, from among Jewish deportees arriving at a Nazi camp, those who were to be used for forced labor and those who were to be killed immediately. The term also refers to the selecting, in ghettos, of Jews to be deported.

seminary   A school dedicated to the training of priests, minister, or rabbis.

Sephardim   Jews expelled from Spain and Portugal in 1492. They and their descendants migrated to North Africa, Italy, western Europe, the Balkans, the Near East, and the Americas.

She'erit ha-Peletah   The "surviving remnant" of Europe's Jews after the Holocaust.

sho'ah   The Hebrew term for "holocaust," or the mass destruction of Jews by the Nazis.

socialism   A governmental system that maintains the beliefs that all goods are owned equally and political power is shared and exercised by the whole community.

sociology   The scientific study of human society, including its origins, development, and organization.

Sonderkommando   Literally "special squad," the term refers to the Jewish units in extermination camps who removed the bodies of those gassed for cremation or burial.

sovereignty   A supreme political power free from external control.

SS   Literally "Protection Squad," originally the term referred to the guard detachments formed in 1925 as Hitler's personal guard. In 1929, under Himmler, the SS developed into the elite units of the Nazi party.

Stahlhelm   In English, "Steel Helmet," the Nationalist organization of former German soldiers founded in 1918.

Stalag   A base camp, or prisoner-of-war camp.

Status Quo Ante   Jewish communities in Hungary that followed neither the Neolog nor the Orthodox trend.

swastika   Ancient symbol originating in South Asia, later appropriated by the Nazis as their emblem.

synagogue   A place of worship and education within the Jewish religion.

tarbut (Heb.: "excursion")   The loosely organized escape of Jews, during World War II, from Slovakia to Hungary, and from Hungary to Romania, Slovakia, and Yugoslavia.

Tatar   A term used to designate a number of Muslim ethnic groups including the Valga Tatars, Crimean Tatars, and the Azeins of Transcaucasia, who lived within Russia.

theology   The scientific study of religion and the nature of God.

tithe   A term, often associated with religion, that refers to one-tenth of one's income. Many religions promote donating a tithe to the church to aid those less fortunate.

totalitarian   A government based on the belief the political authority exercises complete and absolute control over all aspects of the citizen's lives.

Transferstelle   Nazi office in Warsaw that implemented the exchange of goods between the ghetto and the Aryan side of the city.

Transnistria   Province in the southern part of the Ukraine that was occupied and governed by Romania from 1941 to 1944.

Trianon Hungary   Hungary according to the 1920 Treaty of Trianon, which deprived Hungary of more than two-thirds of its territory and about 60 percent of its population after World War I.

tribunal   A special board or committee appointed to make a decision or ruling with regard to a particular matter.

tuberculosis   An infectious disease, characterized by the formation of small lumps within the body, most often the lungs.

typhus   An infectious disease, most often caused by bacteria, with symptoms including severe headaches, high fever, and red rashes.

Umschlagplatz   A place in Warsaw where freight trains loaded and unloaded. During the deportation from the Warsaw ghetto, it was used as an assembly point where Jews were loaded onto cattle cars to be taken to Treblinka.

underground   An organization that works secretly against the ruling government.

United Nations Relief and Rehabilitation Administration (UNRRA)   An organization established on November 9, 1943, by forty-four member nations of the United Nations. After World War II it aided millions of displaced persons.

United Partisan Organization (FPO)   Jewish anti-Nazi underground organization established in Vilna, Lithuania, by the existing Zionist members. The organization remained in Vilna, despite concerns that the majority of the Jews had already been captured by the Nazis. Their goal was to prepare themselves for armed resistance in the event of Nazi invasion. In September 1943, when the ghetto was liquidated, the organization escaped the city through the sewer systems and hid in the forests until the Soviet army liberated Vilna in July 1944.

Ustasa   Croatian nationalist terrorist organization that came to power in April 1941, with the establishment of the Croatian state. It was responsible for the mass murder of Serbs, Jews, and Gypsies.

utilitarian   Something defined or identified based on its usefulness rather than its esthetic appeal.

Vernichtung durch Arbeit   Literally "extermination through work," the term refers to the deliberate policy of gradually killing prisoners in some Nazi camps through starvation and overwork.

Vichy   A spa town in central France. Vichy was the capital of unoccupied France and the headquarters of the regime headed by Marshal Philippe Petain. The Germans occupied Vichy, France, in November 1942.

Volksdeutsche Mittelstelle (VoMi)   The SS welfare and repatriation office for ethnic Germans.

Waffen-SS   Militarized units of the SS.

Wannsee Conference   A meeting called by Reinhard Heydrich and held at Wannsee, a suburb of Berlin. The meeting took place on January 20, 1942, with the purpose of coordinating the "Final Solution."

War Refugee Board   The United States agency established in January 1944 by order of President Franklin D. Roosevelt to rescue people from Nazi-occupied territories.

Wehrmacht   The combined German armed forces.

Weimar Republic   The German republic (1919–33) established after the end of World War I, with its capital in the city of Weimar.

welfare   A public assistance program providing at least a minimum amount of economic aid to individuals who earn less money than is needed to maintain an adequate standard of living.

Yad Vashem   A Holocaust memorial in Jerusalem.

Yalta Conference   The conference held in Yalta, in the Crimea, from February 4 to 11, 1945. The conference was attended by Churchill, Roosevelt, and Stalin, with its purpose to discuss the last stage of the war against Germany.

yeshiva   An elementary or secondary school with a curriculum that focuses on the teachings of the Talmud and Jewish faith.

Yiddish   A language, based on German, that was historically used by people of the Jewish faith who lived in Central and Eastern Europe.

Zegota   Code name used by the Council for Aid to Jews, Zegota was in operation from December 1942 until January 1945. The organization was based in Poland and their main focus was to provide "Aryan" documents to Jews in an effort to avoid Nazi imprisonment.

Zentrum   The Catholic Center party in Germany.

Zionism   A movement aimed at uniting the Jewish people of the exile and settle them in Palestine. Founded in the late 19th century by journalist Theodor Herzl, the organization eventually grew to settle the State of Israel in 1948. Their main goal of statehood was to defend and consolidate Israel and to justify its existence. In the 1970s and 1980s, Zionist aid was turned to Soviet Jews and today guarantees a Jewish nationality to any Jew in need of it.

Zyklon B (hydrogen cyanide)   A pesticide used in the Euthanasia Program and later, especially in the gas chambers of Auschwitz-Birkenau.

Index